NEW
STANDARDS™

PERFORMANCE

Volume 1 ▪ Elementary School

STANDARDS

English Language Arts

Mathematics

Science

Applied Learning

Support for the development of the New Standards performance standards was provided by:

The Pew Charitable Trusts,
John D. and Catherine T. MacArthur Foundation,
William T. Grant Foundation,
and the
New Standards partners.

ISBN 1-889630-51-9

TABLE OF CONTENTS

E   ENGLISH LANGUAGE ARTS 20

M   MATHEMATICS 58

S   SCIENCE 130

A   APPLIED LEARNING 160

INTRODUCTION

ABOUT NEW STANDARDS

New Standards is a collaboration of the Learning Research and Development Center of the University of Pittsburgh and the National Center on Education and the Economy, in partnership with states and urban school districts. The partners are building an assessment system to measure student progress toward meeting national standards at levels that are internationally benchmarked.

The Governing Board includes chief state school officers, governors and their representatives, and others representing the diversity of the partnership, whose jurisdictions enroll nearly half of the Nation's students.

New Standards was founded by Lauren Resnick, Director of the Learning Research and Development Center (LRDC), and Marc Tucker, President of the National Center on Education and the Economy (NCEE). The Executive Director is Eugene Paslov. New Standards staff is based at the LRDC and NCEE as well as the American Association for the Advancement of Science, the Fort Worth Independent School District, the National Council of Teachers of English, and the University of California Office of the President. Technical studies are based at LRDC and Northwestern University, with an advisory committee of leading psychometricians from across the nation.

The New Standards assessment system has three interrelated components: performance standards, an on-demand examination, and a portfolio system.

The **performance standards** are derived from the national content standards developed by professional organizations, e.g., the National Council of Teachers of Mathematics, and consist of two parts:

 Performance descriptions—descriptions of what students should know and the ways they should demonstrate the knowledge and skills they have acquired in the four areas assessed by New Standards—English Language Arts, Mathematics, Science, and Applied Learning—at elementary, middle, and high school levels.

 Work samples and commentaries—samples of student work that illustrate standard-setting performances, each accompanied by commentary that shows how the performance descriptions are reflected in the work sample.

The performance standards were endorsed unanimously by the New Standards Governing Board in June 1996 as the basis for the New Standards assessment system.

The on-demand examination, called the **reference examination** because it provides a point of reference to national standards, is currently available in English Language Arts and Mathematics at grades 4, 8, and 10. It assesses those aspects of the performance standards that can be assessed in a limited time frame under standardized conditions. In English Language Arts, this means reading short passages and answering questions, writing first drafts, and editing. In Mathematics, this means short exercises or problems that take five to fifteen minutes and longer problems of up to forty-five minutes. The reference examination stops short of being able to accommodate longer pieces of work—reading several books, writing with revision, conducting investigations in Mathematics and Science, and completing projects in Applied Learning—that are required by New Standards performance standards and by the national content standards from which they are derived.

The **portfolio system** complements the reference examination. It provides evidence of achievement of the performance standards that depend on extended pieces of work (especially those that show revision) and accumulation of evidence over time. In 1995-96, 3,000 teachers and almost 60,000 students participated in a field trial of the portfolio system. The portfolio system includes instructions for students, teachers, and administrators and example portfolios that contain concrete examples of expectations for students and teachers to refer to as they prepare portfolios.

The 1995-96 portfolio field trial was the second year of field testing the system in English Language Arts and Mathematics, and the first year of developmental testing for Science and Applied Learning. The materials used in the 1995-96 trial were revised to take account of the experience of the first year, with the goal of making the portfolio system easier to understand and implement.

ABOUT THE PERFORMANCE STANDARDS

We have adopted the distinction between content standards and performance standards that is articulated in *Promises to Keep: Creating High Standards for American Students* (1993), a report commissioned by the National Education Goals Panel. Content standards specify "what students should know and be able to do"; performance standards go the next step to specify "how good is good enough."

These standards are designed to make content standards operational by answering the question: how good is good enough?

Where do the performance standards come from?

These performance standards are built directly upon the consensus content standards developed by the national professional organizations for the disciplines. The Mathematics performance standards are based directly on the content standards produced by the National Council of Teachers of Mathematics (1989). (See "Introduction to the Mathematics performance standards," page 58.) Similarly, the performance standards for English Language Arts were developed in concert with the content standards produced by the National Council of Teachers of English and the International Reading Association (1996). (See "Introduction to the English Language Arts performance standards," page 20.)

The Science performance standards are built upon the National Research Council's *National Science Education Standards*. (1996) and the American Association for the Advancement of Science's Project 2061 *Benchmarks for Science Literacy* (1993). (See "Introduction to the Science performance standards," page 130.)

The case of the Applied Learning performance standards is a little different. Applied Learning focuses on connecting the work students do in school with the demands of the twenty-first century workplace. As a newer focus of study, Applied Learning does not have a distinct professional constituency producing content standards on which performance standards can be built. However, the Secretary's Commission on Achieving Necessary Skills (SCANS) laid a foundation for the field in its report, *Learning a Living: A Blueprint for High Performance* (1992), which defined "Workplace Know-how." We worked from this foundation and from comparable international work to produce our own "Framework for Applied Learning" (New Standards, 1994). The Applied Learning performance standards have been built upon this framework. (See "Introduction to the Applied Learning performance standards," page 160.)

STANDARDS FOR STANDARDS

In recent years several reports on standards development have established "standards for standards," that is, guidelines for developing standards and criteria for judging their quality. These include the review criteria identified in *Promises to Keep*, the American Federation of Teachers' "Criteria for High Quality Standards," published in *Making Standards Matter* (1995), and the "Principles for Education Standards" developed by the Business Task Force on Student Standards and published in *The Challenge of Change* (1995). We drew from the criteria and principles advocated in these documents in establishing the "standards" we have tried to achieve in the New Standards performance standards.

Standards should establish high standards for all students.

The New Standards partnership has resolved to abolish the practice of expecting less from poor and minority children and children whose first language is not English. These performance standards are intended to help bring all students to high levels of performance.

Much of the onus for making this goal a reality rests on the ways the standards are implemented. The New Standards partners have adopted a Social Compact, which says in part, "Specifically, we pledge to do everything in our power to ensure all students a fair shot at reaching the new performance standards...This means they will be taught a curriculum that will prepare them for the assessments, that their teachers will have the preparation to enable them to teach it well, and there will be...the resources the students and their teachers need to succeed."

There are ways in which the design of the standards themselves can also contribute to the goal of bringing all students to high levels of performance, especially by being clear about what is expected. We have worked to make the expectations included in these performance standards as clear as possible. For some standards it has been possible to do this in the performance descriptions. For example, the Reading standard includes expectations for students to read widely and to read quality materials. Instead of simply exhorting them to do this, we have given more explicit direction by specifying that students should be expected to read at least twenty-five books each year and that those books should be of the quality and complexity illustrated in the sample reading list provided for each grade level. In Mathematics, we have gone beyond simply listing problem solving among our expectations for students. We set out just what we mean by problem solving and what things we expect students to be able to do in problem solving and mathematical reasoning. In addition, by providing numerous examples we have indicated the level of difficulty of the problems students are expected to solve.

The inclusion of work samples and commentaries to illustrate the meaning of the standards is intended to help make the standards clearer. Most of the standards are hard to pin down precisely in words alone. In the Writing standard, for example, the work samples show the expected qualities of writing for the various kinds of writing required and the commentaries explain how these qualities are demonstrated in the work samples. The work samples and commentaries are an integral part of the performance standards.

The work samples will help teachers, students, and parents to picture work that meets standards and to establish goals to reach for. Students need to know what work that meets standards looks like if they are to strive to produce work of the same quality. They also need to see themselves reflected in the work samples if they are to believe that they too are capable of producing such work. We have included work samples drawn from a diverse range of students and from students studying in a wide variety of settings.

Standards should be rigorous and world class.

Is what we expect of our students as rigorous and demanding as what is expected of young people in other countries—especially those countries whose young people consistently perform as well as or better than ours?

That is the question we are trying to answer when we talk about developing world class standards.

Through successive drafts of these performance standards, we compared our work with the national and local curricula of other countries, with textbooks, assessments, and examinations from other countries and, where possible, with work produced by students in other countries. Ultimately, it is the work students produce that will show us whether claims for world class standards can be supported.

We shared the *Consultation Draft* with researchers in other countries and asked them to review it in terms of their own country's standards and in light of what is considered world class in their field. Included among these countries were Australia, Belgium, Canada, the Czech Republic, Denmark, England and Wales, Finland, France, Germany, Japan, the Netherlands, New Zealand, Norway, Poland, Scotland, Singapore, Sweden, and Switzerland. We asked these reviewers to tell us whether each standard is at least as demanding as its counterparts abroad and whether the set of standards represents an appropriately thorough coverage of the subject areas. We also shared the *Consultation Draft* with recognized experts in the field of international comparisons of education, each of whom is familiar with the education systems of several countries.

Our reviewers provided a wealth of constructive responses to the *Consultation Draft*. Most confined their responses to the English Language Arts, Mathematics, and Science standards, though several commended the inclusion of standards for Applied Learning. The reviewers supported the approach we adopted to "concretize" the performance standards through the inclusion of work samples (similar approaches are being used in some other countries, notably England and Wales and Australia). Some of the reviewers were tentative in their response to the question of whether these performance standards are at least as demanding as their counterparts, noting the difficulty of drawing comparisons in the absence of assessment information, but offered comparative comments in terms of the areas covered by the standards. Some provided a detailed analysis of the performance descriptions together with the work samples and commentaries in terms of the expectations of students at comparable grade levels in other countries.

The reviews confirmed the conclusion we had drawn from our earlier analyses of the curricula, textbooks, and examinations of other countries: while the structure of curricula differs from country to country, the expectations contained in these performance standards represent a thorough coverage of the subject areas. No reviewer identified a case of significant omission. In some cases, reviewers noted that the range of expectations may be greater in the New Standards performance standards than in other countries; for example, few countries expect young people to integrate their learning to the extent required by the standards for investigation in New Standards Mathematics. At the same time, a recent study prepared for the Organisation for Economic Co-operation and Development reports that many countries are moving towards expecting students to engage in practical work of the kind required by the New Standards Science standards (Black and Atkin, 1996). The reviews also suggest that these performance standards contain expectations that are at least as rigorous as, and are in some cases more rigorous than, the demands made of students in other countries. None of the reviewers identified standards for which the expectations expressed in the standards were less demanding than those for students in other countries.

We will continue to monitor the rigor and coverage of the New Standards performance standards and assessments in relation to the expectations of students in other countries. In addition to the continued collection and review of materials from other countries, our efforts will include a review of the New Standards performance standards by the Third International Mathematics and Science Study, collaboration with the Council for Basic Education's plan to collect samples of student work from around the world, continued review of the American Federation of Teachers' series, *Defining World Class Standards*, and collaborative efforts with visiting scholars at the Learning Research and Development Center.

Standards should be useful, developing what is needed for citizenship, employment, and life-long learning.

We believe that the core disciplines provide the strongest foundation for learning what is needed for citizenship, employment, and life-long learning. Thus, we have established explicit standards in the core areas of English Language Arts, Mathematics, and Science. But there is more. In particular, it is critical for young people to achieve high standards in Applied Learning—the fourth area we are working on.

Applied Learning focuses on the capabilities people need to be productive members of society, as individuals who apply the knowledge gained in school and elsewhere to analyze problems and propose solutions, to communicate effectively and coordinate action with others, and to use the tools of the information age workplace.

Applied Learning is not about "job skills" for students who are judged incapable of, or indifferent to, the challenges and opportunities of academic learning. They are the abilities all young people will need, both in the workplace and in their role as citizens. They are the thinking and reasoning abilities demanded both by colleges and by the growing number of high performance workplaces, those that expect people at every level of the organization to take responsibility for the quality of products and services. Some of these abilities are familiar; they have long been recognized goals of schooling, though they have not necessarily been translated clearly into expectations for student performance. Others break new ground; they are the kinds of abilities we now understand will be needed by everyone in the near future. All are skills attuned to the real world of responsible citizenship and dignified work that values and cultivates mind and spirit.

Many reviewers of drafts of these performance standards noted the absence of standards for the core area of social studies, including history, geography, and civics. At the time we began our work, national content standards for those areas were only in early stages of development; we resolved to focus our resources on the four areas we have worked on. As consensus builds around content standards in this additional area, we will examine the possibilities for expanding the New Standards system to include it.

STANDARDS FOR STANDARDS

Standards should be important and focused, parsimonious while including those elements that represent the most important knowledge and skills within the discipline.

As anyone who has been involved in a standards development effort knows, it is easier to add to standards than it is to limit what they cover. It is especially easier to resolve disagreements about the most important things to cover by including everything than it is to resolve the disagreements themselves. We have tried not to take the easier route. We adopted the principle of parsimony as a goal and have tried to practice it. At the same time, we have been concerned not to confuse parsimony with brevity. The performance descriptions are intended to make explicit what it is that students should know and the ways they should demonstrate the knowledge and skills they have acquired. For example, the standards relating to conceptual understanding in Mathematics spell out the expectations of students in some detail.

The approach we have adopted distinguishes between standards as a means of organizing the knowledge and skills of a subject area and as a reference point for assessment, on the one hand, and the curriculum designed to enable students to achieve the standards, on the other. The standards are intended to focus attention on what is important but not to imply that the standards themselves should provide the organizing structure for the curriculum. In English Language Arts, for example, we have established a separate standard for conventions, grammar, and usage. This does not imply that conventions, grammar, and usage should be taught in isolation from other elements of English Language Arts. In fact, all of the work samples included in this book to illustrate the Conventions standard also illustrate parts of the Writing standard. What we are saying is that the work students do should be designed to help them achieve the Conventions standard. This means that conventions, grammar, and usage should not only be among the things assessed but should also be a focus for explicit reporting of student achievement.

Standards should be manageable given the constraints of time.

This criterion follows very closely on the last one, but focuses particularly on making sure that standards are "doable." One of the important features of our standards development effort is the high level of interaction among the people working on the different subject areas. We view the standards for the four areas as a set at each grade level; our publication of the standards by grade level reflects this orientation. This orientation has allowed us to limit the incidence of duplication across subject areas and to recognize and use opportunities for forging stronger connections among subject areas through the work that students do. A key to ensuring the standards are manageable is making the most of opportunities for student work to do "double" and even "triple duty." Most of the work samples included in this book demonstrate the way a single activity can generate

work that allows students to demonstrate their achievement in relation to several standards within a subject area. Several of the work samples show how a single activity can allow students to demonstrate their achievement in relation to standards in more than one subject area. (See, for example, "*Counting on Frank*," page 46 and page 100.)

Standards should be adaptable, permitting flexibility in implementation needed for local control, state and regional variation, and differing individual interests and cultural traditions.

These standards are intended for use in widely differing settings. One approach to tackling the need for flexibility to accommodate local control, state and regional variation, and differing individual interests and cultural traditions, is to make the standards general and to leave the job of translating the standards into more specific statements to the people who use them. We have not adopted that approach. These standards need to be specific enough to guide the New Standards assessment system; we have tried to make them specific enough to do so. We have also tried to achieve the degree of specificity necessary to do this without unduly limiting the kinds of flexibility outlined above. Most of the standards are expressed in a way that leaves plenty of room for local decisions about the actual tasks and activities through which the standards may be achieved.

However, the specificity needed for standards intended to guide an assessment system does place some limits on flexibility. To tackle these apparently contradictory demands on the standards, we have adopted the notion of "substitution." This means that when users of these standards identify elements in the standards that are inconsistent with decisions made at the local level, they can substitute their own. An example of this is the Reading standard in English Language Arts. The Reading standard includes the requirement that students should read the equivalent of twenty-five books each year and specifies that they should read material of the quality and complexity illustrated in the sample reading list. We have included the reading list so as to be clear about the quality of reading material we are talking about at each grade level. But we do not claim that the titles on this list are the only ones that would be appropriate. Thus, users who have established their own reading lists and are satisfied with them can replace the lists provided with their own. There is, however, one important proviso: substitution only works when what is substituted is comparable with the material it replaces both in terms of the quality and the quantity of expectation.

Standards should be clear and usable.

Making standards sufficiently clear so that parents, teachers, and students can understand what they mean and what the standards require of them is essential to the purpose for establishing standards in the first place. It is also a challenge because while all of these groups need to understand what the standards are, the kinds of information they need are different. The most obvious difference is between the way in which the standards need to be presented to elementary school students so that they know what they should be striving to achieve and the way in which those same standards need to be presented to teachers so that they can help their students get there. If the standards were written only in a form that elementary school students could access, we would have to leave out information teachers need to do their job.

These standards are being presented in several formats. This version of the standards is written primarily for teachers. It includes technical language about the subject matter of the standards and terms that educators use to describe differences in the quality of work students produce. It could be described as a technical document. That does not mean that parents and students should not have access to it. We have tried to make the standards clear and to avoid jargon, but they do include language that may be difficult for students to comprehend and more detail than some parents may want to deal with.

The standards are also included in the portfolio materials provided for student use. In these materials, the standards are set out in the form of guides to help students select work to include in their portfolios.

A less technical version of the standards is in preparation. It is being written with parents and the community in general in mind. The standards will be the same but they will be explained in more generally accessible language.

Standards should be reflective of broad consensus, resulting from an iterative process of comment, feedback, and revision including educators and the general public.

This publication is the result of progressive revisions to drafts over a period of eighteen months. Early drafts were revised in response to comment and feedback from reviewers nominated by the New Standards partners and the New Standards advisory committees for each of the subject areas, as well as other educators.

The *Consultation Draft*, published in November 1995, was circulated widely for comment. Some 1,500 individuals and organizations were invited to review the *Draft*. The reviewers included nominees of professional associations representing a wide range of interests in education, subject experts in the relevant fields, experienced teachers, business and industry groups, and community organizations. In addition, we held a series of face-to-face consultations to obtain responses and suggestions. These included detailed discussions with members of key groups and organizations and a series of meetings at which we invited people with relevant experience and expertise to provide detailed critique of the *Consultation Draft*. We also received numerous responses from people who purchased the *Consultation Draft* and who took the trouble to complete and return the response form that was included with each copy.

The process of revision of the performance standards was further informed by a series of independently-conducted focus group meetings with parents and other members of the community in several regions of the country and with teachers who were using the *Consultation Draft*.

The reviewers provided very supportive and constructive commentary on the *Consultation Draft*, both at the broad level of presentation and formatting of the performance standards and at the detailed level of suggestions for refinements to the performance descriptions for some of the standards. These comments have significantly informed the revisions made to the standards in the preparation of this publication.

HOW TO READ THESE PERFORMANCE STANDARDS

The standards for elementary school are set out in an overview on page 19. The overview provides the names of the standards for each of the four areas: English Language Arts, Mathematics, Science, and Applied Learning. To help you navigate your way through the book, a different color is used for each area.

Elementary school level means the end of fourth grade.

The standards for elementary school are set at the level of achievement expected of students at approximately the end of fourth grade. Some students will achieve this level of performance earlier than the end of fourth grade. Some students will reach it later than the end of fourth grade. What is important is that students have the opportunity to meet the standards. (See "Deciding what constitutes a standard-setting performance," page 12.)

Each standard is identified by a symbol.

Turn to the performance descriptions for English Language Arts on pages 22-26. There are five standards for English Language Arts, each identified by a symbol. The symbol for the Reading standard is **E1**. This symbol appears throughout the book wherever there is a reference to this standard.

1 **Most standards are made up of several parts.**
Most of the standards are made up of several parts, for example, the Reading standard has four parts. Each part is identified by a lower case letter; for example, the part of the Reading standard that refers to reading informational materials is **E1c**. These symbols are used throughout the book wherever there is a reference to the relevant part of a standard.

Performance descriptions tell what students are expected to know and be able to do.

Each part of a standard has a performance description. The performance description is a narrative description of what students are expected to know and be able to do. It is shown in color.

2 **Examples are the kinds of work students might do to demonstrate their achievement of the standards.**
Immediately following the performance descriptions for the standard are examples of the kinds of work students might do to demonstrate their achievement. The examples also indicate the nature and complexity of activities that are appropriate to expect of students at the grade level. However, we use the word "example" deliberately. The examples are intended only to show the kinds of work that students might do and to stimulate ideas for further kinds of work. None of the activities shown in the examples is necessarily required to meet the standard.

3 **Cross-references highlight the links between the examples and the performance descriptions.**
The symbols that follow each example show the part or parts of the standard to which the example relates.

4 **Cross-references also highlight links among the standards.**
Often the examples that go with the English Language Arts performance descriptions include cross-references to other parts of the English Language Arts standards.

Cross-references also highlight opportunities for connecting activities across subject areas.

Some cross-references shown following the examples identify parts of standards in other subject areas. These cross-references highlight examples for which the same activity may enable students to demonstrate their achievement in more than one subject matter.

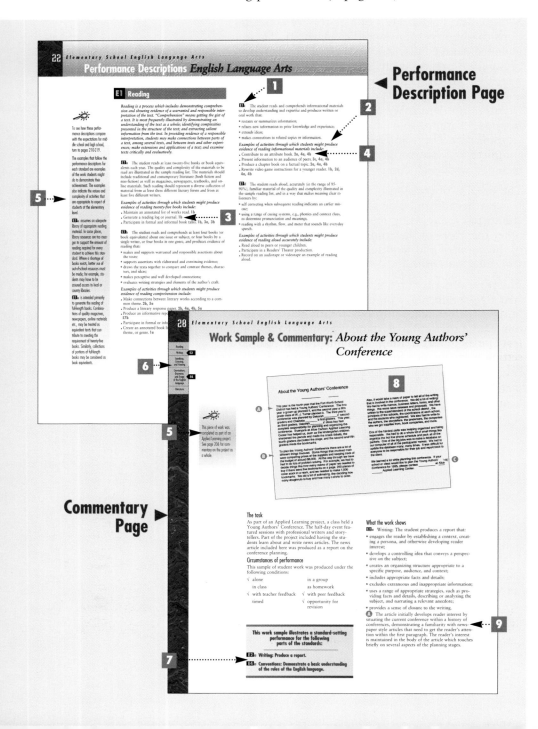

Performance Description Page

Commentary Page

Some cross-references are to Applied Learning.

Some cross-references are to Applied Learning. Applied Learning is not a subject area in its own right. Applied Learning activities are expected to draw on subject matter from English Language Arts, Mathematics, Science, or other subjects. Generally, they will take place as part of studies within one or more subjects. The cross-references show activities that may provide a vehicle for students to demonstrate achievement of standards within one or more subject areas as well as standards for Applied Learning.

Some cross-references also show the possibilities for students to use work from Mathematics or Science to demonstrate their achievement of English Language Arts standards, and vice versa.

We have not tried to highlight every possible cross-reference, only to give an indication of the possibilities. The potential of these examples for realizing the possibilities of enabling students to demonstrate their achievement in more than one subject area depends to a large extent on the specific tasks that are presented to students.

5 Margin notes draw attention to particular aspects of the standards.

The notes in the margin draw attention to particular aspects of the standards, such as the resources to which students need access in order to meet the requirements of the standards.

Comparing the grade levels.

Each page showing performance descriptions has a note in the margin that directs attention to the Appendices which show the performance descriptions at each of the three grade levels: elementary, middle, and high school.

Work samples and commentaries.

Work samples and commentaries appear on the pages immediately following the performance descriptions.

6 Standards are highlighted in the bar at the side of the page.

The bar along the side of the pages showing student work highlights the standards that are illustrated by each work sample.

7 The box at the bottom of the page shows what is illustrated in the work sample.

The shaded box at the bottom of the page lists the parts of the standards that are illustrated in the work sample.

8 Work samples illustrate standard-setting performances.

Each work sample is a genuine piece of student work. We have selected it because it illustrates a standard-setting performance for one or more parts of the standards. (See "Not all performance standards are the same," page 10.)

9 The commentary explains why the work illustrates a standard-setting performance.

The commentary that goes with each work sample identifies the features of the work sample that illustrate the relevant parts of the standards. The commentary explains the task on which the student worked and the circumstances under which the work was completed. It draws attention to the qualities of the work with direct reference to the performance descriptions for the relevant standards.

The commentary also notes our reservations about the work.

The commentary also draws attention to any reservations we have about the student work. (See "Genuine student work," page 12.)

Performance Standards = performance descriptions + work samples + commentaries on the work samples.

Performance standards are, therefore, made up of a combination of performance descriptions, work samples, and commentaries on the work samples:

- The performance descriptions tell what students should know and the ways they should demonstrate the knowledge and skills they have acquired.

- The work samples show work that illustrates standard-setting performances in relation to parts of the standards.

- The commentaries explain why the work is standard-setting with reference to the relevant performance description or descriptions.

Each of these is an essential component of a performance standard.

Most work samples illustrate a standard-setting performance for parts of more than one standard.

Most work samples illustrate the quality of work expected for parts of more than one standard. For example, some of the work samples selected to illustrate parts of **E2**, Writing, also illustrate a standard-setting performance for one or both parts of **E4**, Conventions, Grammar, and Usage of the English Language, or for part of **E5**, Literature, or, possibly, all of these.

"Enchiladas" (see page 37) is an example of a work sample that illustrates parts of more than one standard in English Language Arts.

A work sample may illustrate standards from more than one subject area.

Similarly, a work sample may illustrate parts of standards in more than one subject area. For example, a project completed for **M8**, Putting Mathematics to Work, might also illustrate the report writing part of **E2**, Writing. It might also qualify as a project within the requirements of **A1**, Problem Solving.

"*Counting on Frank*" (see page 46 and page 100) is an example of a work sample that illustrates parts of standards from more than one subject area.

Reading	E1
Writing	E2
Speaking, Listening, and Viewing	E3
Conventions, Grammar, and Usage of the English Language	E4
Literature	E5
Arithmetic and Number Concepts	M1
Geometry & Measurement Concepts	M2
Function & Algebra Concepts	M3
Statistics & Probability Concepts	M4
Problem Solving & Reasoning	M5
Mathematical Skills & Tools	M6
Mathematical Communication	M7
Putting Mathematics to Work	M8
Physical Sciences Concepts	S1
Life Sciences Concepts	S2
Earth and Space Sciences Concepts	S3
Scientific Connections and Applications	S4
Scientific Thinking	S5
Scientific Tools and Technologies	S6
Scientific Communication	S7
Scientific Investigation	S8
Problem Solving	A1
Communication Tools and Techniques	A2
Information Tools and Techniques	A3
Learning and Self-management Tools and Techniques	A4
Tools and Techniques for Working With Others	A5

NOT ALL PERFORMANCE STANDARDS ARE THE SAME

As you read these performance standards, you will notice that the standards are not all the same. The most obvious difference is in the way in which the performance descriptions for the standards are written. We did not impose a single style on the way in which the standards were written although we probably intended to do so when we began work. The reason we abandoned the idea of a single style is that during the course of the development process, it became increasingly apparent that the various standards are different in nature and have different purposes that lend themselves to different kinds of presentation. But the style we have adopted for each standard is not entirely idiosyncratic. There are some patterns that help make sense of the different styles and of the nature and purposes of the standards for which those styles have been used.

The first distinction that most people notice is the difference between the way the performance descriptions for the Mathematics and Science standards are written, on the one hand, and the way the performance descriptions for the English Language Arts and Applied Learning standards are written, on the other. But closer inspection reveals that the differences among the standards do not fall out as neatly as that division would suggest. Each subject area includes different styles of standards and the styles apply across subject areas.

We have identified four categories or kinds of standards, distinguished by their relationship to products of student learning and by the range of evidence required to demonstrate achievement of the standards. The distinctions are broad rather than neat, and we have sought only to define them generally rather than precisely. These differences among the standards have consequences for what it means to "meet a standard" and, therefore, for the ways in which we can use samples of student work to illustrate standard-setting performances.

Standards that describe a piece of work or a performance

One kind of standard is characterized by **E2**, Writing. Each part of this standard literally describes a piece of work that students are expected to produce and the knowledge and skills that should be evident in that work. For this kind of standard there is a one to one relationship between each part of the standard and a piece of work.

Standards that fit this category generally are the parts of **E1**, **E2**, **E3**, **E5**b, **M8**, **S8**, **A1**, **A2**, and **A5**.

Standards of this kind have several features:

• A single piece of work can meet the standard. In fact all of the requirements of the standard usually must be evident in a single piece of work for it to be judged as meeting the standard.

• The qualities that must be evident in a piece of work for it to meet the standard can be stated explicitly and are listed in bullet points as part of the performance description. These qualities can be thought of as assessment criteria or as a rubric for work that meets the standard.

Work samples and commentaries to illustrate standard-setting performances for standards of this kind include: "How to Tap Dance," page 43, "Dream House Project," page 118, "Fire-Belly Newts," page 156, and "Designing and Building a Bike Trailer," page 165.

Standards that describe conceptual understanding

A second kind of standard is characterized by **M1**, Arithmetic and Number Concepts. This standard describes conceptual understanding.

Standards that fit this category are **E5**a, **M1**, **M2**, **M3**, **M4**, **S1**, **S2**, **S3**, and **S4**.

These standards have several features:

• The standard is made up of a number of distinct parts. It is most unlikely that any single piece of work will demonstrate all parts of the standard. In fact, it is common for a single piece of work to relate only to some aspects of one part of the standard. Thus, the standard can usually only be met by multiple pieces of work.

• Conceptual understanding is developmental. Any one piece of work may contain elements of conceptual understanding that are below what is expected for the grade level and elements that either meet or exceed what is expected for the grade level. Judging whether the work is "good enough" often means making an on-balance judgment. The developmental nature of conceptual understanding makes it difficult to specify in more than general terms the qualities that need to be present in a piece of work for it to be judged as "good enough." These expectations need to be defined concept by concept.

In **M1**, **M2**, **M3**, and **M4**, the expectations have been defined more closely through progressive drafts of these performance standards.

S1, **S2**, **S3**, and **S4** are derived from the *National Science Education Standards* and the *Benchmarks for Science Literacy*, each of which contains detailed explication of the concepts and the expectations of students for conceptual understanding at different grade levels.

Work samples and commentaries to illustrate standard-setting performance for standards of this kind include: "Sharing 25," page 66, and "Flinkers" on page 136.

Standards that describe skills and tools

The third kind of standard is made up of the standards that describe skills and tools, such as analytical skills. It is characterized by **S6**, Scientific Tools and Technologies.

Standards that fit this category generally are **E4**, **M5**, **M6**, **M7**, **S5**, **S6**, **S7**, **A3**, and **A4**.

These standards have several features:

• As with the standards that describe conceptual understanding, it is most unlikely that any single piece of work will demonstrate all parts of the standard. In fact, it is common for a single piece of work to relate only to some aspects of one part of the standard. Thus, the standard can only be met by multiple pieces of evidence.

• Also, like conceptual understanding, use of skills and tools is developmental. Any one piece of work may contain evidence of use of skills and tools that is below what is expected for the grade level and evidence of use that either meets or exceeds what is expected for the grade level. Deciding whether the work is "good enough" often means making an on-balance judgment.

• What distinguishes these standards from the other kinds is the body of evidence needed to demonstrate that the standard has been met. Here, sufficiency refers not only to the idea of coverage but also to a notion of consistency of application. We want to be confident that the work in question is representative of a body of work.

Ideally, work that provides evidence for these standards also provides evidence for other standards. This is the case for all of the work samples in this book that illustrate parts of these standards.

Work samples and commentaries to illustrate standard-setting performance for standards of this kind include: "How Many Handshakes?" page 90, "Smiles," page 150, and "Bike Helmet Ordinance," page 181.

Standards that describe an accomplishment based on effort

The fourth category is closely related to the first, standards that describe a piece of work or a performance; it could be regarded as a sub-category of those standards. It is characterized by **E1**a, Read at least twenty-five books or book equivalents each year.

This part of the Reading standard is designed to encourage and reward effort. It is designed on principles similar to those that apply to the merit badges that have long formed a part of the system of encouragement and rewards for young people in community youth organizations like the Boy Scouts of America and the Girl Scouts of the U.S.A. The twenty-five book requirement is designed to encourage students to develop a habit of reading by requiring that they read a lot. The requirement is challenging, especially since the reading is expected to be of the quality of the materials included in the sample

reading list, but it is also confined. This part of the standard is not made more complex by requirements for evidence of depth of reading and comprehension. The message is, if you invest the effort, you will meet the requirement.

An example of a work sample and commentary to illustrate a standard-setting performance for this part of the Reading standard is "Home Reading Record," page 56.

The differences among standards described here have implications for their assessment. (See "How the assessments are connected to the performance standards," page 14.)

THE WORK SAMPLES

The work samples and commentaries form an essential element of the performance standards because they give concrete meaning to the words in the performance descriptions and show the level of performance expected by the standards.

Genuine student work

In all cases, the work samples are genuine student work. While they illustrate standard-setting performances for parts of the standards, many samples are not "perfect" in every respect. Some, for example, include spelling errors, clumsy grammatical constructions, or errors of calculation. We think it is important that the standards be illustrated by means of authentic work samples and accordingly have made no attempt to "doctor" the work in order to correct these imperfections: the work has been included "warts and all." Where errors occur, we have included a note drawing attention to the nature of the mistakes and commenting on their significance in the context of the work. In some cases, for example, the work was produced as a first draft only (in which case it would be expected that the errors would be corrected in work presented as finished work), or there is evidence in the rest of the work to suggest that an error was a slip rather than an error in conceptual understanding.

In other words, we have tried to adopt reasonable expectations for correctness, but not to overlook errors where they arise. We have also resolved to apply those expectations consistently to all the work samples. We have paid attention to spelling, for example, not only in the work samples included to illustrate the English Language Arts standards, but also in those samples included to illustrate standards in the other subject areas. Similarly, we reviewed all work samples for accuracy in relation to mathematical and scientific content.

Work produced by a diverse range of students

The work samples in this book were produced by a diverse range of students in a wide variety of settings. The work comes from places as different from one another as rural communities in Vermont and Iowa, urban communities in Fort Worth, Pittsburgh, San Diego, and New York City, and suburban communities in Washington, California, and Colorado. It comes from students with a wide range of cultural backgrounds, some of whom have a first language other than English. And it comes from students studying in regular programs and from students studying in special education programs. Some of the work was produced under examination conditions in timed settings; most of it was produced in the context of on-going class work and extended projects. Most of the work was produced in school, but some samples were produced through out-of-school programs, such as 4-H and a community youth program.

What unites the work samples is that they all help to illustrate the performance standards by demonstrating standard-setting performances for parts of one or more of the standards.

Deciding what constitutes a standard-setting performance

The work samples published in this book were selected from a much wider range of samples. The samples came from students working on producing New Standards portfolios, from students' work on New Standards reference examinations, from other work produced by students in the classrooms of schools of the states and urban school districts that form the New Standards partnership, and from work produced by students in schools that are involved in related programs.

The collections of student work were reviewed through a variety of strategies to tap the judgment of teachers and subject experts about the "level of performance" at which each of the standards for elementary school should be set. We define the elementary school level as being the expectations for student performance at approximately the end of fourth grade. We used grade level as our reference point because it is in common use and most people understand it. However, "at approximately the end of fourth grade" begs some questions. Do we mean the level at which our fourth graders currently perform? Or, do we mean the level at which our fourth graders might perform if expectations for their performance were higher and the programs through which they learn were designed to help them meet those higher expectations? And, do we mean the level at which the highest-achieving fourth graders perform or the level at which most fourth graders perform?

We established our expectations in terms of what we should expect of students who work hard in a good program; that is, our expectations assume that students will have tried hard to achieve the standards and they will have studied in a program designed to help them to do so. These performance standards are founded on a firm belief that the great majority of students can achieve them, providing they work hard, they study a curriculum designed to help them achieve the standards that is taught by teachers who are prepared to teach it well, and they have adequate resources to succeed.

Some of the work samples included in this book were also included in the *Consultation Draft*; some appeared in earlier drafts as well. The appropriateness of these work samples as illustrating standard-setting performances has been the subject of extensive review, through discussions among our subject advisory committees and through round table discussions among experienced teachers and subject experts. Some of the work samples included in earlier drafts did not pass the scrutiny of these reviews and are not included in this book. Many of the new work samples were identified in the course of meetings set up to score portfolios produced through the New Standards portfolio field trial in 1995-96; others were identified in the process of scoring tasks on New Standards reference examinations. These scoring meetings involve multiple scoring and discussion of samples among experienced teachers and subject experts. Cross-referencing the selection of work samples to illustrate the performance standards with the scoring of work produced through the two elements of the New Standards assessment system is critical to ensuring the development of coherence among all the parts of the system.

We have used this process of progressive iterations of review of work samples in relation to the performance descriptions and in relation to our definition of elementary school level to arrive at agreement about the meaning of elementary school level.

Inevitably, agreement about what work constitutes a standard-setting performance has been easiest to achieve for those parts of the standards that relate to familiar kinds of expectations for student work. The parts of the Writing standard that refer to familiar and often-practiced kinds of writing such as narrative account are good examples of this. Not only did we have access to a wide range of samples from which to choose, but teachers and experts in the field have a long tradition of discussion and assessment of the features of good writing for a narrative account. Work samples to illustrate some other parts of the standards are much harder to find; for example, work samples to illustrate the investigations and projects standards in Mathematics and Science and work samples to illustrate each of the Applied Learning standards. Overall, we had access to relatively few work samples for Science and Applied Learning, since work on these areas within the New Standards system is at an early stage by comparison with the work in English Language Arts and Mathematics.

The comprehensiveness of the work samples

This book contains nearly fifty samples of student work and more are contained in the videotape that accompanies the book. We have sought to include work samples that illustrate standard-setting performances for each of the standards and for as many of the parts of the standards as possible. The range of work samples has been expanded considerably over progressive drafts of the standards. But the collection is still not comprehensive. We have included work samples to illustrate only some parts of the conceptual understanding standards in Mathematics and Science, for example, and work samples to illustrate only some of the kinds of projects and investigations included in those standards.

Limiting the number of samples was a deliberate decision. We decided that we would make best use of a print format by seeking to illustrate as many parts of the standards as possible but restricting the overall number of work samples to a manageable number. We also decided to restrict the work samples to samples that illustrate standard-setting performances in relation to parts of the standards, rather than include work samples that illustrate performances that are not of sufficient quality or that exceed expectations for the standards. (With regard to the latter point, collections of work samples that illustrate performances at a range of performance levels do exist within the New Standards system, as part of the Released Tasks and scoring guides for the reference examinations and in the example portfolios; see page 16.)

It is arguable whether any given collection of work samples, regardless of how large, would be adequate for illustrating every part of the standards. Similarly, it is arguable whether any such collection could also demonstrate the range of ways that students might produce work that illustrates standard-setting performances and illustrate the standards more fully by including work that demonstrates a range of levels of performance. To be really useful, such a collection would also need to be capable of being updated to include more effective illustrations of the standards as work that serves the purpose becomes available— a need that we have already noted exists in relation to some of the standards. A publication format that could perform all of those functions presents a tall order, indeed. However, electronic formats hold the promise of making it possible to build a collection of this sort and to make it easily accessible. We hope to make use of the potential of electronic formats in the future.

HOW WILL THE PERFORMANCE STANDARDS BE USED?

The primary audience for these performance standards is teachers. We hope that teachers will use the standards to:

- Help students and parents understand what work that meets standards looks like;

- Inform discussions with their colleagues as they plan programs to help students learn to high standards;

- Challenge assumptions about what we can expect from students;

- Communicate the meaning of high standards to district administrators, school board members, and the public so they can work together to build learning environments that challenge all students.

New Standards will use the performance standards to provide:

- The basis of design specifications for the New Standards assessment system;

- The basis for reporting student scores on assessments within the New Standards system; and

- The basis for linking the New Standards assessment system with the standards and assessment systems of the members of the New Standards partnership.

Assessment based on standards

Performance standards define a student's academic responsibilities and, by implication, the teaching responsibilities of the school. How do we determine whether students have lived up to their academic responsibilities? We assess their work—is it "good enough" by comparison with the standards.

Assessment that serves the purpose of telling us how well students are performing by comparison with standards (standards-referenced assessment) differs from assessment designed to compare students to average performances (norm-referenced assessment). New Standards assessments are standards-referenced assessments. They start with performance standards and they take seriously the type, quality, and balance of performances spelled out by the standards. Assessment systems of this kind look a lot like a sampling of questions and assignments from a standards-based curriculum.

Common examples of standards-referenced examinations are the Advanced Placement (AP) exams of the College Board. The Scholastic Achievement Test (SAT), also from the College Board, is a contrasting example of a norm-referenced test. The AP exams look like the work (type, quality, and balance) students do in the AP courses whereas the SAT looks very different from the work students do in their college preparatory courses. Other well established standards-based examinations include licensure exams for many occupations such as pilots, architects, and electricians.

Unlike the AP or licensure exams, with explicit courses of study that have been debated and agreed

upon in an open, public forum (e.g., the College Board, the state bar association or the board of realtors), many individual teacher's grades are based solely on their experience as students and teachers. Unless they participate in an external program like the AP or the International Baccalaureate, teachers rarely have the opportunity to see or discuss an end-of-course examination with others who teach the same course, no less to apply common criteria for marking. Even in the case of high school courses with departmental final examinations, the majority of the feedback to students throughout the school year is based on their individual teacher's judgment. And in the vast majority of the instances, especially in the elementary and middle school years, the individual teacher's standards apply almost exclusively.

It can be argued that the teacher, the person closest to the student's work, is in the best position to assess the student's accomplishment. However, the problem with an assessment system based on individual teacher judgment is that students in different classes, with different teachers, in different schools, work to widely varying standards. There is no common reference for teachers, students, or the public to compare performance across individuals or classrooms. This leads to wide variation in expectation and opportunity. Students get good grades one year for trying hard, then fail the following year for being too far below the average on a test.

New Standards has designed an assessment system that provides a common reference point for students, parents, teachers, and the public who want to judge student performance on the quality and quantity of student work that is expected at a particular level. The New Standards assessment system is based on these performance standards. It has three parts: reference examinations, portfolios, and teacher assessment. While each part of the system can be used independently, the most complete picture of performance referenced to the performance standards comes from using all three.

How the assessments are connected to the performance standards

The performance standards define a domain of expected student performances. Take the Reading standard as an example (see page 22). This standard begins with a definition of reading that describes what we expect students to *be able to do* at approximately the end of fourth grade. The performance descriptions go on to spell out expectations for what students *will accomplish* in terms of the quantity, quality, range, and concentration of their reading. Furthermore, students are expected to *put their reading to work* and the standards say so; students have to produce work based on their reading of specific types of text.

We assess the different elements of the domain defined by a standard by using assessment methods appropriate to the expected performance.

In the English Language Arts reference examination

students read a selection of grade-level appropriate passages. The passages include both literary and informational selections. Students answer two types of questions about the passages. One type of question assesses "understanding of the text as a whole" as described in the definition in the Reading standard. These are straightforward questions about the gist of the text. Some of these questions ask students to write a few sentences, some are multiple choice. The second type of question about the same passages asks students to analyze the text, draw reasonable conclusions, and make interpretations—behaviors that characterize what competent readers do.

To demonstrate their achievement of the Reading standard students must also show what they have accomplished—just as people do when they apply for a job. Assessing actual accomplishments means evaluating a selection of student work according to criteria derived directly from the performance descriptions for the standards. New Standards portfolios are organized around "exhibits," each focused on an area of performance. The reading exhibit in the English Language Arts portfolio requires that students include at least four pieces of work that demonstrate their accomplishments in responding to literary and informational texts of appropriate complexity. The portfolio includes criteria for judging the entries in this exhibit. These criteria are drawn directly from the relevant performance descriptions. The criteria can be used by the student for self-assessment, by the teacher for feedback and grading, and by independent external scorers to report on achievement of standards to the public.

A further requirement of the reading exhibit in the portfolio, again based directly on the performance standards, is certification of what the student has read. The first part of the Reading standard (**E1**a) requires that students read at least twenty-five books or book equivalents each year. The reading must include a range of literary forms and works from several writers. Students are also required to read in depth (**E1**b). The appropriate assessor for these requirements is the teacher or another adult close to the student who can verify the student's claims for meeting this requirement. This component of the system for assessing achievement of the Reading standard is designed to work like a merit badge in the style of the awards developed by the Girl Scouts of the U.S.A. and the Boy Scouts of America.

To complete the reading exhibit, students are asked to include evidence that demonstrates reading fluency (**E1**d). This is also provided by means of teacher certification. The portfolio provides teachers and students with simple criteria for assessing reading aloud for fluency, again drawn from the criteria set out in the Reading standard.

In summary, students' achievement of the Reading standard is assessed through a combination of methods:

• The reference examination provides evidence of comprehension, analysis, and interpretation of literary and informational texts, related to the Reading standard as a whole and particularly to **E1**c. (These parts of the reference examination also provide evidence of the first part of the Literature standard, **E5**a.)

• The reading exhibit for the portfolio provides evidence of working with literary and informational texts, related to **E1**b and **E1**c. (Entries included in this exhibit also demonstrate accomplishment in relation to **E5**a and may be used to fulfill part of the requirements of the writing exhibit.)

• Teacher assessment in the form of certification, included in the reading exhibit, provides verification of students' claims regarding the twenty-five book requirement and assessment of reading fluency, related to **E1**a, **E1**b, and **E1**d.

This example of how reading is assessed in the New Standards system illustrates several important points. First, the assessment methods and instruments suit the part of the standard to be assessed. Second, the criteria for judging achievement of the standard are drawn as directly as possible from the performance descriptions of the relevant standard. Third, comprehensive assessment of student achievement of the performance standards requires an appropriate combination of external on-demand assessments like the reference examination, externally-set auditable criteria like the portfolio, and teacher assessment.

The assessments are built on the basic principle that students who work hard in a good program should be able to achieve the performance standards. Students who do what is asked of them, read what they are assigned, do their homework, study for examinations, participate in class, and so on, have a right to expect all this work to pay off in learning. If it does not, there is something wrong with the program.

These standards expect students to work hard. For example, the Science standards include an expectation that every student will complete one science investigation in each of the years leading up to graduation chosen from the following: experiment, fieldwork, design, or secondary research. This requirement is demanding for all students, but doable. Most current college bound students are not asked do this much, let alone students who are not intending to go to college. This is not because these students are not capable of doing the work, but because their programs are not organized to give them the opportunity. However, virtually any student who works hard in a good program can produce investigations such as those identified above that meet standards for quality. By setting expectations like this, standards are raised for all students.

Raising standards for all students has important implications for the quality of curriculum and instruction. Indeed, one of the most important reasons for setting high standards is to challenge the system to perform for the students. Appropriate assessments based on these high standards can give the system feedback on how well it is doing and what it has to do next.

HOW WILL THE PERFORMANCE STANDARDS BE USED?

The reference examinations

Mathematics

The Mathematics reference examinations are targeted for grades 4, 8, and 10. Each examination consists of extended response and short answer items. Student responses are scored both holistically and dimensionally.

Students receive three scores for the Mathematics reference examination: one for understanding of mathematical concepts, one for mathematical skills, and one for problem solving and reasoning and mathematical communication.

Standards defining mathematics scores

SCORE	STANDARDS INCLUDED IN SCORE
Conceptual Understanding	M1, M2, M3, M4
Mathematical Skills	M6
Problem Solving and Reasoning/ Mathematical Communication	M5, M7

English Language Arts

The English Language Arts reference examinations are targeted for grades 4, 8, and 10. Each examination includes open-ended responses, short answer responses, essay questions, and multiple choice items. The student responses are scored holistically on two of these forms; the multiple choice responses are scanned.

Students receive four scores for the English Language Arts reference examination: one for writing, one for reading for basic understanding, one for interpretation and analysis of reading, and one for conventions, grammar, and usage of the English language.

Standards defining English Language Arts scores

SCORE	STANDARDS INCLUDED IN SCORE
Reading: Basic Understanding	E1
Reading: Inference and Analysis	E1
Writing	E2
Writing Conventions	E4

The criteria for scoring each task, for example, the writing sample or responses to the reading questions, are defined by rubrics for each score level (usually 0 to 5) and by anchor examples of student performance at each level. Trained scorers use these rubrics and anchor examples to score responses with high reliability.

Released Tasks from the reference examinations, complete with anchor examples and rubrics, are available to assist teachers and students to prepare for the examinations. The Released Tasks also include examples of student responses scored at each of the performance levels.

Each student's level of performance on the reference examination is determined by decision rules for profiles of scores on sets of items or tasks. These rules were established by panels of judges based on the stated expectations of the performance standards, with allowance made for the usual effects of the test-taking situation.

Levels of performance

For each standards-based score, there are five levels of student performance:

H—Achieved the Standard with Honors means that in addition to meeting the standards, a number of the student's responses exceeded the basic criteria for meeting the standard or displayed features characteristic of advanced knowledge and skill.

S—Achieved the Standard means that the student's performances met the standards as set out in the New Standards performance standards.

N—Nearly Achieved the Standard means that the student's performances almost but did not quite meet the performance standards.

B—Below the Standard means that the student's performances clearly did not meet the performance standards.

L—Little Evidence of Achievement means that the student's performances demonstrated little or none of the knowledge and skill expected by the performance standards.

The portfolio system

The portfolio system complements the reference examination by requiring selections of student work that provide evidence of achievement of the performance standards. The portfolios are organized into exhibits; each focuses on an area of performance and includes clear criteria for assessment. The structure and content of the exhibits parallel the structure of the performance standards. Each exhibit is composed of one or more entries; the entry slips tell students exactly what is required and how it will be assessed. The criteria come directly from the performance descriptions for the standards. For example, the middle school Mathematics portfolio has five exhibits drawn directly from the performance standards as is shown in the chart on the next page.

Mathematics portfolio

EXHIBIT	ENTRIES	STANDARD	EXHIBIT REQUIREMENTS
Conceptual Understanding	• Number and Operations • Geometry and Measurement • Functions and Algebra • Probability and Statistics	**M1** **M2** **M3** **M4**	To demonstrate conceptual understanding, students are required to provide evidence that they can use the concept to solve problems, represent it in multiple ways (through numbers, graphs, symbols, diagrams, or words, as appropriate), and explain it to someone else. The student must include at least two problems, and may include a third if necessary, to provide evidence of all three ways of demonstrating conceptual understanding (using, representing, and explaining).
Problem Solving	• Four problems	**M5**	The student must include four problems which, taken together, show the full range of problem solving required by the performance standard, including formulation, implementation, and conclusion. Problem solving is defined as using mathematical concepts and skills to solve non-routine, usually realistic, problems that challenge the student to organize the steps to follow for a solution.
Skills and Communication	• Skills • Communication Entries submitted for the other three exhibits are cited as evidence. A few additional pieces of work may be included here to fill important gaps.	**M6** **M7**	Entry slips list skills from **M6** (e.g., compute accurately with rational numbers, use equations, formulas, and simple algebraic notation, use geometric shapes and terms correctly) and **M7** (e.g., present mathematical procedures and results clearly, systematically, and correctly; use mathematical language and representations with accuracy: numerical tables and equations, formulas, functions, algebraic equations, charts, graphs, and diagrams).
Project	• At least one large scale project each year	**M8**	This exhibit requires students to put their mathematics to work. Entry slips state criteria, from **M8**, for assessing the following kinds of projects: data study, mathematical model of a physical system, design of a physical structure, management and planning analysis, pure mathematics investigation, and history of a mathematical idea.
Work in Progress	• No entries submitted		Students keep sample work during the year as candidates for selecting as entries.

Portfolios put the standards directly in the hands of students. They help students manage their responsibility for producing work that achieves the performance standards. They also provide a focus for conversations among teachers and students about how the students' work shows evidence of meeting the performance standards and about the further work students need to do to meet the standards.

The portfolio system includes exhibit instructions and entry slips for students, and materials for teachers, including scoring materials. The scoring materials include procedures, criteria, and example exhibits of student work.

Linking the New Standards system with partners' standards and assessment systems

"Linking" is the process of establishing the extent and degree of match between the New Standards system and those of the New Standards partners. It is an essential step in the process of enabling our partners to make decisions about their use of the New Standards system, either in part or as a whole.

Linking is crucial for assuring that student work is assessed according to the same standards that guided its production.

The performance standards provide the initial point of reference for the linking process. While comprehensive linking of assessment systems requires the further step of linking scores on performances, linking standards is a necessary first step and provides a good indication of the potential for linking New Standards with partners' systems.

OVERVIEW OF THE PERFORMANCE STANDARDS

The elementary school standards are set at a level of performance approximately equivalent to the end of fourth grade. It is expected that some students might achieve this level earlier and others later than this grade. (See "Deciding what constitutes a standard-setting performance," page 12.)

E English Language Arts

- **E1** Reading
- **E2** Writing
- **E3** Speaking, Listening, and Viewing
- **E4** Conventions, Grammar, and Usage of the English Language
- **E5** Literature

M Mathematics

- **M1** Arithmetic and Number Concepts
- **M2** Geometry and Measurement Concepts
- **M3** Function and Algebra Concepts
- **M4** Statistics and Probability Concepts
- **M5** Problem Solving and Reasoning
- **M6** Mathematical Skills and Tools
- **M7** Mathematical Communication
- **M8** Putting Mathematics to Work

S Science

- **S1** Physical Sciences Concepts
- **S2** Life Sciences Concepts
- **S3** Earth and Space Sciences Concepts
- **S4** Scientific Connections and Applications
- **S5** Scientific Thinking
- **S6** Scientific Tools and Technologies
- **S7** Scientific Communication
- **S8** Scientific Investigation

A Applied Learning

- **A1** Problem Solving
- **A2** Communication Tools and Techniques
- **A3** Information Tools and Techniques
- **A4** Learning and Self-management Tools and Techniques
- **A5** Tools and Techniques for Working With Others

Introduction to the performance standards for

English Language Arts

The performance standards for English Language Arts define high standards of literacy for American students. The standards focus on what is central to the domain; they are built around reading, writing, speaking, listening, and viewing; and they acknowledge the importance of conventions, literature, public discourse, and functional documents. The standards were developed with the help of classroom teachers and content experts in concert with both the National Council of Teachers of English and the International Reading Association.

The performance standards represent a balanced view of what students should know and the ways they should demonstrate the knowledge and skills they have acquired in this domain. Students are expected to read both literature and informational texts. They are required to produce writing that is traditionally associated with the classroom, including narratives and reports, and they are also expected to exhibit increasing expertise in producing and critiquing public and functional documents. In addition, students are expected to become proficient speakers, to hone their listening skills, and to develop a critical awareness of viewing patterns and the influence of media on their lives. The work that students produce in both written and spoken formats is expected to be of high quality in terms of rhetorical structures as well as the conventions of the English language.

The five standards for English Language Arts are as follows:

E1 Reading;

E2 Writing;

E3 Speaking, Listening, and Viewing;

E4 Conventions, Grammar, and Usage of the English Language;

E5 Literature.

At the high school level, two additional standards are added:

E6 Public Documents;

E7 Functional Documents.

The expansion of literacy at the high school level reflects the growing need for students to understand the range of materials they must deal with throughout their lives. Both public documents and functional documents are introduced in the Reading standard at the middle school level, where students are required to demonstrate a familiarity with these kinds of

texts. It is important that the middle school standard anticipates the advanced degree of understanding expected at the high school level where students are expected both to critique and produce materials of these kinds.

The first part of the Reading standard, **E1**a, requires students to read a wide range of materials by a range of authors on different subjects. The requirement here is fairly simple: read twenty-five books of the quality illustrated in the sample reading list. Too often students are not given the opportunity to read full-length books because of curricular restraints, a lack of resources, or a lack of access to books. The missed opportunity results in a tremendous loss of potential literacy skills that can only be developed when students become habitual readers. The requirement to read twenty-five books a year provides all students the opportunity to become habitual readers and represents a realistic and worthwhile goal that can be reached if students simply invest the effort. The sample reading list is included to provide an indication of the quality and complexity of the materials students are expected to read. Any or all of the specific works on the list may be substituted with other works providing the works that are substituted are of comparable quality and complexity to those that are replaced.

The second part of the Reading standard, **E1**b, requires students to "go deep" in at least one area of interest. We know that students who read regularly tend to read what interests them; note the trends in the work sample, "Home Reading Record," page 56. This part of the Reading standard is intended to encourage all students to do what good readers do and pursue themes, authors, and genres that are of interest to them.

The third part of the Reading standard, **E1**c, requires students to work with informational materials in order to develop understanding and expertise about the topics they investigate. This area of informational materials is of great importance, and for too long it has been neglected in the school curriculum. Its inclusion as a separate part of the Reading standard indicates our desire that more attention be given to reading a broad range of materials written for a variety of audiences and purposes.

The fourth part of the Reading standard, **E1**d, requires students to read aloud proficiently. This requirement is an expectation for elementary school level only.

The Writing standard, **E2**, requires students to demonstrate accomplishment in four types of writing. Each of these writing types is defined by a distinct set of criteria, though there is clearly some overlap. The use of criteria specific to the writing types is meant to ensure that students become familiar with the strategies that characterize specific writing forms and to encourage students to use these criteria when they review and revise their work. All of the commentaries on the work samples related to the Writing standard use the language of these criteria and make explicit how the student work sample illustrates an accomplished example. The types of writing included in this standard are all forms of writing commonly produced both in and out of school.

The Speaking, Listening, and Viewing standard, **E3**, is the only standard that has changed dramatically from previous drafts of these performance standards. The primary change is that the speaking and listening parts of the standard now revolve around a variety of social situations: one-to-one interaction, group discussion, and oral presentation, and that the viewing part of the standard now asks for evidence of an awareness of media influences. The attention to viewing represents a growing awareness that the media play an integral part in most students' lives and that students require increasingly sophisticated tools for dealing with media influences.

The Conventions, Grammar, and Usage of the English Language standard, **E4**, is listed as a separate standard even though the parts of the standard are always assessed in either a written or spoken context. The first part of the standard indicates the expectation that students should be able to represent themselves appropriately using standard English. The second part of the standard reflects the understanding that high quality work most often comes about as a result of a sustained effort represented by numerous drafts of a particular piece of work. In classrooms where high quality work is consistently produced, the revision process is most often an integral part of the curriculum.

The Literature standard, **E5**, like the Conventions standard, is listed separately even though it could easily be broken into two pieces and placed respectively within the Reading and Writing standards. However, for many people who go through school, the study of literature is the only situation in which they have the chance to explore the big ideas and the themes that emerge from social and political conflict, both in their own writing and in the writing of others. An understanding of these ideas and themes is integral for students who will one day be responsible for the negotiation of meaning important to a democracy. The first part of the Literature standard asks students to explore and critique the writing of others with these kinds of critical skills in mind. The second part of the standard asks students to produce literature with the hope that doing this will help students better understand the world that shapes both their literature and the literature of professional writers.

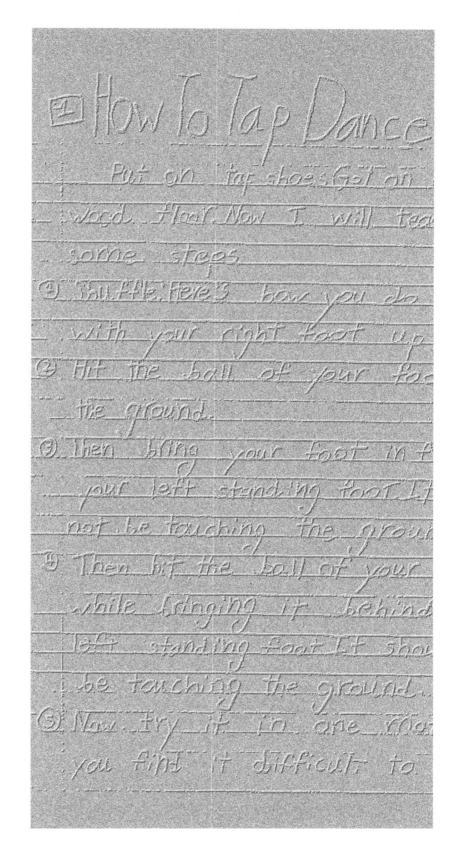

E1 Reading

To see how these performance descriptions compare with the expectations for middle school and high school, turn to pages 210-219.

The examples that follow the performance descriptions for each standard are examples of the work students might do to demonstrate their achievement. The examples also indicate the nature and complexity of activities that are appropriate to expect of students at the elementary level.

E1 a assumes an adequate library of appropriate reading material. In some places, library resources are too meager to support the amount of reading required for every student to achieve this standard. Where a shortage of books exists, better use of out-of-school resources must be made; for example, students may have to be assured access to local or county libraries.

E1 a is intended primarily to generate the reading of full-length books. Combinations of quality magazines, newspapers, on-line materials etc., may be treated as equivalent texts that contribute to meeting the requirement of twenty-five books. Similarly, collections of portions of full-length books may be considered as book equivalents.

Reading is a process which includes demonstrating comprehension and showing evidence of a warranted and responsible interpretation of the text. "Comprehension" means getting the gist of a text. It is most frequently illustrated by demonstrating an understanding of the text as a whole; identifying complexities presented in the structure of the text; and extracting salient information from the text. In providing evidence of a responsible interpretation, students may make connections between parts of a text, among several texts, and between texts and other experiences; make extensions and applications of a text; and examine texts critically and evaluatively.

E1 a The student reads at least twenty-five books or book equivalents each year. The quality and complexity of the materials to be read are illustrated in the sample reading list. The materials should include traditional and contemporary literature (both fiction and non-fiction) as well as magazines, newspapers, textbooks, and on-line materials. Such reading should represent a diverse collection of material from at least three different literary forms and from at least five different writers.

Examples of activities through which students might produce evidence of reading twenty-five books include:
▲ Maintain an annotated list of works read. **1b**
▲ Generate a reading log or journal. **1b**
▲ Participate in formal and informal book talks. **1b, 3a, 3b**

E1 b The student reads and comprehends at least four books (or book equivalents) about one issue or subject, or four books by a single writer, or four books in one genre, and produces evidence of reading that:
• makes and supports warranted and responsible assertions about the texts;
• supports assertions with elaborated and convincing evidence;
• draws the texts together to compare and contrast themes, characters, and ideas;
• makes perceptive and well developed connections;
• evaluates writing strategies and elements of the author's craft.

Examples of activities through which students might produce evidence of reading comprehension include:
▲ Make connections between literary works according to a common theme. **2b, 5a**
▲ Produce a literary response paper. **2b, 4a, 4b, 5a**
▲ Produce an informative report. **1c, 2a, 4a, 4b, M7b, M7e, S7a, S7b**
▲ Participate in formal or informal book talks. **1a, 1c, 3a, 3b, 5a**
▲ Create an annotated book list organized according to author, theme, or genre. **1a**

E1 c The student reads and comprehends informational materials to develop understanding and expertise and produces written or oral work that:
• restates or summarizes information;
• relates new information to prior knowledge and experience;
• extends ideas;
• makes connections to related topics or information.

Examples of activities through which students might produce evidence of reading informational materials include:
▲ Contribute to an attribute book. **2a, 4a, 4b**
▲ Present information to an audience of peers. **3c, 4a, 4b**
▲ Produce a chapter book on a factual topic. **2a, 4a, 4b**
▲ Rewrite video game instructions for a younger reader. **1b, 2d, 4a, 4b**

E1 d The student reads aloud, accurately (in the range of 85-90%), familiar material of the quality and complexity illustrated in the sample reading list, and in a way that makes meaning clear to listeners by:
• self correcting when subsequent reading indicates an earlier miscue;
• using a range of cueing systems, e.g., phonics and context clues, to determine pronunciation and meanings;
• reading with a rhythm, flow, and meter that sounds like everyday speech.

Examples of activities through which students might produce evidence of reading aloud accurately include:
▲ Read aloud to peers or younger children.
▲ Participate in a Readers' Theater production.
▲ Record on an audiotape or videotape an example of reading aloud.

Sample reading list from which students and teachers could select. This list is not exclusive. Acceptable titles also appear on lists produced by organizations such as the National Council of Teachers of English and the American Library Association. Substitutions might also be made from lists approved locally.

Fiction

Brink, *Caddie Woodlawn;*
Cleary, *Ramona and Her Father;*
Coerr, *The Josefina Story Quilt;*
Cohen, *Fat Jack;*
De Saint-Exupery, *The Little Prince;*
Hamilton, *Zeely;*
Hansen, *The Gift-Giver;*
Lord, *In the Year of the Boar and Jackie Robinson;*
Mendez and Byard, *The Black Snowman;*
Naidoo, *Journey to Jo'Burg;*
O'Dell, *Zia;*
Ringgold, *Tar Beach;*
Speare, *The Sign of the Beaver;*
Yep, *Child of the Owl.*

Non-Fiction

Aliki, *Corn Is Maize: The Gift of the Indians;*
Baylor, *The Way to Start a Day;*
Cherry, *The Great Kapok Tree;*
Epstein, *History of Women in Science for Young People;*
Fritz, *And Then What Happened, Paul Revere?;*
Godkin, *Wolf Island;*
Greenfield, *Childtimes: A Three-Generation Memoir;*
Hamilton, *Anthony Burns: The Defeat and Triumph of a Fugitive Slave;*
McGovern, *The Secret Soldier: The Story of Deborah Sampson;*
McKissack, *Frederick Douglass: The Black Lion;*
Politi, *Song of the Swallows;*
Sattler, *Dinosaurs of North America.*

Poetry

Ahlberg, *Heard It in the Playground;*
Blishen and Wildsmith, *Oxford Book of Poetry for Children;*
De Regniers, Moore, White, and Carr, eds., *Sing a Song of Popcorn;*
Giovanni, *Ego-Tripping and Other Poems for Young People;*
Greenfield, *Honey, I Love and Other Love Poems;*
Heard, *For the Good of the Earth and Sun;*
Janeczko, *Strings: A Gathering of Family Poems;*
Koch and Farrell, eds., *Talking to the Sun;*
Lobel, ed., *The Random House Book of Mother Goose;*
Manguel, ed., *Seasons;*
Mathis, *Red Dog, Blue Fly: Football Poems;*
Silverstein, *Where the Sidewalk Ends.*

Folklore

French, *Snow White in New York;*
Goble, *Buffalo Woman;*
Griego y Maestas, *Cuentos: Tales From the Hispanic Southwest;*
Huck and Lobel, *Princess Furball;*
Kipling, *The Elephant's Child;*
Lee, *Legend of the Milky Way;*
Louie and Young, *Yeh-Shen: A Cinderella Story From China;*
Luenn, *The Dragon Kite;*
Steptoe, *Mufaro's Beautiful Daughters;*
Steptoe, *The Story of Jumping Mouse.*

Modern Fantasy and Science Fiction

Andersen, *The Ugly Duckling;*
Bond, *A Bear Called Paddington;*
Dahl, *James and the Giant Peach;*
Grahame, *The Wind in the Willows;*
Lewis, *The Lion, the Witch and the Wardrobe;*
Norton, *The Borrowers;*
Van Allsburg, *Jumanji;*
White, *Charlotte's Web.*

Children's magazines

Action (Scholastic);
Creative Classroom;
News (Scholastic);
Social Studies for the Young Learner;
Weekly Reader;
World (National Geographic).

Other

Newspapers, manuals appropriate for elementary school children, e.g., video game instructions, computer manuals.

Samples of student work that illustrate standard-setting performances for these standards can be found on pages 27-57.

E1 b is intended to encourage students to invest themselves thoroughly in an area that interests them. Such an investment will generate reading from an array of resources, giving students more experience of reading as well as increased understanding of a subject. **E1 b** is not intended to be a cursory experience of doing research on a topic which often requires little more than scanning materials, copying directly from references, and inserting transitional phrases and paragraphs. The challenge with the depth requirement is to encourage a complex understanding developed and enhanced through reading.

The work students produce to meet the English Language Arts standards does not all have to come from an English class. Students should be encouraged to use work from subjects in addition to English to demonstrate their accomplishments. The work samples include some examples of work produced in other classes that meet requirements of these standards. See pages 28, 46, and 48.

These standards allow for oral performances of student work wherever appropriate.

Performance Descriptions *English Language Arts*

E2 Writing

To see how these performance descriptions compare with the expectations for middle school and high school, turn to pages 210-219.

The examples that follow the performance descriptions for each standard are examples of the work students might do to demonstrate their achievement. The examples also indicate the nature and complexity of activities that are appropriate to expect of students at the elementary level.

The cross-references that follow the examples highlight examples for which the same activity, and possibly even the same piece of work, may enable students to demonstrate their achievement in relation to more than one standard. In some cases, the cross-references highlight examples of activities through which students might demonstrate their achievement in relation to standards for more than one subject matter.

E2 b is meant to expand the repertoire of responses children traditionally write when they respond to literature. This type of response requires an understanding of writing strategies.

Writing is a process through which a writer shapes language to communicate effectively. Writing often develops through a series of initial plans and multiple drafts and through access to informed feedback and response. Purpose, audience, and context contribute to the form and substance of writing as well as to its style, tone, and stance.

E2 a The student produces a report that:

• engages the reader by establishing a context, creating a persona, and otherwise developing reader interest;
• develops a controlling idea that conveys a perspective on the subject;
• creates an organizing structure appropriate to a specific purpose, audience, and context;
• includes appropriate facts and details;
• excludes extraneous and inappropriate information;
• uses a range of appropriate strategies, such as providing facts and details, describing or analyzing the subject, and narrating a relevant anecdote;
• provides a sense of closure to the writing.

Examples of reports include:
▲ An informative report. **1b, 1c, 4a, 4b, M7b, M7e, S7a, S7b**
▲ An attribute book (a book on a single subject, not necessarily developed by chapters, sometimes called an "all-about," e.g., "all about whales," "all about earthquakes"). **1b, 1c, 4a, 4b**
▲ A chapter book. **4a, 4b**

E2 b The student produces a response to literature that:

• engages the reader by establishing a context, creating a persona, and otherwise developing reader interest;
• advances a judgment that is interpretive, analytic, evaluative, or reflective;
• supports judgment through references to the text, references to other works, authors, or non-print media, or references to personal knowledge;
• demonstrates an understanding of the literary work;
• provides a sense of closure to the writing.

Examples of responses to literature include:
▲ A literary response paper. **1b, 4a, 4b, 5a**
▲ A book review. **1b, 4a, 4b, 5a**
▲ A parody. **1b, 4a, 4b, 5a**
▲ A literary analysis paper. **1b, 4a, 4b, 5a**
▲ A comparison of a children's literary classic with a televised version of the same work. **3d, 4a, 4b, 5a**

E2 c The student produces a narrative account (fictional or autobiographical) that:

• engages the reader by establishing a context, creating a point of view, and otherwise developing reader interest;
• establishes a situation, plot, point of view, setting, and conflict (and for autobiography, the significance of events);
• creates an organizing structure;
• includes sensory details and concrete language to develop plot and character;
• excludes extraneous details and inconsistencies;
• develops complex characters;
• uses a range of appropriate strategies, such as dialogue and tension or suspense;
• provides a sense of closure to the writing.

Examples of narrative accounts include:
▲ An autobiographical account. **4a, 4b**
▲ An imaginative story. **4a, 4b, 5b**
▲ A narrative picture book. **4a, 4b, 5b**
▲ A retelling of a traditional tale from an alternative point of view. **4a, 4b, 5b**

E2 d The student produces a narrative procedure that:

• engages the reader by establishing a context, creating a persona, and otherwise developing reader interest;
• provides a guide to action that anticipates a reader's needs; creates expectations through predictable structures, e.g., headings; and provides transitions between steps;
• makes use of appropriate writing strategies such as creating a visual hierarchy and using white space and graphics as appropriate;
• includes relevant information;
• excludes extraneous information;
• anticipates problems, mistakes, and misunderstandings that might arise for the reader;
• provides a sense of closure to the writing.

Examples of narrative procedures include:
▲ A set of rules for organizing a class meeting. **4a, 4b**
▲ A chapter book developed around procedures, e.g., how to have a safe vacation, with chapters on safe swimming, safe games, and other issues of safety. **4a, 4b, S4c**
▲ A how-to report to accompany a board game. **4a, 4b**
▲ A set of procedures for accessing information in the library. **4a, 4b, A1a**
▲ A rewrite of video game instructions for a younger reader. **1b, 1c, 4a, 4b**

E3 Speaking, Listening, and Viewing

Speaking, listening, and viewing are fundamental processes which people use to express, explore, and learn about ideas. The functions of speaking, listening, and viewing include gathering and sharing information; persuading others; expressing and understanding ideas; coordinating activities with others; and selecting and critically analyzing messages. The contexts of these communication functions include one-to-one conferences, small group interactions, large audiences and meetings, and interactions with broadcast media.

E3a The student participates in one-to-one conferences with a teacher, paraprofessional, or adult volunteer, in which the student:

- initiates new topics in addition to responding to adult-initiated topics;
- asks relevant questions;
- responds to questions with appropriate elaboration;
- uses language cues to indicate different levels of certainty or hypothesizing, e.g., "what if...," "very likely...," "I'm unsure whether...";
- confirms understanding by paraphrasing the adult's directions or suggestions.

Examples of one-to-one interactions include:
- Book talks with a teacher or parent. **1a, 1b, 1c, 5a**
- Analytical discussions of a movie or television program with a teacher or parent. **3d**
- Conferences regarding a draft of an essay, the student's progress on a mathematics assignment, or the status of a science project. **4b**
- Discussion with an adult of a collection of the student's work. **4b**

E3b The student participates in group meetings, in which the student:

- displays appropriate turn-taking behaviors;
- actively solicits another person's comment or opinion;
- offers own opinion forcefully without dominating;
- responds appropriately to comments and questions;
- volunteers contributions and responds when directly solicited by teacher or discussion leader;
- gives reasons in support of opinions expressed;
- clarifies, illustrates, or expands on a response when asked to do so; asks classmates for similar expansions.

Examples of activities involving group meetings include:
- Create a plan for a group project (e.g., sketching out a multiple-authored picture book; organizing a presentation to be made to the class).
- Develop and discuss class rubrics.
- Engage in classroom town meetings.
- Participate in book talks with other students. **1a, 1b, 1c, 5a**
- Work as part of a group to solve a complex mathematical task.
- Role-play to better understand a certain historical event. **1c**
- Participate in peer writing response groups. **4b**

E3c The student prepares and delivers an individual presentation, in which the student:

- shapes information to achieve a particular purpose and to appeal to the interests and background knowledge of audience members;
- shapes content and organization according to criteria for importance and impact rather than according to availability of information in resource materials;
- uses notes or other memory aids to structure the presentation;
- engages the audience with appropriate verbal cues and eye contact;
- projects a sense of individuality and personality in selecting and organizing content, and in delivery.

Examples of presentations include:
- A report of research on a topic of general interest to the class. **1c, 4a, 4b**
- A presentation of project plans or a report for an Applied Learning project. **4a, 4b, A2a**
- A recounting of various anecdotes in an attempt to persuade the class to change a class policy. **4a**
- A presentation to parents about a project created for a science fair. **4a, 4b, S7c, S8a, S8b, S8c, S8d**

E3d The student makes informed judgments about television, radio, and film productions; that is, the student:

- demonstrates an awareness of the presence of the media in the daily lives of most people;
- evaluates the role of the media in focusing attention and in forming an opinion;
- judges the extent to which media provide a source of entertainment as well as a source of information;
- defines the role of advertising as part of media presentation.

Examples of activities through which students might produce evidence of making informed judgments about television, radio, and film productions include:
- Present a paper or report on reasons for selecting one media choice over another. **1c, 2a, 3c, 4a, 4b**
- Prepare a report on the benefits obtained (including information learned) from media exposure. **1c, 2a, 4a, 4b**
- Maintain a week's log to document personal viewing habits and analyze the information collected in the log.
- Summarize patterns of media exposure in writing or in an oral report. **1c, 2a, 3c, 4a, 4b**
- Analyze the appeal of particularly memorable commercials. **2a, 3c, 4a, 4b**

Samples of student work that illustrate standard-setting performances for these standards can be found on pages 27-57.

For samples of student work that illustrate standard-setting performances for **E3a** and **E3b** refer to the videotape accompanying this book.

Performance Descriptions *English Language Arts*

To see how these performance descriptions compare with the expectations for middle school and high school, turn to pages 210-219.

The examples that follow the performance descriptions for each standard are examples of the work students might do to demonstrate their achievement. The examples also indicate the nature and complexity of activities that are appropriate to expect of students at the elementary level.

The cross-references that follow the examples highlight examples for which the same activity, and possibly even the same piece of work, may enable students to demonstrate their achievement in relation to more than one standard. In some cases, the cross-references highlight examples of activities through which students might demonstrate their achievement in relation to standards for more than one subject matter.

E4 Conventions, Grammar, and Usage of the English Language

Having control of the conventions and grammar of the English language means having the ability to represent oneself appropriately with regard to current standards of correctness (e.g., spelling, punctuation, paragraphing, capitalization, subject-verb agreement). Usage involves the appropriate application of conventions and grammar in both written and spoken formats.

E4a The student demonstrates a basic understanding of the rules of the English language in written and oral work, and selects the structures and features of language appropriate to the purpose, audience, and context of the work. The student demonstrates control of:

- grammar;
- paragraph structure;
- punctuation;
- sentence construction;
- spelling;
- usage.

Examples of activities through which students might demonstrate an understanding of the rules of the English language include:

▲ Demonstrate in a piece of writing the ability to manage the conventions, grammar, and usage of English so that they aid rather than interfere with reading. **2a, 2b, 2c, 2d, 5a, 5b**

▲ Proofread acceptably the student's own writing or the writing of others, using dictionaries and other resources, including the teacher or peers as appropriate. **2a, 2b, 2c, 2d, 5a, 5b**

▲ Observe conventions of language during formal oral presentations. **3c**

E4b The student analyzes and subsequently revises work to clarify it or make it more effective in communicating the intended message or thought. The student's revisions should be made in light of the purposes, audiences, and contexts that apply to the work. Strategies for revising include:

- adding or deleting details;
- adding or deleting explanations;
- clarifying difficult passages;
- rearranging words, sentences, and paragraphs to improve or clarify meaning;
- sharpening the focus;
- reconsidering the organizational structure.

Examples of activities through which students might produce evidence of analyzing and revising work include:

▲ Incorporate into revised drafts, as appropriate, suggestions taken from critiques made by peers and teachers. **2a, 2b, 2c, 2d, 5a, 5b**

▲ Produce a series of distinctly different drafts that result in a polished piece of writing or a presentation. **2a, 2b, 2c, 2d, 5a, 5b**

▲ Consider and respond to the critiques of peers and teachers. **2a, 2b, 2c, 2d, 5a, 5b**

▲ Critique the writing or presentation of a peer.

E5 Literature

Literature consists of poetry, fiction, non-fiction and essays as distinguished from instructional, expository, or journalistic writing.

E5a The student responds to non-fiction, fiction, poetry, and drama using interpretive, critical, and evaluative processes; that is, the student:

- identifies recurring themes across works;
- analyzes the impact of authors' decisions regarding word choice and content;
- considers the differences among genres;
- evaluates literary merit;
- considers the function of point of view or persona;
- examines the reasons for a character's actions, taking into account the situation and basic motivation of the character;
- identifies stereotypical characters as opposed to fully developed characters;
- critiques the degree to which a plot is contrived or realistic;
- makes inferences and draws conclusions about contexts, events, characters, and settings.

Examples of activities through which students might produce evidence of responding to literature include:

▲ Determine why certain characters (either fictional or non-fictional) behave the way they do. **1b, 2b**

▲ Make connections between literary works according to a common theme. **1b, 2b**

▲ Produce a creative retelling of a familiar fairy tale for a group of adults. **1b**

▲ Create a verse by verse paraphrase of a poem. **1b**

▲ Compare a children's literary classic with a televised version of the same work. **2b, 3d**

▲ Participate in formal or informal book talks. **1a, 1b, 1c, 3a, 3b**

E5b The student produces work in at least one literary genre that follows the conventions of the genre.

Examples of literary genres include:
▲ A poem. **4a, 4b**
▲ A short play. **4a, 4b**
▲ A picture book. **4a, 4b**
▲ A story. **2c, 4a, 4b**

Work Sample & Commentary: Brothers of the Heart

The task

Students were asked to read *Brothers of the Heart* by Joan Blos and then produce five pieces: a character list along with a brief annotation about each character; a summary of the story; a recounting of the book's various themes; a book review; and a Venn diagram showing the relationships among several of the main characters. Only the book review is included here.

Circumstances of performance

This sample of student work was produced under the following conditions:

√ alone   in a group

   in class   √ as homework

   with teacher feedback   with peer feedback

   timed   √ opportunity for revision

What the work shows

E2 b Writing: The student produces a response to literature that:

• engages the reader by establishing a context, creating a persona, and otherwise developing reader interest;

• advances a judgment that is interpretive, analytic, evaluative, or reflective;

• supports judgment through references to the text, references to other works, authors, or non-print media, or references to personal knowledge;

• demonstrates an understanding of the literary work;

• provides a sense of closure to the writing.

A The book report gets the reader's attention in the first sentence by highlighting the general idea of the story. The report retains the reader's interest by keeping the writing focused and to the point.

B The report connects Shem's experiences with a theme common to many books, biographies and movies: people in search of their purpose and/or destiny.

Book Review

A ⟶ Joan W. Blos created a story which shows two worlds. On¹ is the white man's world, and the second, the Native American world. Her story was touching, rich and beautiful. Although the book had a simple plot, it had many rich symbols.

The hero of the book, Shem, was a character who became real. You wanted to help him find his place in the world. Her other characters were also described very well. Through the many letters and impressions in the book, you could also understand some of the pioneer life.

This book was about finding destiny and purpose. By the end of the book, Shem had found his place in the world. Altough he lived in the white man's world, he also honored his connection to the Native ⟵ **C** American world. I believe we all find our destiny and purpose, and

B ⟶ although some of us don't empathize with other worlds, we can all

D ⟶ feel brotherhood and kinship, and find our own brother of the heart.

C The writer supports her judgments by making connections between relationships described in the book and those common to real life experiences.

The book report demonstrates an understanding of the text as a whole through references to Shem's struggles and conflicts and by drawing parallels to real life.

D The report ends on a personal note, providing the reader with the understanding that the book has personal significance for the student. The implication is that the book may have significance for others as well.

Work Sample & Commentary: *About the Young Authors' Conference*

This piece of work was completed as part of an Applied Learning project. See page 206 for commentary on the project as a whole.

About the Young Authors' Conference

A This year is the fourth year that the Fort Worth School District has had a Young Authors' Conference. The first year a grown-up planned it, and the second year a fifth grade class at W. J. Turner planned it. The third year's conference was planned by Deborah _____'s second graders and Charlotte _____'s first graders. This year, as third graders, Deborah _____'s class has had complete responsibility for planning and organizing the conference. Everyone at Alice Carlson Applied Learning Center has helped us, such as the kindergarten children sharpened the pencils and made the snack tickets, the fourth graders decorated the stage, and the second and fifth graders made the bookmarks.

B To plan the Young Authors' Conference there are a lot of different things involved. Some things that involved math were comparing prices of the supplies and keeping track of the budget of around $8,000. All the way through we have had to do lots of problem solving. For example, we had to decide things like how many reams of paper we needed to buy if there were five bookmarks on a page, 250 pieces of cover stock in a ream, and we needed to make 1,000 bookmarks. We did a lot of estimating, like deciding how many doughnuts to buy and how many t-shirts to order.

Also, it would take a ream of paper to tell all of the writing that is involved in the conference. We did a lot of writing! We had to write memos, business letters, forms, and other things. We wrote news releases and proposals. We have written to the superintendent of the school district, the principals of the schools, the coordinators at each school, and the students who registered. We also had to write to the authors, the storytellers, the presenters, the companies who we got supplies from, book companies, and more.

One of the hardest parts was keeping organized and being responsible. We had to do a whole lot of small things like organize the hot line phone schedule and pack all of the packets. One of the big jobs was to make a database on our computer of all of the participants' names. We had to update the database many, many times. It was difficult for everyone to be responsible for their job and report back to the class.

C We learned a lot while planning this conference. If your school or class would like to plan the Young Authors' Conference for 1995, please contact _____ at Alice _____ Applied Learning Center.

The task

As part of an Applied Learning project, a class held a Young Authors' Conference. The half-day event featured sessions with professional writers and storytellers. Part of the project included having the students learn about and write news articles. The news article included here was produced as a report on the conference planning.

Circumstances of performance

This sample of student work was produced under the following conditions:

√ alone
  in a group
  in class
  as homework
√ with teacher feedback
√ with peer feedback
  timed
√ opportunity for revision

This work sample illustrates a standard-setting performance for the following parts of the standards:

E2 a **Writing: Produce a report.**

E4 a **Conventions: Demonstrate a basic understanding of the rules of the English language.**

What the work shows

E2 a **Writing:** The student produces a report that:

- engages the reader by establishing a context, creating a persona, and otherwise developing reader interest;
- develops a controlling idea that conveys a perspective on the subject;
- creates an organizing structure appropriate to a specific purpose, audience, and context;
- includes appropriate facts and details;
- excludes extraneous and inappropriate information;
- uses a range of appropriate strategies, such as providing facts and details, describing or analyzing the subject, and narrating a relevant anecdote;
- provides a sense of closure to the writing.

A The article initially develops reader interest by situating the current conference within a history of conferences, demonstrating a familiarity with newspaper style articles that need to get the reader's attention within the first paragraph. The reader's interest is maintained in the body of the article which touches briefly on several aspects of the planning stages.

About the Young Authors' Conference

Reading

E2 Writing

Speaking,
Listening,
and Viewing

Conventions,
Grammar,
and Usage
of the English
Language **E4**

Literature

The perspective established in the report addresses several related purposes:

B to report on the general nature of the planning process for the conference; and

C to put out a call for another class to handle the planning in the coming year.

The student organized the article in such a way as to make the task described both interesting and doable.

The article includes facts and details at the appropriate level of specificity for a newspaper report.

C The final paragraph puts forth the idea that the students' learning was the main benefit of having planned the conference. The article then addresses the reader directly and asks who might be interested in planning the following year's conference. This combination of summary and request provides a fitting conclusion for the report.

E4 a Conventions, Grammar, and Usage of the English Language: The student demonstrates a basic understanding of the rules of the English language in written and oral work, and selects the structures and features of language appropriate to the purpose, audience, and context of the work. The student demonstrates control of:

• grammar;

• paragraph structure;

• punctuation;

• sentence construction;

• spelling;

• usage.

The article demonstrates control of spelling, usage, and paragraphing.

The student organized the list of chores involved in preparing for the conference into readable sentences which demonstrate an understanding of the structural features of written language.

Work Sample & Commentary: *My Life as a Sea Horse*

Reading **E1**

Writing **E2**

Speaking, Listening, and Viewing

Conventions, Grammar, and Usage of the English Language **E4**

Literature

The task

Following a month long unit focused on various aspects of the ocean, students were asked to write a paper about an ocean creature. In the following report, a student chose to write from an ocean creature's point of view.

Circumstances of performance

This sample of student work was produced under the following conditions:

√ alone   in a group

in class   √ as homework

√ with teacher feedback   with peer feedback

timed   √ opportunity for revision

What the work shows

E1c Reading: The student reads and comprehends informational materials to develop understanding and expertise and produces written or oral work that:

- restates or summarizes information;
- relates new information to prior knowledge and experience;
- extends ideas;
- makes connections to related topics or information.

The student organized and restated information from a variety of sources in a manner appropriate for an informational piece of writing.

A The report establishes a connection between prior knowledge about reproduction and the reproductive behavior of sea horses.

B The ideas gathered through reading and research are recast within a story that incorporates the ideas in a new context. The idea that sea horses need special attention if they are kept as pets leads to the conclusion that they must be happier living in the ocean.

C The report provides a connection between the information presented and the feasibility of having a sea horse as a pet.

This work sample illustrates a standard-setting performance for the following parts of the standards:

E1c Reading: Read and comprehend informational materials.

E2a Writing: Produce a report.

E4a Conventions: Demonstrate a basic understanding of the rules of the English language.

My Life as a Sea Horse

E1 ▶ Reading

E2 ▶ Writing

Speaking, Listening, and Viewing

Conventions, Grammar, and Usage of the English Language

E4 ▶

Literature

E2 a Writing: The student produces a report that:

- engages the reader by establishing a context, creating a persona, and otherwise developing reader interest;

- develops a controlling idea that conveys a perspective on the subject;

- creates an organizing structure appropriate to a specific purpose, audience, and context;

- includes appropriate facts and details;

- excludes extraneous and inappropriate information;

- uses a range of appropriate strategies, such as providing facts and details, describing or analyzing the subject, and narrating a relevant anecdote;

- provides a sense of closure to the writing.

The report establishes a context in the explanation that the sea horse is trying to make her way "around a school of fish," and that, as she tries to "make her way home," she will talk with the reader.

D **E** The friendly, conversational tone and the use of a female persona develop reader interest. The persona is maintained throughout the piece and the attitudes expressed by the persona are consistent with the factual data and with a distinctive personality.

F The use of the first person to relay information creates an informal yet informative tone.

Facts and details are grouped and organized in an appropriate manner.

G The majority of the scientific details are accurate and details that are inconsistent with the persona or inappropriate for the report's purpose are avoided.

H The framing device of the sea horse narrator is maintained throughout the piece and referred to again in the conclusion, providing a sense of closure to the work.

E4 a Conventions, Grammar, and Usage of the English Language: The student demonstrates a basic understanding of the rules of the English language in written and oral work, and selects the structures and features of language appropriate to the purpose, audience, and context of the work. The student demonstrates control of:

- grammar;

- paragraph structure;

- punctuation;

- sentence construction;

- spelling;

- usage.

The student made use of:

I introductory words;

J rhetorical questions;

and a humorous tone to imitate the structures and features of speech. The organization, spelling, usage and sense of syntax demonstrate fluency with the conventions of the written language.

Work Sample & Commentary: *A Rainbow of Your Own*

Reading

Writing   E2

Speaking, Listening, and Viewing

Conventions, Grammar, and Usage of the English Language   E4

Literature

The quality of writing in this work sample owes much to the student's opportunities to revise the work. The final document emerged from many revisions, each of which led progressively to the high quality of the final draft.

The task

Students were asked to work through a series of drafts to produce an essay.

Circumstances of performance

This student chose initially to present information on the topic in an oral report, then used audience feedback to rethink the project and produce the final draft.

√ alone   in a group
√ in class   √ as homework
√ with teacher feedback   √ with peer feedback
  timed   √ opportunity for revision

What the works shows

E2 a   Writing: The student produces a report that:

• engages the reader by establishing a context, creating a persona, and otherwise developing reader interest;

• develops a controlling idea that conveys a perspective on the subject;

• creates an organizing structure appropriate to a specific purpose, audience, and context;

• includes appropriate facts and details;

• excludes extraneous and inappropriate information;

• uses a range of appropriate strategies, such as providing facts and details, describing or analyzing the subject, and narrating a relevant anecdote;

• provides a sense of closure to the writing.

A   The work develops reader interest with an appealing title, "A Rainbow of Your Own," and with an intriguing first sentence that poses a question in the form of a riddle.

B   The opening paragraph establishes that the controlling idea of the piece is to persuade the reader that a love bird would be a perfect pet.

A → **A Rainbow of Your Own**   [FINAL DRAFT]

B → Have you ever seen a rainbow with two beady, black eyes? I have, it's my pet Salsa! He's a lovebird. A lovebird would be the perfect pet for you.

I'm sure that some of you like to bird watch right? If you have a lovebird you can see all the brilliant colors of birds at home. They come in every shade of every color, so you can pick the one you like best.

Lovebirds are extremely smart. They can be taught amazing tricks. They can even learn to talk! I know what you think, oh, they're

E → too loud. Well, that is a disadvantage, but their noises are either talking or nice singing. This can be very enjoyable. Another great thing about lovebirds is that after they are used to their

---

This work sample illustrates a standard-setting performance for the following parts of the standards:

E2 a   Writing: Produce a report.

E4 b   Conventions: Analyze and subsequently revise written work.

A Rainbow of Your Own

Reading

▶ Writing

Speaking,
Listening,
and Viewing

Conventions,
Grammar,
and Usage
of the English
Language

Literature

names, they come when you call, just like dogs. Lovebirds are also very curious. They are always discovering new things, that can make you laugh.

C ▶ Lovebirds are very hardy and can live up to fifteen years. This is a lot longer than mice or hamsters. Love birds don't eat as much as dogs or cats, because they have much smaller stomachs! I know you're thinking, they have to poop sometimes. Well, they do, but you can paper train them and if you don't it doesn't really bother you. When thinking of birds, lots of people think of big, extremely loud macaws or tiny singing canaries. Lovebirds are just the right size to hold and enjoy. Another good thing about lovebird is that they can stay home when you go on a trip for a few days. If you go away for longer,

it is easy just to take your bird's cage to a friend's house.

Lovebirds become very attached to you. They are loyal and always want to be with you. They are also pretty cute. Most lovebirds have good personalities and are full of energy. You've probably heard that lovebirds bite. Well, that is true, but if you spend a lot of time with your bird, that **D** ◀ nippiness disappears. They are also very funny. For instance, my bird, Salsa, makes funny faces and he is always ready for another hilarious battle with one of his toys. Salsa is very soft, and cudily. His feathers are like fluffy clouds.

I think "lovebird" is a great name for these
F ▶ pets. If you had one, you'd think so too. They are really lovable!

C The student arranged reasons, examples, and anecdotes persuasively, e.g., in paragraph four, the argument begins with the hardiness of love birds, moves on to a comparison of the feeding needs of love birds and other pets, to paper training, to size, and finally to the ease of having love birds cared for while the owner is away.

D The work includes the appropriate amount of information for a prospective love bird owner and supports the main points by citing personal experience and opinions, such as the belief that love birds are "very funny."

Draft of introduction
and conclusion

intro — Have you ever seen a rainbow with to black beady eyes? I have, it's my pet Salsa! He's a lovebird. A lovebird would be a perfect pet for you.

I think lovebird is a great name for these birds. If you had one you'd think to

con — that too. They're really loveable

A Rainbow of Your Own

Reading

Writing ◄ E2

Speaking,
Listening,
and Viewing

Conventions,
Grammar,
and Usage
of the English
Language ◄ E4

Literature

Draft 2

Love Birds

Hello ladies and Gentlemen. Tonight I am
going to tell you why love birds are good pets.
I'm sure that some of you like to bird watch right?
Anyway. If you have a love bird you can see all
the brilliant colors of birds at home.
① Lovebirds become very attached to you. They
are very loyal and always want to be with you.
②They of the birds can be taught amazing tricks. This is a lot
love birds are to very hardy and can live up to 15 years.
longer than mice or hamsters. Love birds don't eat
as much as dogs or cats because they have
much smaller stomachs!
1. Love birds are extremely smart. They
even
can learn to talk! I know what you think

oh, they're too loud. Well, that is a disadvantage,
2 but their noises are either talking or nice singing.
This can be very enjoyable. They come in
every shade of every color so you can pick the
one you like the best. Lovebirds are also
②They
pretty. they are very pretty. Lovebirds are
also pretty cute. You've probably heard
that they bite. Well, that is true, but
your bird
if you spend alot of time with that nipping
4
③Most Lovebirds
disappears. Lovebirds
have good personalities and are full
⑧
of energy. (Lots of people when thinking of
birds think of big, extremely loud macaws
or tiny singing canaries. Lovebirds are just the

to add and enjoy,
are just the right size, small enough that
their cages aren't as big as a couch, but
big enough that they aren't really chirpy and tweety.
⑤ They are also very funny. For instance, my bird,
Salsa, makes funny faces and his always
ready for another hilarious battle with one
of his toys. Salsa is very soft and cuddly.
⑥ His feathers are like clouds. I know what
you're thinking, they have to go to the bath-
3 room same time. Well, they do but you can
paper
easily train them and if you don't, it doesn't
really bother you.
Another thing that is great about
that
lovebirds is after they get used to their

E The details of pet care, the anticipation of problems and solutions for these problems, and the anecdotes about the bird, Salsa, develop the argument for liking love birds as pets.

F The final paragraph provides a sense of closure by reiterating the main point of the argument.

A Rainbow of Your Own

Reading

E2 Writing

Speaking,
Listening,
and Viewing

Conventions,
Grammar,
and Usage
of the English
Language

E4

Literature

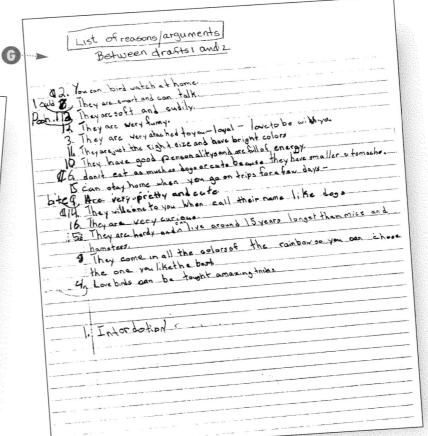

name they come when you call just like dogs. ④Another good thing about love birds is that they can stay home when you go on a trip for a few days. If you go away for longer than that it is easy for a friend to take care of them because. Lovebirds are also very curious. They are always discovering new things. that can make you laugh they like

Again I would like to say Lovebirds make great pets!

List of reasons/arguments
Between drafts 1 and 2

I cald ② You can bird watch at home.
Pooh ⑧ They are smart and can talk.
⑪ They are soft and cudily.
③ They are very funny.
They are very attached to you—loyal — love to be with you
⑯ They are just the right size and have bright colors
⑩ They have good personalitys and are full of energy
⑥ don't eat as much as dogs or cats because they have smaller stomachs.
⑮ can stay home when you go on trips for a few days—
btere ⑦ Are very pretty and cute
⑭ They will come to you when call their name like dogs
⑯ They are very curious.
⑤ They are hardy and live around 15 years longer than mice and hamsters.
⑨ They come in all the colors of the rainbow so you can choose the one you like the best.
④ Love birds can be taught amazing tricks

1. Intoduction

DRAFT 1

Highlight only reasons why lovebirds make good pets.

Birds

Hello, ladies and gentalmen tonight I am here to tell you why to have birds for pets. In the last epasode wrote why to bird watch have your own bird you can bird watch right at your home.

In my house we have three birds, two cockitails and one love bird, the love bird is mine. Our three birds names are Dandy, Billy and Salsa. I know what your thinking, oh Salsa is the best name, thats because he is my bird and I thought up his name all by my self.

E4 b Conventions, Grammar, and Usage of the English Language: The student analyzes and subsequently revises work to clarify it or make it more effective in communicating the intended message or thought. The student's revisions should be made in light of the purposes, audiences, and contexts that apply to the work. Strategies for revising include:

- adding or deleting details;
- adding or deleting explanations;
- clarifying difficult passages;
- rearranging words, sentences, and paragraphs to improve or clarify meaning;
- sharpening the focus;
- reconsidering the organizational structure.

G The student added details and reconsidered prior ideas over the course of producing the various drafts, e.g., after the first draft the student listed fifteen points according to the sequence in which they might subsequently be used in later drafts.

The student revised the work in terms of audience and purpose through multiple versions. The first draft includes information and anecdotes about various birds and lists four reasons why birds make good pets. This information appears in different forms in subsequent drafts.

A Rainbow of Your Own

Lots of people want dogs and lots of people have dogs and they think, oh, my dog's so smart he can roll over ~~Haha birds are more smarter they can talk.~~ My bird Salsa is very funny what he does is he stands on his perch and swings down then he hits his head on the floor of his cage. Then he lets go of is pearch and climbs back on again. He does this over and over. He also has battels with his toys, it's a very funny intrasting sight to see.

When you get a bird you should pick the one that pays the most atechen

to you when you are picking one out. As soon as you get home you should spend a lot of time with. If you dont do that it will bond to someone else that means that it away wants to be with with another person. ~~Birds are very soft and cudily~~ ~~espisily the hand fed ones.~~ You can get hand fed love birds and cockitails at critter land. ~~Critter land is in Mill Valley~~ it is a cross from 7eleven and if you dont know where 7eleven is ~~I think you need to get your brain check.~~

I know what your thinking they just sit in their cage and chirp and sing. Well, that's not the truth ~~Salsa is very cudily he reads with me and watches television with me. basikly~~ he goes every where I go. Well, I mean in my house and in my back yard.

Again I would like to say birds are great pets.

The End

The drafts treat the information from a variety of perspectives. In the second draft, the title was changed from "Birds" to "Love Birds," and the piece took the form of a speech. The final draft takes the form of a persuasive essay.

The writing incorporates critiques from teachers and adults, e.g., the list of fifteen reasons to have a pet lovebird was created as the result of a suggestion by an adult.

The student responded and then reorganized the final draft in response to suggestions from peers that the speech was disorganized.

The drafts progress from a set of facts through a disorganized speech to a polished essay. This progression suggests an understanding of the stages of writing and a willingness to make substantive changes as needed.

Reading

E2 Writing

Speaking,
Listening,
and Viewing

Conventions,
Grammar,
and Usage
of the English
Language

E5 Literature

Work Sample & Commentary: *Enchiladas*

The task

Students were asked to select a topic to which they had a commitment in their lives and then to choose a genre in which to express that commitment. Students were required to revise and edit their writing before "publishing" the complete texts. The work shown here is one recipe and an anecdote from a much longer project in which a series of recipes and anecdotes were compiled into a book titled, "La Mesa Esta Puesta (The Table Is Set)." This student also produced the work in Spanish.

Circumstances of performance

This sample of student work was produced under the following conditions:

√ alone   in a group

√ in class   √ as homework

√ with teacher feedback √ with peer feedback

  timed   √ opportunity for
          revision

What the work shows

E2 d Writing: The student produces a narrative procedure that:

- engages the reader by establishing a context, creating a persona, and otherwise developing reader interest;

- provides a guide to action that anticipates a reader's needs; creates expectations through predictable structures, e.g., headings; and provides transitions between steps;

- makes use of appropriate writing strategies such as creating a visual hierarchy and using white space and graphics as appropriate;

- includes relevant information;

- excludes extraneous information;

- anticipates problems, mistakes, and misunderstandings that might arise for the reader;

- provides a sense of closure to the writing.

The work engages the reader with the title of the larger project, "La Mesa Esta Puesta (The Table Is Set)," and a colorful cover to identify the project as a Spanish/English recipe book. The work includes both the recipes and the accompanying anecdotes, with each providing an interesting context for the other.

A The work provides a guide to action through the recognizable form of a recipe.

B The instructions are clear and are organized chronologically with specific guidelines about when to move on to the next step.

This work sample illustrates a standard-setting performance for the following parts of the standards:

E2 c Writing: Produce a narrative account.

E2 d Writing: Produce a narrative procedure.

E5 b Literature: Produce work in at least one literary genre that follows the conventions of the genre.

Enchiladas

Reading

Writing E2

Speaking, Listening, and Viewing

Conventions, Grammar, and Usage of the English Language

Literature E5

Enchiladas

Ingredients:
5 red chiles
2 packages of tortillas
2 chopped onions (finely)
3 finely chopped fresh cheeses
½ garlic head
1 cup of oil
salt to taste

To begin you put the red chiles in boiling water. When they are soft you put them in the blender and add a little bit of water, garlic and salt. The chile paste needs to be strained, in order to separate the juice from the seeds. You then fry the tortillas a bit so that they are soft. When you take them out of the oil, you pass them through the chile. You then fill

them up with cheese and onions and roll them like a taco.

The day my mother made enchiladas all the neighbors came to visit us. They say that it is because the smell of the chile cooking creeps out the windows. Toña, one of my comadres came in with her baby crying. Maria, well "Mariquita" to the ones that knew her came in chatting away, as always. The other two comadres "the religious ones" forgot about church and walked in with their Bibles. On this occasion my mom started talking as she cooked. All the ladies were sitting in the kitchen around the table. My mom got into the talking so much that

she forgot the enchiladas, so they burned. ~~When~~ But, my mom still served them like that. When the ladies tasted them they looked at each other and started getting up excusing themselves. From that day on, no one ever came back for my mom's enchiladas. Now, we can eat them all ourselves.

C The student used appropriate strategies for relating a recipe, which include identifying the logical steps involved in cooking, and then presenting them as a series of statements in clear, concise language.

D The recipe section concludes by creating a visual image of what the enchiladas will look like.

Enchiladas

Reading

E2 Writing

Speaking,
Listening,
and Viewing

Conventions,
Grammar,
and Usage
of the English
Language

E5 Literature

E2 c Writing: The student produces a narrative account (fictional or autobiographical) that:

* engages the reader by establishing a context, creating a point of view, and otherwise developing reader interest;

* establishes a situation, plot, point of view, setting, and conflict (and for autobiography, the significance of events);

* creates an organizing structure;

* includes sensory details and concrete language to develop plot and character;

* excludes extraneous details and inconsistencies;

* develops complex characters;

* uses a range of appropriate strategies, such as dialogue and tension or suspense;

* provides a sense of closure to the writing.

The anecdote engages the reader by establishing the reader as an observer of the events in the kitchen.

The plot sequence includes all the appropriate elements—rising action: arrival of the various guests who serve as distracters; conflict: conversation instead of cooking; climax: burning the enchiladas; conclusion: the guests excusing themselves.

E The conflict in the story (the burning of the enchiladas) develops as a result of the socializing, but the story still ends with a positive and, therefore, somewhat ironic result.

The anecdote is organized chronologically within a brief period of time.

F The student included detailed descriptions of the tastes and smells in the kitchen appropriate to a story about cooking.

G The student used brief characterizations to introduce each of the women who came into her mother's kitchen.

H The anecdote ends by indicating that the women's leaving in disgust was actually the best thing that could have happened, because it meant the family could eat all of the enchiladas by themselves.

E5 b Literature: The student produces work in at least one literary genre that follows the conventions of the genre.

The student replicated the format of a picture book by including text accompanied by illustrations that depict the context of the story.

The few mistakes in this work are more likely "slips" than actual errors, e.g., whereas no apostrophe is used in the line "one of my moms..." the same construction is later used properly.

Work Sample & Commentary: *The Stained Glass Tree*

Reading

Writing E2

Speaking,
Listening,
and Viewing

Conventions,
Grammar,
and Usage E4
of the English
Language

Literature E5

The quality of writing in this work sample owes much to the student's opportunities to revise the work. The final document emerged from many revisions, each of which led progressively to the high quality of the final draft.

The task

Students were asked to take an entry from their writer's notebook and develop it into a picture book. This student chose two entries describing her grandmother's house. After reciting them as a story in a small response group, she wrote a rough draft that eventually developed into the picture book she titled "The Stained Glass Tree."

Circumstances of performance

This sample of student work was produced under the following conditions:

√ alone   in a group

√ in class   √ as homework

√ with teacher feedback   √ with peer feedback

  timed   √ opportunity for
                             revision

What the works shows

E2 c Writing: The student produces a narrative account (fictional or autobiographical) that:

• engages the reader by establishing a context, creating a point of view, and otherwise developing reader interest;

• establishes a situation, plot, point of view, setting, and conflict (and for autobiography, the significance of events);

• creates an organizing structure;

• includes relevant details and concrete language to develop plot and character;

• excludes extraneous details and inconsistencies;

• develops complex characters;

• uses a range of appropriate strategies, such as dialogue and tension or suspense;

• provides a sense of closure to the writing.

The work engages the reader by establishing the point of view of the narrator walking the reader through her grandmother's home while providing a detailed description of the house.

This work sample illustrates a standard-setting performance for the following parts of the standards:

E2 c **Writing: Produce a narrative account.**

E4 a **Conventions: Demonstrate a basic understanding of the rules of the English language.**

E5 b **Literature: Produce work in at least one literary genre that follows the conventions of the genre.**

This is my grandmother's door. The front door with the stained glass tree. Two plants stand on either side hiding the doorbell which you ring.

You hear it play "Yankee Doodle" and the dog barking. The door opens making bells on the doorknob ring.

A ⟶ Now you are standing on a slate platform. To your right is the kitchen, a step up. To your left is the hall a step down and straight in front of you is the carpeted living room, a step up. You look around. A chiming clock rings joined by another soon after.

You turn to the right into the kitchen. A red, orange and brown pattern on the floor catches your eye. You try to figure out what the pattern is. It's too confusing.

You look up into the double oven to see what you smell. It's just the smell of the kitchen. You take one step forward and look at the stove. You look up to see an assortment of pots/pans and muffin tins.

You turn around and see cabinets, sink and a refrigerator.

D ⟶ You open the refrigerator. You see apricots and peaches galore. You close the refrigerator.

You look up at the hanging baskets over the sink, filled with garlic, peaches and more apricots.

You walk away to the table and look at the new flower arrangement. Today it is daylilies.

You turn because you don't want to look into the messy garage. This room is the cat room. It smells of cat litter.

You look at the window which is covered with cat flower pots.

You hear a crackling noise. You turn around to see what's making the noise. It's Boots, your grandmother's cat on the scratching post. Then you hear the low rumble of the washing machine.

You walk out the door onto the patio, your grandfather is lying on the sun chair, with a paper over his head.

You look at the patio table with its white and yellow umbrella.

The process of moving through the house provides the organizing structure for the work. The short paragraphs represent a halt in the movement while the narrator and the reader pause to look at or listen to something.

The work includes the appropriate details to describe the house and its contents. In addition, the narrative stays focused on the tour, rather than veering off on other subjects.

A **B** The impression of repeatedly starting and stopping allows the narrator to communicate a wide variety of impressions regarding the objects or rooms being considered.

C The title, "The Stained Glass Tree," orients the reader and creates a focal point for the plot sequence. At the end, the narrative returns to the focal point, reorienting a reader who toured behind the stained glass tree, and providing a sense of closure to the work.

The Stained Glass Tree

Reading

Writing

Speaking,
Listening,
and Viewing

Conventions,
Grammar,
and Usage
of the English
Language

Literature

E4 a Conventions, Grammar, and Usage of the English Language: The student demonstrates a basic understanding of the rules of the English language in written and oral work, and selects the structures and features of language appropriate to the purpose, audience, and context of the work. The student demonstrates control of:

- grammar;
- paragraph structure;
- punctuation;
- sentence construction;
- spelling;
- usage.

The student demonstrated an age-appropriate control of written language. The sentences are simple, subject-verb-object constructions which focus the reader's attention on the descriptions. This simple construction has the additional advantage of being appropriate for the intended audience, and it provides a rhythm for the picture book.

E5 b Literature: The student produces work in at least one literary genre that follows the conventions of the genre.

The picture book tells an effective story and uses a full color format consistent with picture books produced by professional writers and artists.

D Using "you" as the subject of the sentences (and therefore the beginning word in most of the paragraphs) draws the reader into the text. This device also provides a narrative rhythm that is characteristic of picture books.

You go in, but you go in the sliding door of the living room. You turn to your right, past the table to the cupboard with the cups in it. You look at all the tea cups for at least five minutes.

Then walk through the living room with all its boxes, coasters, violets and lamps that turn on when you touch them.

You walk down two steps to the bar. The bar is a small room containing an ice box, cabinets, a table, chairs, bunches of wine holders and a speaker.

You walk through the folding doors into the family room. You remember doing needlepoint and making strings of paper clips and hanging them up with unused floss.

You look at the double rocker. It's really a small couch that has rockers on it.

B You step into the dark hall. Bark! You jump, then kneel down to apologize to the little black dog on which you've just stepped.

Down the hall farther and turn right. You step into the room in which you sleep.

You look at the white wicker chest of drawers with all its photos. You walk over to the book shelf and pick out a book called *Helen Keller*. You've been reading about her and would like to know more about her.

After a while you stop reading and go into the bathroom to look at all the soaps, perfumes and other beauty necessities. You remember locking yourself in here once and smelling every single perfume in the room.

Later that evening you walk down your grandmother's long driveway with your grandfather to pick nectarines and apricots.

In the dusk light you feel the apricots trees' small soft apricots with their fuzzy feeling. You hear a soft rustle when you pull on the apricot.

You walk back up the long driveway.
You walk down the hallway to the family room. Before you pick up your needlepoint you look out the window down on the lighted seaside. The last boat of the day blows its whistle. It's a long, low whistle.

You pick up your needlepoint and slowly thread the needle then run the needle through the canvas diagonally. Your grandfather starts flipping

through the TV channels. You hear bits of conversations on the different channels.

F It's time for bed, you hear your mother say. You look out the window one last time at the lighted seaside which now looks like a Fourth of July fireworks show that has been paused.

You pick up the blanket which has been thrown on you. And walk down the hallway to the kitchen to say goodnight to the three pets after you've said goodnight to your grandparents.

Then back down the hallway to your room and you listen to a story your father is reading. The story ends. Your father says goodnight and then sits down quietly until your sister is asleep and then leaves. All you can hear is the quiet hum of the fan above you and the chirping of the crickets sounding far off in the distance. You listen to both of them until sleep overtakes you.

The next morning after breakfast you walk outside the front door with the stained glass tree on it.

Onto the front porch and into the lawn wet with dew that drips over your feet. You walk up to the low white fence and now feel the roughness of gravel under your feet.

You look down at the hillside of ivy. You see the various fruit trees abruptly cutting off the ivy, then the ivy starts again, this time being cut off by the road.

C You turn in the direction of your grandmother's door. The front door with the stained glass tree.

The Stained Glass Tree

Reading

Writing   **E2**

Speaking, Listening, and Viewing

Conventions, Grammar, and Usage of the English Language   **E4**

Literature   **E5**

You go in but you go in the sliding door of the living room. You turn to your right past the table to the cupboard, with the cups in it. You look at all the tea cups for at least five minutes.

E The sensory details become visual in the pictures accompanying the text, e.g., a picture of the entire cabinet, viewed from afar, and a picture of a single large tea cup, viewed up close, accompany the line, "You look at all the tea cups for at least five minutes." These drawings provide a clear context for the text.

F The use of poetic imagery is appropriate to both the tone and the setting of the piece.

Reading

▶ **E2** Writing

Speaking,
Listening,
and Viewing

E4 ▶ Conventions,
Grammar,
and Usage
of the English
Language

Literature

Work Sample & Commentary: *How to Tap Dance*

The task

Students were asked to write an "I know how to…" paper about something they understood well. They were asked to think about things they had learned and would like to teach others. Then they were encouraged to think about an audience who had little or no knowledge of the process they would write about, and to write the essay for that audience. The work was begun as an in-class assignment and was finished that evening as homework.

Circumstances of performance

This sample of student work was produced under the following conditions:

√ alone   in a group

√ in class   √ as homework

   with teacher feedback   with peer feedback

   timed   √ opportunity for revision

What the work shows

E2 d Writing: The student produces a narrative procedure that:

* engages the reader by establishing a context, creating a persona, and otherwise developing reader interest;

* provides a guide to action that anticipates a reader's needs; creates expectations through predictable structures, e.g., headings; and provides transitions between steps;

* makes use of appropriate writing strategies such as creating a visual hierarchy and using white space and graphics as appropriate;

* includes relevant information;

* excludes extraneous information;

* anticipates problems, mistakes, and misunderstandings that might arise for the reader;

* provides a sense of closure to the writing.

A The simple title establishes a context for the main idea of the work.

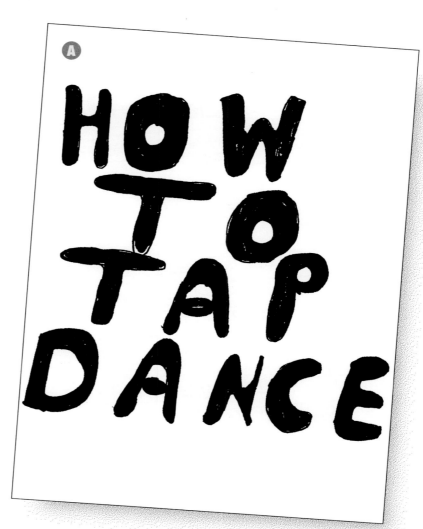

A

HOW
TO
TAP
DANCE

This work sample illustrates a standard-setting performance for the following parts of the standards:

E2 d Writing: Produce a narrative procedure.

E4 a Conventions: Demonstrate a basic understanding of the rules of the English language.

How to Tap Dance

1 **How To Tap Dance**

B ► Put on tap shoes.Get on a hard wood floor.Now I will teach you some steps.

C ► ① Shuffle.Here's how you do it.Start with your right foot up in back
② Hit the ball of your foot on the ground.

B ► ③ Then bring your foot in front of your left standing foot.It should not be touching the ground.
④ Then hit the ball of your foot while bringing it behind your left standing foot.It should not be touching the ground.
⑤ Now try it in one motion.If you find it difficult to do this,

2 than start back from step 1 and try it again.Here is another step that you might find easier

C ► Flap.Here's how you do it.
① Pick your foot up off the ground and hit the ball of your foot on the ground right where you picked it up.
② Then pick up the same foot and hit the ball of your foot right in front of you.If you find that difficult then start back at step

D ► 1 of flap.Here is a step that you could put after a shuffle or a flap.

C ► Ballchange.Here's how you do it.

① Take one of your feet and step behind the other foot.
② When the foot that stepped hits the ground, lift your other off the ground.
③ Then last but not least, step with the foot that's in the air.If you

E ► don't understand this step, start back from step one of ballchange. Here is a step that you might find fun called boogie woogie.Here is how you do it.
① Stand with your feet flat on the ground.
② Lift your right heel off the ground.
③ Then drop your right heel and

B The use of imperatives in the opening and throughout the piece establishes the stance of the writer as an authority on tap dancing.

The work reflects an appropriate organizational strategy for a reader with little prior tap dancing experience. Paragraphs of one or two sentences describe each individual foot movement. Each paragraph is numbered for easy reference.

C **D** The instructions become a guide to action by using appropriate transitional phrases and embedded headings to guide the reader from the simplest step through to the most difficult step.

The amount of information included is sufficient to inform readers without overwhelming them with irrelevant details.

How to Tap Dance

Reading

E2 Writing

Speaking, Listening, and Viewing

Conventions, Grammar, and Usage of the English Language

E4

Literature

4

pop your left heel up. The arms
to this step are...
① Stick your index fingers out and
put your hands by your sides.
② When your right heel goes down
put your right hand down. You
should still have your index fingers
sticking out.
③ When your left heel goes down
your left hand goes down. Here
is one of the more difficult
steps that I know.

C ➤ ② Tap riff. Here's how you do
it. I'll count the sounds. Pick up your
right foot

Sound① Hit the ball of your right foot.

E The work anticipates where the reader might become frustrated or confused, and, where necessary, provides solutions to possible problems.

F The work ends by describing a difficult step and then stating that it is the last step the student can teach the reader.

E4 a Conventions, Grammar, and Usage of the English Langauge: The student demonstrates a basic understanding of the rules of the English language in written and oral work, and selects the structures and features of language appropriate to the purpose, audience, and context of the work. The student demonstrates control of:

• grammar;

• paragraph structure;

• punctuation;

• sentence construction;

• spelling;

• usage.

The student described a series of complicated physical movements in clear, concise English. He broke apart each step and conveyed the various parts with the appropriate written language. The use of imperatives and simple sentence structures contributed to the successful accomplishment of the task of making difficult directions accessible for a reader who has little experience in the particular dance form.

5

Sound② Then hit your right heel.
Sound③ The drop your left standing heel.
Sound④ Brush your right heel back crossing over your standing leg.
Sound⑤ Brush back on your right ball of the foot.
Sound⑥ Drop standing left heel again.
Then repeat these six sounds again wrapping your foot the other way, 12 sounds in all. Now for 13,14, and 15. you repeat the first three sounds I told you making a total of 15 sounds so far.

6

Sound⑯ Place the right heel down.
Sound⑰ Drop the right toe down. For 18,19, 20, and 21 drop the back left heel, then front right heel, back left heel, front right heel. The total is 21 sounds. Then use your left foot to reverse the 21 tap riff. This is considered an advanced tap step. That is the last step I

F ➤ can teach you. Bye.

Work Sample & Commentary: Counting on Frank

Reading

Writing E2

Speaking, Listening, and Viewing

Conventions, Grammar, and Usage of the English Language

Literature

The task

Students were asked to read *Counting on Frank* by Rod Clement and to write a letter to the author commenting on at least one example of the mathematical claims made.

Circumstances of performance

This sample of student work was produced under the following conditions:

This work sample is also included among the work samples that illustrate the Mathematics performance standards. See page 100.

√ alone

in class

√ with teacher feedback

timed

in a group

√ as homework

with peer feedback

√ opportunity for revision

What the work shows

E2 d Writing: The student produces a narrative procedure that:

- engages the reader by establishing a context, creating a persona, and otherwise developing reader interest;

- provides a guide to action that anticipates a reader's needs; creates expectations through predictable structures, e.g., headings; and provides transitions between steps;

- makes use of appropriate writing strategies such as creating a visual hierarchy and using white space and graphics as appropriate;

- includes relevant information;

- excludes extraneous information;

- anticipates problems, mistakes, and misunderstandings that might arise for the reader;

- provides a sense of closure to the writing.

The detailed steps of the mathematical procedure engage the reader by clearly recounting the steps the student followed.

A The context of a letter allows for a constructive critique of several mathematical procedures employed by the author.

Dear Rod Clement,
I read your book, Counting On Frank, I thought it was a great book. I would recommend this to any kids or even adults who just love math. All of the math claims in the book are just waiting for kids to try. I think you didn't think that anybody would try these problems a second time, but I did.
You'll see from the work below that I tried 3 of the claims. There were many more in the book, but these seemed to be easier to try. Even though your math claims were really exaggerated, I still thought this was a hilarious, great book.

Bathroom pg.6
We measured our school sink. It was just under a cubic ft. We timed the water and how long it took to fill it all. It took forty seconds to fill it all. The Book said that it had 2 faucets running. We only had one faucet running so that means that you divide 40÷2=20 seconds. After that we asked a contractor what is the average size of a bathroom? He said 8x8 and most average ceilings are 8 ft. high. To find out the cubic feet in a bathroom multiply 8x8x8 which is 512 cubic ft. The I multiplied 512 cubic ft. x 20 seconds= 10,240 seconds. I needed to know

B Brief anecdotes at the conclusion of each section develop reader interest and support the claims made by the procedures described.

C The strategy of announcing that the writer has tried the problems establishes a believable voice for the writer and serves to get the reader's attention.

D The headings that begin each of the three sections, along with the appropriate transition words within each section, provide a guide to action for the text.

This work sample illustrates a standard-setting performance for the following part of the standards:

E2 d Writing: Produce a narrative procedure.

Counting on Frank

minutes. so I divided by 60 and I got 170 min. which is almost 3 hrs. The boy said it took 11 hours and 45 min which is definetely way off. Or maybe he has a huge bathroom. He says it took 705 min. If I could fill 3 cu.ft. in one min. 705 min. x 3 cu.ft. was what he filled. If I figured that a bathroom ceiling is 8' tall I would Divide the height and get the area which is 264 sq. ft. To find out the area there are millions of possibilities. Here are some that are close 20x13, 16x16, 26x10 these are huge bathrooms. I have proved him wrong.

Peas pg.8

In the story it said he would knock off 15 peas per day off his plate x 7 days in a week x 52 weeks x 8 yrs. = 43,680 peas. With a large bag of peas has about 3,325 peas in a bag, bags are done by weight not just counting so this is an estimate. I used 1 coffee cup of peas it could take 700 peas in it. so 4 3/4 c. are in one bag. After I was done one cup I just filled it up because I know what the number on so I. multiplied 700 peas times four cups = 2800 then three quarters of 700 equals 525. (2800) + 525 = 3,325. (4 cups) 3/4 (Peas in a bag)

I divided 43,680 Peas (Number of peas in 8 yrs.) ÷ by 3,325 (1 bag) = 13.13 bags of peas.

If 13 bags of peas do not even fill 1 grocery bag how would it be level with their table (like it said in the story) His whole kitchen would be small like a grocery bag or the peas are as big as softballs. I have proved him wrong again.

Pen pg1

In the story the boy said the average ball point pen draws a line twenty-three hundred yards long before the ink runs out. I measured an ink tube - it was 9 cm high. Then I drew a line 3000 ft long (30 times up and down a 100 ft. piece of paper). After I was done drawing the lines I measured the ink again I had used 2 cm. of ink. If I used 2 cm. for 3000 ft. then I estimate 1 cm. would be 1,500. Then I would multiplig 1500ft x 9cm.= 13,500 ft. then I would divide my answer (13,500 yds.) by 3 = 4,500 yds. because 3ft. in one yd. The boys estimate was 2300 so I was about 1/2 off. I used a brand new papermate pen, Which I think is the average pen. I have proved him wrong a third time.

The letter is written clearly and logically. This avoids the risk of the reader misunderstanding the procedures described and avoids the need to use examples or parallel situations to clarify the points made.

E The conclusion of the letter appropriately restates the original claim. The conclusion also exhibits a sensitivity to the author of the book by recognizing the value of the author's work in an enthusiastic manner and recommending the book to others.

I'm wondering if all the other math in the book is as exaggerated as the 3 claims that I tried. Did you try out the mathematical claims that you made or were you just trying to be funny? I think that you exaggerated the numbers to make the book hilarious. Even though your math isn't very good in this book, I still really liked the story.

Sincerely,

Work Sample & Commentary: *How Many Handshakes?*

Reading

Writing E2

Speaking,
Listening,
and Viewing

Conventions,
Grammar,
and Usage
of the English
Language

Literature

The task

In a mathematics class, the teacher gave students the following instructions:

Five people enter a room and introduce themselves to each other. If everyone shakes everyone else's hand just once, what is the total number of handshakes that occurred?

Circumstances of performance

This work sample is also included among the work samples that illustrate the Mathematics performance standards. See page 90.

This sample of student work was produced under the following conditions:

√ alone   in a group

√ in class   as homework

  with teacher feedback   with peer feedback

  timed   opportunity for revision

A ····▸

A way you can always figure it out, without a chart, is by using a math sentence. Starting at the highest of your number, or the lowest, going up or down then adding all of them together. Remember not to include the person who can't shake his own hand. For exsample if you had 30 people. You might start with a 29 because 30 cannot shake his own hand. Then you would count down to 1. Then add all the numbers together and that would equal the correct answer.

◂···· **B**

◂···· **C**

What the work shows

E2 d Writing: The student produces a narrative procedure that:

- engages the reader by establishing a context, creating a persona, and otherwise developing reader interest;

- provides a guide to action that anticipates a reader's needs; creates expectations through predictable structures, e.g., headings; and provides transitions between steps;

- makes use of appropriate writing strategies such as creating a visual hierarchy and using white space and graphics as appropriate;

- includes relevant information;

- excludes extraneous information;

- anticipates problems, mistakes, and misunderstandings that might arise for the reader;

- provides a sense of closure to the writing.

The description of the procedure communicates a mathematical concept in a clear, simple voice.

A The student used appropriate transition words to guide the reader through the mathematical process being explained.

B The student anticipated problems a reader might encounter in working through the problem by suggesting that the reader, "Remember not to include the person who can't shake his own hand." He then provided a clarifying example.

C A sense of closure is provided with the indication that if the procedure has been carefully followed the answer should be correct and the problem solved.

This work sample illustrates a standard-setting performance for the following part of the standards:

E2 d Writing: The student produces a narrative procedure.

Work Sample & Commentary: *Media Viewing Log*

The task

Students were asked to keep a log of the television programs they viewed for one week. The log sheets provided asked students to list the programs they watched and to consider some of the implications of their viewing habits.

Circumstances of performance

This sample of student work was produced under the following conditions:

√ alone   in a group

   in class   √ as homework

   with teacher feedback   with peer feedback

   timed   opportunity for revision

What the work shows

E3 d Speaking, Listening, and Viewing: The student makes informed judgments about television, radio, and film productions; that is, the student:

• demonstrates an awareness of the presence of the media in the daily lives of most people;

• evaluates the role of the media in focusing attention and in forming an opinion;

• judges the extent to which media provide a source of entertainment as well as a source of information;

• defines the role of advertising as part of media presentation.

The student indicated that watching television has a variety of purposes for her and that being aware of the reason for watching is valuable.

Name _____

Media Viewing Log

Page ___1___ of ___

	Time Spent	Program Viewed	Other Activities Done While Viewing	Activities Not Done in Favor of Viewing	Benefits of Viewing	Detriments of Viewing
Mon	1 hr	Diary of Anne Frank	Ø	Playing on Computer	Learned more about Anne Frank	Less time to get ready for bed
Tues	10 min.	Alvin and the chipmunks	none	playing the piano	I killed time.	none
Wed	15 min.	Odd Couple	none	Playing the piano	I killed time	I could have been practicing
Thurs	10 min	Gumby	none	playing on computer	none	I could have been practicing
Sat	30 min.	Bewitched	none	playing on computer	none	I could have been practicing
Sat	1 hr	Les Miserables in Concert	none	playing the piano	none	I could have been practicing
Sun	15 min	Alex Mack	I dealt a deck of cards.	playing on Computer	none	none

New Standards Copyright © 1996

Portfolio Media Viewing Log

T.V.

By _____

In doing this television log, I learned many things. Not all t.v. is bad. It depends partly on the program that you are watching. There are some programs such as Schoolhouse Rock or Square One T.V. Math Talk that many people think is perfectly okay to watch. There some shows that don't really teach you anything but that can't do you any harm to watch.

Another thing that I learned was that if there were other things that were more important than watching t.v. or that needed to be done first it is probably not good to watch t.v. before doing those things.

Another thing that I learned was that whether watching t.v. is bad or not also partly depends on how long you watch t.v. If you watch to much t.v. at a time then it is not good. But if you are not watching for too long then it is not really bad depending on what you are watching.

I always try to find something fun to do other than watch t.v. I don't think that the greatest thing to do is watch t.v., but there are some shows on t.v. that I enjoy watching.

I am glad that I did this log, and I learned a lot from it. I think it will make me more aware of the choices I make in the future that concern t.v.

This work sample illustrates a standard-setting performance for the following part of the standards:

E3 d Speaking, Listening, and Viewing: The student makes informed judgments about television, radio, and film productions.

Reading

Writing

Speaking,
Listening,
and Viewing

Conventions,
Grammar,
and Usage
of the English
Language

Literature ◄ **E5**

Work Sample & Commentary: I Discover Columbus

The task

Students were asked to read *I Discover Columbus* by Robert Lawson and to separate the historical facts from the fictional elements in a report.

Circumstances of performance

This sample of student work was produced under the following conditions:

√ alone   in a group

   in class   √ as homework

   with teacher feedback   with peer feedback

   timed   √ opportunity for
                                        revision

What the work shows

E5 a Literature: The student responds to non-fiction, fiction, poetry, and drama using interpretive, critical, and evaluative processes; that is, the student:
• identifies recurring themes across works;
• analyzes the impact of authors' decisions regarding word choice and content;
• considers the differences among genres;
• evaluates literary merit;
• considers the function of point of view or persona;
• examines the reasons for a character's actions, taking into account the situation and basic motivation of the character;
• identifies stereotypical characters as opposed to fully developed characters;
• critiques the degree to which a plot is contrived or realistic;
• makes inferences and draws conclusions about contexts, events, characters, and settings.

A The lists indicate a clear distinction between those events the author borrowed from history and those events which were contrived by the author to make the story interesting.

B The work attests to the value of the author's decision to use the bird as the narrator by suggesting that this technique keeps the reader interested and adds humor to the book.

C The recognition that the book is not simply a historical account or a humorous tale demonstrates a knowledge of various genres.

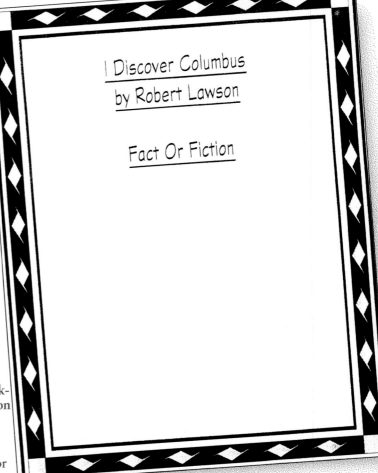

I Discover Columbus
by Robert Lawson

Fact Or Fiction

This work sample illustrates a standard-setting performance for the following part of the standards:

E5 a **Literature: Respond to non-fiction, fiction, poetry, and drama.**

Elementary School English Language Arts 51

Reading

Writing

Speaking,
Listening,
and Viewing

Conventions,
Grammar,
and Usage
of the English
Language

E5   Literature

I Discover Columbus

Fact

1) He was born in Genoa, Italy.
2) He was born poor.
3) He wanted honor and riches.
4) He was a great navigator and organizer of expeditions.
5) He had an audience with the king and queen.
6) Ferdinand and Isabella were very excited about finding a new land.
7) Torquamada was a real person.
8) He was made "admiral of the ocean sea".
9) The trip was going to be very expensive, and Isabel and Ferdinand did not have 1,700 gulden to pay for it.
10) They raised enough money for the expedition.
11) There were 3 ships: the Nina, the Pinta, and the Santa Maria.
12) The fleet left on Aug.3,1492.
13) Columbus sailed on the Santa Maria.
14) There was a parade when he left Spain.
15) The journal that he wrote describes that the voyage was stormy and dangerous.
16) Columbus prepared plans for the expedition including maps, books, instruments, and lists.

17) The Santa Maria was chartered by Juan de la Cosa and he came along as a sailing partner.
18) Columbus's crew was planning a mutiny because the trip was so long.
19) Conditions on the boat were bad. There was little food and water.
20) Columbus first landed on an island called Guanahani, later renamed San Salvador.
21) The Santa Maria was wrecked on a sandbar.
22) Vincent Pinzon was captain of the Nina.
23) Martin Pinzon was captain of the Pinta.

Fiction

1) Birds cannot fly from the Amazon River to Spain.
2) Aurelio is a bird and cannot talk.
3) Aurelio and Columbus taught each other different languages.
4) Aurelio gave Columbus the idea to discover a new land.
5) Columbus owned Aurelio and became famous for owning a talking bird.
6) Aurelio was responsible for the meeting between Columbus and King Ferdinand and Queen Isabella.
7) The king wanted to see the famous egg trick.
8) The king threw Columbus out of the castle because the egg cracked in his face.
9) Aurelio pawned the Queen's jewels to raise money for the expedition.
10) Aurelio stole jewels from the people of Spain to give to the Queen so she could raise more money .
11) Columbus was seasick.
12) Dona Mercedes was not a stowaway on the ship.
13) There was no wedding on the ship.
14) Dona Mercedes did not help Columbus write his journal and diary.
15) Admiral Don Manuel Nicosa did not exist. Juan

Opinion

I Discover Columbus, by Robert Lawson, was a very interesting book. It combined history with a sense of humor and was very tongue in cheek. Some parts of the book are difficult to understand because it is unclear if the facts are true or false. But, by writing in this way, the author makes the book much more interesting. Using Aurelio as the narrator of the story was a very funny idea and helped keep me interested in the story. Also, the artwork was very good.
I would definitely recommend this book for anyone who would like to read about Columbus and learn about his expedition.

Work Sample & Commentary: *Drift Aways*

The task

Students were asked to write a poem with strong imagery. Prior to writing their own poems, the students spent a week reading from various collections of poems and studying imagery, rhythm, poetic language, and form.

Circumstances of performance

This sample of student work was produced under the following conditions:

√ alone

√ in class

   with teacher feedback

   timed

   in a group

√ as homework

√ with peer feedback

√ opportunity for revision

What the work shows

E4 a Conventions, Grammar, and Usage of the English Language: The student demonstrates a basic understanding of the rules of the English language in written and oral work, and selects the structures and features of language appropriate to the purpose, audience, and context of the work. The student demonstrates control of:
• grammar;
• paragraph structure;
• punctuation;
• sentence construction;
• spelling;
• usage.

A The student identified three misspelled words in the second version (see circled words) and corrected them for the final version.

The student demonstrated, through virtually error free writing, the ability to manage the conventions of the English language.

Draft 1

Jan. 12, 1996

'Feelings, Drift Aways

When you know you can't forget someone
Because of how you miss them so much,
And no matter how much you try
You can't.

When you know you can't forget someone
Even though because they died,
They're making your life miserable
You can't.

When you know you can't forget someone
Even if you know they can't come back,
But you wish with all your heart they could,
They can't.

To: Uncle Jerry, who I
wish would come back
with all my heart,
please, come back.

E4 b Conventions, Grammar, and Usage of the English Language: The student analyzes and subsequently revises work to clarify it or make it more effective in communicating the intended message or thought. The student's revisions should be made in light of the purposes, audiences, and contexts that apply to the work. Strategies for revising include:
• adding or deleting details;
• adding or deleting explanations;
• clarifying difficult passages;
• rearranging words, sentences, and paragraphs to improve or clarify meaning;
• sharpening the focus;
• reconsidering the organizational structure.

The student made effective changes in the form of the poem. The early three stanza draft has long sentences that imitate prose in form and rhythm. The final four

---

This work sample illustrates a standard-setting performance for the following parts of the standards:

E4 a Conventions: Demonstrate a basic understanding of the rules of the English language.

E4 b Conventions: Analyze and subsequently revise written work.

E5 b Literature: Produce work in at least one literary genre that follows the conventions of the genre.

Draft 2

Mar. 9, 1995

²Drift Aways

Wicked women!
Small cat.
Poor (defenceless) creature. — **A**
When you know you can't forget someone
Even if (there) all of a sudden just drift,
Drift away.

When you know you can't forget someone
Even if (there) just a cat. — **A**
Tiny cat,
Giant jump,
Three story jump,
Down,
    Down,
        Down, 'hole.
I nto the
I Likemy Uncle Jerry,
That cat, Bunnie, — **A**
(Which) I still have hope for,
Just drifted away.

        Drift Aways.

Draft 3

Drift Aways

Mar. 9, 1995

²Drift Aways

Wicked women!
Small cat.
Poor defenseless creature.
When you know you can't forget someone
Even if they all of a sudden just drift
Drift away.

When you know you can't forget someone
Even if they're just a cat,
Tiny cat,
Giant jump,
Three story jump,
Down,
    Down,
        Down,
I nto the 'hole.
Likemy Uncle Jerry, — **B**
That cat, Bunnie,
Which I still have hope for,
Just drifted away.

    Drift aways.

---

stanza format makes use of imagery, line breaks, and white space to create mood and rhythm.

B The student made appropriate and substantive changes from draft to draft, e.g., adding the parallel between the loss of the cat and the death of her uncle.

E5 b Literature: The student produces work in at least one literary genre that follows the conventions of the genre.

The student draws an analogy between an occurrence she once witnessed and the larger question concerning the finality of death.

C D The poetic devices used in the poem, such as alliteration, repetition, and the gentle image of drifting away as a metaphor for death, suggest an understanding of poetic language and how to make proper use of it.

E The use of line breaks and white space to produce a strong poetic form, e.g., "Down, Down, Down," demonstrates an understanding of poetic form.

2Drift Aways

C → Wicked woman!
Small cat.
Poor defenseless creature
When you know you can't forget someone
D → Even if they all of a sudden just drift
Drift away.

When you know you can't forget someone
Even if they're just a cat,
Tiny cat,
Giant jump,
Three story jump,
Down,   ← **E**
    Down,
        Down,
Into the hole.
B → Like my uncle Jerry,
That cat, Bunnie,
Which I still have hope for,
D → Just drifted away.

    Drift aways.

Work Sample & Commentary: *A Flash of Lightning and Silent Pond*

Reading

Writing

Speaking, Listening, and Viewing

Conventions, Grammar, and Usage of the English Language

Literature   E5

The task

Students participated in a poetry study lasting several weeks, after which they were asked to write their own poems. As part of the unit, the students read and analyzed poetry during workshops that focused on various elements of poetry, such as figurative language, imagery, and form.

Circumstances of performance

This sample of student work was produced under the following conditions:

√ alone   in a group

   in class   √ as homework

   with teacher feedback   √ with peer feedback

   timed   √ opportunity for
                              revision

What the work shows

E5 b Literature: The student produces work in at least one literary genre that follows the conventions of the genre.

The student chose brief images to reflect upon in these poems. He tried to capture a moment of time in words that evoke the memory of lightning and of a still pond.

A "A Flash of Lightning" deals with an image of lightning in each of the five stanzas.

The work demonstrates an understanding of the conventions of poetry by the use of line breaks as punctuation;

B the use of repetition to imitate sound;

C the play with various rhyme forms such as slant rhyme; and

D alliteration.

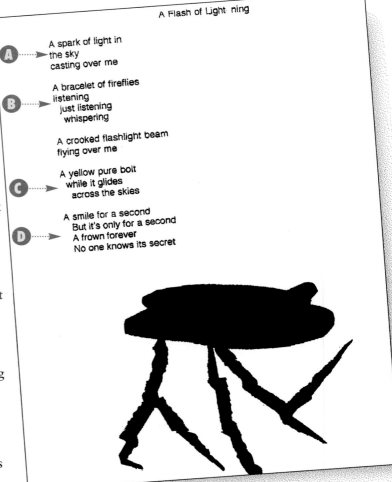

A Flash of Lightning

A A spark of light in
the sky
casting over me

B A bracelet of fireflies
listening
just listening
whispering

A crooked flashlight beam
flying over me

C A yellow pure bolt
while it glides
across the skies

D A smile for a second
But it's only for a second
A frown forever
No one knows its secret

The careful use of language creates quick snapshots of the event. Each stanza begins with a metaphor for lightning—a spark, a bracelet, a flashlight beam, a bolt, and a smile—most of which present lightning as a benevolent entity. The verbs convey a calm, peaceful mood as well as action—"casting," "flying," "glides." The final two lines disrupt the mood and hint at the true nature of the phenomenon, "A frown forever?/No one knows its secret."

This work sample illustrates a standard-setting performance for the following part of the standards:

E5 b Literature: Produce work in at least one literary genre that follows the conventions of the genre.

A Flash of Lightning and Silent Pond

The use of metaphors throughout "Silent Pond" demonstrates an understanding of poetic techniques.

E Beginning both stanzas with an image involving shiny metals creates a certain degree of symmetry.

The personification of the puddle as lying on the ground and listening to the wind creates the principal image of the poem. In this poem, brief lines create a series of related images rather than a prolonged thought or story.

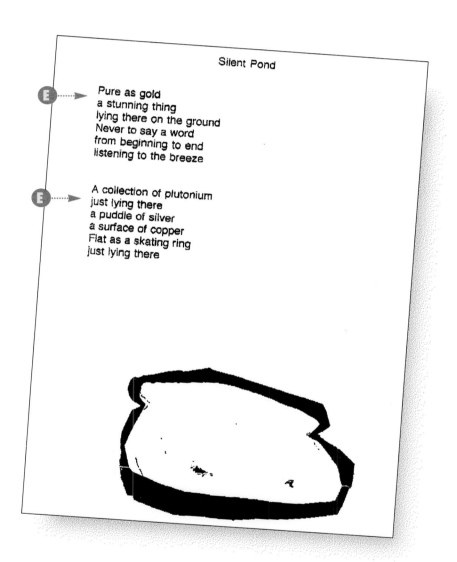

Silent Pond

E →
Pure as gold
a stunning thing
lying there on the ground
Never to say a word
from beginning to end
listening to the breeze

E →
A collection of plutonium
just lying there
a puddle of silver
a surface of copper
Flat as a skating ring
just lying there

Work Sample & Commentary: *Home Reading Record*

Reading **E1**
Writing
Speaking, Listening, and Viewing
Conventions, Grammar, and Usage of the English Language
Literature

The task

Students were asked to keep a record of their reading throughout the course of the year. Both a teacher and a parent were asked to certify that the reading record represented what the student had actually read. An excerpt of the record is included here.

Circumstances of performance

This sample of student work was produced under the following conditions:

√ alone   in a group

√ in class   √ as homework

    with teacher feedback   with peer feedback

    timed   opportunity for revision

Home Reading Record for _____

Date Begun	Type	Title and Author	Date Finished
7-24-95	P	The Twits by Roald Dahl	7-27-95
6-15-95	C	The Indian in the cupboard Lynne Reid Banks	7-28-95
7-29-95	C	The Return of the Indian Lynne Reid Banks	8-10-95
8-3-95	P	Aladdin by Disney	8-3-95
8-10-95	C	The Secret of the Indian Lynne Reid Banks	8-21-95
8-22-95	C	The Mystery of the Cupboard Lynne Reid Banks	9-3-95
9-4-95		The Wonderful Story of Henry Sugar Roald Dahl	

Type Codes: P= piece of cake, J= just right, C= challenging   Parent Signature _____

What the work shows

E1 a Reading: The student reads at least twenty-five books or book equivalents each year. The quality and complexity of the materials to be read are illustrated in the sample reading list. The materials should include traditional and contemporary literature (both fiction and non-fiction) as well as magazines, newspapers, textbooks, and on-line materials. Such reading should represent a diverse collection of material from at least three different literary forms and from at least five different writers.

This reading log is an excerpt of an entire year's log. The entire reading log provides evidence that the student met the goal of reading twenty-five books of an appropriate quality for the elementary standard. The reading log also shows the variety of texts the student read, including mysteries, fiction, non-fiction/biography, and fairy tales.

E1 b Reading: The student reads and comprehends at least four books (or book equivalents) about one issue or subject, or four books by a single writer, or four books in one genre, and produces evidence of reading that:
- makes and supports warranted and responsible assertions about the texts;
- supports assertions with elaborated and convincing evidence;
- draws the texts together to compare and contrast themes, characters, and ideas;
- makes perceptive and well developed connections;
- evaluates writing strategies and elements of the authors's craft.

The reading log shows evidence that the student read in depth from four or more books from one author and four or more texts in one genre.

This work sample illustrates a standard-setting performance for the following parts of the standards:

E1 a Reading: Read at least twenty-five books or book equivalents each year.

E1 b Reading: Read in depth.

Home Reading Record

Home Reading Record for _____

Date Begun	Type	Title and Author	Date Finished
9/20	C	The Wonderful Story of Henry Sugar (And six more) / Roald Dahl	
10/19	J	Harris and Me / Gary Paulsen	10/17
11/7	J	Number the Stars / Lois Lowry	11/?6
11/29	P	The Vicar of Nibbleswicke / Roald Dahl	11/27
11/30		The BFG - Roald Dahl Chapter 6	11/29

Type Codes: P= piece of cake, J= just right, C= challenging   Parent Signature_____

Home Reading Record for _____

Date	Type	Title and Author	Genre	# pages	Completed
11/30	J	The BFG - Roald Dahl	action/ Adventure	208	12/11
12/16	P	How I Got My Shrunken Head / R.L. Stine	Mystery	119	12/18
12/19	P	Revenge of the Lawn Gnomes / R.L. Stine	Mystery	119	12/20
12/21	J	Charlie and the Great Glass Elevator / Roald Dahl	action/ adventure	163	1/15
1/16	C	Danny the Champion of the World / Roald Dahl	action/ adventure	198	1/21
1/22	P	The Magic Finger / Roald Dahl	action/ Adventure	64	1/22
1/23	C	Mr. Tucket / Gary Paulsen	action/ adventure	166	1/30
1/31	J	The Witches / Roald Dahl	fairy tale	208	2/10

Type Codes: P= piece of cake, J= just right, C= challenging   Parent Signature_____
Genres: Historical, science, or realistic fiction, non-fiction, biography, poetry, fairy tale, folk tale, mystery, action/adventure, etc.

Home Reading Record for _____

Date	Type	Title and Author	Genre	# pages	Completed
2/11	J	Soccer Halfback / Matt Christopher	realistic fiction	182	2/21
2/22	C	Boy / Roald Dahl	Non-fiction Biography	176	3/4
3/5	J	Everywhere / Bruce Brooks	Realistic fiction	70	

Type Codes: P= piece of cake, J= just right, C= challenging   Parent Signature_____
Genres: Historical, science, or realistic fiction, non-fiction, biography, poetry, fairy tale, folk tale, mystery, action/adventure, etc.

Home Reading Record for _____

Date	Type	Title and Author	Genre	# pages	Completed
3/20	J	THERE'S A GHOST IN THE BOYS' BATHROOM / Tom B. Stone	Mystery	99	4/2
4/5	J	Wayside school gets a little stranger / Louis Sachar	Wacky realistic fiction	168	4/11
4/12	J	Stay out of the Bathroom / R.U. Slime/Robert Hughes	realistic fiction	129	4/20
4/21	J	Eat Cheese and Barf / R.U. Slime/Robert Hughes	realistic fiction	129	5/3
5/4	J	Dinn Dredel's wagon of wonders / Bill Britian	fairy tale	179	5/8
5/9	J	Devil's Donkey / Bill Britian	fairy tale	120	5/12
5/13	J	Professor Popkin's Prodigous Polish / Bill Britian	fairy tale	152	

Type Codes: P= piece of cake, J= just right, C= challenging   Parent Signature_____
Genres: Historical, science, or realistic fiction, non-fiction, biography, poetry, fairy tale, folk tale, mystery, action/adventure, etc.

Introduction to the performance standards for

Mathematics

Building directly on the National Council of Teachers of Mathematics (NCTM) Curriculum Standards, the Mathematics performance standards present a balance of conceptual understanding, skills, and problem solving.

The first four standards are the important conceptual areas of mathematics:

M1 Arithmetic and Number Concepts;

M2 Geometry and Measurement Concepts;

M3 Function and Algebra Concepts;

M4 Statistics and Probability Concepts.

These conceptual understanding standards delineate the important mathematical content for students to learn. To demonstrate understanding in these areas, students need to provide evidence that they have used the concepts in a variety of ways that go beyond recall. Specifically, students show progressively deeper understanding as they use a concept in a range of concrete situations and simple problems, then in conjunction with other concepts in complex problems; as they represent the concept in multiple ways (through numbers, graphs, symbols, diagrams, or words, as appropriate) and explain the concept to another person.

This is not a hard and fast progression, but the concepts included in the first four standards have been carefully selected as those for which the student should demonstrate a robust understanding. These standards make explicit that students should be able to demonstrate understanding of a mathematical concept by using it to solve problems, representing it in multiple ways (through numbers, graphs, symbols, diagrams, or words, as appropriate), and explaining it to someone else. All three ways of demonstrating understanding—use, represent, and explain—are required to meet the conceptual understanding standards.

Complementing the conceptual understanding standards, M5 - M8 focus on areas of the mathematics curriculum that need particular attention and a new or renewed emphasis:

M5 Problem Solving and Reasoning;

M6 Mathematical Skills and Tools;

M7 Mathematical Communication;

M8 Putting Mathematics to Work.

Establishing separate standards for these areas is a mechanism for highlighting the importance of these areas, but does not imply that they are independent of conceptual understanding. As the work samples that follow illustrate, good work usually provides evidence of both.

Like conceptual understanding, the definition of problem solving is demanding and explicit. Students use mathematical concepts and skills to solve non-routine problems that do not lay out specific and detailed steps to follow; and solve problems that make demands on all three aspects of the solution process—formulation, implementation, and conclusion. These are defined in **M5**, Problem Solving and Reasoning.

The importance of skills has not diminished with the availability of calculators and computers. Rather, the need for mental computation, estimation, and interpretation has increased. The skills in **M6**, Mathematical Skills and Tools, need to be considered in light of the means of assessment. Some skills are so basic and important that students should be able to demonstrate fluency, accurately and automatically; it is reasonable to assess them in an on-demand setting, such as the New Standards reference examination. There are other skills for which students need only demonstrate familiarity rather than fluency. In using and applying such skills they might refer to notes, books, or other students, or they might need to take time out to reconstruct a method they have seen before. It is reasonable to find evidence of these skills in situations where students have ample time, such as in a New Standards portfolio. As the margin note by the examples that follow the performance descriptions indicates, many of the examples are performances that would be expected when students have ample time and access to tools, feedback from peers and the teacher, and an opportunity for revision. This is true for all of the standards, but especially important to recognize with respect to **M6**.

M7 includes two aspects of mathematical communication—using the language of mathematics and communicating about mathematics. Both are important. Communicating about mathematics is about ideas and logical explanation. The travelogue approach adopted by many students in the course of describing their problem solving is not what is intended.

M8 is the requirement that students put many concepts and skills to work in a large-scale project or investigation, at least once each year, beginning in the fourth grade. The types of projects are specified; for each, the student identifies, with the teacher, a clear purpose for the project, what will be accomplished, and how the project involves putting mathematics to work; develops a question and a plan; writes a detailed description of how the project was carried out, including mathematical analysis of the results; and produces a report that includes acknowledgment of assistance received from parents, peers, and teachers.

The examples

The purpose of the examples listed under the performance descriptions is to show what students might do or might have done in achieving the standards, but these examples are not intended as the only ways to demonstrate achievement of the standard. They are meant to illustrate good tasks and they begin to answer the question, "How good is good enough?" "Good enough" means being able to solve problems like these.

Each standard contains several parts. The examples below are cross-referenced to show a rough correspondence between the parts of the standard and the examples. These are not precise matches, and students may successfully accomplish the task using concepts and skills different from those the task designer intended, but the cross-references highlight examples for which a single activity or project may allow students to demonstrate accomplishment of several parts of one or more standards.

The purpose of the samples of student work is to help explain what the standards mean and to elaborate the meaning of a "standard-setting performance." Few pieces of work are so all-encompassing as to qualify for the statement, "meets the standard." Rather, each piece of work shows evidence of meeting the requirements of a selected part or parts of a standard. Further, most of these pieces of work provide evidence related to parts of more than one standard. It is essential to look at the commentary to understand just how the work sample helps to illuminate features of the standards.

Resources

We recognize that some of the standards presuppose resources that are not currently available to all students. The New Standards partners have adopted a Social Compact, which says, in part, "Specifically, we pledge to do everything in our power to ensure all students a fair shot at reaching the new performance standards...This means that they will be taught a curriculum that will prepare them for the assessments, that their teachers will have the preparation to enable them to teach it well, and there will be an equitable distribution of the resources the students and their teachers need to succeed."

The NCTM standards make explicit the need for calculators of increasing sophistication from elementary to high school and ready access to computers. Although a recent National Center for Education Statistics survey confirmed that most schools do not have the facilities to make full use of computers and video, the New Standards partners have made a commitment to create the learning environments where students can develop the knowledge and skills that are delineated here. Thus, **M6**, Mathematical Skills and Tools, assumes that students have access to computational tools at the level spelled out by NCTM. This is not because we think that all schools *are* currently equipped to provide the experiences that would enable students to meet these performance standards, but rather that we think that all schools *should be* equipped to provide these experiences. Indeed, we hope that making these requirements explicit will help those who allocate resources to understand the consequences of their actions in terms of student performance.

The elementary school performance standards are set at a level of performance that is approximately equivalent to the end of fourth grade. It is expected, however, that some students might achieve this level earlier and others later than this grade. The work samples that follow, however, were all done by students who were, in fact, in the fourth grade.

Performance Descriptions *Mathematics*

M1 Arithmetic and Number Concepts

To see how these performance descriptions compare with the expectations for middle school and high school, turn to pages 220-231.

The examples that follow the performance descriptions for each standard are examples of the work students might do to demonstrate their achievement. The examples also indicate the nature and complexity of activities that are appropriate to expect of students at the elementary level. Depending on the nature of the task, the work might be done in class, for homework, or over an extended period.

The cross-references that follow the examples highlight examples for which the same activity, and possibly even the same piece of work, may enable students to demonstrate their achievement in relation to more than one standard. In some cases, the cross-references highlight examples of activities through which students might demonstrate their achievement in relation to standards for more than one subject matter.

The student demonstrates understanding of a mathematical concept by using it to solve problems, representing it in multiple ways (through numbers, graphs, symbols, diagrams, or words, as appropriate), and explaining it to someone else. All three ways of demonstrating understanding—use, represent, and explain—are required to meet this standard.

The student produces evidence that demonstrates understanding of arithmetic and number concepts; that is, the student:

M1 a Adds, subtracts, multiplies, and divides whole numbers, with and without calculators; that is:

• adds, i.e., joins things together, increases;

• subtracts, i.e., takes away, compares, finds the difference;

• multiplies, i.e., uses repeated addition, counts by multiples, combines things that come in groups, makes arrays, uses area models, computes simple scales, uses simple rates;

• divides, i.e., puts things into groups, shares equally; calculates simple rates;

• analyzes problem situations and contexts in order to figure out when to add, subtract, multiply, or divide;

• solves arithmetic problems by relating addition, subtraction, multiplication, and division to one another;

• computes answers mentally, e.g., 27 + 45, 30 x 4;

• uses simple concepts of negative numbers, e.g., on a number line, in counting, in temperature, "owing."

M1 b Demonstrates understanding of the base ten place value system and uses this knowledge to solve arithmetic tasks; that is:

• counts 1, 10, 100, or 1,000 more than or less than, e.g., 1 less than 10,000, 10 more than 380, 1,000 more than 23,000, 100 less than 9,000;

• uses knowledge about ones, tens, hundreds, and thousands to figure out answers to multiplication and division tasks, e.g., 36 x 10, 18 x 100, 7 x 1,000, 4,000 ÷ 4.

M1 c Estimates, approximates, rounds off, uses landmark numbers, or uses exact numbers, as appropriate, in calculations.

M1 d Describes and compares quantities by using concrete and real world models of simple fractions; that is:

• finds simple parts of wholes;

• recognizes simple fractions as instructions to divide, e.g., ¼ of something is the same as dividing something by 4;

• recognizes the place of fractions on number lines, e.g., in measurement;

• uses drawings, diagrams, or models to show what the numerator and denominator mean, including when adding like fractions, e.g., ⅛ + ⅝, or when showing that ¾ is more than ⅛;

• uses beginning proportional reasoning and simple ratios, e.g., "about half of the people."

M1 e Describes and compares quantities by using simple decimals; that is:

• adds, subtracts, multiplies, and divides money amounts;

• recognizes relationships among simple fractions, decimals, and percents, i.e., that ½ is the same as 0.5, and ½ is the same as 50%, with concrete materials, diagrams, and in real world situations, e.g., when discovering the chance of a coin landing on heads or tails.

M1 f Describes and compares quantities by using whole numbers up to 10,000; that is:

• connects ideas of quantities to the real world, e.g., how many people fit in the school's cafeteria; how far away is a kilometer;

• finds, identifies, and sorts numbers by their properties, e.g., odd, even, multiple, square.

Examples of activities through which students might demonstrate conceptual understanding of arithmetic and number include:

▲ Use examples and drawings to show a third grader who is having trouble understanding multiplication why 3 x 6 = 6 x 3. **1a**

▲ Use base ten blocks and numerals or other models and representations to solve 43 x 38, and show how the numbers get taken apart in the process of solving such a problem, e.g., 43 can become 40 + 3, or 38 can become 40 - 2. **1a, 1b**

▲ Figure out how many Valentine's Day cards would be exchanged in total, if there are 30 students in the class and if everyone gave everyone else one card. **1a, 1b, 1c**

▲ Draw and explain many different ways to make 263, using tens, hundreds and ones. **1a, 1b, 1c**

▲ Organize a budget for a project. **1a, 1b, 1c, 1d, 1e, 1f, A1a, A1b, A1c**

▲ Solve the following problem: "You have a book to read that is 100 pages long. You must read it in five days. How many pages should you read each day?" **1a, 1b, 1c, 1f**

▲ Determine the possible number of objects in a group given this information: when put in groups of three, none is left over; when put in groups of two, one is left over; when put in groups of five, one is left over; there are fewer than 40 objects altogether. **1a, 1b, 1c, 1f**

▲ Make reasonable estimates and then calculate accurately the number of beans in a cup, seeds in a pumpkin, ceiling tiles in a room, and wheels on 37 tricycles. **1a, 1b, 1c, 1f**

▲ Show and explain to a classmate the different coin combinations that make 75¢, excluding pennies. **1a, 1b, 1c, 1f**

▲ Find one possible answer for addends that equal the sum of 8,829, when the digits 1, 2, 3, 4, 5, 6, 7, and 8 are used only once in the solution. **1a, 1b, 1c, 5a, 5b, 5c**

▲ Analyze seasonal variations in temperature, including negative values. **1a, 1c, 1f, S3c, A1a**

▲ Put together fraction pieces to make a whole in different ways, e.g., ⅛ + ⅛ + ¾. **1c, 1d**

▲ Draw diagrams to explain how three pizzas can be shared equally by four people. **1c, 1d**

▲ Make approximate counts of different kinds of animals in different zones of a small tide pool area. **1c, 1f, S6b**

▲ Draw and label diagrams to show the fractional value of each piece of a set of tangram pieces, if all seven pieces (i.e., the whole set) are equal to one whole. **1d**

▲ Pretend you see a highway sign that reads, "Exit A, 1 mile. Exit B, 2¼ miles," and shortly thereafter you see a sign that reads, "Exit A, ¼ mile." Figure out how far away exit B must now be. (Balanced Assessment) **1d, 1f**

▲ Make up stories that go with number sentences, e.g., 5 x 9 = 45; 27 x 6 = ?. **1f**

M2 Geometry and Measurement Concepts

The student demonstrates understanding of a mathematical concept by using it to solve problems, representing it in multiple ways (through numbers, graphs, symbols, diagrams, or words, as appropriate), and explaining it to someone else. All three ways of demonstrating understanding—use, represent, and explain—are required to meet this standard.

The student produces evidence that demonstrates understanding of geometry and measurement concepts; that is, the student:

M2a Gives and responds to directions about location, e.g., by using words such as "in front of," "right," and "above."

M2b Visualizes and represents two dimensional views of simple rectangular three dimensional shapes, e.g., by showing the front view and side view of a building made of cubes.

M2c Uses simple two dimensional coordinate systems to find locations on a map, and represent points and simple figures.

M2d Uses many types of figures (angles, triangles, squares, rectangles, rhombi, parallelograms, quadrilaterals, polygons, prisms, pyramids, cubes, circles, and spheres) and identifies the figures by their properties, e.g., symmetry, number of faces, two- or three-dimensionality, no right angles.

M2e Solves problems by showing relationships between and among figures, e.g., using congruence and similarity, and using transformations including flips, slides, and rotations.

M2f Extends and creates geometric patterns using concrete and pictorial models.

M2g Uses basic ways of estimating and measuring the size of figures and objects in the real world, including length, width, perimeter, and area.

M2h Uses models to reason about the relationship between the perimeter and area of rectangles in simple situations.

M2i Selects and uses units, both formal and informal as appropriate, for estimating and measuring quantities such as weight, length, area, volume, and time.

M2j Carries out simple unit conversions, such as between cm and m, and between hours and minutes.

M2k Uses scales in maps, and uses, measures, and creates scales for rectangular scale drawings based on work with concrete models and graph paper.

Examples of activities through which students might demonstrate conceptual understanding of geometry and measurement include:

▲ Locate a point on a map using its distance away from another given point, the map's scale, and compass point directions, e.g., N, NE, E, SE, etc. **2a, 2c, 2k**

▲ Given views of three faces of a three dimensional figure made of stacked cubes, represent the views of the other faces and figure out the total number of cubes used to construct the figure. **2b**

▲ Explain and show why a square is not a cube. **2d**

▲ Describe a shape from among the following, using as few attributes as possible to distinguish it from the others: right triangle, equilateral triangle, trapezoid, and parallelogram. **2d**

▲ Design and label a quilt square which includes two lines of symmetry, four congruent shapes, and two similar shapes; then make a final version at twice the original size, i.e., a "two to one" scale, and add color while maintaining symmetry. **2d, 2e, 2f, 2k**

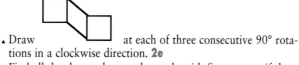

▲ Draw   at each of three consecutive 90° rotations in a clockwise direction. **2e**

▲ Find all the shapes that can be made with five squares if the sides touch completely. **2e**

▲ Figure out the approximate area and perimeter of the bottom of a shoe. **2g**

▲ Solve the following problem, using concrete materials as appropriate: "Given a diagram of a fenced-in, rectangular garden plot with dimensions three meters by eight meters, find its area and perimeter; design a second garden plot using less fencing, but providing greater area; design a third plot using more fencing, but providing less area. Of all possible rectangular designs using the original amount of fencing, which provides the greatest area?" **2g, 2h, 2i**

▲ Put five objects, such as books, rocks, or pumpkins, in rank order by weight, first by estimating and then by measuring exactly. **2i**

▲ Figure out exactly how much time would you gain for the completion of a project by waking up at 6:15 rather than 7:00 for five school days. **2i, 2j**

Samples of student work that illustrate standard-setting performances for these standards can be found on pages 66-129.

Performance Descriptions *Mathematics*

To see how these performance descriptions compare with the expectations for middle school and high school, turn to pages 220-231.

The examples that follow the performance descriptions for each standard are examples of the work students might do to demonstrate their achievement. The examples also indicate the nature and complexity of activities that are appropriate to expect of students at the elementary level. Depending on the nature of the task, the work might be done in class, for homework, or over an extended period.

The cross-references that follow the examples highlight examples for which the same activity, and possibly even the same piece of work, may enable students to demonstrate their achievement in relation to more than one standard. In some cases, the cross-references highlight examples of activities through which students might demonstrate their achievement in relation to standards for more than one subject matter.

M3 Function and Algebra Concepts

The student demonstrates understanding of a mathematical concept by using it to solve problems, representing it in multiple ways (through numbers, graphs, symbols, diagrams, or words, as appropriate), and explaining it to someone else. All three ways of demonstrating understanding—use, represent, and explain—are required to meet this standard.

The student produces evidence that demonstrates understanding of function and algebra concepts; that is, the student:

M3 a Uses linear patterns to solve problems; that is:

- shows how one quantity determines another in a linear ("repeating") pattern, i.e., describes, extends, and recognizes the linear pattern by its rule, such as, the total number of legs on a given number of horses can be calculated by counting by fours;
- shows how one quantity determines another quantity in a functional relationship based on a linear pattern, e.g., for the "number of people and total number of eyes," figure out how many eyes 100 people have all together.

M3 b Builds iterations of simple non-linear patterns, including multiplicative and squaring patterns (e.g., "growing" patterns) with concrete materials, and recognizes that these patterns are not linear.

M3 c Uses the understanding that an equality relationship between two quantities remains the same as long as the same change is made to both quantities.

M3 d Uses letters, boxes, or other symbols to stand for any number, measured quantity, or object in simple situations with concrete materials, i.e., demonstrates understanding and use of a beginning concept of a variable.

Examples of activities through which students might demonstrate conceptual understanding of functions and algebra include:

- Find, make, and describe linear patterns on the 99-chart, e.g., 4, 14, 24, 34. **3a**
- Given the situation described in the Christmas carol, "The Twelve Days of Christmas," determine how many gifts would have been given in total; describe any pattern you notice that helps in solving the problem. **3a, 3b**
- Show how the letters "aab, aab,...," can represent the pattern "metal, metal, plastic,...," "leaf, leaf, rock,...," or many other patterns. **3a, 3d**
- Solve the following problem: When building a staircase out of cubes, one step uses a total of one cube, two steps a total of three cubes, three steps a total of six cubes, etc. Find how many cubes are used for six steps, nine steps, n steps. Describe the pattern. **3b**
- Observe and record, in a two-column table, multiplicative patterns with concrete materials, e.g., how many regions are produced by increasing the numbers of folds of paper; and recognize that this type of pattern does not proceed in a linear way, i.e., not 2, 4, 6, 8, etc., but 2, 4, 8, 16, etc. **3b**
- Build the fourth, fifth, and sixth iterations in the following

  sequence: □ ⊞ ⊞ ; use any given number to make a square number; and recognize that the number of little squares in the pattern does not proceed in a linear fashion. **3b**
- Given x + y = 10 (or, say, Δ + □ = 10), figure out all the whole numbers that will make the equation true, i.e., use the variables to show all the ways to make ten by adding two whole numbers together. **3c, 3d**
- Plot points on a coordinate graph according to the convention that (x, y) refers to the intersection of a given vertical line and a given horizontal line. **3d**

M4 Statistics and Probability Concepts

The student demonstrates understanding of a mathematical concept by using it to solve problems, representing it in multiple ways (through numbers, graphs, symbols, diagrams, or words), and explaining it to someone else. All three ways of demonstrating understanding—use, represent, and explain—are required to meet this standard.

The student produces evidence that demonstrates understanding of statistics and probability concepts in the following areas; that is, the student:

M4 a Collects and organizes data to answer a question or test a hypothesis by comparing sets of data.

M4 b Displays data in line plots, graphs, tables, and charts.

M4 c Makes statements and draws simple conclusions based on data; that is:

- reads data in line plots, graphs, tables, and charts;
- compares data in order to make true statements, e.g., "seven plants grew at least 5 cm";
- identifies and uses the mode necessary for making true statements, e.g., "more people chose red";
- makes true statements based on a simple concept of average (median and mean), for a small sample size and where the situation is made evident with concrete materials or clear representations;
- interprets data to determine the reasonableness of statements about the data, e.g., "twice as often," "three times faster";
- uses data, including statements about the data, to make a simple concluding statement about a situation, e.g., "This kind of plant grows better near sunlight because the seven plants that were near the window grew at least 5 cm."

M4 d Gathers data about an entire group or by sampling group members to understand the concept of sample, i.e., that a large sample leads to more reliable information, e.g., when flipping coins.

M4 e Predicts results, analyzes data, and finds out why some results are more likely, less likely, or equally likely.

M4 f Finds all possible combinations and arrangements within certain constraints involving a limited number of variables.

Examples of activities through which students might demonstrate conceptual understanding of statistics and probability include:

- Generate survey questions, such as: How many people are in your family? What is your hair color? What do you do at recess? Predict the survey results, carry out the survey, graph the data, and write true statements about the data. **4a, 4b, 4c, 4d**
- Figure out a need, e.g., the librarian's purchase of new library books; and collect data in order to make a recommendation. **4a, 4b, 4c, 4d**
- Make conjectures, after sampling the particular situation, about how many raisins are in a given box taken from a set of boxes or what colors of tiles are in a bag. **4a, 4b, 4c, 4d**
- Investigate the temperature over the entire school year. **4a, 4b, 4c, 4d, S3c, A1a**
- Investigate the possible and likely or unlikely outcomes when rolling two number cubes and recording the sums. **4d, 4e, 4f**
- Design spinners with regions red, blue and green, according to the following instructions: Spinner #1: red will certainly win; Spinner #2: red cannot win; Spinner #3: red is likely to win; Spinner #4: red, blue and green are equally likely to win; Spinner #5: red or blue will probably win. **4e**
- Find all of the different combinations possible using three ice cream flavors, two sauces, and one topping; then discover which would allow the most new combinations—an additional ice cream flavor or a new topping. (Balanced Assessment) **4f**

M5 Problem Solving and Reasoning

The student demonstrates logical reasoning throughout work in mathematics, i.e., concepts and skills, problem solving, and projects; demonstrates problem solving by using mathematical concepts and skills to solve non-routine problems that do not lay out specific and detailed steps to follow; and solves problems that make demands on all three aspects of the solution process—formulation, implementation, and conclusion.

Formulation

M5a Given the basic statement of a problem situation, the student:

• makes the important decisions about the approach, materials, and strategies to use, i.e., does not merely fill in a given chart, use a pre-specified manipulative, or go through a predetermined set of steps;

• uses previously learned strategies, skills, knowledge, and concepts to make decisions;

• uses strategies, such as using manipulatives or drawing sketches, to model problems.

Implementation

M5b The student makes the basic choices involved in planning and carrying out a solution; that is, the student:

• makes up and uses a variety of strategies and approaches to solving problems and uses or learns approaches that other people use, as appropriate;

• makes connections among concepts in order to solve problems;

• solves problems in ways that make sense and explains why these ways make sense, e.g., defends the reasoning, explains the solution.

Conclusion

M5c The student moves beyond a particular problem by making connections, extensions, and/or generalizations; for example, the student:

• explains a pattern that can be used in similar situations;

• explains how the problem is similar to other problems he or she has solved;

• explains how the mathematics used in the problem is like other concepts in mathematics;

• explains how the problem solution can be applied to other school subjects and in real world situations;

• makes the solution into a general rule that applies to other circumstances.

Examples of activities through which students might demonstrate facility with problem solving and reasoning include:

▲ Suppose you are given a string that is sixteen inches long. If you cut or fold it in any two places, will it always make a triangle? **5a, 5b, 5c**

▲ Figure out how many handshakes there will be altogether if five people in a room shake each other's hand just once. **5a, 5b, 5c**

▲ Prove or disprove a classmate's claim that ¾ and ⅚ are really the same because both have one piece missing. **5a, 5b, 5c**

▲ Given an unopened bag of chocolate chip cookies, with cookies arranged in rows, show and explain whether the manufacturer's claim of "More than 1,000 chips in every bag!" is reasonable. **5a, 5b, 5c**

▲ Figure out the value of each tangram piece if the small tangram triangle is worth one cent and the value is proportional to the area. **5a, 5b, 5c**

▲ For the sum of 8,829, find one possible answer for addends when the digits 1, 2, 3, 4, 5, 6, 7, and 8 are used only once in the solution. **5a, 5b, 5c**

Samples of student work that illustrate standard-setting performances for these standards can be found on pages 66-129.

Performance Descriptions *Mathematics*

M6 Mathematical Skills and Tools

The student demonstrates fluency with basic and important skills by using these skills accurately and automatically, and demonstrates practical competence and persistence with other skills by using them effectively to accomplish a task, perhaps referring to notes, books, or other students, perhaps working to reconstruct a method; that is, the student:

M6a Adds, subtracts, multiplies, and divides whole numbers correctly; that is:

• knows single digit addition, subtraction, multiplication, and division facts;

• adds and subtracts numbers with several digits;

• multiplies and divides numbers with one or two digits;

• multiplies and divides three digit numbers by one digit numbers.

M6b Estimates numerically and spatially.

M6c Measures length, area, perimeter, circumference, diameter, height, weight, and volume accurately in both the customary and metric systems.

M6d Computes time (in hours and minutes) and money (in dollars and cents).

M6e Refers to geometric shapes and terms correctly with concrete objects or drawings, including triangle, square, rectangle, side, edge, face, cube, point, line, perimeter, area, and circle; and refers with assistance to rhombus, parallelogram, quadrilateral, polygon, polyhedron, angle, vertex, volume, diameter, circumference, sphere, prism, and pyramid.

M6f Uses $+, -, \times, \div, /, \overline{)}$, $, ¢, %, and . (decimal point) correctly in number sentences and expressions.

M6g Reads, creates, and represents data on line plots, charts, tables, diagrams, bar graphs, simple circle graphs, and coordinate graphs.

M6h Uses recall, mental computations, pencil and paper, measuring devices, mathematics texts, manipulatives, calculators, computers, and advice from peers, as appropriate, to achieve solutions; that is, uses measuring devices, graded appropriately for given situations, such as rulers (customary to the ⅛ inch; metric to the millimeter), graph paper (customary to the inch or half-inch; metric to the centimeter), measuring cups (customary to the ounce; metric to the milliliter), and scales (customary to the pound or ounce; metric to the kilogram or gram).

Examples of activities through which students might demonstrate facility with mathematical skills and tools include:

▲ Know that 6 x 7 = 42. **6a**

▲ Use an efficient mental approach to estimate the total cost of items costing $2.94, $1.28 and $0.74. **6a, 6b, 6d, 6h**

▲ Mentally add two digit numbers correctly during problem solving. **6a, 6h**

▲ Decide whether to use a calculator, paper and pencil or mental arithmetic to figure out 6 x 6,000. **6a, 6h**

▲ Figure out rectangular areas correctly when designing a floor plan for a "dream house." **6b, 6c**

▲ Measure the circumference of a pumpkin accurately by using a piece of yarn, and then laying it next to a ruler. **6c, 6e**

▲ Use a calculator to check the arithmetic in a project.

▲ Use a table to record functions such as how many chairs fit at how many tables. **6g**

▲ Use a Venn diagram to record students who wore a sweater to school and students who walked to school. **6g**

▲ Make a bar graph or simple circle graph to show how many students like different kinds of vegetables. **6g, 6f**

M7 Mathematical Communication

The student uses the language of mathematics, its symbols, notation, graphs, and expressions, to communicate through reading, writing, speaking, and listening, and communicates about mathematics by describing mathematical ideas and concepts and explaining reasoning and results; that is, the student:

M7a Uses appropriate mathematical terms, vocabulary, and language, based on prior conceptual work.

M7b Shows mathematical ideas in a variety of ways, including words, numbers, symbols, pictures, charts, graphs, tables, diagrams, and models.

M7c Explains solutions to problems clearly and logically, and supports solutions with evidence, in both oral and written work.

M7d Considers purpose and audience when communicating about mathematics.

M7e Comprehends mathematics from reading assignments and from other sources.

Examples of activities through which students might demonstrate facility with mathematical communication include:

▲ Use words, numbers, or diagrams to explain how to take numbers apart in order to solve problems using mental math, e.g., 25 x 6. One way is "20 x 6 is 120, and 5 x 6 is 30; 120 + 30 = 150." Or, "25 x 4 is 100, and 25 x 2 is 50, and so the answer is 150 because 100 + 50 = 150." **7a, 7b, 7c**

▲ Explain why 34 + 17 ≠ 3417 to a first grader or to a visitor from outer space. **7a, 7b, 7c, 7d**

▲ Show ½ + ¾ in pictures and diagrams so a younger student could understand the sum. **7a, 7b, 7c, 7d**

▲ Use clear, correct mathematical language to describe a shape composed of several geometric solids so that it could be reproduced exactly by a person who cannot see the shape. **7a, 7b, 7c, 7d**

▲ Represent survey data about student school lunch preferences in graphical, written, and numerical form in order to make a clear and effective recommendation to kitchen staff about menu changes. **7a, 7b, 7c, 7d**

▲ Give an oral presentation of a preliminary investigation of classification of shapes, in order to get peer feedback; then revise the classification scheme to make it clearer. **7a, 7b, 7c, 7d, E3c**

▲ Prepare a report, including graphs, charts, and diagrams, on the optimal number and location of recycling containers, based on data from the classroom and the entire school. **7a, 7b, 7c, 7d, 7e, E2a, S4b, S6d, S7a, A1b**

To see how these performance descriptions compare with the expectations for middle school and high school, turn to pages 220-231.

The examples that follow the performance descriptions for each standard are examples of the work students might do to demonstrate their achievement. The examples also indicate the nature and complexity of activities that are appropriate to expect of students at the elementary level. Depending on the nature of the task, the work might be done in class, for homework, or over an extended period.

The cross-references that follow the examples highlight examples for which the same activity, and possibly even the same piece of work, may enable students to demonstrate their achievement in relation to more than one standard. In some cases, the cross-references highlight examples of activities through which students might demonstrate their achievement in relation to standards for more than one subject matter.

M8 Putting Mathematics to Work

The student conducts at least one large scale project each year, beginning in fourth grade, drawn from the following kinds and, over the course of elementary school, conducts projects drawn from at least two of the kinds.

A single project may draw on more than one kind.

M8a Data study, in which the student:

* develops a question and a hypothesis in a situation where data could help make a decision or recommendation;
* decides on a group or groups to be sampled and makes predictions of the results, with specific percents, fractions, or numbers;
* collects, represents, and displays data in order to help make the decision or recommendation; compares the results with the predictions;
* writes a report that includes recommendations supported by diagrams, charts, and graphs, and acknowledges assistance received from parents, peers, and teachers.

M8b Science study, in which the student:

* decides on a specific science question to study and identifies the mathematics that will be used, e.g., measurement;
* develops a prediction (a hypothesis) and develops procedures to test the hypothesis;
* collects and records data, represents and displays data, and compares results with predictions;
* writes a report that compares the results with the hypothesis; supports the results with diagrams, charts, and graphs; acknowledges assistance received from parents, peers, and teachers.

M8c Design of a physical structure, in which the student:

* decides on a structure to design, the size and budget constraints, and the scale of design;
* makes a first draft of the design, and revises and improves the design in response to input from peers and teachers;
* makes a final draft and report of the design, drawn and written so that another person could make the structure; acknowledges assistance received from parents, peers, and teachers.

M8d Management and planning, in which the student:

* decides on what to manage or plan, and the criteria to be used to see if the plan worked;
* identifies unexpected events that could disrupt the plan and further plans for such contingencies;
* identifies resources needed, e.g., materials, money, time, space, and other people;
* writes a detailed plan and revises and improves the plan in response to feedback from peers and teachers;
* carries out the plan (optional);
* writes a report on the plan that includes resources, budget, and schedule, and acknowledges assistance received from parents, peers, and teachers.

M8e Pure mathematics investigation, in which the student:

* decides on the area of mathematics to investigate, e.g., numbers, shapes, patterns;
* describes a question or concept to investigate;
* decides on representations that will be used, e.g., numbers, symbols, diagrams, shapes, or physical models;
* carries out the investigation;
* writes a report that includes any generalizations drawn from the investigation, and acknowledges assistance received from parents, peers, and teachers.

Examples of projects include:

▲ Develop questions and a hypothesis for a study of students' diets; collect, organize, display, and analyze the data; and make recommendations to the school community based on the data. **8a, S2a, S4c, A1b**

▲ Compare the growth of a set of plants under a variety of conditions, e.g., amount of water, fertilizer, duration and exposure to sunlight. **8b, S2a**

▲ Make a design for a tree house that accounts for physical and financial constraints. **8c, A1a**

▲ Plan a class camping trip, including making a schedule, researching costs and facilities, developing a budget. **8d, S2a, S2c, S4b, S4c, A1c**

▲ Plan and conduct a probability study that compares the results from three different spinners, e.g.,

. **8e**

Samples of student work that illustrate standard-setting performances for these standards can be found on pages 66-129.

Work Sample & Commentary: *Sharing 25*

Arithmetic and Number Concepts **M1**

Geometry & Measurement Concepts

Function & Algebra Concepts

Statistics & Probability Concepts

Problem Solving & Reasoning

Mathematical Skills & Tools **M6**

Mathematical Communication

Putting Mathematics to Work

The quotations from the Mathematics performance descriptions in this commentary are excerpted. The complete performance descriptions are shown on pages 60-65.

The task

The following written prompt appeared on an examination:

In each situation below, four friends want to "share 25" as equally as possible. Show or explain how to "share 25" in each situation.

1. Four friends shared 25 balloons as equally as possible.

2. Four friends shared $25 as equally as possible.

3. Four friends shared 25 cookies as equally as possible.

Circumstances of performance

This sample of student work was produced under the following conditions:

√ alone   in a group

√ in class   as homework

   with teacher feedback   with peer feedback

√ timed   opportunity for revision

This five minute task was part of a field test for the New Standards Reference Examination: Mathematics (Elementary).

Sharing 25…

In each situation below, four friends want to "share 25" as equally as possible. Show or explain how to "share 25" in each situation.

1. Four friends shared 25 balloons as equally as possible.

   A ⟶ 3 people get 6 and one person got 7

2. Four friends shared $25 as equally as possible.

   B ⟶ Each person gets $6.25

3. Four friends shared 25 cookies as equally as possible.

   C ⟶ Each person gets 6 and a quarter

Reprinted from *Writing in Math Class*, pp. 76-78. ©1995 by Math Solutions Publications. Used by permission.

This work sample illustrates a standard-setting performance for the following parts of the standards:

M1 a Arithmetic and Number Concepts: Add, subtract, multiply, and divide whole numbers.

M1 c Arithmetic and Number Concepts: Estimate, approximate, round off, use landmark numbers, or use exact numbers in calculations.

M1 d Arithmetic and Number Concepts: Describe and compare quantities by using simple fractions.

M1 e Arithmetic and Number Concepts: Describe and compare quantities by using simple decimals.

M6 a Mathematical Skills and Tools: Add, subtract, multiply, and divide whole numbers correctly.

M6 d Mathematical Skills and Tools: Compute time and money.

M6 f Mathematical Skills and Tools: Use +, -, x, ÷, /, ‾ , $, ¢, %, and . (decimal point) correctly in number sentences and expressions.

What the work shows

M1 a Arithmetic and Number Concepts: The student adds, subtracts, multiplies, and divides whole numbers, with and without calculators; that is:

• divides, i.e., puts things into groups, shares equally….

A B C

• analyzes problem situations and contexts in order to figure out when to add, subtract, multiply, or divide.

A B C The student demonstrated conceptual understanding by applying arithmetic skills differently, and appropriately, in a variety of situations.

Sharing 25

M1c Arithmetic and Number Concepts: The student estimates, approximates, rounds off, uses landmark numbers, or uses exact numbers, as appropriate, in calculations.

Ⓐ Ⓑ Ⓒ The correct answers demonstrate rounding off or use of exact number, as appropriate, in each situation.

M1d Arithmetic and Number Concepts: The student describes and compares quantities by using concrete and real world models of simple fractions; that is:

• finds simple parts of wholes....

Ⓑ Ⓒ

M1e Arithmetic and Number Concepts: The student describes and compares quantities by using simple decimals; that is:

• adds, subtracts, multiplies, and divides money amounts....

Ⓑ

M6a Mathematical Skills and Tools: The student adds, subtracts, multiplies, and divides whole numbers correctly....

Ⓐ Ⓑ Ⓒ

M6d Mathematical Skills and Tools: The student computes...money (in dollars and cents).

Ⓑ

M6f Mathematical Skills and Tools: The student uses...$...and . (decimal point) correctly....

Ⓑ

 Arithmetic and Number Concepts

Geometry & Measurement Concepts

Function & Algebra Concepts

Statistics & Probability Concepts

Problem Solving & Reasoning

 Mathematical Skills & Tools

Mathematical Communication

Putting Mathematics to Work

Work Sample & Commentary: *Arithmetic*

Arithmetic and Number Concepts **M1**

Geometry & Measurement Concepts

Function & Algebra Concepts

Statistics & Probability Concepts

Problem Solving & Reasoning

Mathematical Skills & Tools **M6**

Mathematical Communication **M7**

Putting Mathematics to Work

The quotations from the Mathematics performance descriptions in this commentary are excerpted. The complete performance descriptions are shown on pages 60-65.

The tasks

These tasks all focus on the same arithmetic and number concepts and skills, although they were drawn from four different classrooms.

In Sample 1, the teacher included the following instructions on a classroom test:

Using what you know about multiplication, find the answer to the equation below. Show all your work and clearly explain how you got your answer.

63 x 46 =

In Sample 2, the teacher gave the following written instructions as part of a class exercise:

Solve each problem two ways.

522 - 367 =

87 x 9 =

Sample 1

Two Digit Multiplication

5. Using what you know about multiplication, find the answer to the equation below. Show all your work and clearly explain how you got your answer.

63 x 46 = 2,898

63 - 1 time
63 - 1 time
126 - 2 times
126 - 2 times
252 - 4 times
252 - 4 times
504 - 8 times
504 - 8 times
1008 - 16 times
1,008 - 16 times
2,016 - 32 times
126 - 2 times
2,142 - 34 times
504 - 8 times
2,646 - 42 times
252 - 4 times
2,898 - 46 times

A

How I got the answer 2,898 was I knew that I could add 63 46 times but it would take to much time so I decided to do it with doubling. But when I got to 32 times I couldn't double because I would have added 63 64 times insted of 46 times. Then I added 63 2, 8, and 4 more times to get 46 times.

These work samples illustrate standard-setting performances for the following parts of the standards:

M1 a Arithmetic and Number Concepts: Add, subtract, multiply, and divide whole numbers.

M1 b Arithmetic and Number Concepts: Demonstrate understanding of the base ten value system and use this knowledge to solve arithmetic tasks.

M1 c Arithmetic and Number Concepts: Estimate, approximate, round off, use landmark numbers, or use exact numbers in calculations.

M1 d Arithmetic and Number Concepts: Describe and compare quantities by using simple fractions.

M6 a Mathematical Skills and Tools: Add, subtract, multiply, and divide whole numbers correctly.

M6 f Mathematical Skills and Tools: Use +, -, x, ÷, /, ⎺, $, ¢, %, and . (decimal point) correctly in number sentences and expressions.

M6 h Mathematical Skills and Tools: Use recall, mental computations, and pencil and paper to achieve solutions.

M7 a Mathematical Communication: Use appropriate mathematical terms, vocabulary, and language.

M7 b Mathematical Communication: Show mathematical ideas in a variety of ways.

M7 c Mathematical Communication: Explain solutions to problems clearly and logically.

In Sample 3, the teacher gave the following oral instructions at the end of a long unit of work:

Make a catalogue of all the ways the class has come up with to multiply large numbers.

Make up a two digit by two digit multiplication problem and use these ways to find the answer.

In Sample 4, a specialist read the following written instructions to an individual student:

Four children had three bags of M & M's.

They decided to open all three bags of candy and share the M & M's fairly.

There were 52 M & M candies in each bag.

How many M & M candies did each child get?

Circumstances of performance

These samples of student work were produced under the following conditions:

√ alone   in a group

√ in class   as homework

 with teacher feedback   with peer feedback

 timed   opportunity for revision

Sample 1 was part of a classroom test. For Samples 2 and 3, students were permitted to talk as they worked. Sample 4 was produced when a specialist interviewed the student as the student was completing the work.

Arithmetic

Sample 1 was produced before the class had received any instruction about two digit by two digit multiplication, although they had experience in developing strategies for simpler computation.

Sample 2 was produced in a classroom where students' computation strategies were regularly shared, and several were posted on the wall.

Sample 3 was produced after a long unit of work in which students created, developed, and learned a range of strategies for single and double digit multiplication.

Sample 4 was produced before the class had received any instruction about division, but they had extensive experience with developing and explaining strategies for other computation problems.

What the work shows

M1a Arithmetic and Number Concepts: The student adds, subtracts, multiplies, and divides whole numbers, with and without calculators; that is:

• adds, i.e., joins things together, increases.

A B C D E All students added as they solved larger problems.

• subtracts, i.e., takes away, compares, finds the difference.

F G

• multiplies, i.e., uses repeated addition, counts by multiples, combines things that come in groups, makes arrays....

A The student combined doubling with repeated addition.

C The student used repeated addition of 85.

H The student showed how the problem could be solved by making 62 circles with 85 stars in each circle.

I The student drew a base ten block array.

• divides, i.e., puts things into groups, shares equally....

J The student "split" 80 into 40 and 40 in order to multiply.

E K The student began to divide 156 by 4 by putting down 20 four times.

• analyzes problem situations and contexts in order to figure out when to add, subtract, multiply, or divide.

E In Sample 4, the instructions give no indication about how arithmetic can be used to solve the problem: the student figured it all out.

• solves arithmetic problems by relating addition, subtraction, multiplication, and division to one another.

A C The students related addition to multiplication.

Sample 2

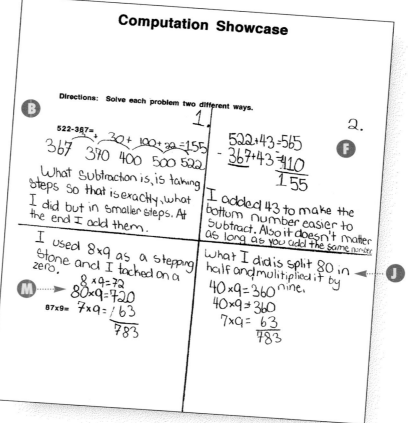

Computation Showcase

Directions: Solve each problem two different ways.

Arithmetic

B F These parts of the work demonstrate using addition to solve a subtraction problem.

L The student counted by twos in the process of multiplying.

D The student counted by multiples to solve a division problem.

• computes answers mentally, e.g., 27 + 45, 30 x 4.

A B C E All students used mental computation effectively throughout all of their work.

Sample 3

M1b Arithmetic and Number Concepts: The student demonstrates understanding of the base ten place value system and uses this knowledge to solve arithmetic tasks; that is:

• counts 1, 10, 100, or 1,000 more than or less than, e.g., 1 less than 10,000, 10 more than 380, 1,000 more than 23,000, 100 less than 9,000.

B The student counted 3, 30, and 100 more.

D The student counted by twenties, tens, and ones.

Each sample includes evidence that demonstrates this kind of understanding.

• uses knowledge about ones, tens, hundreds, and thousands to figure out answers to multiplication and division tasks, e.g., 36 x 10, 18 x 100, 7 x 1,000, 4,000 ÷ 4.

I J L M The students broke the numbers apart, e.g., 40 x 9; 60 x 80; 3 x 50.

M1c Arithmetic and Number Concepts: The student estimates, approximates, rounds off, uses landmark numbers, or uses exact numbers, as appropriate, in calculations.

B The student used landmark numbers to go from 367 to 370 to 400 to 500.

G The student rounded off in order to make the problem easier.

Each sample demonstrates the use of exact numbers to finish the tasks.

M1d Arithmetic and Number Concepts: The student describes and compares quantities by using concrete and real world models of simple fractions; that is:

• finds simple parts of wholes.

J The student applied concrete knowledge to split "80 in half."

Arithmetic

M6 a Mathematical Skills and Tools: The student adds, subtracts, multiplies, and divides whole numbers correctly; that is:

• knows single digit addition, subtraction, multiplication, and division facts.

Ⓐ Ⓒ Ⓛ Ⓜ Here as in many places, the students' knowledge of basic facts is demonstrated in correct solutions to larger problems.

• adds and subtracts numbers with several digits.

Ⓐ Ⓑ Ⓒ Ⓔ Here, as in other places, the samples demonstrate correct work.

• multiplies and divides numbers with one or two digits.

Ⓐ Ⓙ Ⓜ Ⓝ Here, as in many other places, the samples demonstrate correct work.

• multiplies and divides three digit numbers by one digit numbers.

Ⓔ In elementary school, it may be appropriate for students to work through a solution to division problems; multiplication and division with multi-digit numbers is not expected to be routine at this level.

M6 f Mathematical Skills and Tools: The student uses +, -, x...correctly in number sentences and expressions.

Ⓕ Ⓘ These parts of the samples demonstrate correct use of symbols. This is also evident throughout the samples.

M6 h Mathematical Skills and Tools: The student uses recall, mental computations, pencil and paper...to achieve solutions.

Ⓐ Ⓑ Ⓒ Ⓔ

M7 a Mathematical Communication: The student uses appropriate mathematical terms, vocabulary, and language, based on prior conceptual work.

Ⓐ Ⓑ Ⓒ Ⓔ

M7 b Mathematical Communication: The student shows mathematical ideas in a variety of ways, including words, numbers, symbols, pictures, charts, graphs, tables, diagrams, and models.

Ⓐ Ⓑ Ⓒ Ⓔ

M7 c Mathematical Communication: The student explains solutions to problems clearly and logically, and supports solutions with evidence, in both oral and written work.

Ⓐ Ⓑ Ⓓ Ⓖ

In Sample 3, the student spelled a few words inconsistently, e.g., "multiplied" is correct while "multiplyed" is not; and misspelled others, e.g., "Catalouge" instead of "Catalogue." All of the samples were taken from work done in class which was not edited for spelling.

Ⓜ Arithmetic and Number Concepts

Geometry & Measurement Concepts

Function & Algebra Concepts

Statistics & Probability Concepts

Problem Solving & Reasoning

Ⓜ Mathematical Skills & Tools

Ⓜ Mathematical Communication

Putting Mathematics to Work

Sample 4

Four children had three bags of M & M's. They decided to open all three bags of candy and share the M & M's fairly. There were 52 M & M candies in each bag. How many M & M candies did each child get?

Darrell asked for the problem to be read aloud to him three times. Then Darrell considered the problem for a moment before he began talking as he wrote.

Darrell: *Four people.*

So I said, uhh. ... So I took. ... First, I did this. I numbered the four people.. And then I put, then I put 3 times 52.

Then I said, equals.

Ⓛ➤ *And that equals ... 3 times 52 equals ... 150 ... 152, 154, 156. And that equals 156.*

Ⓚ➤ *So, since there's four children, I split the 156 and I said, 20, 20, 20, 20.*

Ⓓ➤ *I said, 20, ... so I added all the 20's up. 20, 40, 60, 80. ... Then I said, 85, 90, 95, 100. Then I said 10, 20; 30, 40. These are tens.*

... 141, 142, 143, 144,

... 145, 146, 147, 148,

... 149, 150, 151, 152,

... 153, 154, 155, 156. And so, ... so each, each child got, ... 30, 35. Each child got 20,

30,

35,

36, 37, 38, 39.

Each child got 39 M & M's.

[Writes 11 12 13 14].

[Writes 3 x 52]

[Writes =.]

[Writes 156.]

[Writing 20's as he speaks.]

[Writing 5's in each column.]
[Writing 10's in each column.]
[Writing 1's in each column.]
[Writing 1's in each column.]
[Writing 1's in each column.]

[Pointing to 20 in the first column.]
[Pointing to 10 in the first column.]
[Pointing to 5 in the first column.]
[Pointing to 1's in the first column.]

Work Sample & Commentary: *3-D to 2-D*

The quotations from the Mathematics performance descriptions in this commentary are excerpted. The complete performance descriptions are shown on pages 60-65.

The tasks

These work samples are drawn from two different classrooms, but focus on the same concept of visualizing and representing three dimensional objects in two dimensions.

In Sample 1, the teacher gave the following written instruction to the students:

Andre built a shape with blocks. What would be the front view?

In Sample 2, the teacher gave the students Student Sheets 15 and 16 (from *Seeing Solids and Silhouettes*, a book in the series, *Investigations in Number, Data and Space*, Dale Seymour Publications, 1995) which had these written instructions:

Choose two or three buildings. Draw their silhouettes from the front, top, and right side. (Student Sheet 15)

Draw the front, top, and side silhouettes for three cube buildings. Put the number of the building above its silhouettes. (Student Sheet 16)

Circumstances of performance

These samples of student work were produced under the following conditions:

√ alone	in a group
√ in class	as homework
√ with teacher feedback	with peer feedback
timed	√ opportunity for revision

Both students were developing a New Standards Elementary Mathematics Portfolio. Because of this, they knew the criteria in this system for work that shows conceptual understanding. The criteria require the student to use, represent, and explain the concept. The students used the tasks as opportunities to show what they understood about the concept of visualizing and representing three dimensional objects in two dimensions.

Sample 1 was completed in Spanish in a bilingual classroom. The translation was provided by the teacher.

What the work shows

M2 a Geometry and Measurement Concepts: The student gives and responds to directions about location, e.g., by using words such as "in front of," "right," and "above."

A B Both students used location words in their explanations of their thinking and understanding.

M2 b Geometry and Measurement Concepts: The student visualizes and represents two dimensional views of simple rectangular three dimensional shapes, e.g., by showing the front view and side view of a building made of cubes.

C D Both students produced two dimensional views to represent three dimensional objects.

E Sample 2 includes a small mistake that does not detract from the evidence of an overall understanding of this concept.

These work samples illustrate standard-setting performances for the following parts of the standards:

M2 a Geometry and Measurement Concepts: Give and respond to directions about location.

M2 b Geometry and Measurement Concepts: Visualize and represent two dimensional views of simple rectangular three dimensional shapes.

M2 d Geometry and Measurement Concepts: Use many types of figures.

M7 a Mathematical Communication: Use appropriate mathematical terms, vocabulary, and language.

Arithmetic and Number Concepts

Geometry & Measurement Concepts **M2**

Function & Algebra Concepts

Statistics & Probability Concepts

Problem Solving & Reasoning

Mathematical Skills & Tools

Mathematical Communication **M7**

Putting Mathematics to Work

3-D to 2-D

Arithmetic and Number Concepts

M2 Geometry & Measurement Concepts

Function & Algebra Concepts

Statistics & Probability Concepts

Problem Solving & Reasoning

Mathematical Skills & Tools

M7 Mathematical Communication

Putting Mathematics to Work

Sample 1

Name _____

Andre built a shape with blocks. What would be the front view?

Front

C

A

La razon por la que pienso esta es porque me imagine voltiar la forma sin ver los otros culos que quedavan. Yo se q esta bien porque de la izquierda ala derech. ay 3 culos. Y arriba de los 3 culos ay otros 3 culos entoses de la derecha ala iquierda ay 6 culos afrente en total. Y ala derecha ay un culo arriba. Y ala izquiero ay un culo arriba diagonal. Entoses en f.nte ay 3 culos en total.

Translation

A

The reason why I think this is because I imagined turning around the form without seeing the other cubes remaining. I know this is right because from the left to the right there are 3 cubes. And on top of the 3 cubes there are 3 other cubes so from the right to the left there are a total of 6 cubes. And on the right there is one cube above. And on the left there is one cube above diagonal. So in front there are a total of 8 cubes.

M2 d Geometry and Measurement Concepts: The student uses many types of figures (...squares,...cubes...) and identifies the figures by their properties, e.g., symmetry, number of faces, two- or three-dimensionality, no right angles.

3-D to 2-D

Sample 2

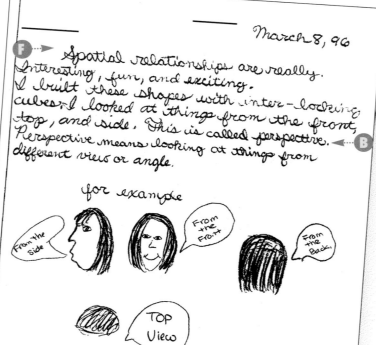

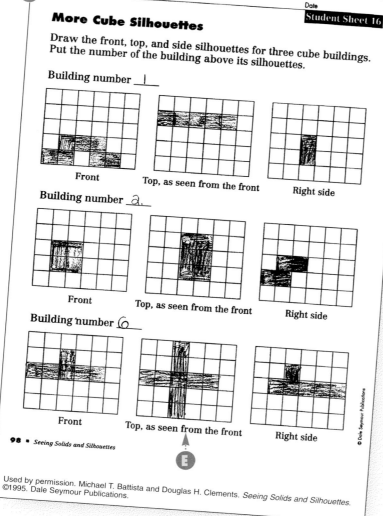

More Cube Buildings

Choose two or three buildings. Draw their silhouettes from the front, top, and right side.

Seeing Solids and Silhouettes ▪ **97**

M7a Mathematical Communication: The student uses appropriate mathematical terms, vocabulary, and language, based on prior conceptual work.

A Sample 1 includes appropriate use of location words (e.g., "from the right to the left") and shape words ("cube").

B Sample 2 includes a good elementary definition of perspective, supported with a clearly explained example.

F Sample 2 includes some unnecessary and superfluous communication. While this kind of communication is fairly common for students as they develop their capacity to explain their thinking, reasoning, and understanding, it does not add any mathematical communication to the response.

Work Sample & Commentary: *Patterns*

The task
The teacher asked students to respond in their mathematics journals to the following question: What is a mathematical pattern?

Circumstances of performance
This sample of student work was produced under the following conditions:

√ alone   in a group

√ in class   as homework

   with teacher feedback   with peer feedback

   timed   opportunity for revision

What the work shows

M3 a Function and Algebra Concepts: The student uses linear patterns to solve problems; that is, shows how one quantity determines another in a linear ("repeating") pattern, i.e., describes, extends, and recognizes the linear pattern by its rule, such as the total number of legs on a given number of horses can be calculated by counting by fours.

A B The student explained what patterns are, and noted that a pattern can be linear, i.e., that it "may or may not repeat itself." The student gave an example of a linear pattern and extended it.

M3 b Function and Algebra Concepts: The student builds iterations of simple non-linear patterns, including multiplicative and squaring patterns (e.g., "growing" patterns) with concrete materials, and recognizes that these patterns are not linear.

A The student explained what patterns are, and noted that a pattern can "grow or lower itself," i.e., be non-linear.

C D The student went on to give two examples of different kinds of non-linear patterns: one in which the numbers get larger by adding the next odd number in sequence; the other in which the numbers get larger by adding "numbers in sequence."

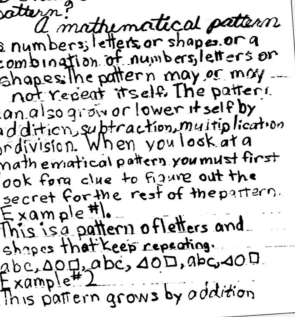

The quotations from the Mathematics performance descriptions in this commentary are excerpted. The complete performance descriptions are shown on pages 60-65.

M7 a Mathematical Communication: The student uses appropriate mathematical terms, vocabulary, and language, based on prior conceptual work.

A B C D These parts of the work provide evidence of appropriate use of mathematical terms and vocabulary. This evidence is supported throughout the work.

This work sample illustrates a standard-setting performance for the following parts of the standards:

M3 a Function and Algebra Concepts: Use linear patterns to solve problems.

M3 b Function and Algebra Concepts: Build iterations of simple non-linear patterns.

M7 a Mathematical Communication: Use appropriate mathematical terms, vocabulary, and language.

Work Sample & Commentary: *Pumpkin Activity*

The task

The teacher gave these instructions:

- Estimate and then measure the height, diameter, circumference, and weight of your group's pumpkin. Use the pieces of yarn, rulers, and a bathroom scale.

- Record your estimated and actual measurements in a clear and organized way.

- Explain how you made the measurements of each feature you are measuring.

- Estimate the number of seeds in your pumpkin, decide on a counting method, and then count the seeds.

- Record what true statements or conclusions you can make about the data from all eight class pumpkins.

The quotations from the Mathematics performance descriptions in this commentary are excerpted. The complete performance descriptions are shown on pages 60-65.

Arithmetic and Number Concepts

Geometry & Measurement Concepts **M2**

Function & Algebra Concepts

Statistics & Probability Concepts **M4**

Problem Solving & Reasoning

Mathematical Skills & Tools **M6**

Mathematical Communication **M7**

Putting Mathematics to Work

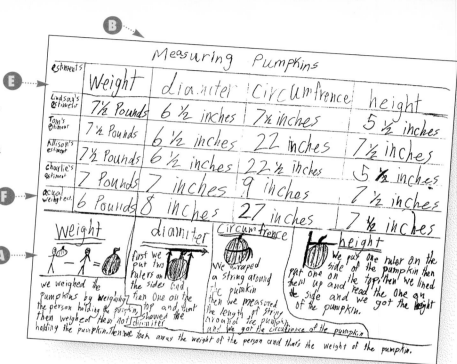

This work sample illustrates a standard-setting performance for the following parts of the standards:

M2 g Geometry and Measurement Concepts: Use basic ways of estimating and measuring the size of figures and objects in the real world.

M4 b Statistics and Probability Concepts: Display data.

M4 c Statistics and Probability Concepts: Make statements and draw simple conclusions based on data.

M6 b Mathematical Skills and Tools: Estimate numerically and spatially.

M6 c Mathematical Skills and Tools: Measure accurately.

M6 g Mathematical Skills and Tools: Read, create, and represent data.

M6 h Mathematical Skills and Tools: Use measuring devices.

M7 a Mathematical Communication: Use appropriate mathematical terms, vocabulary, and language.

M7 b Mathematical Communication: Show mathematical ideas in a variety of ways.

Circumstances of performance

This sample of student work was produced under the following conditions:

√ alone   √ in a group

√ in class   as homework

√ with teacher feedback   √ with peer feedback

   timed   opportunity for revision

While students shared pumpkins in groups of four, they made their estimates and recorded the data individually. The teacher verified that students measured correctly.

What the work shows

M2 g Geometry and Measurement Concepts: The student uses basic ways of estimating and measuring the size of figures and objects in the real world including length, width, perimeter, and area.

A The student estimated, measured, recorded, and described the weight, diameter, circumference, and height of a pumpkin.

M4 b Statistics and Probability Concepts: The student displays data in...tables and charts.

B C The student produced a chart and a table that provide clear displays of data about the group's estimates and measurements and about the data from the whole class.

Pumpkin Activity

C

Pumpkin number	1st 1	2nd 2	3rd 3	4th 4	5th 5	6th 6	7th 7	8th 8
Weight	table 5 8 lbs.	table 3 6 lbs.	table 4 6 lbs.	table 6 6 lbs.	table 5 5 lbs.	table 8 5 lbs.	table 4 lbs.	table 4 lbs.
diameter	table 4 8 inches	table 5 8 inches	table 3 8 inches	table 6 8 inches	table 7½	table 7 inches	table 2 6½ inches	table 7 6½ inches
circumfrence	table 4 22 inches	table 5 24 inches	table 3 22 inches	table 6 21½ inches	table 8 21½ inches	table 7 21 inches	table 2 21 inches	table 21 inches
height	table 8 9 inches	table 5 8 inches	table 7 8 inches	table 2 7½ in.	table 7 7½ in.	table 7½ in.	table 7¼ in.	table 6 5½ in.

D

Conclusions   4/3/94

Our pumpkin was largest in circumfrence and diamiter
(our pumpkin was table 4) but 6th place in height
and 3rd place in # of seeds and weight. Also
One of them was 3rd place in height, but last
place in diamiter. One of them was last in seeds'
weight and diamiter, but 3rd place in height, but
table 5 was second an all of them acsept for
weight and it was first in that. Table 6 was 4th
in diamiter and weight, but last in height.
The second heaviest had the most seeds and
the heaviest had the second most seeds. Table 6
had 6 pounds, was 6 inches in diamiter but was only
21" in circumfreuce and 5½ inches in height.)

M4 c Statistics and Probability Concepts: The student makes statements...based on data; that is, reads data in...tables and charts; compares data in order to make true statements....

D The student read the data about the class pumpkins in order to make comparisons and produce true statements about them.

M6 b Mathematical Skills and Tools: The student estimates numerically and spatially.

E The student estimated weight, diameter, circumference, and height.

M6 c Mathematical Skills and Tools: The student measures length,...circumference, diameter,...weight accurately....

F The student measured weight, diameter, circumference, and height accurately. These measurements were verified by the teacher during the activity.

M6 g Mathematical Skills and Tools: The student reads, creates, and represents data on...charts, tables....

B C The chart and table are correctly drawn.

M6 h Mathematical Skills and Tools: The student uses...measuring devices...to achieve solutions.

A F The student used rulers and yarn to find measurements.

M7 a Mathematical Communication: The student uses appropriate mathematical terms, vocabulary, and language, based on prior conceptual work.

D True statements based on the data are communicated clearly.

M7 b Mathematical Communication: The student shows mathematical ideas in a variety of ways, including words, numbers, symbols, pictures, charts, graphs, tables, diagrams, and models.

A B C The process of measurement is explained in multiple ways (words, diagrams, symbolic notation) and the data are represented in a clear and easily interpreted chart and table.

The work includes some misspelled words. This sample represents work done in class which was not further edited for spelling. The errors occur in words that represented relatively new concepts for the student, e.g., "estiment" for "estimate" and "circumfrence" for "circumference."

The following table shows the number of seeds in each pumpkin reported by table groups. The student referred to these data in the "Conclusions" section of the response.

	Table 1	Table 2	Table 3	Table 4	Table 5	Table 6	Table 7	Table 8
Number of seeds	369	600	824	738	793	562	233	486

Arithmetic and Number Concepts

M2 Geometry & Measurement Concepts

Function & Algebra Concepts

M4 Statistics & Probability Concepts

Problem Solving & Reasoning

M6 Mathematical Skills & Tools

M7 Mathematical Communication

Putting Mathematics to Work

Work Sample & Commentary: *Height Measurement Statistics*

The task

The teacher gave the following instructions:

• Collect everyone's height measurement in inches.

• Make a line plot with the data.

• Write about what you noticed about the data.

Circumstances of performance

This sample of student work was produced under the following conditions:

The quotations from the Mathematics performance descriptions in this commentary are excerpted. The complete performance descriptions are shown on pages 60-65.

√ alone	√ in a group
√ in class	as homework
√ with teacher feedback	with peer feedback
timed	√ opportunity for revision

What the work shows

M4a Statistics and Probability Concepts: The student collects and organizes data to answer a question....

Ⓐ Ⓑ The student began with the question of how tall her classmates were, and collected and organized data to answer this question.

M4b Statistics and Probability Concepts: The student displays data in line plots....

Ⓑ

M4c Statistics and Probability Concepts: The student makes statements and draws simple conclusions based on data; that is, the student:

• reads data in line plots....

Ⓑ

• compares data in order to make true statements, e.g., "seven plants grew at least 7 cm."

Ⓒ The student made true statements about the range, "bumps," "holes," outlier, and median.

This work sample illustrates a standard-setting performance for the following parts of the standards:

M4a Statistics and Probability Concepts: Collect and organize data to answer a question.

M4b Statistics and Probability Concepts: Display data.

M4c Statistics and Probability Concepts: Make statements and draw simple conclusions based on data.

M7a Mathematical Communication: Use appropriate mathematical terms, vocabulary, and language.

Feb. 6, 96

Ⓐ The assignment was to figure out how tall each person was by measuring them in inches. I wrote everyones height on my Data Collection sheet. **Ⓒ** Then I made a Line Plot. Here's what I noticed. The Range of the **Ⓓ** heights were 53½ to 68½. Also the bumps were at 58 and 57. The bumps are where the x on the Line Plot rose. The holes were at 56½, 59, 59½, 60, 62, 63½, 64, 64½, 65, 65½, 66, 66½, 67, 67½, and 68. The holes are on the Line Plot wear no x are. That means no one is that height. The outlier on our sheet was 68½ inches. An outlier is a x on a Line Plot wear no one is around (anotrer x.) The median was 57½ in our class. I enjoyed doing this project + would like to do something like this again.
By

You did a wonderful job with this. I especially like the way you've explained your terms This could be even better if you'd also explain median and what we did to figure it out

Ⓕ Revision A median is the middle of our line plots we got it by taking one x away from each side. The last X is the median.

• identifies and uses the mode necessary for making true statements, e.g., "more people chose red."

Ⓓ

• makes true statements based on a simple concept of average (median and mean), for a small sample size and where the situation is made evident with concrete materials or clear representations.

Ⓔ

Ⓕ The revision provides further evidence of the student's understanding.

Arithmetic and Number Concepts

Geometry & Measurement Concepts

Function & Algebra Concepts

Statistics & Probability Concepts ◄ **M4**

Problem Solving & Reasoning

Mathematical Skills & Tools

Mathematical Communication ◄ **M7**

Putting Mathematics to Work

Height Measurement Statistics

M7 a Mathematical Communication: The student uses appropriate mathematical terms, vocabulary, and language, based on prior conceptual work.

A C D E Appropriate use of mathematical terms and vocabulary is evident in these parts of the work particularly, and is supported by evidence throughout the work.

Arithmetic and Number Concepts

Geometry & Measurement Concepts

Function & Algebra Concepts

M4 Statistics & Probability Concepts

Problem Solving & Reasoning

Mathematical Skills & Tools

M7 Mathematical Communication

Putting Mathematics to Work

A

"inches means

Heights of Classmates

PJ 53½"
Emil 58½"
Sue 54½"
Tony 54½"
Jon 57"
Will 63"
Matt 61½"
Caitlin 61"
Ashanti 61"
Michelle 58½"
Jenni 57"
Sommer 57½"
Nick 55½"
Diane 60½"
Jennifer 62½"
Mike 54"
Sarah 56"
Santana 55½"
Caleb 58"
Derek 57"
Emilio 55"
Mrs. McFeaters 68½"
David 58"
Dawn 58"

Data Collection Sheet.

B

Line Plot

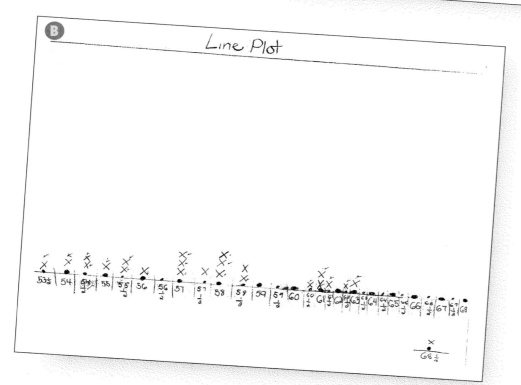

Work Sample & Commentary: *Two Dice Sums*

The quotations from the Mathematics performance descriptions in this commentary are excerpted. The complete performance descriptions are shown on pages 60-65.

Arithmetic and Number Concepts **M1**

Geometry & Measurement Concepts

Function & Algebra Concepts

Statistics & Probability Concepts **M4**

Problem Solving & Reasoning

Mathematical Skills & Tools **M6**

Mathematical Communication **M7**

Putting Mathematics to Work

The task

After students had many chances to roll two dice and record the sums, the teacher gave the following instructions for this multi-part probability activity:

1. Think of a way to figure out all the combinations (sums) for two dice rolled together. Write a title and explain what you did. We will discuss the various strategies you came up with, and look at what works well.

2. Use a 6 x 6 grid to figure out the combinations for two dice sums to check that you found all the ways. (The teacher provided an example of a 6 x 6 grid, without supplying the numbers in the inner cells.)

When you are finished, show how each sum can be shown as a fraction of the total number of combinations that are possible.

3. Play this game with a partner several times:

• Draw a chart with spaces under the sums for two dice.

• Draw 11 circles in any of the 11 spaces in any combination you want.

• Write the reason why you put the circles where you did. Try to use fractions to explain your choices.

• With a partner, take turns rolling the dice. Each time you roll a sum, put Xs in all the circles you have for that sum. You win when all your circles are crossed off.

This game is based on an activity from *A Collection of Math Lessons, 3 - 6*, Marilyn Burns, Math Solution Publications, 1987.

> ### This work sample illustrates a standard-setting performance for the following parts of the standards:
>
> **M1 d Arithmetic and Number Concepts: Describe and compare quantities by using simple fractions.**
>
> **M4 e Statistics and Probability Concepts: Predict results and find out why some results are more likely, less likely, or equally likely.**
>
> **M4 f Statistics and Probability Concepts: Find all possible combinations.**
>
> **M6 g Mathematical Skills and Tools: Read, create, and represent data.**
>
> **M7 b Mathematical Communication: Show mathematical ideas in a variety of ways.**
>
> **M7 c Mathematical Communication: Explain solutions to problems clearly and logically.**

Circumstances of performance

This sample of student work was produced under the following conditions:

√ alone   √ in a group

√ in class   as homework

√ with teacher feedback   √ with peer feedback

timed   opportunity for revision

Students had prior experience of making their own charts and using conventional fractional notation, and had explored probability using dice and other materials. The activities were spread out over two days.

What the work shows

M1 d Arithmetic and Number Concepts: The student describes and compares quantities by using concrete and real world models of simple fractions; that is, finds simple parts of wholes....

A All possible sums for paired dice are represented and compared as simple fractions.

M4 e Statistics and Probability Concepts: The student predicts results, analyzes data, and finds out why some results are more likely, less likely, or equally likely.

A B C The student organized the possible outcomes in order to make predictions about the likelihood of rolling particular two dice sums.

M4 f Statistics and Probability Concepts: The student finds all possible combinations and arrangements within certain constraints involving a limited number of variables.

D The student created a way to find all possible combinations for the sums of two dice.

Two Dice Sums

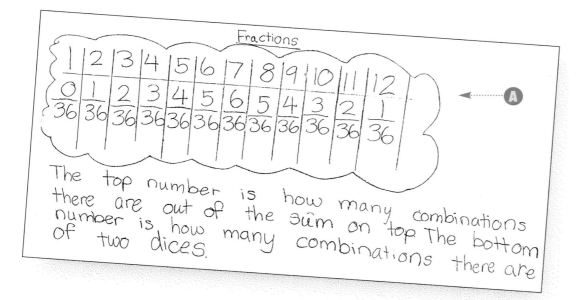

Fractions

1	2	3	4	5	6	7	8	9	10	11	12
$\frac{0}{36}$	$\frac{1}{36}$	$\frac{2}{36}$	$\frac{3}{36}$	$\frac{4}{36}$	$\frac{5}{36}$	$\frac{6}{36}$	$\frac{5}{36}$	$\frac{4}{36}$	$\frac{3}{36}$	$\frac{2}{36}$	$\frac{1}{36}$

The top number is how many combinations there are out of the sum on top. The bottom number is how many combinations there are of two dices.

M6 g Mathematical Skills and Tools: The student reads, creates, and represents data on…charts, tables….

A **D** The student-created charts, especially the horizontal tables under "Combinations" and the fractions chart, are appropriate, clear, and complete.

M7 b Mathematical Communication: The student shows mathematical ideas in a variety of ways, including words, numbers, symbols,…charts,… tables….

D **E** The student used words to explain how the chart works. Numbers, symbols ("A" and "B"), and a table are used to communicate the combinations.

M7 c Mathematical Communication: The student explains solutions to problems clearly and logically, and supports solutions with evidence, in… written work.

B **C** The written explanations are sufficiently clear and logical for the elementary level. The student provided evidence in support of the game strategy by referring back to the data contained in the tables.

The work includes several errors in usage and grammar, e.g., "two dices," "loosed" for "lost," and "come" for "came." This was a class assignment and was not intended to be further edited.

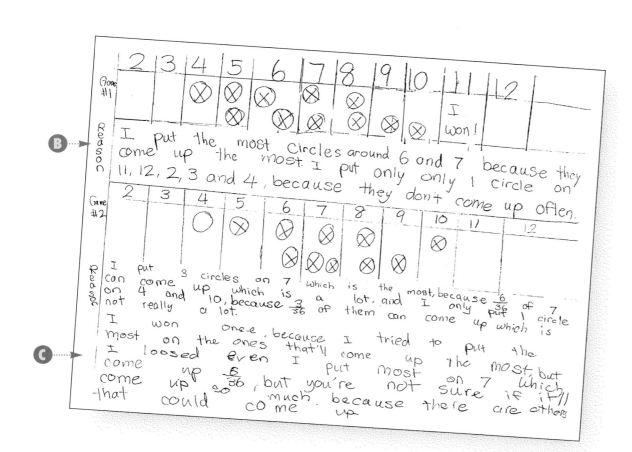

Arithmetic and Number Concepts

Geometry & Measurement Concepts

Function & Algebra Concepts

Statistics & Probability Concepts

Problem Solving & Reasoning

Mathematical Skills & Tools

Mathematical Communication

Putting Mathematics to Work

Work Sample & Commentary: *Creatures*

Arithmetic
and Number
Concepts

Geometry &
Measurement
Concepts

Function &
Algebra
Concepts

Statistics &
Probability
Concepts   ◀ M4

Problem
Solving &
Reasoning   ◀ M5

Mathematical
Skills & Tools

Mathematical
Communication   ◀ M7

Putting
Mathematics
to Work

The quotations from the Mathematics performance descriptions in this commentary are excerpted. The complete performance descriptions are shown on pages 60-65.

The task

The teacher asked the class to draw four Halloween characters (a ghost, a witch, a skeleton, and a pumpkin-headed scarecrow). She then instructed them to cut the figures into four heads and four bodies and to staple each set into a small "flip book."

The teacher asked: How many characters could you possibly come up with by combining the different parts in various ways? Show and explain in detail all the combinations you could make.

Circumstances of performance

This sample of student work was produced under the following conditions:

√ alone   in a group
  in class   √ as homework
  with teacher feedback   with peer feedback
  timed   opportunity for
                           revision

The task was assigned as a two-day homework "problem of the week." There had been no prior work by the class with similar discrete mathematics or logic tasks.

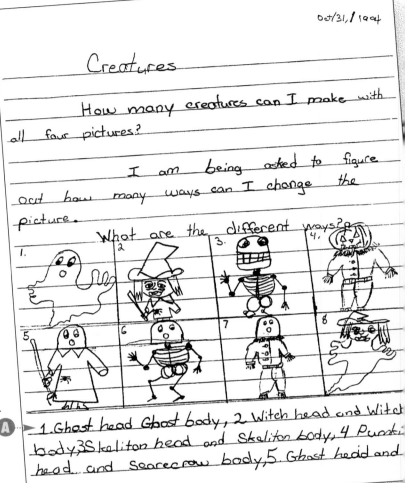

Ⓐ ▶

This work sample illustrates a standard-setting performance for the following parts of the standards:

M4 f **Statistics and Probability Concepts: Find all possible combinations.**

M5 b **Problem Solving and Reasoning: Implementation.**

M5 c **Problem Solving and Reasoning: Conclusion.**

M7 b **Mathematical Communication: Show mathematical ideas in a variety of ways.**

M7 c **Mathematical Communication: Explain solutions to problems clearly and logically.**

Mathematics required by the task

In this task the teacher instructed students to make and use a "flip book" as a tool to help find all possible combinations. So, while the task calls for extensive problem solving and reasoning, important decisions about what materials and approach to use in formulating the problem were made for the students.

For this reason the task does not provide an opportunity for students to demonstrate the formulation part (**M5 a**) of the Problem Solving and Reasoning standard. The task does, however, provide an opportunity for students to demonstrate the implementation (**M5 b**) and conclusion (**M5 c**) parts of the standard.

What the work shows

M4 f Statistics and Probability Concepts: The student finds all possible combinations and arrangements within certain constraints involving a limited number of variables.

Ⓐ The student found all the possible combinations of the four heads and four bodies.

Creatures

M5 b Problem Solving and Reasoning: The student makes the basic choices involved in planning and carrying out a solution; that is,...

• makes up and uses a variety of strategies and approaches to solving problems....

B The student used two approaches to solve the problem: a "flip book"/systematic listing and a student-created multiplicative formula.

• makes connections among concepts in order to solve problems....

C The student made connections among different conceptual approaches: "I know that my [systematic listing] solution is correct because there are four monsters, so that means there are four bodies [and four heads] and four times four equals sixteen."

• solves problems in ways that make sense and explains why these ways make sense....

B **C** **D** The student explained why the solution made sense in several ways by setting out clearly both of the approaches used.

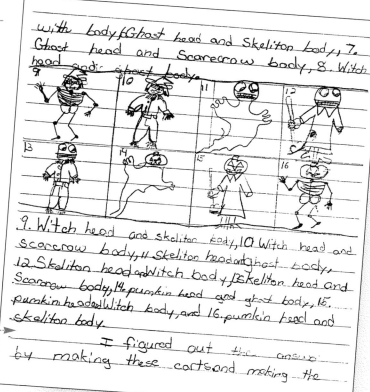

B ▸

with body, 6 Ghost head and Skeliton body, 7. Ghost head and Scarecrow body, 8. Witch head and ghost body. 9

9. Witch head and skeliton body, 10 Witch head and scarecrow body, 11 Skeliton head and ghost body, 12 Skeliton head and Witch body, 13 Skeliton head and Scarecrow body, 14 pumkin head and ghost body, 15. pumkin head and Witch body, and 16 pumkin head and skeliton body.

I figured out the answer by making these carts and making the

body

D ▸

hole and then flipping the different body's with one head and then when I've tryed ever body with that head I switch to the next head.
I got started by filping the stapled book like it says above.
I got stuck drawin the details on the witch but other than that I did fine.
I got help by looking at the picture harder.
I did this way because it is easy to understand.
The answer is 16 ways to create a monster with this recipe book.

C ▸

I know my solution is correct because there are four monsters so that means there are four bodys and four times

Arithmetic and Number Concepts

Geometry & Measurement Concepts

Function & Algebra Concepts

M4 Statistics & Probability Concepts

M5 Problem Solving & Reasoning

Mathematical Skills & Tools

M7 Mathematical Communication

Putting Mathematics to Work

Creatures

four equals sixteen:

4 monster heads
× 4 different bodys to put them on
16 different ways

x 4 ●●●●
4 ●●●● = 16
●●●●
●●●●

There is not a different solution (believe me I checked!) unless you make them headless!

This reminded me of a book I have called Croc-gu-phant were you switch the panels and get different weird aniamals!

I think if there were 5 cards there would be 25 ways!

M5 c Problem Solving and Reasoning: The student moves beyond the particular problem by making…extensions, and/or generalizations; for example,…makes the solution into a general rule that applies to other circumstances.

E The student moved beyond the particular problem by defining a general rule (four heads times four bodies) and applying it in a different circumstance: "I think if there were five cards there would be 25 ways."

M7 b Mathematical Communication: The student shows mathematical ideas in a variety of ways, including words, numbers, symbols, pictures….

A C The systematic listing makes use of both pictures and sentences. Numbers and a diagram are used to represent the multiplicative formula.

M7 c Mathematical Communication: The student explains solutions to problems clearly and logically, and supports solutions with evidence….

A C D The explanation is clear, logical, and supported with diagrammatic, numeric, pictorial, and narrative evidence.

The work includes several misspelled words in the written portion of the work (e.g., "skeliton," "pumkin," and "carts" instead of "charts"). This was a homework assignment and was not intended to be further edited for spelling.

Work Sample & Commentary: *¿Se hace un triangulo?*

The task

The teacher gave the students the following instructions:

Suppose you were given a string that is sixteen inches long. If you cut or fold it in any two places, will it always make a triangle?

Circumstances of performance

This sample of student work was produced under the following conditions:

√ alone   in a group

√ in class   as homework

√ with teacher feedback   with peer feedback

   timed   √ opportunity for revision

This sample was completed in Spanish in a bilingual classroom. The translation was provided by the teacher.

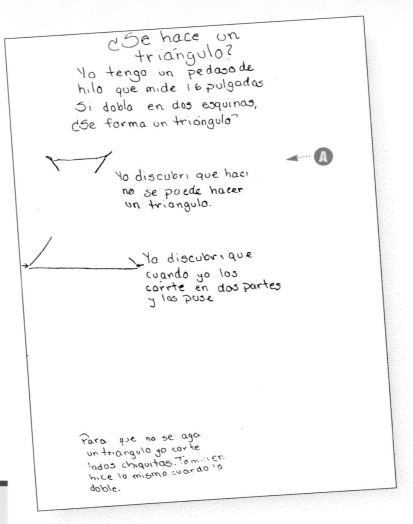

¿Se hace un triángulo?

Yo tengo un pedaso de hilo que mide 16 pulgadas Si dobla en dos esquinas, ¿Se forma un triángulo?

Yo discubri que haci no se puede hacer un triangulo.

Yo discubri que cuando yo los corrte en dos partes y los pose

Para que no se aga un triangulo yo corte lados chiquitas. Tambien hice lo mismo cuando lo doble.

This work sample illustrates a standard-setting performance for the following parts of the standards:

M2 d Geometry and Measurement Concepts: Use many types of figures.

M2 e Geometry and Measurement Concepts: Solve problems by showing relationships between and among figures.

M2 g Geometry and Measurement Concepts: Use basic ways of estimating and measuring the size of figures and objects in the real world.

M2 i Geometry and Measurement Concepts: Select and use units for estimating and measuring length.

M5 a Problem Solving and Reasoning: Formulation.

M5 b Problem Solving and Reasoning: Implementation.

M5 c Problem Solving and Reasoning: Conclusion.

M6 e Mathematical Skills and Tools: Refer to geometric shapes and terms correctly.

M7 b Mathematical Communication: Show mathematical ideas in a variety of ways.

M7 c Mathematical Communication: Explain solutions to problems clearly and logically.

What the work shows

M2 d Geometry and Measurement Concepts: The student uses many types of figures (angles, triangles...) and identifies the figures by their properties....

A B C The student used angles and triangles throughout this problem solving activity.

D The student did not merely identify, but discovered a property for, triangles: "if the two sides add up to more than the bottom side, it will make a triangle."

M2 e Geometry and Measurement Concepts: The student solves problems by showing relationships between and among figures....

A B C The student searched for and showed relationships among sides of triangles.

D The student summarized relationships among sides of triangles in a general rule.

The quotations from the Mathematics performance descriptions in this commentary are excerpted. The complete performance descriptions are shown on pages 60-65.

Arithmetic and Number Concepts

M2 Geometry & Measurement Concepts

Function & Algebra Concepts

Statistics & Probability Concepts

M5 Problem Solving & Reasoning

M6 Mathematical Skills & Tools

M7 Mathematical Communication

Putting Mathematics to Work

¿Se hace un triangulo?

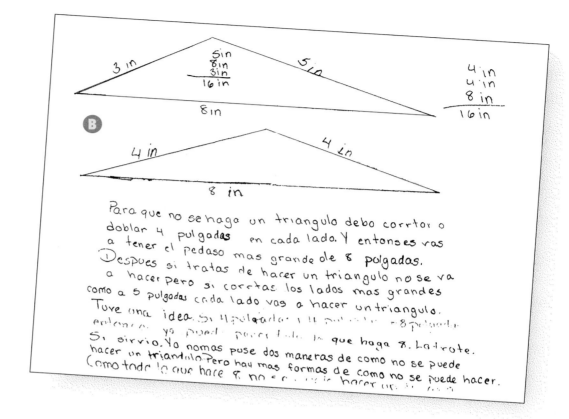

Para que no se haga un triangulo debo corrtar o
doblar 4 pulgadas en cada lado. Y entonses vas
a tener el pedaso mas grande de 8 pulgadas.
Despues si tratas de hacer un triangulo no se va
a hacer pero si corrtas los lados mas grandes
como a 5 pulgadas cada lado vas a hacer un triangulo.
Tuve una idea. Si 4pulgadas ... ... =8 pulgadas
entonce. yo pued pero ... ... que haga 8. La trote.
Si sirvio.Yo nomas puse dos maneras de como no se puede
hacer un triandulo.Pero hay mas formas de como no se puede hacer.
Como todo lo que hace 8 no se ... ... hacer un ...

M2 g Geometry and Measurement Concepts: The student uses basic ways of estimating and measuring the size of figures and objects in the real world, including length,…perimeter….

A B C

M2 i Geometry and Measurement Concepts: The student selects and uses units, both formal and informal as appropriate, for estimating and measuring quantities such as…length….

B C

M5 a Problem Solving and Reasoning: Formulation. Given the basic statement of a problem situation, the student:

• makes the important decisions about the approach, materials, and strategies to use, i.e., does not merely fill in a given chart, use a pre-specified manipulative, or go through a predetermined set of steps.

A The student decided to use a trial-and-error approach, which later became more systematic. The student also decided to use string, scissors, and a ruler.

• uses previously learned strategies, skills, knowledge, and concepts to make decisions.

A The student used knowledge about triangles and measurement to develop the approach.

• uses strategies, such as using manipulatives or drawing sketches, to model problems.

A B

M5 b Problem Solving and Reasoning: Implementation. The student makes the basic choices involved in planning and carrying out a solution; that is, the student:

• makes up and uses a variety of strategies and approaches to solving problems and uses or learns approaches that other people use, as appropriate.

B The student used measurement strategies to solve the problem.

• makes connections among concepts in order to solve problems.

B C The student made connections between measurement and geometry concepts to solve the problem.

• solves problems in ways that make sense and explains why these ways make sense, e.g., defends the reasoning, explains the solution.

A B C

M5 c Problem Solving and Reasoning: Conclusion. The student moves beyond a particular problem by making connections, extensions, and/or generalizations; for example, the student:…

• makes the solution into a general rule that applies to other circumstances.

D The student went beyond the problem by finding a rule that would work for making any triangle.

¿Se hace un triangulo?

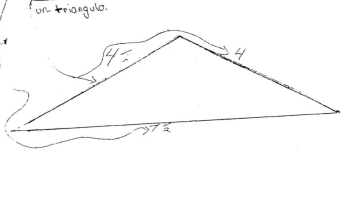

C ···▶ Si pones 7½, 4½, 4 si se hace un triangulo.
Pero si pones 8, 4 y 4 no se hace un triangulo. Haci
es que si pongo aqui un numero menos que 8 aqui si se
va a hacer un triangulo. La regla es que si lo dos

D ···▶ lados suman mas que el lado de abajo si se hace
un triangulo.

Translation

A ···▶ **Page 1:** I have a piece of string that measures 16 inches. If I fold it in two places, will it always form a triangle?

First I found that like this you can't make a triangle.

I found that when I cut it in two parts and put in on the two corners you can't make a triangle.

Later I discovered that if I put the short string near the long string, I could make a triangle.

To not be able to make a triangle I cut short sides. I did the same when I folded it.

B ···▶ **Page 2:** To not be able to make a triangle I must cut or fold 4 inches on each side. Then the largest side will be 8 inches. Then if you try to make a triangle you can't. But if you cut the sides larger, like 5 inches each side, you will be able to make a triangle. I had an idea. If 4 inches plus 4 inches equals 8 inches, then I could put everything that equals 8. I tried it. It worked. I only show two ways that don't make a triangle, but there are more. Everything that equals 8 will not make a triangle.

C ···▶ If you put 7 1/2, 4 1/2, 4 it will make a triangle. But if you put 8,4 and 4 it will not make a triangle. So if I put here (arrow pointing to base of triangle) a number less

D ···▶ than 8, then it will make a triangle. The rule is that if the two sides add up to more than the bottom side, it will make a triangle.

M6e Mathematical Skills and Tools: The student refers to geometric shapes and terms correctly with concrete objects or drawings, including triangle,…side….
Ⓐ Ⓑ Ⓒ Ⓓ

M7b Mathematical Communication: The student shows mathematical ideas in a variety of ways, including words, numbers,…pictures,…diagrams….
Ⓐ Ⓑ Ⓒ Ⓓ

M7c Mathematical Communication: The student explains solutions to problems clearly and logically, and supports solutions with evidence, in both written and oral work.
Ⓐ Ⓑ Ⓒ Ⓓ

Arithmetic and Number Concepts

M2 Geometry & Measurement Concepts

Function & Algebra Concepts

Statistics & Probability Concepts

M5 Problem Solving & Reasoning

M6 Mathematical Skills & Tools

M7 Mathematical Communication

Putting Mathematics to Work

Work Sample & Commentary: *The Great Fish Dilemma*

The quotations from the Mathematics performance descriptions in this commentary are excerpted. The complete performance descriptions are shown on pages 60-65.

The task

The teacher gave students the following written prompt:

How many different ways can you put nine fish in two bowls?

Show all your work and at the end explain why you made the decisions you did as you solved the problem.

Circumstances of performance

These samples of student work were produced under the following conditions:

√ alone   in a group

√ in class   as homework

   with teacher feedback   with peer feedback

   timed   opportunity for revision

Students could choose to include their work in the Vermont statewide portfolio assessment. They had been instructed in the specific criteria that the Vermont system uses in scoring problem solving work, so they knew what was expected. (See Marge Petit and Beth Hulbert, *Learning How to Show Your Best*, Exemplars, RR1, Box 7390, Underhill, VT 05489.)

What the work shows

M5 a Problem Solving and Reasoning: Formulation. Given the basic statement of a problem situation, the student:

- makes the important decisions about the approach, materials, and strategies to use, i.e., does not merely fill in a given chart, use a pre-specified manipulative, or go through a predetermined set of steps.

(A) (B) (C) In Sample 1, the student made a chart. In Sample 2, the student used cubes and blocks, and then drew pictures.

- uses previously learned strategies, skills, knowledge, and concepts to make decisions.

(A) (B) In Sample 1, the student used an organized chart as a strategy. In Sample 2, the student used cubes and blocks to make decisions.

Name _____
Date _____

The Great Fish Dilemma

How many different ways can you put nine fish in two bowls?
   Show all your work and at the end explain why you made the decisions you did as you solved the problem.

Used by permission. Exemplars: A Teachers Solution, RR 1 Box 7390, Underhill, VT 05489.

- uses strategies, such as using manipulatives or drawing sketches, to model problems.

(A) (B) (C)

M5 b Problem Solving and Reasoning: Implementation. The student makes the basic choices involved in planning and carrying out a solution; that is, the student:

- makes up and uses a variety of strategies and approaches to solving problems and uses or learns approaches that other people use, as appropriate.

(A) (B) (C) (D) (E) In Sample 1, the student analyzed the chart to refine the solution. In Sample 2, the student used cubes, blocks, pictures, patterns, and a concept of "dividing" to solve the problem.

- makes connections among concepts in order to solve problems.

(A) (C) (D) Both students made connections between number concepts and the probability concept of finding all possible combinations. In Sample 2, the student also connected the concept of patterns to the concept of finding all possible combinations.

- solves problems in ways that make sense and explains why these ways make sense, e.g., defends the reasoning, explains the solution.

(E) (F) In Sample 1, the student explained why all of the possibilities "aren't good." In Sample 2, the student explained why the problem really only involved "dividing 7 fish."

These work samples illustrate standard-setting performances for the following parts of the standards:

M5 a Problem Solving and Reasoning: Formulation.

M5 b Problem Solving and Reasoning: Implementation.

M5 c Problem Solving and Reasoning: Conclusion.

Arithmetic and Number Concepts

Geometry & Measurement Concepts

Function & Algebra Concepts

Statistics & Probability Concepts

Problem Solving & Reasoning **M5**

Mathematical Skills & Tools

Mathematical Communication

Putting Mathematics to Work

The Great Fish Dilemma

Sample 1

A →

There are nine fish and I think they are all the same. They are goldfish just like the one at my house. I made a chart to solve the problem.

Bowl 1 Bowl 2

number of fish {

Bowl 1	Bowl 2
0	9
1	8
2	7
3	6
4	5
5	4
6	3
7	2
8	1
9	0

← best

Even though I found 10 possibitys. Some aren't good. The only reason to pit all fish in one bowl is if cleaning other bowl. The best choises are the ones I cirkled so they have room to move. ← **F**

Sample 2

B →

We hav 9 fish and 2 bowls. Som of the fish, are frent. Two of the fish are Simese Fighting fish, and the rest are neons. The Simese fish can't be tageter ever or they kill each other. The neons can be with anyone. I drewn pictures to show my anser. First I used cups and blocks—read for Simese fish and bloe for neons —to solve it.

C →

s = simese   n = neon

These are all the ways because I foloed a padern. The padern was to put ← **D** I simese fish in each bowl then start in bowl 1 with all the neons and the next time just have 6 neons in bowl 1 and 1 in bowl 2. I always had to put a simese fish in each bowl so I was ← **E** really only divideing 7 fish (the neons). There are 8 difrent ways for my problem. Som are to cronded like ← **G** number 1 and number 8. Neons have lots of babies then well realy be in truble.

M5 ‹ Problem Solving and Reasoning: Conclusion. The student moves beyond a particular problem by making connections, extensions, and/or generalizations; for example, the student:

• explains a pattern that can be used in similar situations.

D

• explains how the problem solution can be applied to other school subjects and in real world situations.

F **G** In Sample 1, the student related the solution to the real world situation of cleaning the fishbowl. In Sample 2, the student related the solution to the real world situation of overcrowding the fish and what would happen when the fish had "babies."

Each sample includes some misspelled words, such as "choises" for "choices" and "read" for "red." The work was completed as a class exercise and was not edited to correct spelling mistakes.

Work Sample & Commentary: *How Many Handshakes?*

Arithmetic and Number Concepts

Geometry & Measurement Concepts

Function & Algebra Concepts **M3**

Statistics & Probability Concepts **M4**

Problem Solving & Reasoning **M5**

Mathematical Skills & Tools

Mathematical Communication **M7**

Putting Mathematics to Work

The quotations from the Mathematics performance descriptions in this commentary are excerpted. The complete performance descriptions are shown on pages 60-65.

The final paragraph of work sample 1 is also included among the work samples that illustrate the English Language Arts performance standards. See page 48.

The task

The teacher gave the students the following instructions:

Five people enter a room and introduce themselves to each other. If everyone shakes everyone else's hand just once, what is the total number of handshakes that occurred?

For Sample 1, the instructions were given in written form. For Sample 2, the instructions were given orally.

Circumstances of performance

These samples of student work were produced under the following conditions:

√ alone   in a group

√ in class   as homework

   with teacher feedback   with peer feedback

   timed   opportunity for revision

This problem was a non-routine problem for the students in both of the classrooms, which made this an appropriate problem solving task.

Sample 2 was completed in Spanish in a bilingual classroom. The translation was provided by the teacher.

> ### These work samples illustrate standard-setting performances for the following parts of the standards:
>
> **M3** b Function and Algebra Concepts: Build iterations of simple non-linear patterns.
>
> **M4** f Statistics and Probability Concepts: Find all possible combinations.
>
> **M5** a Problem Solving and Reasoning: Formulation.
>
> **M5** b Problem Solving and Reasoning: Implementation.
>
> **M5** c Problem Solving and Reasoning: Conclusion.
>
> **M7** b Mathematical Communication: Show mathematical ideas in a variety of ways.
>
> **M7** c Mathematical Communication: Explain solutions to problems clearly and logically.

What the work shows

M3 b *Function and Algebra Concepts: The student builds iterations of simple non-linear patterns....*

A B C D E F G In both samples, the students build the solution by building the pattern. They both extend this pattern into a general rule as well.

M4 f *Statistics and Probability Concepts: The student finds all possible combinations and arrangements within certain constraints involving a limited number of variables.*

A B H I The drawings throughout both samples show that the students found all the possible combinations of handshakes.

M5 a *Problem Solving and Reasoning: Formulation. Given the basic statement of a problem situation, the student:*

- makes the important decisions about the approach, materials, and strategies to use, i.e., does not merely fill in a given chart, use a pre-specified manipulative, or go through a predetermined set of steps.

A B H I Both students decided to use diagrams, lists, and equations.

- uses previously learned strategies, skills, knowledge, and concepts to make decisions.

A B H I Both samples demonstrate use of simple addition, as well as skill in drawing diagrams and making lists.

- uses strategies, such as using manipulatives or drawing sketches, to model problems.

A B H I

How Many Handshakes?

Sample 1

How Many Handshakes?

Five people enter a room and introduce themselves to each other. If everyone shakes everyone else's hand just once, what is the total number of handshakes that occurred.

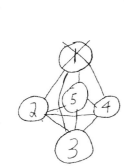

number 1 shakes 4 people
number 2 shakes 3 People
number 3 shakes 2 People
number 4 shakes 1 People
and number 5 shakes 0 People

A ········▶

$$4 + 3 + 2 + 1 = 10$$

J ········▶ At first I made a chart using five bubbles, numbering each. I did this to find the answer. Number one would shake 4, not shaking his own hand. I then drawed four lines to 4, 3, 2 and 1. Then I did the egzact same routine on 4, 3 and 2 and 1. I did not shake any ones hand. Then I counted the lines. and added them and it equaled 10. That is how many hand shakes in all.

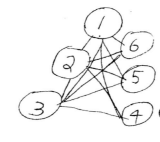

I shook 5 people hands
2 shook 4 People hands
3 shook 3 People hands
4 shook 2 People hands
5 shook 1 People hands
6 shook no hands

B ········▶

$$5 + 4 + 3 + 2 + 1 = 15$$

M5b Problem Solving and Reasoning: Implementation. The student makes the basic choices involved in planning and carrying out a solution; that is, the student:

• makes up and uses a variety of strategies and approaches to solving problems and uses or learns approaches that other people use, as appropriate.
A B H I Both students used diagrams, lists, and equations.

• makes connections among concepts in order to solve problems.
A B C E F H I Both students made connections between simple number concepts and patterns to solve the problem.

• solves problems in ways that make sense and explains why these ways make sense, e.g., defends the reasoning, explains the solution.
A B C E F H I J

C ········▶ I noticed a pattern. Since you don't have 6 shake any hands, you write 5, then add 4 then 3 then 2 then 1. and then it equals 15. That pattern helps me to realize not to use a chart on 7 because I can use my way like I did on the pattern. If there where 7 people I would just have to make a math sentence like this:

$$6 + 5 + 4 + 3 + 2 + 1 = 21$$

D ········▶ A way you can always figure it out, without a chart, is by using a math sentence starting at the highest of your number, or the lowest, going up or down then adding all of them together. Remember not to include the person who can't shake his own hand. For exsample if you had 30 people. You might start with 29 because 30 can not shake his own hand. Then you would count down to 1. Then add all the numbers together and that would equal the correct answer.

(side tabs)

Arithmetic and Number Concepts

Geometry & Measurement Concepts

M3 Function & Algebra Concepts

M4 Statistics & Probability Concepts

M5 Problem Solving & Reasoning

Mathematical Skills & Tools

M7 Mathematical Communication

Putting Mathematics to Work

How Many Handshakes?

M5c Problem Solving and Reasoning: Conclusion. The student moves beyond a particular problem by making connections, extensions, and/or generalizations; for example, the student:…

• makes the solution into a general rule that applies to other circumstances.

D G Both students went beyond the problem by finding a rule that would work for any number of people.

M7b Mathematical Communication: The student shows mathematical ideas in a variety of ways, including words, numbers,…pictures,…diagrams….

A B C D E F G H I J

Arithmetic and Number Concepts

Geometry & Measurement Concepts

Function & Algebra Concepts **M3**

Statistics & Probability Concepts **M4**

Problem Solving & Reasoning **M5**

Mathematical Skills & Tools

Mathematical Communication **M7**

Putting Mathematics to Work

Sample 2

H →

5 personas saludan un al otro. Si cada persona saluda a cada quien solo una ves, cCuantos saludos son?

El hizo 4 + 3 + 2 + 1 + 0 = 10
saludos

Son 10 saludos

El 1 hizo 4 saludas
El 2 hizo 3 saludos
        2
        1
        0

E →
Primero yo hice 5 caritas y luego puse cuantos saludos. Despues puse el numero 1 saludo a 2,3,4 y 5. Y el 2 saludo al 3,4 y5 y el 3 saludo a el 4 y5 y el 4 saludo al 5 y el 5 a nadie. Sume los saludos y la respuesta era 10. 4+3+2+1+0=10.

How Many Handshakes?

Sample 2 continued

7 Personas saludan a uno al otro solamente una vez, ¿Cuantos saludos son?

6+5+4+3+2+1+0=21

El 1 hizo 6 saludos
El 2 hizo 5 saludos
El 3 hizo 4 saludos
El 4 hizo 3 saludos
El 5 hizo 2 saludos
El 6 hizo 1 saludo
El 7 hizo 0 saludos

Primero puse 7 caritas y luego puse cuantos saludos. Despues puse el numero 1 saludo 2,3, 4,5,6 y 7 y tambien hise lo mismo con 2,3,4, 5,6 y 7. Despues los sume: 6+5+4+3+2+1+0=21

Es fácil. Sólo tengo que empeza con el número que es uno menos y sumar los demas Por ejemplo: si son 39 tengo que empesar con el 38.

Sample 2 Translation

E ▸ First I made 5 faces and then I put how many handshakes. After that I put that number 1 shakes the hand of 2,3,4, and 5. And number 2 shakes 3.4. and 5 and number 3 shakes 4 and 5 and number 4 shakes 5 and number 5 shakes nobody's hand. I added the handshakes and the answer is 10.
4+3+2+1+0 =10

F ▸ First I put 7 faces and then I put how many handshakes. I put that number 1 shakes the hand of 2,3,4,5,6 and 7 and also I did the same with 2,3,4,5,6 and 7. After that I added:
6+5+4+3+2+1+0 = 21

G ▸ It is easy. I only have to start with the number that is one less and add the rest. For example: If there are 39 I have to start with 38.

M7 ◂ Mathematical Communication: The student explains solutions to problems clearly and logically, and supports solutions with evidence, in both written and oral work.
Ⓐ Ⓑ Ⓒ Ⓓ Ⓔ Ⓕ Ⓖ Ⓗ Ⓘ Ⓙ

Arithmetic and Number Concepts

Geometry & Measurement Concepts

M3 ▸ Function & Algebra Concepts

M4 ▸ Statistics & Probability Concepts

M5 ▸ Problem Solving & Reasoning

Mathematical Skills & Tools

M7 ▸ Mathematical Communication

Putting Mathematics to Work

Work Sample & Commentary: *Tangram Dispute*

Arithmetic
and Number   **M1**
Concepts

Geometry &
Measurement **M2**
Concepts

Function &
Algebra
Concepts

Statistics &
Probability
Concepts

Problem
Solving &   **M5**
Reasoning

Mathematical
Skills & Tools **M6**

Mathematical **M7**
Communication

Putting
Mathematics
to Work

The task
The teacher gave students the prompt (the diagrams were the size of tangram pieces) illustrated here.

Circumstances of performance
This sample of student work was produced under the following conditions:

√ alone   in a group

√ in class   as homework

√ with teacher feedback   √ with peer feedback

   timed   √ opportunity for
                              revision

The quotations from the Mathematics performance descriptions in this commentary are excerpted. The complete performance descriptions are shown on pages 60-65.

Students had previously worked with tangrams. They had begun to study area relationships and fractions.

This student was preparing a New Standards Elementary Mathematics Portfolio and was aware of the requirements for the portfolio. In providing evidence of problem solving work, students using New Standards mathematics portfolios must show that they can go beyond the problem and make connections, extensions or generalizations (**M5** c).

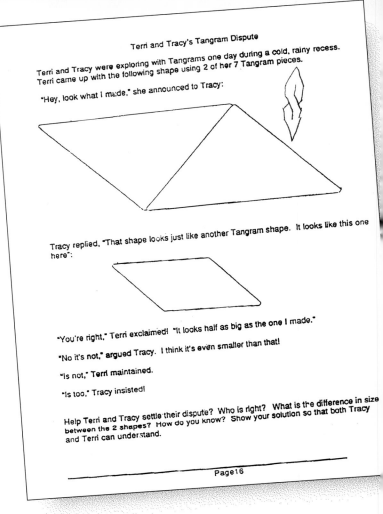

Terri and Tracy's Tangram Dispute

Terri and Tracy were exploring with Tangrams one day during a cold, rainy recess. Terri came up with the following shape using 2 of her 7 Tangram pieces.

"Hey, look what I made," she announced to Tracy:

Tracy replied, "That shape looks just like another Tangram shape. It looks like this one here":

"You're right," Terri exclaimed! "It looks half as big as the one I made."

"No it's not," argued Tracy. I think it's even smaller than that!

"Is not," Terri maintained.

"Is too," Tracy insisted!

Help Terri and Tracy settle their dispute? Who is right? What is the difference in size between the 2 shapes? How do you know? Show your solution so that both Tracy and Terri can understand.

Page 16

This work sample illustrates a standard-setting performance for the following parts of the standards:

M1 d **Arithmetic and Number Concepts:** Describe and compare quantities by using simple fractions.

M2 e **Geometry and Measurement Concepts:** Solve problems by showing relationships between and among figures.

M5 a **Problem Solving and Reasoning: Formulation.**

M5 b **Problem Solving and Reasoning: Implementation.**

M5 c **Problem Solving and Reasoning: Conclusion.**

M6 e **Mathematical Skills and Tools:** Refer to geometric shapes and terms correctly.

M7 b **Mathematical Communication:** Show mathematical ideas in a variety of ways.

M7 c **Mathematical Communication:** Explain solutions to problems clearly and logically.

What the work shows

M1 d Arithmetic and Number Concepts: The student describes and compares quantities by using concrete and real world models of simple fractions; that is:

• finds simple parts of wholes.

A The student explained and showed in a model that there can be four equal (parallelogram) parts within the whole (parallelogram).

• uses drawings, diagrams, or models to show what the numerator and denominator mean, including when adding like fractions, e.g., ⅛ + ⅝, or when showing that ¾ is more than ⅜.

B **C** The student used two models to show that one small parallelogram is equivalent to one out of four equal parts of the whole parallelogram, i.e., that "Tracy's shape was ¼ not a ½ of Terri's shape."

Tangram Dispute

M2 e Geometry and Measurement Concepts: The student solves problems by showing relationships between and among figures, e.g., using congruence and similarity....

D The student explained and modeled that "...one big shape can equal (i.e., be congruent to) four little of the same (i.e., a similar) shape."

M5 a Problem Solving and Reasoning: Formulation. Given the basic statement of a problem situation, the student:

• makes the important decisions about the approach, materials, and strategies to use, i.e., does not merely fill in a given chart, use a pre-specified manipulative, or go through a predetermined set of steps.

A **B** **C** **D** Given a problem situation with many possible approaches, the student decided what materials to use (pattern blocks and tiles) and what approach to follow.

• uses previously learned strategies, skills, knowledge, and concepts to make decisions.

A The student used knowledge about the relationship between simple parts and wholes to decide who was correct in the dispute.

• uses strategies, such as using manipulatives or drawing sketches, to model problems.

B **C** **D**

M5 b Problem Solving and Reasoning: Implementation. The student makes the basic choices involved in planning and carrying out a solution; that is, the student:

• makes up and uses a variety of strategies and approaches to solving problems and uses or learns approaches that other people use, as appropriate.

B **C** The student used fractional and geometric strategies to solve the problem.

• makes connections among concepts in order to solve problems.

A **B** **C** **D** The student made connections between number and geometry concepts to solve the problem.

• solves problems in ways that make sense and explains why these ways make sense, e.g., defends the reasoning, explains the solution.

A **B** **C**

Arithmetic and Number Concepts **M1**

Geometry & Measurement Concepts **M2**

Function & Algebra Concepts

Statistics & Probability Concepts

Problem Solving & Reasoning **M5**

Mathematical Skills & Tools **M6**

Mathematical Communication **M7**

Putting Mathematics to Work

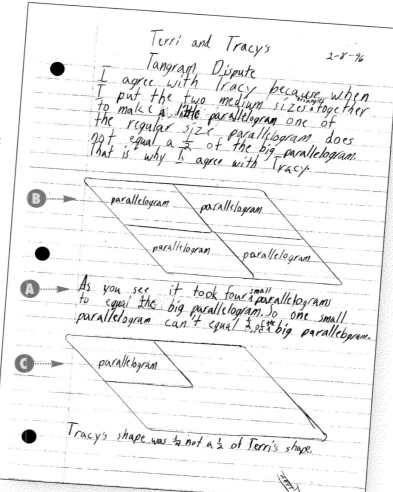

Terri and Tracy's
Tangram Dispute   2-8-96

I agree with Tracy because when I put the two medium sizes triangles together to make a little parallelogram one of the regular size parallelogram does not equal a ½ of the big parallelogram. That is why I agree with Tracy.

B → parallelogram   parallelogram
          parallelogram   parallelogram

A → As you see it took four small parallelograms to equal the big parallelogram. So one small parallelogram can't equal ½ of the big parallelogram.

C → parallelogram

Tracy's shape was ½ not a ½ of Terri's shape.

Tangram Dispute

M5 c Problem Solving and Reasoning: Conclusion. The student moves beyond a particular problem by making connections, extensions, and/or generalizations; for example, the student:…

• explains how the problem is similar to other problems he or she has solved….

D The student went beyond the problem by illustrating that the same approach and concepts can be used in a different situation.

M6 e Mathematical Skills and Tools: The student refers to geometric shapes and terms correctly with concrete objects or drawings, including triangle,…parallelogram….

B The student referred correctly to the parallelogram, which is not mentioned by name in the task.

M7 b Mathematical Communication: The student shows mathematical ideas in a variety of ways, including words, numbers,…pictures….

A B C D

M7 c Mathematical Communication: The student explains solutions to problems clearly and logically, and supports solutions with evidence, in both written and oral work.

A The solution is explained clearly.

B C The conclusion is supported by diagrammatic evidence.

Arithmetic and Number Concepts **M1**

Geometry & Measurement Concepts **M2**

Function & Algebra Concepts

Statistics & Probability Concepts

Problem Solving & Reasoning **M5**

Mathematical Skills & Tools **M6**

Mathematical Communication **M7**

Putting Mathematics to Work

As you can see 1 big shape can equal **D** four little of the same shape. So Tracy is right it can't equal 1/2 of the big shape. This square is showing that four little squares equal one big square. Two little square equal 1/2 of the big square. So it is the same with a parallelogram, two parallelograms equal the half, not one.

Work Sample & Commentary: *Feverish Freddy*

The task

The teacher gave students the following prompt:

Freddy, a very precise real estate appraiser, was sent to appraise some lots on a local property. Freddy appraised lot A for $88,000, but then came down with the flu and was unable to determine the fair market value of the other lots. Help Freddy determine the values so he does not lose his job!

Using the value Freddy determined for lot A, figure the fair value of each of the other lots in relation to lot A. Write a report to Freddy informing him of your mathematical determinations. Show Freddy how you reached your conclusion, so he will have faith in your determination. Represent your determination mathematically, and use appropriate math language and representations to support your conclusion. Share with Freddy any mathematically relevant observations you make, as well as any recommendations.

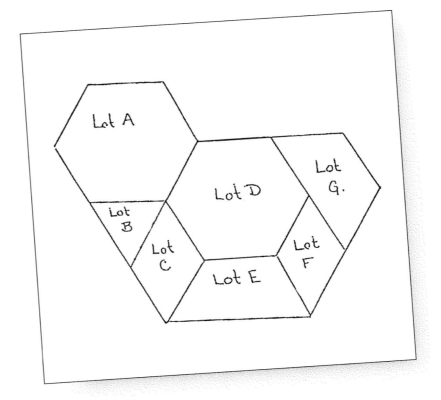

In the actual task, this diagram matched the size of pattern blocks.

Circumstances of performance

This sample of student work was produced under the following conditions:

√ alone   in a group

√ in class   as homework

√ with teacher feedback   √ with peer feedback

    timed   opportunity for revision

Students had prior experience working with pattern blocks and were familiar with their fractional equivalents (with the hexagon equal to one whole).

What the work shows

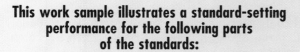 **Arithmetic and Number Concepts:** The student adds, subtracts, multiplies, and divides whole numbers, with and without calculators; that is:…

- analyzes problem situations and contexts in order to figure out when to add, subtract, multiply, or divide.

Ⓐ The student, given a problem situation with many possible approaches, figured out which arithmetic operations to use in order to come to a correct solution (evident throughout the work, without citing a specific operation).

- solves arithmetic problems by relating addition, subtraction, multiplication, and division to one another.

Ⓑ

The quotations from the Mathematics performance descriptions in this commentary are excerpted. The complete performance descriptions are shown on pages 60-65.

This work sample illustrates a standard-setting performance for the following parts of the standards:

M1 a Arithmetic and Number Concepts: Add, subtract, multiply, and divide whole numbers.

M1 d Arithmetic and Number Concepts: Describe and compare quantities by using simple fractions.

M2 e Geometry and Measurement Concepts: Solve problems by showing relationships between and among figures.

M3 d Function and Algebra Concepts: Use letters, boxes, or other symbols to stand for any number, measured quantity, or object in simple situations.

M5 a Problem Solving and Reasoning: Formulation.

M5 b Problem Solving and Reasoning: Implementation.

M5 c Problem Solving and Reasoning: Conclusion.

M6 e Mathematical Skills and Tools: Refer to geometric shapes and terms correctly.

M6 g Mathematical Skills and Tools: Read, create, and represent data.

M6 h Mathematical Skills and Tools: Use manipulatives and calculators to achieve solutions.

M7 b Mathematical Communication: Show mathematical ideas in a variety of ways.

Arithmetic and Number Concepts — M1

Geometry & Measurement Concepts — M2

Function & Algebra Concepts — M3

Statistics & Probability Concepts

Problem Solving & Reasoning — M5

Mathematical Skills & Tools — M6

Mathematical Communication — M7

Putting Mathematics to Work

Feverish Freddy

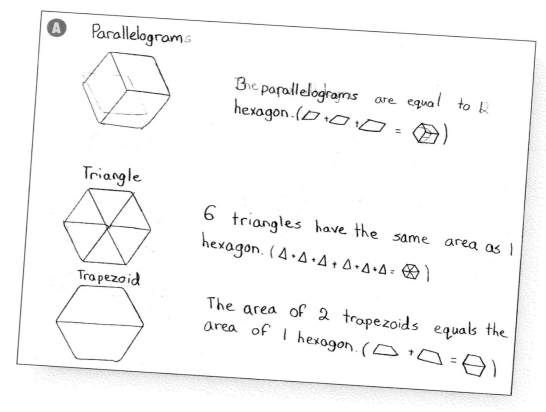

M1 d Arithmetic and Number Concepts: The student describes and compares quantities by using concrete and real world models of simple fractions; that is:
• finds simple parts of wholes….

M2 e Geometry and Measurement Concepts: The student solves problems by showing relationships between and among figures, e.g., using congruence….

C The student compared congruent fractional parts of hexagons to determine the relative value of each part.

M3 d Function and Algebra Concepts: The student uses letters, boxes, or other symbols to stand for any number, measured quantity, or object in simple situations with concrete materials, i.e., demonstrates understanding and use of a beginning concept of a variable.

B

M5 a Problem Solving and Reasoning: Formulation. Given the basic statement of a problem situation, the student:

• makes the important decisions about the approach, materials, and strategies to use, i.e., does not merely fill in a given chart, use a pre-specified manipulative, or go through a predetermined set of steps.

A The student decided which approach (finding simple parts of hexagons and determining their relative value) and material (pattern blocks) to use.

• uses previously learned strategies, skills, knowledge, and concepts to make decisions.

A C The student used knowledge of the fractional equivalents among pattern block pieces to make decisions about the value of each piece (i.e., each lot).

• uses strategies, such as using manipulatives or drawing sketches, to model problems.

A

M5 b Problem Solving and Reasoning: Implementation. The student makes the basic choices involved in planning and carrying out a solution; that is, the student:

• makes up and uses a variety of strategies and approaches to solving problems….

A B The student used pictorial, geometric, narrative, and arithmetic approaches in the solution.

• makes connections among concepts in order to solve problems.

A C D The student connected the fractional concepts with geometric concepts of congruence and whole number concepts of value to solve the problem.

• solves problems in ways that make sense and explains why these ways make sense, e.g., defends the reasoning, explains the solution.

C The student explained the process used to reach the solution, without stating explicitly how the exact dollar value of each lot was derived.

E The work provides evidence of making sense of what to do with the cents that were left over.

Feverish Freddy

E → On lot B, C and F there was a certain amount of cents. I didn't add them to the main number because I didn't think it was important.

C → On the lots 3 lot Fs or Gs would equal 1 lot A or D. 1 lot G and 1 lot E is equal to 1 lot A or D. Lot B is equal to 1½ of lot F or C. 3 lot Bs have the same area as 1 lot E or G.

$$3F = A$$
$$E + G = A$$
$$B = \frac{F}{2}$$

Each of the letters equal 1 lot put into a number sentence.

B →
$$3B = G$$
$$2F + 2B = A$$
$$F + B = E$$
$$A - 2F - B = B$$
$$D - 3B = G$$
$$G + C + B = D$$

D

Shape of lot	Cost	Lot letter(s)	total cost
hexagon	88,000	A and D	176,000
Parallelogram	29,333	C and F	58,666
triangle	14,666	B	14,666
trapezoid	44,000	E and G	88,000

M5 ◄ Problem Solving and Reasoning: Conclusion. The student moves beyond a particular problem by making connections, extensions, and/or generalizations....

B The student extended the problem by listing algebraic equations that show the fractional relationships among the lots. Expressing mathematical relationships algebraically goes beyond what most elementary students know and can be expected to do.

M6 e Mathematical Skills and Tools: The student refers to geometric shapes and terms correctly with concrete objects or drawings, including triangle,...parallelogram....

A **D**

M6 g Mathematical Skills and Tools: The student reads, creates, and represents data on...charts, tables, diagrams....

A **D** The student created a chart and diagram to organize and represent information.

M6 h Mathematical Skills and Tools: The student uses...manipulatives, calculators,...as appropriate, to achieve solutions.

A **D** The student used pattern blocks and a calculator (in "Cost" and "Total cost") to achieve a solution. The teacher verified that the student used a calculator.

M7 b Mathematical Communication: The student shows mathematical ideas in a variety of ways, including words, numbers, symbols, pictures, charts, graphs, tables, diagrams, and models.

A **B** **C** **D**

Lot A 88,000
Lot B 14,666
Lot C 29,333
Lot D 88,000
Lot E 44,000
Lot F 29,333
Lot G 44,000

M1 Arithmetic and Number Concepts

M2 Geometry & Measurement Concepts

M3 Function & Algebra Concepts

Statistics & Probability Concepts

M5 Problem Solving & Reasoning

M6 Mathematical Skills & Tools

M7 Mathematical Communication

Putting Mathematics to Work

Work Sample & Commentary: Counting on Frank

The task

Students were asked to read *Counting on Frank* by Rod Clement and to write a letter to the author commenting on at least one example of the mathematical claims made.

Circumstances of performance

This sample of student work was produced under the following conditions:

√ alone   √ in a group

√ in class   √ as homework

√ with teacher feedback   with peer feedback

     timed   √ opportunity for revision

Four students discussed the mathematics in *Counting on Frank* in depth before they wrote their analyses. The students spent class time as well as many recesses figuring out how to test the claims in the book. For example, the students discussed how to use the classroom sink to test the claim in the book about the bathroom filling up with water. The students worked together to develop strategies for testing the claims about the peas and the ball-point pen. The teacher encouraged the students' discussions, and provided time and materials in school for them to work out their reasoning. The students met outside of class to work together on the writing. Students completed the writing individually, at home.

The students completed this activity near the end of the school year. Earlier in the year, the students had studied area and perimeter concepts in depth, as well as applications of multiplication and division in problem solving activities.

The quotations from the Mathematics performance descriptions in this commentary are excerpted. The complete performance descriptions are shown on pages 60-65.

This work sample is also included among the work samples that illustrate the English Language Arts performance standards. See page 46.

Arithmetic and Number Concepts **M1**

Geometry & Measurement Concepts **M2**

Function & Algebra Concepts

Statistics & Probability Concepts

Problem Solving & Reasoning **M5**

Mathematical Skills & Tools **M6**

Mathematical Communication **M7**

Putting Mathematics to Work

This work sample represents a standard-setting performance for the following parts of the standards:

M1 a Arithmetic and Number Concepts: Add, subtract, multiply, and divide whole numbers.

M1 b Arithmetic and Number Concepts: Demonstrate understanding of the base ten place value system and use this knowledge to solve arithmetic tasks.

M1 c Arithmetic and Number Concepts: Estimate, approximate, round off, use landmark numbers, or use exact numbers, as appropriate, in calculations.

M1 d Arithmetic and Number Concepts: Describe and compare quantities by using concrete and real world models of simple fractions.

M1 e Arithmetic and Number Concepts: Describe and compare quantities by using simple decimals.

M1 f Arithmetic and Number Concepts: Describe and compare quantities by using whole numbers up to 10,000.

M2 g Geometry and Measurement Concepts: Use basic ways of estimating and measuring the size of figures and objects in the real world.

M2 i Geometry and Measurement Concepts: Select and use units for estimating and measuring quantities.

M2 j Geometry and Measurement Concepts: Carry out simple unit conversions.

M5 a Problem Solving and Reasoning: Formulation.

M5 b Problem Solving and Reasoning: Implementation.

M5 c Problem Solving and Reasoning: Conclusion.

M6 a Mathematical Skills and Tools: Add, subtract, multiply, and divide whole numbers correctly.

M6 b Mathematical Skills and Tools: Estimate numerically and spatially.

M6 c Mathematical Skills and Tools: Measure accurately.

M6 d Mathematical Skills and Tools: Compute time.

M6 f Mathematical Skills and Tools: Use +, -, x, ÷, /,...and . (decimal point) correctly in number sentences and expressions.

M6 h Mathematical Skills and Tools: Use recall, mental computations, pencil and paper, measuring devices, manipulatives, calculators and advice from peers, as appropriate, to achieve solutions.

M7 a Mathematical Communication: Use appropriate mathematical terms, vocabulary, and language.

M7 b Mathematical Communication: Show mathematical ideas in a variety of ways.

M7 c Mathematical Communication: Explain solutions to problems clearly and logically.

M7 d Mathematical Communication: Consider purpose and audience when communicating about mathematics.

M7 e Mathematical Communication: Comprehend mathematics from reading assignments and from other sources.

Counting on Frank

What the work shows

M1 a Arithmetic and Number Concepts: The student adds, subtracts, multiplies, and divides whole numbers, with and without calculators; that is:...

• multiplies, i.e.,...uses simple rates.

A B C D E F The consistent and effective use of multiplication throughout the student work shows a deep understanding at the elementary level.

• divides, i.e., puts things into groups, shares equally; calculates simple rates.

G H I J

• analyzes problem situations and contexts in order to figure out when to add, subtract, multiply, or divide....

K L M The student successfully figured out how and when to use arithmetic in these multi-step problems. The analysis is particularly strong because the situations were general claims made by a character in a book, i.e., there was no hint about how to proceed to test the claims.

• solves arithmetic problems by relating addition, subtraction, multiplication, and division to one another.

E The student added to complete a multiplication problem. The teacher also verified that the student divided 700 by 4 and multiplied the answer by 3 with a calculator to figure out that "three quarters of 700 equals 525."

• computes answers mentally....

D G N O The student, as verified by the teacher, computed some of the arithmetic mentally, here and in other places in the work.

M1 b Arithmetic and Number Concepts: The student demonstrates understanding of the base ten place value system and uses this knowledge to solve arithmetic tasks; that is:...uses knowledge about ones, tens, hundreds, and thousands to figure out answers to multiplication and division tasks, e.g., 36 x 10, 18 x 100, 7 x 1,000, 4,000 ÷ 4.

D E N

M1 c Arithmetic and Number Concepts: The student estimates, approximates, rounds off, uses landmark numbers, or uses exact numbers, as appropriate, in calculations.

J N O P Q R The student used a well-developed sense of when it is appropriate to round off or estimate in these situations. Elsewhere, the student successfully used exact numbers in calculations.

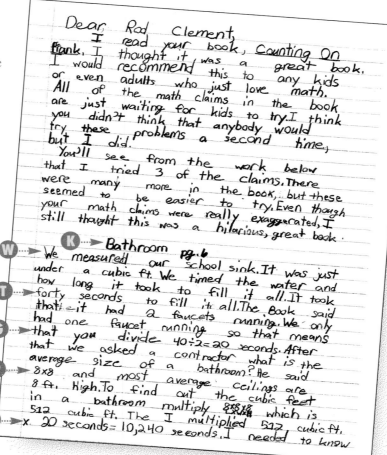

M1 d Arithmetic and Number Concepts: The student describes and compares quantities by using concrete and real world models of simple fractions; that is, finds simple parts of wholes....

E The student used coffee cups and measured out 4¾ cups. The computation ("three quarters of 700 is 525") is advanced for this level.

M1 e Arithmetic and Number Concepts: The student describes and compares quantities by using simple decimals....

J The student took part of the decimal answer to a division problem (13.13) and used the nearest whole number (13) to make sense of the given situation, i.e., bags of peas.

Arithmetic and Number Concepts

Geometry & Measurement Concepts

Function & Algebra Concepts

Statistics & Probability Concepts

Problem Solving & Reasoning

Mathematical Skills & Tools

Mathematical Communication

Putting Mathematics to Work

Counting on Frank

M1 f
Arithmetic
and Number
Concepts **M1**

Geometry &
Measurement
Concepts **M2**

Function &
Algebra
Concepts

Statistics &
Probability
Concepts

Problem
Solving &
Reasoning **M5**

Mathematical
Skills & Tools **M6**

Mathematical
Communication **M7**

Putting
Mathematics
to Work

M1 f Arithmetic and Number Concepts: The student describes and compares quantities by using whole numbers up to 10,000; that is, connects ideas of quantities to the real world....

K **L** **M** The student called the author's bluff by actually connecting the ideas in the book to the real world.

A **C** **J** In each problem, the student dealt successfully with quantities larger than 10,000 (10,240 seconds; 43,680 peas; 13,500 feet). The clarity and thoroughness of communication provides evidence of understanding of these quantities and represents a strong performance for this level.

M2 g Geometry and Measurement Concepts: The student uses basic ways of estimating and measuring the size of figures and objects in the real world, including length, width, perimeter, and area.

P The student went beyond the standards by measuring the volume of the bathroom in cubic feet. The teacher verified that the students had constructed the formula for area themselves earlier in the year through conceptual activities. The students' motivation to test the claim about the bathroom led them to a discussion of how to measure the size of the sink and the bathroom, and they constructed the idea of "layers" of length times width. The teacher then supplied them with the formula L x W x H.

Q The student demonstrated understanding of area by listing some of the "millions of possibilities...that are close" for 264 square feet. The student also demonstrated understanding by applying the concept of area to the size of a bathroom floor, and noticing that an area of 264 square feet would be "huge."

D **S** The student measured the length of the pen and the length of the line and used these measurements to solve the problem.

M2 i Geometry and Measurement Concepts: The student selects and uses units, both formal and informal as appropriate, for estimating and measuring quantities such as...length, area, volume, and time.

D **S** The student used centimeters to measure the pen, and feet to measure the line.

R The student used a coffee cup to measure volume.

T The student used seconds to measure time.

(H) minutes. so I divided by 60 and I got 170 min. which is almost 3 hrs. The boy said it took 11 hours and 45 min. which is definitely war off. Or maybe he has a huge bathroom.

(F) He says it took 705 min. If I could fill 3 cu. ft. in one min. That would equal up to 2115 cuft. in one min. 705 min. X 3cu. ft.

(I) was what he filled. If I figured that a bathroom ceiling is 8' tall I would Divide the height and get the area which is 264 sq. ft. To find out the area there

(Q) are millions of possibilities. Here are some that are close -20x13, 16x16, 26x10 these are huge bathrooms. I have proved him wrong.

(L) → Peas pg.8
In the story it said he would knock

(B) off 15 peas per day off his plate x 7 days in a week x 52 weeks x 8 yrs.= 43,680

(R) 3,325 peas in a bag. bags are done by weight not just counting so this is an estimate. I used 1 coffee cup

(E) of peas it could take 700 peas in it. so 4 3/4 c. are in one bag. After I was done one cup I just filled it up because I know what the number on So I. multiplied 700 peas times four cups = 2800 then three quarters of 700 equals 525. (2800 + 525 = 3,325. (4 cups) 3/4 (Peas in a bag)

(J) → I divided 43,680 peas (Number of peas in 8 yrs.) by 3,325 (1 bag) = 13.13 bags of peas.

If 13 bags of peas do not even fill the grocery bag how would it be level with their table (like it said in the story) His whole kitchen would be small like a grocery bag or the peas are as big as softballs.

(V) → I have proved him wrong again.

(M) → Pen pg.1
In the story the boy said the average ball point pen draws a line twenty-three hundred yards long before the ink runs out. I measured

(S) an ink tube - it was 9cm high. Then

(D) I drew a line 3000 ft. long (30 times up and down a 100 ft. piece of paper).

(N) After I was done drawing the lines I measured the ink again. I had used 2 cm. of ink. If I

(C) used 2cm. for 3000 ft. then I estimate 1 cm. would be 1,500. Then I would multiply 1500ft x 9cm.= 13,500 ft. then I would divide my answer (13,500 yds)

(U) by 3 = 4,500 yds. because 3ft. in one yd. The boys estimate was 2,300 so I

(O) was about off. I used a brand new papermate pen, which I think is the average pen. I have proved him wrong a third time.

Counting on Frank

M2 j Geometry and Measurement Concepts: The student carries out simple unit conversions, such as between cm and m, and between hours and minutes.

B H U The student converted peas per day to peas per year, seconds to minutes, minutes to hours, and feet to yards.

M5 a Problem Solving and Reasoning: Formulation. Given the basic statement of a problem situation, the student:

• makes the important decisions about the approach, materials, and strategies to use, i.e., does not merely fill in a given chart, use a pre-specified manipulative, or go through a predetermined set of steps.

K L M The student made the decisions to use the sink, the peas, the coffee cup, the ball-point pen, and the 100 feet long piece of paper.

• uses previously learned strategies, skills, knowledge, and concepts to make decisions.

K L M Throughout the three problems, the student drew upon knowledge and skills related to multiplication, division, and measurement (i.e., length, area, and volume).

• uses strategies, such as using manipulatives or drawing sketches, to model problems.

K L M The student devised effective strategies, such as timing how long the water took to fill the sink, using the coffee cup to measure the peas, and measuring the decrease in length of the ink in the pen.

M5 b Problem Solving and Reasoning: Implementation. The student makes the basic choices involved in planning and carrying out a solution; that is, the student:

• makes up and uses a variety of strategies and approaches to solving problems….

K L M

• makes connections among concepts in order to solve problems.

K L M There are many connections between arithmetic and measurement throughout the work.

• solves problems in ways that make sense and explains why these ways make sense, e.g., defends the reasoning, explains the solution.

O Q V Statements like, "His whole kitchen would be small like a grocery bag or the peas are as big as softballs," show that the student made sense of the problem. Throughout the work, the student impressively, consistently, and accurately explicates the reasoning used.

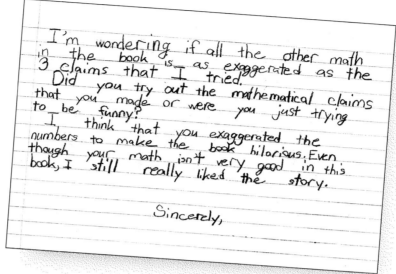

M5 c Problem Solving and Reasoning: Conclusion. The student moves beyond a particular problem by making connections, extensions, and/or generalizations….

L M The assignment asked the student to focus on one claim made in the book. The student chose to extend the assignment by analyzing and writing about more than one claim. This is a reasonable extension for elementary school level.

M6 a Mathematical Skills and Tools: The student adds, subtracts, multiplies, and divides whole numbers correctly; that is:

• knows single digit addition, subtraction, multiplication, and division facts.

D E G N The student showed a command of basic facts, which was needed to carry out these and other calculations.

• adds…numbers with several digits.

E

• multiplies and divides numbers with one or two digits.

G H

• multiplies and divides three digit numbers by one digit numbers.

E

M6 b Mathematical Skills and Tools: The student estimates numerically and spatially.

N O Q R

M6 c Mathematical Skills and Tools: The student measures length, area,…height,…and volume accurately in both the customary and metric systems.

D N S W The teacher verified the accuracy of the measurements.

M1 Arithmetic and Number Concepts

M2 Geometry & Measurement Concepts

Function & Algebra Concepts

Statistics & Probability Concepts

M5 Problem Solving & Reasoning

M6 Mathematical Skills & Tools

M7 Mathematical Communication

Putting Mathematics to Work

Counting on Frank

Arithmetic and Number Concepts **M1**

Geometry & Measurement Concepts **M2**

Function & Algebra Concepts

Statistics & Probability Concepts

Problem Solving & Reasoning **M5**

Mathematical Skills & Tools **M6**

Mathematical Communication **M7**

Putting Mathematics to Work

M6 d Mathematical Skills and Tools: The student computes time (in hours and minutes)....

H

M6 f Mathematical Skills and Tools: The student uses +, -, x, ÷, /,...and . (decimal point) correctly in number sentences and expressions.

A B C E F G J P Q

M6 h Mathematical Skills and Tools: The student uses recall, mental computations, pencil and paper, measuring devices,...manipulatives, calculators...and advice from peers, as appropriate, to achieve solutions....

K L M The student drew upon many resources to complete the assignment.

M7 a Mathematical Communication: The student uses appropriate mathematical terms, vocabulary, and language, based on prior conceptual work.

K L M The student used many mathematical terms appropriately, including "estimate," "measure," "average," "multiply," "divide," "seconds," "minutes," "area," "long," "high," "equal," "cm," "ft."

P The use of the term "cubic feet" and the formula for volume go beyond what is required at this level.

U The student wrote "yds" after 13,500, but this mislabeling did not interfere with the correct mathematics in the work.

M7 b Mathematical Communication: The student shows mathematical ideas in a variety of ways, including words, numbers, and symbols....

K L M

M7 c Mathematical Communication: The student explains solutions to problems clearly and logically, and supports solutions with evidence, in both oral and written work.

K L M

M7 d Mathematical Communication: The student considers purpose and audience when communicating about mathematics.

K L M The student focused consistently on the purpose of disputing the claims in the book and wrote directly to the author.

M7 e Mathematical Communication: The student comprehends mathematics from reading assignments and from other sources.

K L M The student even comprehended mathematical information from a contractor about the average size of a bathroom.

The student misspelled a few words (e.g., "definitely") and made some grammatical mistakes (e.g., capitalizing "book" in the middle of the sentence). The teacher did not require the students to fix the errors.

Work Sample & Commentary: *School Uniforms Project*

The task

The teacher asked students to come up with a question for a data study that they would then carry out.

This student chose to survey the children of her school about their opinions on the following questions:

Would you like to have uniforms at this school?

What colors would you like the uniforms to be:

• white and red?

• white and magenta?

• white and blue?

This work sample illustrates a standard-setting performance for the following parts of the standards:

M1 a Arithmetic and Number Concepts: Add, subtract, multiply, and divide whole numbers.

M1 c Arithmetic and Number Concepts: Estimate, approximate, round off, use landmark numbers, or use exact numbers in calculations.

M1 d Arithmetic and Number Concepts: Describe and compare quantities by using concrete and real world models of simple fractions.

M1 e Arithmetic and Number Concepts: Describe and compare quantities by using simple decimals.

M4 a Statistics and Probability Concepts: Collect and organize data to answer a question.

M4 b Statistics and Probability Concepts: Display data.

M4 c Statistics and Probability Concepts: Make statements and draw simple conclusions based on data.

M4 d Statistics and Probability Concepts: Gather data about an entire group or by sampling group members to understand the concept of sample.

M5 a Problem Solving and Reasoning: Formulation.

M6 a Mathematical Skills and Tools: Add, subtract, multiply, and divide whole numbers correctly.

M6 g Mathematical Skills and Tools: Read, create, and represent data.

M7 d Mathematical Communication: Consider purpose and audience when communicating about mathematics.

M8 a Putting Mathematics to Work: Data study.

Circumstances of performance

This sample of student work was produced under the following conditions:

alone	√ in a group
√ in class	as homework
√ with teacher feedback	√ with peer feedback
timed	√ opportunity for revision

The student developed and carried out this project with three classmates, but wrote an individual report. The class had not previously worked with collecting survey data.

In this classroom, students had been using New Standards Elementary Mathematics Portfolios. The teacher intended for students to be able to use this data survey to satisfy requirements for the project exhibit of the portfolio. According to the instructions for the project exhibit, students completing a data study should do the following things.

• Think of a situation where data can help you make a decision or recommendation. Describe the situation and the question you will ask.

• Decide on the groups and numbers of people you will survey.

• Predict the results of your study using specific fractions, percents, numbers, etc.

• Collect and organize your data in a chart. You may need to reorganize it.

• Compare your result to your prediction. Write down what was the same or different.

• Organize your data into a chart, graph, or diagram that shows your result.

• Record how your results help you make your recommendation or decision.

• Write a report that includes your decision or recommendation. Include all your work.

This sample was completed in Spanish in a bilingual classroom. The translation was provided by the teacher.

The quotations from the Mathematics performance descriptions in this commentary are excerpted. The complete performance descriptions are shown on pages 60-65.

M1 Arithmetic and Number Concepts

Geometry & Measurement Concepts

Function & Algebra Concepts

M4 Statistics & Probability Concepts

M5 Problem Solving & Reasoning

M6 Mathematical Skills & Tools

M7 Mathematical Communication

M8 Putting Mathematics to Work

School Uniforms Project

What the work shows

M1a Arithmetic and Number Concepts: The student…divides whole numbers, with and without calculators; that is:

- divides, i.e., puts things into groups, shares equally; calculates simple rates.

A

- analyzes problem situations and contexts in order to figure out when to…divide.

A The student figured out that it was necessary to divide the number of children in the sample by the number of grades in the school in order to get an equal sampling from each grade.

M1c Arithmetic and Number Concepts: The student estimates, approximates, rounds off,…as appropriate, in calculations.

B The student made the appropriate choice of rounding off in order to more easily compute 10%.

M1d Arithmetic and Number Concepts: The student describes and compares quantities by using concrete and real world models of simple fractions; that is:

- uses beginning proportional reasoning and simple ratios….

C The student used fractions to represent a simple concept of proportion ("⁹⁶⁄₁₀₀…96 out of 100 children said…").

M1e Arithmetic and Number Concepts: The student describes and compares quantities by using simple decimals; that is:

- recognizes relationships among simple fractions, decimals, and percents, i.e., that ½ is the same as 0.5, and ½ is the same as 50%, with concrete materials, diagrams, and in real world situations….

B

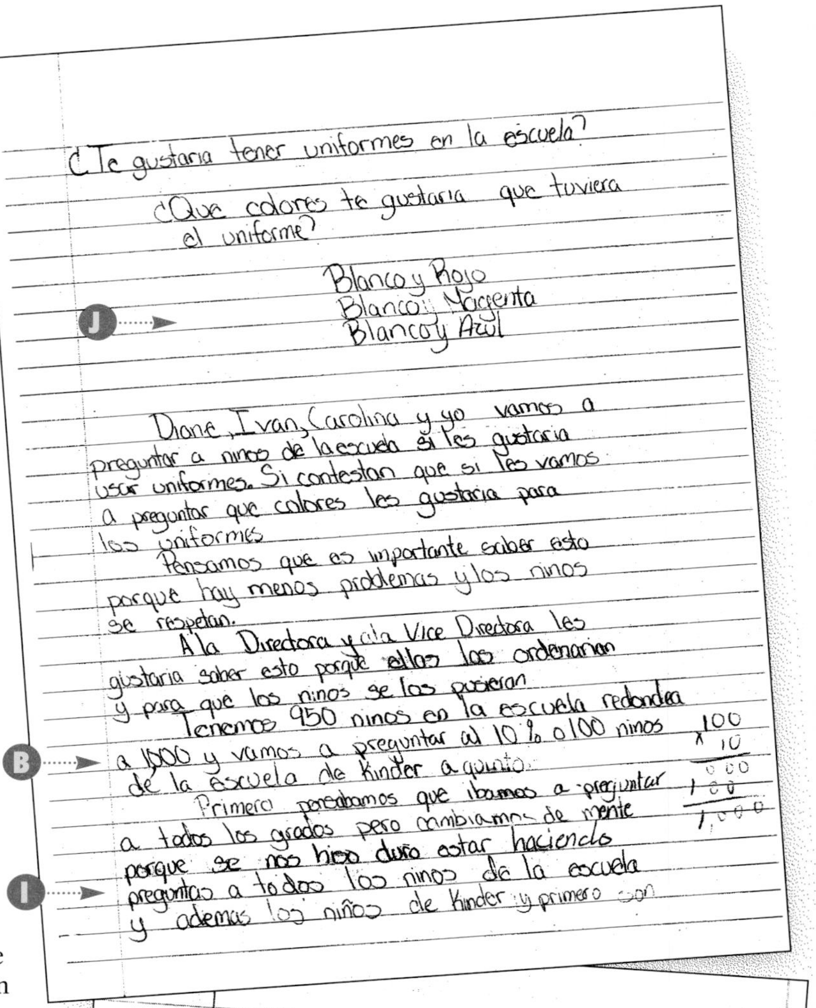

Sidebar navigation:
- Arithmetic and Number Concepts **M1**
- Geometry & Measurement Concepts
- Function & Algebra Concepts
- Statistics & Probability Concepts **M4**
- Problem Solving & Reasoning **M5**
- Mathematical Skills & Tools **M6**
- Mathematical Communication **M7**
- Putting Mathematics to Work **M8**

First handwritten page:

¿Te gustaria tener uniformes en la escuela?

¿Que colores te gustaria que tuviera el uniforme?

J →
Blanco y Rojo
Blanco y Magenta
Blanco y Azul

Diane, Ivan, Carolina y yo vamos a preguntar a niños de la escuela si les gustaria usar uniformes. Si contestan que si les vamos a preguntar que colores les gustaria para los uniformes.

Pensamos que es importante saber esto porque hay menos problemas y los niños se respetan.

A la Directora y a la Vice Directora les gustaria saber esto porque ellos los ordenarian y para que los niños se los pusieron.

B → Tenemos 950 niños en la escuela redondea a 1000 y vamos a preguntar al 10% o 100 niños de la escuela de Kinder a quinto.

×100
×10
000
100
1,000

Primera pensabamos que ibamos a preguntar a todos los grados pero cambiamos de mente porque se nos hizo duro estar haciendo

I → preguntas a todos los niños de la escuela y ademas los niños de Kinder y primero son

---

Second handwritten page:

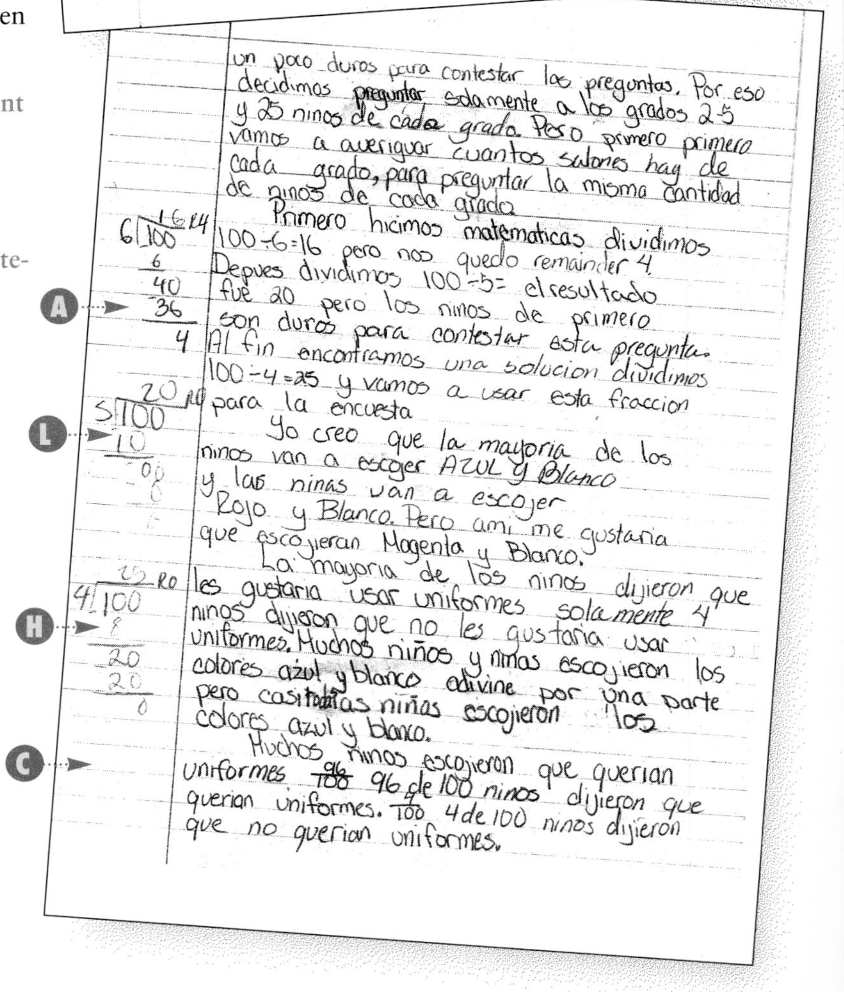

un poco duros para contestar las preguntas. Por eso decidimos preguntar solamente a los grados 25 y 25 niños de cada grado. Pero primero primera vamos a averiguar cuantos salones hay de cada grado, para preguntar la misma cantidad de niños de cada grado.

Primero hicimos matematicas dividimos

A →
6 | 100   16 r4
   6
   40
   36
    4

100÷6=16 pero nos quedo remainder 4. Despues dividimos 100÷5= el resultado fue 20 pero los niños de primero son duros para contestar esta pregunta. Al fin encontramos una solucion dividimos 100÷4=25 y vamos a usar esta fraccion para la encuesta

L →
5 | 100   20 r0
   10
    00

Yo creo que la mayoria de los niños van a escoger AZUL y Blanco y las niñas van a escojer Rojo y Blanco. Pero a mi me gustaria que escojieran Magenta y Blanco.

La mayoria de los niños dijieron que

H →
4 | 100   25 r0
    8
   20
   20
    0

les gustaria usar uniformes solamente 4 niños dijieron que no les gustaria usar uniformes. Muchos niños y niñas escojieron los colores azul y blanco adivine por una parte pero casi todas las niñas escojieron los colores azul y blanco.

Muchos niños escojieron que querian uniformes. ⁹⁶⁄₁₀₀ 96 de 100 niños dijieron que

C → querian uniformes. ⁴⁄₁₀₀ 4 de 100 niños dijieron que no querian uniformes.

School Uniforms Project

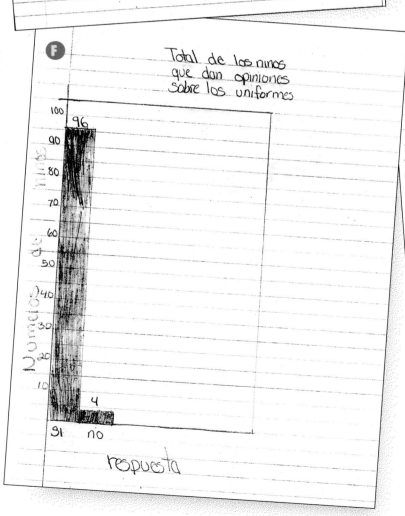

23/96   23 de 96 niños escojieron los colores rojo y blanco.

37/96   37 de 96 niños escojieron los colores magenta o guinda con blanco.

40/96   40 de 96 niños escojieron los colores azul y blanco.

K ► Yo le recomiendo a la Directora y Vice Directora que ordenen los uniformes de los colores azul y blanco.

Puse 96 para estas fracciones porque 4 niños dijieron que no querian uniformes y reste 100-4= y la respuesta fue 96 a los niños que dijieron que no querian uniformes no les preguntamos que colores les gustaria pas los uniformes.

M4 a Statistics and Probability Concepts: The student collects and organizes data to answer a question or test a hypothesis by comparing sets of data.

D **E** The student collected data to test a hypothesis.

F **G** The student organized the data.

M4 b Statistics and Probability Concepts: The student displays data in...graphs, tables, and charts.

F **G**

M4 c Statistics and Probability Concepts: The student makes statements and draws simple conclusions based on data; that is:...

• compares data in order to make true statements....

C

• uses data, including statements about the data, to make a simple concluding statement about a situation....

H The student used the data to make simple concluding statements. Most of the statements made (e.g., "Most of the children…" for 96%) are accurate. One conclusion ("…almost all the girls…" for 25 out of 57 sampled) is not accurate.

Arithmetic and Number Concepts **M1**

Geometry & Measurement Concepts

Function & Algebra Concepts

Statistics & Probability Concepts **M4**

Problem Solving & Reasoning **M5**

Mathematical Skills & Tools **M6**

Mathematical Communication **M7**

Putting Mathematics to Work **M8**

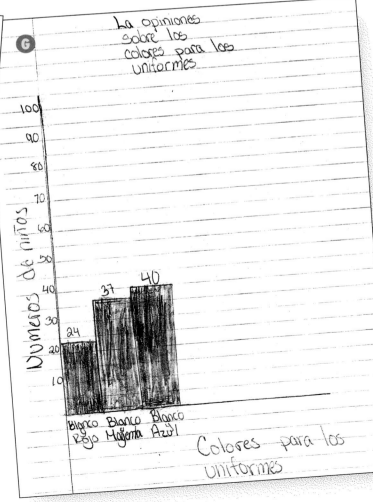

F

Total de los niños que dan opiniones sobre los uniformes

Numero de niños

100, 96, 90, 80, 70, 60, 50, 40, 30, 20, 10, 4

si   no

respuesta

G

La opiniones sobre los colores para los uniformes

Numeros de niños

100, 90, 80, 70, 60, 50, 40, 30, 20, 10

24   37   40

Blanco Blanco Blanco
Rojo Magenta Azul

Colores para los uniformes

School Uniforms Project

M4 d Statistics and Probability Concepts: The student gathers data about an entire group or by sampling group members to understand the concept of sample, i.e., that a large sample leads to more reliable information....

I The reasoning behind choosing to sample roughly 10% of the school is clearly explained.

M5 a Problem Solving and Reasoning: Formulation. Given the basic statement of a problem situation, the student.

• makes the important decisions about the approach, materials, and strategies to use, i.e., does not merely fill in a given chart, use a pre-specified manipulative, or go through a predetermined set of steps.

A **B** **D** **E** **F** **G** The student made decisions about the sampling method, and the charts and graphs to be used.

• uses previously learned strategies, skills, knowledge, and concepts to make decisions.

B The student used the concept of percent in making decisions.

M6 a Mathematical Skills and Tools: The student adds, subtracts, multiplies, and divides whole numbers correctly; that is:...

• multiplies and divides three digit numbers by one digit numbers.

A

M6 g Mathematical Skills and Tools: The student reads, creates, and represents data on...charts, tables, diagrams, and bar graphs....

D **E** **F** **G**

M7 d Mathematical Communication: The student considers purpose and audience when communicating about mathematics.

J The report enables readers to understand the project.

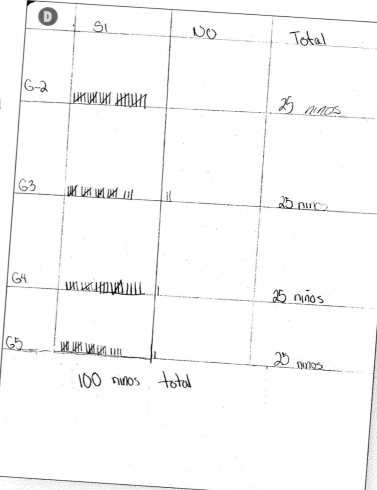

School Uniforms Project

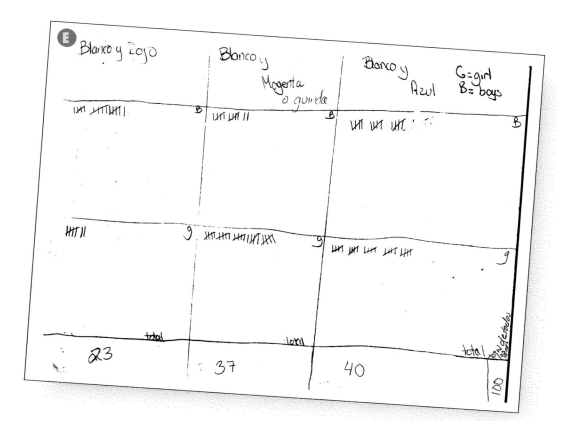

M8 a Putting Mathematics to Work: Data study, in which the student:

• develops a question and a hypothesis in a situation where data could help make a decision or recommendation.

J K The student showed clearly that the question could lead directly to a real recommendation.

The project does not entirely fulfill this criterion for the data study, because the question is not expressed as a hypothesis. Nevertheless, the student accomplished the important purposes of a large scale mathematics project. The purpose of the Putting Mathematics to Work standard is for students to make important decisions about using mathematics and to put extensive mathematics to work in realistic situations.

• decides on a group or groups to be sampled and makes predictions of the results, with specific percents, fractions, or numbers.

B I L The student used clear arithmetic and logical reasons in choosing the group and numbers used in the sample. The prediction applied to only one of the two questions posed. The prediction included no specific numbers. This lack of specificity does not of itself restrict the project from meeting the standard for a data study.

• collects, represents, and displays data in order to help make the decision or recommendation; compares the results with the predictions.

F G H

• writes a report that includes recommendations supported by diagrams, charts, and graphs, and acknowledges assistance received from parents, peers, and teachers.

A B C D E F G H I J K L

Arithmetic and Number Concepts

Geometry & Measurement Concepts

Function & Algebra Concepts

Statistics & Probability Concepts

Problem Solving & Reasoning

Mathematical Skills & Tools

Mathematical Communication

Putting Mathematics to Work

School Uniforms Project

Translation

Would you like to have uniforms at this school?

What colors would you like the uniforms to be?

J
white and red
white and magenta
white and blue

Diane, Ivan, Carolina and I are going to ask the children of the school if they would like uniforms. If they answer yes, we are going to ask them what colors they would like the uniforms to be.

We think that it is important to know this because there are less problems and the children will respect one another.

The principal and the vice-principal would like to know this because they would order them and because the children would wear them.

B
We have 950 children in the school rounded off to 1,000 and we are going to ask 10% or 100 children in the school from kindergarten to fifth.

I
At first we thought we were going to ask all the grades but we changed our minds because it was hard for us to be asking questions of all the kids in the school and besides the children in kindergarten and first have a little trouble answering the questions. That's why we decided to ask only grades 2-5 and 25 children at each grade. But first we need to find out how many rooms there are at each grade, so we can ask the same quantity of children at each grade.

A
First we did some mathematics we divided 100 by 6 but there was a remainder of 4. Next we divided 100 by 5 and the result was 20 but the children in first grade have a hard time answering the question. Finally we found the solution we divided 100 by 4 = 25 and we are going to use this fraction for our survey.

L
I think that most of the boys are going to choose blue and white and the girls are going to choose red and white. But I would like it if they chose magenta and white.

H
Most of the children said that they would like to have uniforms only 4 children said that they would not like to have uniforms. Many boys and girls chose the colors blue and white, I guessed part of it but almost all the girls chose blue and white.

C
Many children chose that they would like uniforms $\frac{96}{100}$ 96 out of 100 children said they wanted uniforms. $\frac{4}{100}$ 4 out of 100 children said they did not want uniforms.

$\frac{23}{96}$ 23 out of 96 children chose the colors red and white.

$\frac{37}{96}$ 37 out of 96 children chose the colors magenta or guinda with white.
< Note: guinda is just another word for magenta>
(by teacher)

$\frac{40}{96}$ 40 out of 96 children chose the colors blue and white.

K
I recommend to the principal and the vice-principal that they order blue and white uniforms.

I put 96 for these fractions because 4 children said that they didn't want uniforms and I subtracted 100-4= and the anwer was 96 with the children that said they did not want uniforms we did not ask them what colors they would like.

Graph titled: Total of children who give opinions about uniforms

Graph titled. Opinions about the colors of the uniforms

tally sheet for the surveying of the children by grade

tally sheet for the surveying of the children separated by boy/girl

Arithmetic and Number Concepts — M1

Geometry & Measurement Concepts

Function & Algebra Concepts

Statistics & Probability Concepts — M4

Problem Solving & Reasoning — M5

Mathematical Skills & Tools — M6

Mathematical Communication — M7

Putting Mathematics to Work — M8

Work Sample & Commentary: *Catapult Investigation*

The task

After each student had built an individual catapult according to the teacher's design, the teacher gave the following instructions:

Use your catapults to determine which setting (on the catapult) is best for shooting a wet sponge the furthest. To complete the project you will need to:

• design and carry out a test that determines the optimum setting for shooting a wet sponge the furthest;

• include all information that would be necessary for anyone reading this response to follow your work completely.

Circumstances of performance

This sample of student work was produced under the following conditions:

√ alone   √ in a group

√ in class   as homework

√ with teacher feedback   √ with peer feedback

     timed   √ opportunity for revision

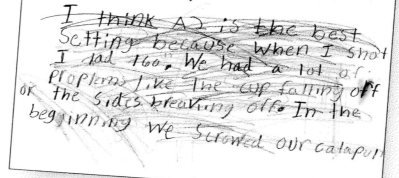

CATAPULTS

11/8/95

Which setting is the best for shooting a wet sponge the furthest?

Design and carry out a test that determines the optimum setting for shooting wet sponges the furthest. Include all information that would be necessary for anyone reading this response to follow your work completely.

I think A2 is the best setting because when I shot I had 160". We had a lot of problems like the cup falling off or the sides breaking off. In the beginning we screwed our catapult

---

This work sample illustrates a standard-setting performance for the following parts of the standards:

M4 a Statistics and Probability Concepts: Collect and organize data to answer a question.

M4 b Statistics and Probability Concepts: Display data.

M4 c Statistics and Probability Concepts: Make statements and draw simple conclusions based on data.

M4 f Statistics and Probability Concepts: Find all possible combinations.

M5 a Problem Solving and Reasoning: Formulation.

M5 b Problem Solving and Reasoning: Implementation.

M6 c Mathematical Skills and Tools: Measure accurately in both the customary and metric systems.

M6 g Mathematical Skills and Tools: Read, create, and represent data.

M6 h Mathematical Skills and Tools: Use measuring devices and calculators to achieve solutions.

M7 b Mathematical Communication: Show mathematical ideas in a variety of ways.

M8 b Putting Mathematics to Work: Science study.

Students completed this project as part of a unit on simple machines and had explored levers and fulcrums. The class took several days to complete the testing of catapult-setting variables and to write up the results as a report. Students worked with partners in the testing of their catapults.

What the work shows

M4 a Statistics and Probability Concepts: The student collects and organizes data to answer a question...by comparing sets of data.

A **B** The student collected, organized, and compared data in order to determine which catapult setting sends wet sponges the furthest.

M4 b Statistics and Probability Concepts: The student displays data in line plots, graphs, tables, and charts.

A Data are displayed in a clear table.

B Data are displayed in a graph. The data for settings A1 and A2 were placed off line but this does not detract from the overall clarity of the graph.

M4 c Statistics and Probability Concepts: The student makes statements and draws simple conclusions based on data; that is:...

• compares data in order to make true statements....

C The student compared the data to make true statements: "A2 was the best setting because (it) shot very far...It had an average of 123 inches...C2 is the worst setting...."

The quotations from the Mathematics performance descriptions in this commentary are excerpted. The complete performance descriptions are shown on pages 60-65.

Arithmetic and Number Concepts

Geometry & Measurement Concepts

Function & Algebra Concepts

M4 Statistics & Probability Concepts

M5 Problem Solving & Reasoning

M6 Mathematical Skills & Tools

M7 Mathematical Communication

M8 Putting Mathematics to Work

Catapult Investigation

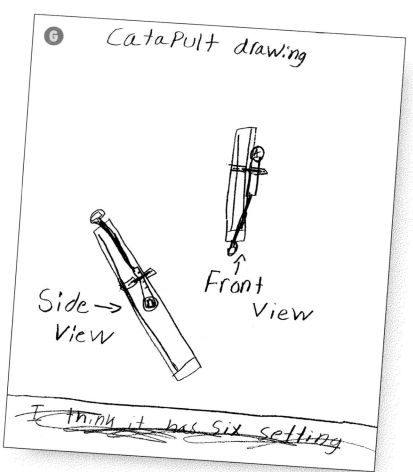

G Catapult drawing

Side → View

Front View

I think it has six setting

- uses previously learned strategies, skills, knowledge, and concepts to make decisions.

C The student used the previously learned concept of average to decide on the best setting.

- uses strategies, such as using manipulatives or drawing sketches, to model problems.

G **H** **I**

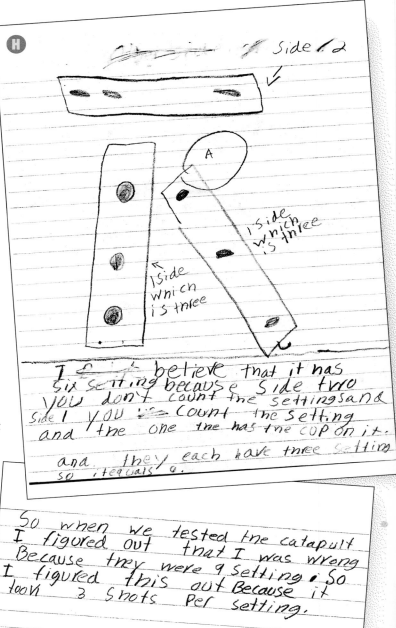

H

Side 2

A

Iside which is three

Iside which is three

I believe that it has six setting because side two you don't count the settings and side I you count the setting and the one the has the cup on it. and they each have three settin so it equals 6.

So when we tested the catapult I figured out that I was wrong Because they were 9 setting. So I figured this out Because it took 3 shots per setting.

- makes true statements based on a simple concept of average (median and mean), for a small sample size....

A **C**

- uses data, including statements about the data, to make a simple concluding statement about a situation....

D

M4 f Statistics and Probability Concepts: The student finds all possible combinations and arrangements within certain constraints involving a limited number of variables.

E In the course of testing the settings, the student found all the possible combinations of settings.

M5 a Problem Solving and Reasoning: Formulation. Given the basic statement of a problem situation, the student:

- makes the important decisions about the approach, materials, and strategies to use, i.e., does not merely fill in a given chart, use a pre-specified manipulative, or go through a predetermined set of steps.

A **B** **C** **E** **F** The student decided on the methods for determining, recording, and representing the most effective setting.

Sidebar (left margin):

Arithmetic and Number Concepts

Geometry & Measurement Concepts

Function & Algebra Concepts

Statistics & Probability Concepts **M4**

Problem Solving & Reasoning **M5**

Mathematical Skills & Tools **M6**

Mathematical Communication **M7**

Putting Mathematics to Work **M8**

Catapult Investigation

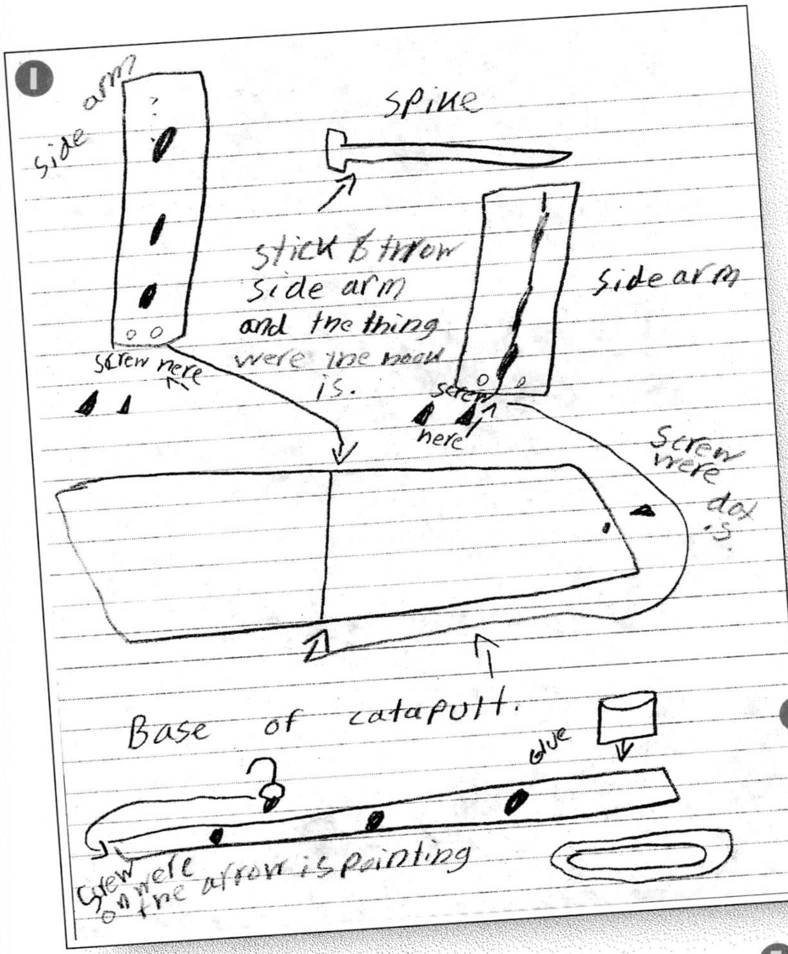

M6 g Mathematical Skills and Tools: The student reads, creates, and represents data on...charts, tables, diagrams....

A B

M5 b Problem Solving and Reasoning: Implementation. The student makes the basic choices involved in planning and carrying out a solution; that is, the student:

• makes up and uses a variety of strategies and approaches to solving problems and uses or learns approaches that other people use, as appropriate.

A B C E F The student created an approach for testing the settings.

• makes connections among concepts in order to solve problems.

A E The student made connections among statistics concepts (e.g., finding all combinations of settings and averaging like results) to answer the question.

• solves problems in ways that make sense and explains why these ways make sense, e.g., defends the reasoning, explains the solution.

C D E F

M6 c Mathematical Skills and Tools: The student measures length...accurately in both the customary and metric systems.

A The student measured the lengths of firings. The teacher verified the accuracy of measurements.

Side bar navigation:

Arithmetic and Number Concepts

Geometry & Measurement Concepts

Function & Algebra Concepts

M4 Statistics & Probability Concepts

M5 Problem Solving & Reasoning

M6 Mathematical Skills & Tools

M7 Mathematical Communication

M8 Putting Mathematics to Work

Student work:

F In the beginning we scrowed our catapults together. Then we talked about the problem there would be and how we would solve them. One day we went outside to test and to prove How many setting there were. When we fired them catapults figured out they were nine setting so I was wrong.*

E They were nine setting because you have to fire like A1 A2 A3 there's three settings then B1 B2 B3 there's six settings then C1 C2 C3 and there's nine sitting when you add all togther. We solved most of the problem's but there more problem's. We dicided that A1 was at the top and b was in midak and c was at boddem. Three is by the two is in the middle and 1 is at the end. We averaged because

C It was the onfailesl way. I thought A2 was the best setting because shot very far. I think I had an average of 123 inches!

*because I thought there were 6

D A2 shoots far because you have the most leverage. C2 is the worst setting because you can't lift the lever high.

Catapult Investigation

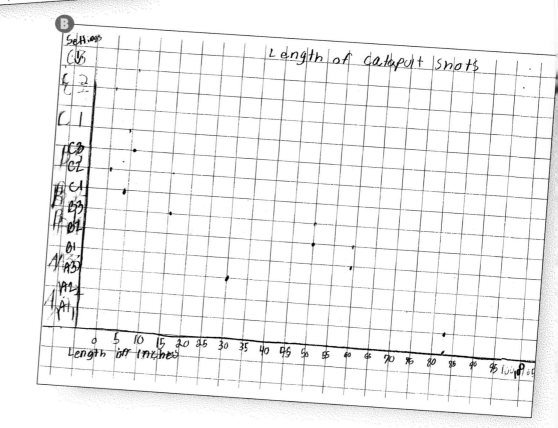

A

Catapult Data Table

Setting	Trial 1	Trial 2	Trial 3	Average
A1	63"	91"	105"	88"
A2	79"	165"	131"	123"
A3	39"	37"	14"	30"
B1	49"	74"	55"	59"
B2	41"	71"	35"	50"
B3	27"	7"	16"	16"
C1	3"	5"	5"	4"
C2	3"	0"	6"	1"
C3	9"	8"	3"	7"

B

Settings

Length of catapult shots

Length off inches

M6 h Mathematical Skills and Tools: The student uses...measuring devices...calculators,...as appropriate, to achieve solutions.

A The student used measuring devices to achieve a solution.

A The student used a calculator (as verified by the teacher) to compute averages.

M7 b Mathematical Communication: The student shows mathematical ideas in a variety of ways, including words, numbers, symbols, pictures, charts, graphs, tables, diagrams, and models.

A B F G H I The student showed his ideas in multiple ways. Some of the diagrams in particular are unlabeled, labeled confusingly, or difficult to interpret (see the three diagrams of the catapult). Overall, however, the ideas are communicated with sufficient clarity.

Catapult Investigation

M8 b Putting Mathematics to Work: The student conducts a science study, in which the student:

• decides on a specific science question to study and identifies the mathematics that will be used, e.g., measurement.

A **B** **C** **E** **F** The student investigated a science question and decided what mathematics should be used.

• develops a prediction (a hypothesis) and develops procedures to test the hypothesis.

E **F** **G** **H** **I** This investigation does not entirely fit the criteria for a "Science Study," because it does not ask the student for a hypothesis. The purpose of the Putting Mathematics to Work standard is for students to put extensive mathematics to work in realistic situations. The investigation clearly accomplishes this central purpose of a large scale mathematics project.

• collects and records data, represents and displays data, and compares results with predictions.

A **B** **C** The data are recorded, represented, and compared. Since the teacher called for students to answer a question in this investigation, the results of the data collection are used to this end, rather than to make a prediction.

• writes a report that compares the results with the hypothesis; supports the results with diagrams, charts, and graphs; acknowledges assistance received from parents, peers, and teachers.

The report is clear and uses the results to answer the question. The teacher did not ask students to acknowledge assistance; nevertheless, the student acknowledged his partner's assistance in making certain decisions.

Arithmetic and Number Concepts

Geometry & Measurement Concepts

Function & Algebra Concepts

M4 Statistics & Probability Concepts

M5 Problem Solving & Reasoning

M6 Mathematical Skills & Tools

M7 Mathematical Communication

M8 Putting Mathematics to Work

Work Sample & Commentary: *The Never Ending Four*

The quotations from the Mathematics performance descriptions in this commentary are excerpted. The complete performance descriptions are shown on pages 60-65.

The task

The teacher asked students to complete a large scale mathematics project chosen from among five kinds. This student chose to do a "Pure Mathematics Investigation." The teacher gave the student the written instructions illustrated here.

Circumstances of performance

This sample of student work was produced under the following conditions:

√ alone   in a group
  in class   √ as homework
√ with teacher feedback   √ with peer feedback
  timed   √ opportunity for revision

In this classroom students were using the New Standards Elementary Mathematics Portfolio. The teacher intended students to be able to use their chosen projects to fulfill the requirements for the project exhibit in the portfolio.

What the work shows

M3b Function and Algebra Concepts: The student builds iterations of simple non-linear patterns, including multiplicative and squaring patterns (e.g., "growing" patterns) with concrete materials, and recognizes that these patterns are not linear.

This work sample illustrates a standard-setting performance for the following parts of the standards:

M3b Function and Algebra Concepts: Build iterations of simple non-linear patterns and recognize that these patterns are not linear.

M4a Statistics and Probability Concepts: Collect and organize data to answer a question.

M5a Problem Solving and Reasoning: Formulation.

M6g Mathematical Skills and Tools: Read, create, and represent data.

M7b Mathematical Communication: Show mathematical ideas in a variety of ways.

M7c Mathematical Communication: Explain solutions to problems clearly and logically.

M7d Mathematical Communication: Consider purpose and audience when communicating about mathematics.

M8e Putting Mathematics to Work: Pure mathematics investigation.

Pure Math Investigation

Follow these instructions to complete a pure math investigation. Use complete sentences because this will help you write your report later!

1. Decide on what kind of math you will investigate. Will it involve numbers, shapes, patterns, all of these, or something else? Write down your idea and briefly describe it.

2. As you investigate a mathematical idea, try to discover something that you didn't know before, or didn't understand in the same way. Write down what you want to find out or understand better.

3. In order to present your investigation, you will need to use more than just words. You may use numbers, symbols, diagrams, shapes, and/or physical models like blocks or cubes. These are called representations. Write down what representations you will use.

4. Carry out your investigation. Find out all that you can about the idea that you are studying.

5. Write down what you found out or understand better. If you come up with any general rules, write them down. Make sure to use representations.

Write a report that includes all of your work from these questions and instructions. Include a title. Explain how you investigated your idea, and explain and show all that you found out. Make your report neat and organized! Attach this sheet and all your papers!

A The student built (again and again) the non-linear pattern generated by this "trick" question (i.e., that the numbers appearing before a four turns up are always five or nine).

M4a Statistics and Probability Concepts: The student collects and organizes data to answer a question…by comparing sets of data.

B The student represented data in a table in order to further explore the number relationships.

M5a Problem Solving and Reasoning: Formulation. Given the basic statement of a problem situation, the student:

• makes the important decisions about the approach, materials, and strategies to use, i.e., does not merely fill in a given chart, use a pre-specified manipulative, or go through a predetermined set of steps.

A B C D E The student made all decisions regarding how to proceed with this entirely unformulated project.

M6g Mathematical Skills and Tools: The student reads, creates, and represents data on charts, tables, diagrams….

B

M7b Mathematical Communication: The student shows mathematical ideas in a variety of ways, including words, numbers, symbols,…charts, tables, diagrams….

A B C D E

M7c Mathematical Communication: The student explains solutions to problems clearly and logically, and supports solutions with evidence, in both oral and written work.

The Never Ending Four

The Never Ending Four

For my math investigation I investigated how it is that everytime someone picks any number, and they spell out that number, and then count how many letters are in that number. Then write that number down and spell that number out, then continue the same process they had done before and will always end with a four. This is an interesting trick because I was always trying to get something other than a four but then I found out that it was impossible. That's why this trick is called The Never Ending Four.

In order to understand this trick lets try an example. Say you pick a hard number like 2,345. The first thing you need to do is write the number down.
Okay, the number is TWO THOUSAND THREE HUNDRED FORTY FIVE.
Then, count the letters and they total 32. Then spell out thirty two.
Okay, THIRTY TWO.
Now, count the letters.
They total 8 letters.
Then, spell out eight.
EIGHT.
Then, you count the letters.
They equal 5.
Spell out 5.
FIVE.
Then, count the letters.
There are 4 letters.
Spell out 4
FOUR
At four you can't get out of it and will continue to get four as the answer.

Most of the numbers you may first pick will come out at less than 30 numbers. Now lets look at these 30 numbers and see what they come out to:

1	one	3	three	5	five	4	four ect		
2	two	3	three	5	five	4	four **4**	**four**, ect...	
3	three	5	five	4	four **4**	**four**, ect.			
4	four **4**	**four**, ect...							
5	five **4**	**four**, ect...							
6	six	3	three	5	five	4	four **4**	**four**, ect	
7	seven	5	five	4	four **4**	**four**, ect			
8	eight	5	five	4	four **4**	**four**,ect			
9	nine	4	four	4	**four**, ect				
10	ten	3	three	5	five	4	four **4**	**four** , ect	

If you notice the number before four is mostly five. Let's try numbers 11-30:

11	eleven	6	(look at 6 above)
12	twelve	6	(look at 6 above)
13	thirteen	6	(look at 6 above)
14	fourteen	9	(look at 9 above)
15	fifteen	8	(look at 8 above)
16	sixteen	7	(look at 7 above)
17	seventeen	7	(look at 7 above)
18	eighteen	9	(look at 9 above)
19	nineteen	8	(look at 8 above)
20	twenty	8	(look at 8 above)
21	twenty-one	6	(look at 6 above)
22	twenty-two	9	(look at 9 above)
23	twenty-three	9	(look at 9 above)
24	twenty-four	11	(look at 11 above)
25	twenty-five	10	(look at 10 above)
26	twenty-six	10	(look at 10 above)
27	twenty-seven	9	(look at 9 above)
28	twenty-eight	11	(look at 11 above)
29	twenty-nine	11	(look at 11 above)
30	thirty	10	(look at 10 above)
		7	(look at 7 above)

B C The student used a narrative description and tables to illustrate the nature of the "problem" (or, in this case, "trick").

M7d Mathematical Communication: The student considers purpose and audience when communicating about mathematics.

D E The student clearly explained the nature of the project as well as how it would be conveyed to the classroom audience.

M8e Putting Mathematics to Work: The student conducts a pure mathematics investigation, in which the student:

• decides on the area of mathematics to investigate, e.g., numbers, shapes, patterns.

D

• describes a question or concept to investigate.

D

• decides on representations that will be used, e.g., numbers, symbols, diagrams, shapes, or physical models.

A B C D E

• carries out the investigation.

A B C D E

• writes a report that includes any generalizations drawn from the investigation, and acknowledges assistance received from parents, peers, and teachers.

A B C D E

Three errors in counting the letters (32, 13, and 30) do not detract from the project.

A
In my investigation I want to find out why the number always has a four at the end. In the beginning I also thought that the number before four was five. It turned out sometimes it was and sometimes it wasn't. But it was either a five or a nine. This is a pattern I want to investigate as well.

Now if you compare these from the other ones you could see that you have less five's in these graph than the other one's. What I found out is that if the number keeps growing you will see more nines then fives.

The reason why any number you pick will always end in a four is that even if you pick a very large number when you spell the number the number of letters will always be less then the number. It keeps on going down. Finally, when you get to less than 30 letters you can see what happens above, it will keep on going down, and down until it gets to four.

I am going to present my investigation to the class by giving each person in my group a card. Then I will ask them all of these instructions.

Write down any number.
Please spell out that number.
E Write the number of letters in that number
Please spell out that number
Write the number of letters in that number...
If you get to four please raise your hand and keep it raised.

I will continue until all the hands are raised. The person that raises their hand the last wins. Everyone will see that this trick is true and will all have the number four.

Work Sample & Commentary: *Dream House Project*

Arithmetic
and Number   **M1**
Concepts

Geometry &
Measurement   **M2**
Concepts

Function &
Algebra
Concepts

Statistics &
Probability   **M4**
Concepts

Problem
Solving &
Reasoning

Mathematical **M6**
Skills & Tools

Mathematical **M7**
Communication

Putting
Mathematics   **M8**
to Work

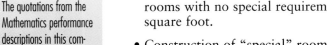

The quotations from the Mathematics performance descriptions in this commentary are excerpted. The complete performance descriptions are shown on pages 60-65.

The task

The teacher gave students the following instructions, and clarified them through an extended discussion:

Plan and design your own "dream house" within certain cost constraints. Here are the budget, cost, and building rules you will have to work with.

- You will have $200,000 to spend altogether.

- The land for the house costs $100,000.

- Construction of "regular" rooms (traditional rooms with no special requirements) costs $75 per square foot.

- Construction of "special" rooms (requiring special wiring, plumbing, or unusual materials) costs $150 per square foot.

- All houses must include a kitchen, bathroom, bedroom, and living room.

This work sample illustrates a standard-setting performance for the following parts of the standards:

M1 a **Arithmetic and Number Concepts: Add, subtract, multiply, and divide whole numbers.**

M2 b **Geometry and Measurement Concepts: Visualize and represent two dimensional views of simple rectangular three dimensional shapes.**

M2 g **Geometry and Measurement Concepts: Use basic ways of estimating and measuring the size of figures and objects in the real world.**

M2 k **Geometry and Measurement Concepts: Use scales in maps and scale drawings.**

M4 c **Statistics and Probability Concepts: Make statements and draw simple conclusions based on data.**

M6 a **Mathematical Skills and Tools: Add, subtract, multiply, and divide whole numbers correctly.**

M6 c **Mathematical Skills and Tools: Measure length, area, and perimeter accurately.**

M6 h **Mathematical Skills and Tools: Use measuring devices.**

M7 a **Mathematical Communication: Use appropriate mathematical terms, vocabulary, and language.**

M7 b **Mathematical Communication: Show mathematical ideas in a variety of ways.**

M7 d **Mathematical Communication: Consider purpose and audience when communicating about mathematics.**

M8 c **Putting Mathematics to Work: Design a physical structure.**

- Rooms and hallways must have reasonable areas.

- The overall design must be convenient and practical (e.g., provide easy access to rooms, allow for privacy, include doors and hallways in practical locations, etc.).

- The number of sides to your floor plan should be limited, to avoid a sprawling, awkward design.

To get started, you will:
- Complete a rough draft of your floor plan by cutting out the rooms from half-inch graph paper.

- Record the calculations of the area and cost on the cut-out of the room.

- Track your budget on a running budget sheet ("Budget Update").

- Meet in a response group to see if your rough draft is reasonable.

To finish, you will:
- Make a final draft of your floor plan without graph paper, using a ruler and protractor, and following the scale exactly.

- Draw a front and side view of your dream house based on your floor plan.

Circumstances of performance

This sample of student work was produced under the following conditions:

√ alone	in a group
√ in class	as homework
√ with teacher feedback	√ with peer feedback
timed	√ opportunity for revision

Students completed this project over the course of four weeks. They worked individually except when initially measuring the classroom as part of a pre-project activity ("Scale Model of Room 14"). They also met once in small peer response groups, and once with an editing partner.

The teacher reviewed students' progress on this project daily, and created the "House Project Response Group Meeting Notes" and the "Editing Checklist for House Description" in order to help students complete the project.

The students had worked with two digit multiplication and the concept of area prior to beginning the project. They were allowed to use calculators to check calculations and for multiplication with multipliers of three or more digits.

Dream House Project

What the work shows

M1 a Arithmetic and Number Concepts: The student adds, subtracts, multiplies...whole numbers with and without calculators; that is:

• adds, i.e., joins things together, increases.

A The student added costs of rooms to determine the amount remaining in the budget.

• subtracts, i.e., takes away, compares, finds the difference.

B The student subtracted to determine the amount of the budget remaining.

• multiplies, i.e., uses repeated addition, counts by multiples....

C The student multiplied the area of rooms by cost per square foot to determine the total cost of each room.

M2 b Geometry and Measurement Concepts: The student visualizes and represents two dimensional views of simple rectangular three dimensional shapes....

D The student visualized and represented the two dimensional house floor plan in side and front views, i.e., as if in three dimensions.

M2 g Geometry and Measurement Concepts: The student uses basic ways of estimating and measuring the size of figures and objects in the real world, including length, width, perimeter, and area.

E The student measured the length and width of the classroom in order to determine area.

Scale Model oof Room 14

Plan:
First, we measure the length and the width of the room. Then we mutiply the length and the width to find out the area. Then we mutiply the area and 75 dollars, because 75 dollars is the cost of each square foot. So we can find out the total cost. Daniel L and Meryl are measuring and michal and I are calculating.

Measuring: Length 36 feet, 6 inches rounded off 37 feet
width: 24 feet 4 ininches rounded off 24 feet
cost total: 66,600   24×3v-888   sq ft

I know 24×37 makes sense, because instead of doing 24 rows of 37, I just mutiply 24×37. Ther answer is 888.

M1 ▶ Arithmetic and Number Concepts

M2 ▶ Geometry & Measurement Concepts

Function & Algebra Concepts

M4 ▶ Statistics & Probability Concepts

Problem Solving & Reasoning

M6 ▶ Mathematical Skills & Tools

M7 ▶ Mathematical Communication

M8 ▶ Putting Mathematics to Work

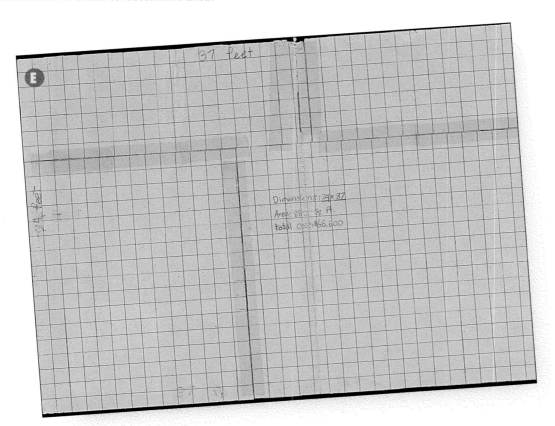

37 feet

24 feet

Dimensions: 24×37
Area: 88? sq ft.
total cost: $66,600

Dream House Project

M2 k Geometry and Measurement Concepts: The student uses...scales...for rectangular scale drawings based on work with concrete models and graph paper.

E **C** The student used half-inch square graph paper to create a ½ inch: 1 foot scale model of a room.

M4 c Statistics and Probability Concepts: The student makes statements and draws simple conclusions based on data; that is, reads data in line plots....

F The student interpreted line plot data in order to make decisions about reasonable areas of rooms in the floor plan.

M6 a Mathematical Skills and Tools: The student adds, subtracts, multiplies...whole numbers correctly.

A **B** **C** There is evidence of accurate calculations in these parts of the work and throughout.

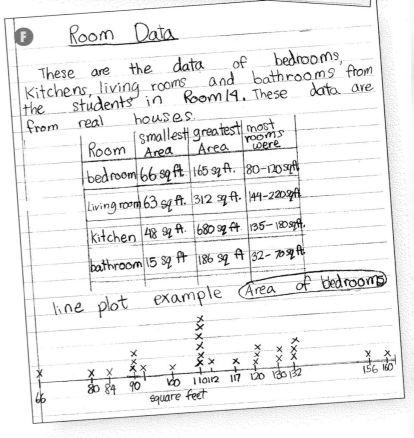

special room

12 ft.

Hot or Tub room

A
  12
 x12
 144 sq ft ← answer

12 ft.

B 144
  x 50
  # 7,600 dollars ← answer

I think this is the perfect size, because it's not too big and not too small for a hot tub indoors and it doesn't cost too much also.

F Room Data

These are the data of bedrooms, Kitchens, living rooms and bathrooms from the students in Room 14. These data are from real houses.

Room	smallest Area	greatest Area	most rooms were
bedroom	66 sq ft	165 sq ft.	80-120 sq ft
Living room	63 sq ft.	312 sq ft.	144-220 sq ft.
kitchen	48 sq ft.	680 sq ft	135-180 sq ft.
bathroom	15 sq ft	186 sq ft	32-70 sq ft.

line plot example (Area of bedrooms)

square feet
66 80 84 90 100 101 112 117 120 130 132 156 160

Dream House Project

Building Contract

- Name of homeowner: _____
- Total budget: $200,000
- Cost of land: $100,000
- Amount left to spend on house construction: $100,000
- Rooms required by room 14 code:
    - 1 bedroom (at least)
    - kitchen
    - living room
    - bathroom
- Cost to build regular rooms per square foot: $75 /sq.ft.
- All rooms that need special materials or extra work are called 'special rooms'. These rooms cost twice as much to build.
  Cost of special rooms: $150 /sq.ft.
- List some 'special rooms' you may want:
    - waterslide splash pool room
    - pet room
    - ice cream room
    - snow room
    - playground room
    - camping room
- I agree to plan and design my house according to this contract.

M6 c Mathematical Skills and Tools: The student measures length, area,...perimeter...accurately in...the customary...system.

C **E** These parts of the work provide evidence of accurate calculations that are supported by the calculations shown in the rough and final drafts.

M6 h Mathematical Skills and Tools: The student...uses measuring devices graded appropriately for given situations, such as rulers (customary to the ⅛ inch...), graph paper (customary to the inch or half-inch...)....

C **E** **G** The student used a ruler and graph paper to measure lengths of sides of rooms.

M7 a Mathematical Communication: The student uses appropriate mathematical terms, vocabulary, and language, based on prior conceptual work.

H The student used appropriate mathematical vocabulary to describe the process involved in completing the project, e.g., "area," "unit," "reasonable."

M1 ▶ Arithmetic and Number Concepts

M2 ▶ Geometry & Measurement Concepts

Function & Algebra Concepts

Statistics & Probability Concepts

Problem Solving & Reasoning

M6 ▶ Mathematical Skills & Tools

M7 ▶ Mathematical Communication

M8 ▶ Putting Mathematics to Work

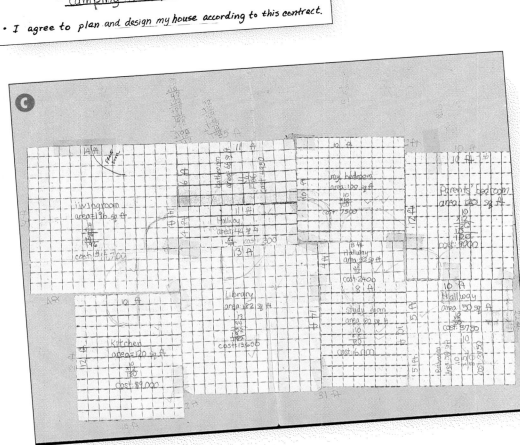

Dream House Project

B BUDGET UPDATE

Name: _____

Required Room	Area	Cost
· bathroom	45 sq ft	3375 ⁰⁰
· bedroom	100 sq ft	7500 ⁰⁰
· Kitchen	120 sq ft	9000 ⁰⁰
· Livingroom	196 sq ft	14 700 ⁰⁰

Total cost of 4 required rooms (SHOW CALCULATIONS)👀

```
 3375
 7500        3375+7500+9000+14700 =34575
 9000
+14700       answer
 34575
```

Amount of your building budget that is left (SHOW CALCULATIONS)👀

```
 100,000
-34575       100,000 - 34575 = 65425
 65425       answer
```

Other room	Area	Cost per sq.ft.	Cost	Budget Remaining
Library	182 sq ft	75 ⁰⁰	13650	51775 ⁰⁰
study room	80 sq ft	75 ⁰⁰	6000	

M7 b Mathematical Communication: The student shows mathematical ideas in a variety of ways, including words, numbers…graphs…tables….

B E F H

M7 d Mathematical Communication: The student considers purpose and audience when communicating about mathematics.

I The student communicated the purpose and explained the process for completing the project clearly enough for the project to be understood by an otherwise uninformed peer.

Arithmetic and Number Concepts **M1**
Geometry & Measurement Concepts **M2**
Function & Algebra Concepts
Statistics & Probability Concepts **M4**
Problem Solving & Reasoning
Mathematical Skills & Tools **M6**
Mathematical Communication **M7**
Putting Mathematics to Work **M8**

A

What is the exact amount of money I have left in my budget?

```
 14700        100000
+13650       - 78900
 28350        21100
  9000
 +6000
 43350
  3750
 +4950
 52050
  3300
  7500
 62850
  9900
  3750
 +2400
 78900
```

J

HOUSE PROJECT RESPONSE GROUP MEETING NOTES

Name: _____

· Are all the required rooms present ? YES ☑
  NO ☐ , needs _____

· Are the <u>areas</u> for the rooms <u>realistic</u> ?

  (O.K.)

· Is the <u>perimeter</u> of the house (the outside walls) <u>simple</u> or <u>complicated</u> ? (How many sides does house have ?)

  (O.K.)

· Are rooms, hallways and doors <u>convenient</u> ?

· Exactly how much budget is left over? $21,100

· NEXT STEPS:

  – What will you revise about your house plan ?
  I will revise nothing about my house plan

  – If you are not revising anything, why not ?
  because I had done everything right and [The Teacher] had checked it and he thinks everything is "O.K."

Dream House Project

M1 Arithmetic and Number Concepts

M2 Geometry & Measurement Concepts

Function & Algebra Concepts

M4 Statistics & Probability Concepts

Problem Solving & Reasoning

M6 Mathematical Skills & Tools

M7 Mathematical Communication

M8 Putting Mathematics to Work

Page 1

House Project— ROUGH DRAFT DESCRIPTION   Name: _____

¶ #1: Explain the project.... What is this? What's it about? How much did you have to spend? How much does one square foot cost? What rooms did you have to have? Was the land free? What is the SCALE (how long is one foot on your plan?)

The project is a house project. It's about buildin our own dream house. The total we could spend for our house is 100,000.00 and the land cost $100,000.00 too (the land is not free, of course) so all together including the house and the land, it cost $200,000.00. One square foot cost 75.00 for a regular room like a bedroom or a livingroom, but one square foot cost 150.00 for a special room like a swimmin pool. ½ inch is 1 square foot.

¶ #2: Explain about AREA .... What is area? What units do you use to measure area? Give a clear example – use one of your rooms to explain how you know how to figure out the area....

Area is how big is the whole thing. We use one square foot as one unit. My bedroom is 100 square feet, I did it by multip -lying it. I count how many squares are on one side and then, I count how many squares are on the top, then I mutiply it together and I get the answer of the

Page 2

whole room. I do that with the other rooms too. The answer I got of every room is how many square feet there are.

¶ #3: Show how you know how to use 2-digit multipli- cation to calculate a room's area.... (like 16 ft. x 12 ft.). Show how to figure out how much a room costs (explain clearly... If you used a calculator, explain how .... Explain how you could still figure it out even without a calculator)

Diagrams   numbers   pictures   words

If one of my room is 13 ft x 14 ft, I first do 3x4 =12. So I write the 2 and add the 10 to the 10x4 which is 40 but if I add a 10 to the 40 it be 50 so I write the 5 on the left side of 2, it's 52. Then I do 3x10 equals to 30. I write the 3 under the 5 on top from 52. Then I do 10x10=100 and I write the 1 on the left side of 3. Then I add the 52 and 130 together and I got the answer of 182 sq ft. Here's what it looks like:

$$\begin{array}{r} 13 \\ \times 14 \\ \hline 52 \\ 13 \\ \hline 182 \end{array}$$

Page 3

To find out the cost of a regular room you mutiply the total sq ft to 75.00 because each square foot of a regular room is 75.00 so I do the total square foot of the room times 75.00 and if it's a special room, you also use the total square feet of that room times 150.00 because that's how much one square foot cost of a special room

¶ #4: Explain how you know that your rooms have a reasonable area (you can use the notes you already have on the back of your first draft rooms... just give a few examples – you don't need to explain about every room)

I know my rooms have a reasonable area because I looked at the rooms chart that my class had made, those rooms are real rooms that the class had measured. Anyway, I compared my rooms to the charts the class had made, and see if it is too big or too small or perfect, my rooms always turns out to be perfect and another way I could tell is by cutting out fake furnitures to put in the rooms and see if it fits.

Page 4

¶ #5: Explain:
• How many square feet does your finished house have?
• How much does it cost, altogether? (explain where your calculations are so they can be looked at)
• How much money is leftover in your budget? (explain how you figured this out)

My finished house have 1052 square feet, because I added up every room's total square feet and I got the answer. Then I check it with the other paper where I wrote down my exact square feet of my whole house and it's the same. Then I time 1040 with 75, becau: that's how many square feet each squar feet cost. I used the calculator. I got the answer of 78000.00, that's how much money I spend. I used the calculator. I still have 22000.00 left I used the calculator, but I also have those answer in the other sheet of paper. The whole perimeter of my house is 142 ft. I did it by countin; the walls of my house.

Dream House Project

K

EDITING CHECKLIST FOR HOUSE DESCRIPTION

Name: _____
Editing partner: Annie
Date: 3-29-95

¶ #1:

✓ Uses <u>complete</u> <u>sentences</u> ☑
✓ Paragraph begins with a <u>topic sentence</u> ☑
✓ Would a parent or a 4th grader from another class understand the project by reading ¶#1? ☑

✓ Explains about the budget clearly ☑
✓ Explains cost of one square foot for <u>both</u> special and regular rooms ☑
✓ Clearly explains what the <u>scale</u> of the house plan is ($\frac{1}{2}$ inch = 1 foot and $\frac{1}{4}$ square inch = 1 square foot) ☑

¶ #2:

✓ Explains clearly what AREA <u>is</u> ☑
✓ Explains what kind of units are used to measure area ☑

✓ Uses an example of how he or she figured out the area of one of their rooms. ☑

✓ Uses complete sentences ☑
✓ Begins with a topic sentence ☑

¶. #3:

✓ Uses numbers, words, and diagrams to explain how to use long multiplication to figure out area (like 16 x 12 or 18 x 9...) ☑

✓ Explains <u>how</u> to figure out a room's cost ☑

✓ Uses <u>complete sentences</u> and a <u>topic sentence</u> ☑

¶ #4:

✓ Explains why he or she knows for sure that rooms are a <u>reasonable area</u> (for example, explains how furniture could fit, or how room compares to real room areas on our line plots...) ☑

✓ Uses <u>complete sentences</u> and a <u>topic sentence</u> ☑

¶ #5:

✓ Gives the <u>total area</u> of the entire house in square feet ☑
✓ Gives the total house cost ☑
✓ Gives the amount remaining in budget (amount leftover + cost <u>should</u> = $100,000) ☑
✓ Gives total <u>perimeter</u> of house in feet (<u>not</u> square feet...) ☑

M8 ‹ Putting Mathematics to Work: The student conducts a project to design a physical structure, in which the student:
• decides on a structure to design, the size and budget constraints, and the scale of design.

G The student made the important decisions in planning the dream house.

• makes a first draft of the design, and revises and improves the design in response to input from peers and teachers.

C I J K The student made revisions to the rough draft floor plan and to the rough draft description on the basis of feedback from peers and the teacher.

• makes a final draft and report of the design, drawn and written so that another person could make the structure....

I G

There are several spelling and grammatical errors in the rough draft work. Only the final draft description and floor plan were edited for spelling and grammar. A few errors remain in the final draft work; however, the errors do not detract from its accuracy or clarity (e.g., "mutiply" for "multiply").

Arithmetic and Number Concepts **M1**

Geometry & Measurement Concepts **M2**

Function & Algebra Concepts

Statistics & Probability Concepts **M4**

Problem Solving & Reasoning

Mathematical Skills & Tools **M6**

Mathematical Communication **M7**

Putting Mathematics to Work **M8**

Dream House Project

I

—Designed House.

The project is a house project. It's about building our own dream house. The total we could spend for our house is $100,000 and the land cost $100,000 too, (the land is not free, of course) so all together including the house and the land, it cost $200,000. One square foot cost $75.00 for a regular room like a bedroom or a livingroom, but one square foot cost $150.00 for a special room like a swimming pool. ½ inch is one foot in the design.

H

Area is space covered in the whole thing. We use one square foot as one unit. My bedroom is 100 square feet. I did it by mutiplying it. I count how many feet there are on one side and then I count how many feet there are on the top, then I mutiply it together and I get the answer of how many **square** feet there are in the whole room. I do that with all the other rooms too.

If one of my rooms is 13 ft × 14 ft, I first do 3×4=12 so I write the 2 and add the 10 to the 4X10 which is 40, but if I add a 10 to the 40, it'll be 50 so I write the 5 on the left side of 2, it's 52. Then I do 3X10 equals to 30 I write the 3 under the 5 on top from 52. Then I do 10X10 and I write the 1 on the left side of 3. Then I add the 52 and 130 together and I got the answer of 182 square feet. Here's what it looks like:

$$\begin{array}{r} 13 \\ \times 4 \\ \hline 52 \\ +13 \\ \hline 182 \end{array}$$

To find out the cost of a regular room, you mutiply the total square feet to $75.00, because each square foot of a regular room is $75.00 so I do the total square foot of the room times $75.00 and if the room is a special room, you then use the total square fet of that room times $150.00, because that's how much one square foot cost for a special room.

I **know** all my rooms have a reasonable area, because I looked at the rooms chart that my class had made, those rooms are real rooms that the class had measured. Anyway, I compared my rooms to the charts the class had made and see if it is too big or too small or just perfect, my rooms always turns out to be perfect. Another way I could tell is by cutting out fake furnitures to put in the rooms and see if it fits.

My finished house have 1040 square feet, because I added up every room's total square feet and I got the answer. Then I check it with the other paper where I wrote down my exact square feet of my whole house and it's the same. Then I times 1040 with 75, because that's how much each square feet costs for a regular room. I used the calculator, I got the answer of $78,000. That's how much money I'll spend. I still have $22,000 left, but I also have those answer in the

---

other sheet of paper. The whole perimeter of my house is 142 ft. I did it by counting the walls of my house and adding it together.

Dream House Project

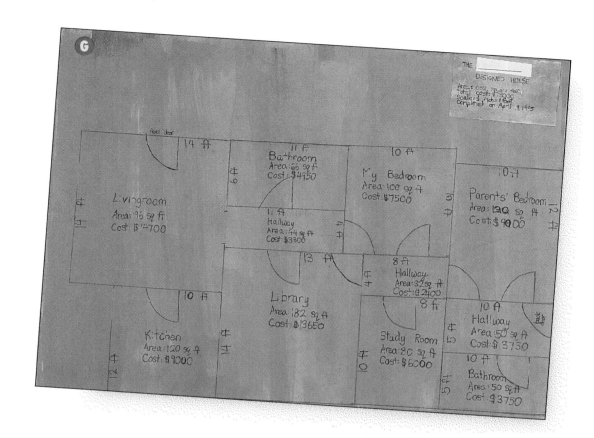

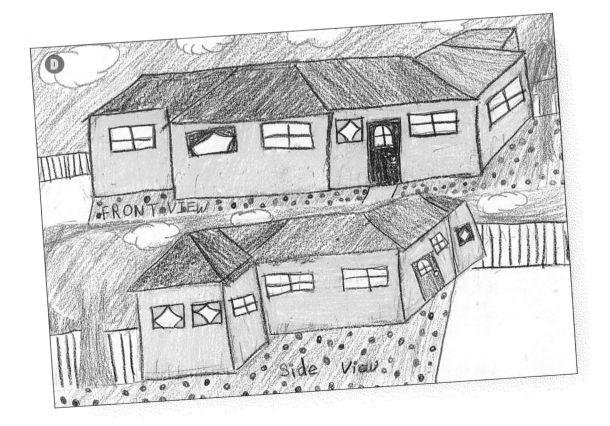

Work Sample & Commentary: *Constructing a Polyhedron*

The task

The teacher gave students the following instructions, and clarified them through an extended discussion:

Look at the polyhedra on this poster. Choose one of them to construct. You will be able to use a diagram of the net in order to help you see how the shapes fit together. You will also:

• Choose a length for the side of the polygons that will be the faces of your polyhedron.

• Use a compass to make a template of the polygons that make the faces of your polyhedron. The main face you will use will be an equilateral triangle.

• Extend the sides to make flaps, and then join the faces together by using rubber bands on the flaps.

• Write about your construction.

The main choices of polyhedra to construct included the regular octahedron (a figure with eight equilateral triangles as faces), the regular icosahedron (a figure with 20 equilateral triangles as faces), and the cuboctahedron (a figure with six squares and eight triangles as faces).

The student in this sample constructed a snub icosadodecahedron. This polyhedron was not offered as a choice for students to construct, because it was considered too complex for elementary students. The snub icosadodecahedron is a polyhedron made of 80 triangles and 12 pentagons. (Its name is derived from the dodecahedron, which is composed of pentagons, and the icosahedron, which is composed of equilateral triangles.)

In order to complete this task, the student voluntarily:

• figured out the net for the polyhedron, with assistance from the teacher;

• received additional instruction from the teacher about how to use a protractor to measure the angles and how to construct a pentagon;

• spent several hours beyond the allotted time for the project, including before and after school and during lunch recesses.

Circumstances of performance

This sample of student work was produced under the following conditions:

√ alone   in a group
√ in class   as homework
√ with teacher feedback   with peer feedback
  timed   √ opportunity for revision

Before beginning this project, students had been working with two dimensional geometry concepts, especially symmetry, congruence, quadrilaterals, triangles, circles, and diameter. They had constructed two dimensional "stained glass windows," according to specifications about the geometry required.

This student's work illustrates parts of the standard for Geometry and Measurement Concepts. In addition, the sample helps to illustrate what it means for an elementary student to exceed the standard in some areas, e.g., the student constructs and works with pentagons, measuring the angles of the pentagon in degrees.

The quotations from the Mathematics performance descriptions in this commentary are excerpted. The complete performance descriptions are shown on pages 60-65.

This work sample illustrates a standard-setting performance for the following parts of the standards:

M2 d Geometry and Measurement Concepts: Use many types of figures.

M2 f Geometry and Measurement Concepts: Extend and create geometric patterns using concrete and pictorial models.

M2 g Geometry and Measurement Concepts: Use basic ways of estimating and measuring the size of figures and objects in the real world.

M2 i Geometry and Measurement Concepts: Select and use units for estimating and measuring length.

M6 b Mathematical Skills and Tools: Estimate numerically and spatially.

M6 c Mathematical Skills and Tools: Measure accurately.

M6 e Mathematical Skills and Tools: Refer to geometric shapes and terms correctly.

M6 h Mathematical Skills and Tools: Use measuring devices.

Arithmetic and Number Concepts

M2 ▸ Geometry & Measurement Concepts

Function & Algebra Concepts

Statistics & Probability Concepts

Problem Solving & Reasoning

M6 ▸ Mathematical Skills & Tools

Mathematical Communication

Putting Mathematics to Work

Constructing a Polyhedron

E ➤ First thing I did was make the SNUB ICOSIDODECAHEDRON. Then When I was done making it I notice some stuff. One thing I notice was that the faces on my snub icosidodecahedron were pentigons and triangles. And faces means sides. Then I notice that the vertex was 4. the vertex means the points that met together. An example is on the next page. Then I notice that all around the pentigon is triangles and that there are 15 that fit around a pentigon. Then I notice that a pentigon never touch another pentigon. And to make it you had to make 78 triangles and 12 pentigons to make the Snub Icosidodecahedron. But I notice some of that stuff I had to know before I started.

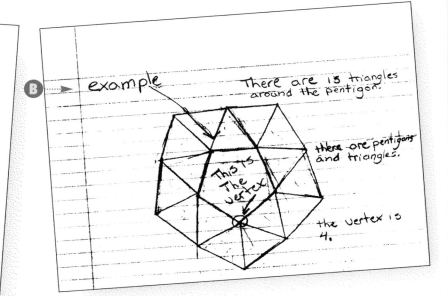

B ➤ example

There are 15 triangles around the pentigon.

This is The vertex

there are pentigons and triangles.

the vertex is 4.

What the work shows

M2 d Geometry and Measurement Concepts: The student uses many types of figures (angles, triangles,...polygons) and identifies the figures by their properties....

A The student used triangles; her use of the pentagon and snub icosadodecahedron represents work that exceeds the standard for this level.

M2 f Geometry and Measurement Concepts: The student extends and creates geometric patterns using concrete and pictorial models.

B The student found a pattern in this polyhedron.

M2 g Geometry and Measurement Concepts: The student uses basic ways of estimating and measuring the size of figures and objects in the real world....

A C In order to construct the triangles and pentagons, the student measured the length of the sides.

M2 i Geometry and Measurement Concepts: The student selects and uses units, both formal and informal as appropriate, for estimating and measuring quantities such as...length....

A The use of inches is appropriate for this level; the use of degrees exceeds the standard for this level.

M6 b Mathematical Skills and Tools: The student estimates numerically and spatially.

A D The successful completion of the icosadodecahedron provides evidence that the student estimated spatially and numerically, as both kinds of estimation were clearly required in the construction.

M6 c Mathematical Skills and Tools: The student measures length...accurately in...the customary... system.

A C

M6 e Mathematical Skills and Tools: The student refers to geometric shapes and terms correctly with concrete objects or drawings, including triangle,...side,...face,...point, line...; and refers with assistance to...polygon, polyhedron, angle, vertex....

E The student refers correctly to angle, triangle, pentagon, and icosadodecahedron. The student appears to have a working understanding of the term "vertex" but has not yet developed a clear definition. (The writing of "4½" is also incorrect in some places.)

M6 h Mathematical Skills and Tools: The student uses...measuring devices...to achieve solutions.

A C The use of a ruler is appropriate for this level; the use of the compass and protractor exceeds the standard.

If this project were written up in a more systematic way, it would illustrate an example of a pure mathematics investigation, one of the projects described in **M6**.

Several words are misspelled in the written portion of the work. This was a class assignment and was not intended to be further edited for spelling or grammar. The focus of the assignment was the construction. The spelling and grammar errors are reasonable for first draft work, e.g., "notice" for "noticed" and "pentigon" for "pentagon."

Readers who build this figure will discover that there are actually 80 triangles, not 78, as the student reports.

Constructing a Polyhedron

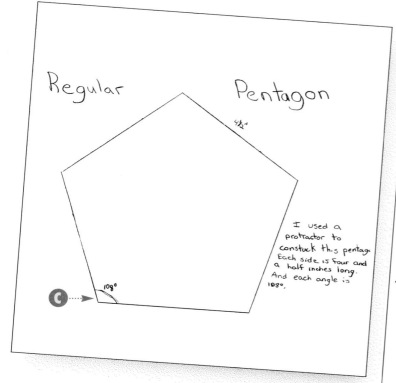

Regular Pentagon

4½"

I used a protractor to constuck this pentago. Each side is four and a half inches long. And each angle is 108°.

C ····▶ 108°

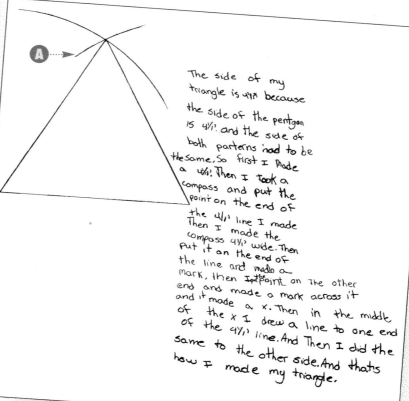

A ····▶

The side of my triangle is 4½" because the side of the pentgon is 4½" and the side of both parterns had to be the same. So first I made a 4½". Then I took a compass and put the point on the end of the 4½" line I made Then I made the compass 4½" wide. Then put it on the end of the line and made a mark. then I put point on the other end and made a mark across it and it made a x. Then in the middle of the x I drew a line to one end of the 4½" line. And Then I did the same to the other side. And thats how I made my triangle.

Arithmetic and Number Concepts

M2 ▶ Geometry & Measurement Concepts

Function & Algebra Concepts

Statistics & Probability Concepts

Problem Solving & Reasoning

M6 ▶ Mathematical Skills & Tools

Mathematical Communication

Putting Mathematics to Work

D

Introduction to the performance standards for

Science

There are two widely used and respected national documents in science which we have taken into account: the National Research Council (NRC) *National Science Education Standards* (1996) and the American Association for the Advancement of Science (AAAS) Project 2061 *Benchmarks for Science Literacy* (1993). We found the AAAS analysis of the Benchmarks and the NRC Draft to be helpful in seeing the substantial degree of agreement between the two documents. We also consulted New Standards partner statements about standards and international documents, including the work of the Third International Mathematics and Science Study and the Organisation for Economic Co-operation and Development. Many of these sources, like the *Benchmarks*, give greater emphasis to technology and the applications of science than does the NRC.

The framework for the Science performance standards reflects New Standards partner representatives' distillation of these several sources of guidance:

S1 Physical Sciences Concepts;

S2 Life Sciences Concepts;

S3 Earth and Space Sciences Concepts;

S4 Scientific Connections and Applications;

S5 Scientific Thinking;

S6 Scientific Tools and Technologies;

S7 Scientific Communication;

S8 Scientific Investigation.

As the amount of scientific knowledge explodes, the need for students to have deep understanding of fundamental concepts and ideas upon which to build increases; as technology makes information readily available, the need to memorize vocabulary and formulas decreases. There is general agreement among the science education community, in principle, that studying fewer things more deeply is the direction we would like to go. The choices about what to leave out and what to keep are hotly debated. There are 855 benchmarks and the content standards section of the NRC standards runs nearly 200 pages, so there are still choices to be made in crafting a reasonable set of performance standards.

When the goal is deep understanding, it is necessary to revisit concepts over time. Students show progressively deeper understanding as they use the concept in a range of familiar situations to explain observations and make predictions, then use the concept in unfamiliar situations; as they represent the concept in multiple ways (through words, diagrams, graphs, or charts), and explain the concept to another person. The conceptual understanding standards make explicit that students should be able to demonstrate understanding of a scientific concept "by using a concept accurately to explain observations and make predictions and by representing the concept in multiple ways (through words, diagrams, graphs, or charts, as appropriate)." Both aspects of understanding—explaining and representing—are required to meet these standards.

For most people and most concepts, there is a progression from phenomenological to empirical to theoretical, or from a qualitative to a quantitative understanding. We have chosen one important concept, density, to illustrate the progression. To do this we use "Flinkers" at the elementary school level (see page 136), "Discovering Density" at the middle school level (see Volume 2, page 101), and "The Density of Sand" at the high school level (see Volume 3, page 84). The expectation for any particular concept at any particular level can only be described with a satisfactory degree of precision and accuracy in the degree of detail adopted by AAAS and NRC; we strongly urge users of these performance standards to consult either or both of those documents for guidance on other concepts.

Complementing the conceptual understanding standards, S5 - S8 focus on areas of the science curriculum that need particular attention and a new or renewed emphasis:

S5 Scientific Thinking;

S6 Scientific Tools and Technologies;

S7 Scientific Communication;

S8 Scientific Investigation.

Establishing separate standards for these areas is a mechanism for highlighting the importance of these areas, but does not imply that they are independent of conceptual understanding. The NRC standards, by declaring that inquiry is not only a teaching method but also an object of study, should put the time-worn "content versus process" debate to rest, and focus effort on combining traditionally defined content with process. As the work samples that follow illustrate, good work usually provides evidence of both.

Resources

Reviewers of drafts of these performance standards have pointed out that our expectations are more demanding, both in terms of student time and access to resources, than they consider reasonable for all students. We acknowledge the distance between our goals and the status quo, and the fact that there is a tremendous disparity in opportunities between the most and least advantaged students. We think that there are at least two strategies that must be pursued to achieve our goals—making better use of existing, out-of-school resources and making explicit the connection between particular resources and particular standards.

Best practice in science has always included extensive inquiry and investigation, but it is frequently given less emphasis in the face of competing demands for student time and teacher resources. An elementary teacher faced with the unfamiliar territory of project work in science or a secondary teacher faced with the prospect of guiding 180 projects and investigations can legitimately throw up his or her hands and cry, "Help!" Youth and community-based organizations, such as the Boy Scouts of America, Girl Scouts of the U.S.A., and 4-H, have science education on their agenda. Thus, we have incorporated examples of projects and investigations that are done outside of school to make clear that help is available.

We acknowledge that some of the performance descriptions and examples presuppose resources that are not currently available to all students, even those who take advantage of the out-of-school opportunities available to them. Yet, New Standards partners have adopted a Social Compact, which says, in part, "Specifically, we pledge to do everything in our power to ensure all students a fair shot at reaching the new performance standards…This means that they will be taught a curriculum that will prepare them for the assessments, that their teachers will have the preparation to enable them to teach it well, and there will be an equitable distribution of the resources the students and their teachers need to succeed."

All of the district, state, and national documents in science make explicit the need for students to have hands-on experience and to use information tools. Thus, for example, **S6**, Scientific Tools and Technologies, makes explicit reference to using telecommunications to acquire and share information. A recent National Center for Education Statistics survey recently reported that only 50% of schools and fewer than 9% of instructional rooms currently have access to the Internet. We know that this is an equity issue—that far more than 9% of the homes in the United States have access to the Internet and that schools must make sure that students' access to information and ideas does not depend on what they get at home—so we have crafted performance standards that would use the Internet so that people will make sure that all students have access to it. Since the New Standards partners have made a commitment to create the learning environments where students can develop the knowledge and skills that are delineated here, we hope that making these requirements explicit will help those who allocate resources to understand the consequences of their actions in terms of student performance.

Performance Descriptions *Science*

To see how these performance descriptions compare with the expectations for middle school and high school, turn to pages 232-239.

The Science standards are founded upon both the National Research Council's *National Science Education Standards* and the American Association for the Advancement of Science's Project 2061 *Benchmarks for Science Literacy*. These documents, each of which runs to several hundred pages, contain detail that amplifies the meaning of the terms used in the performance descriptions.

S1 Physical Sciences Concepts

The student demonstrates conceptual understanding by using a concept accurately to explain observations and make predictions and by representing the concept in multiple ways (through words, diagrams, graphs, or charts, as appropriate). Both aspects of understanding—explaining and representing—are required to meet this standard.

The student produces evidence that demonstrates understanding of:

S1a Properties of objects and materials, such as similarities and differences in the size, weight, and color of objects; the ability of materials to react with other substances; and different states of materials.

S1b Position and motion of objects, such as how the motion of an object can be described by tracing and measuring its position over time; and how sound is produced by vibrating objects.

S1c Light, heat, electricity, and magnetism, such as the variation of heat and temperature; how light travels in a straight line until it strikes an object or how electrical circuits work.

Examples of activities through which students might demonstrate conceptual understanding of physical sciences include:

▲ Investigate the browning process of apple slices and the factors that slow or speed up the process. **1a**

▲ Use physical properties such as color, texture, or hardness to sort objects into two or more categories; change the categories to include a new object; and explain the rule to another student. **1a, 4a**

▲ Use diagrams to explain the characteristics of ice melting, water boiling, and steam condensing; and illustrate how these kinds of characteristics can affect environments and the organisms that live in them. **1a, 2a, 2b, 2c**

▲ Predict the bouncing pattern of a basketball under different throwing conditions using previous observations of force and motion. **1b**

▲ Make a musical instrument, explain the relationship between sound and shape, and compare this to a structure/function relationship in an organism. **1b, 2a**

▲ Investigate heat and friction by burning, rubbing, or mixing substances together; explain similarities and differences. **1c**

▲ Use knowledge of magnetism to predict what materials will be attracted, repelled, or unaffected by a magnet, then conduct an experiment to confirm or reject their predictions. **1c, 3a**

S2 Life Sciences Concepts

The student demonstrates conceptual understanding by using a concept accurately to explain observations and make predictions and by representing the concept in multiple ways (through words, diagrams, graphs, or charts, as appropriate). Both aspects of understanding—explaining and representing—are required to meet this standard.

The student produces evidence that demonstrates understanding of:

S2a Characteristics of organisms, such as survival and environmental support; the relationship between structure and function; and variations in behavior.

S2b Life cycles of organisms, such as how inheritance and environment determine the characteristics of an organism; and that all plants and animals have life cycles.

S2c Organisms and environments, such as the interdependence of animals and plants in an ecosystem; and populations and their effects on the environment.

S2d Change over time, such as evolution and fossil evidence depicting the great diversity of organisms developed over geologic history.

Examples of activities through which students might demonstrate conceptual understanding of life sciences include:

▲ Predict how long a plant will live planted in a closed glass jar located by a window; and explain what additional information regarding the plant and the surrounding environment would be needed to improve the prediction. **2a, 1a, 3a, 3b**

▲ Complete a 4-H animal care project; write a report explaining the growth and development of the animal and present the animal at the county-wide fair. **2a, 2b, 2c, 7a, 8b**

▲ Make drawings of observations showing the life cycle of a plant or animal. **2b**

▲ Explain the differences between inherited and environmental features of individuals such as flower colors or bike riding ability and describe the physical characteristics of the environment that could affect these features. **2a, 2b, 2c, 2d, 1a, 4a**

▲ Plan the supplies and equipment needed for a camping trip and explain their purposes. **2a, 2c, 4b, 4d, M8d, A1c**

▲ Explain how organisms, both human and other, cause changes in their environments and how some of these changes can be detrimental to other organisms. **2a, 2b, 2c, 2d, 1a, 4a, 4b**

▲ Use more than one medium such as models, text, drawings, or oral explanations to show how various organisms have changed over time to fill a variety of niches. **2c, 2d, 4a**

▲ Describe the similarities and differences between fossils and related contemporary organisms and explain how environmental factors contributed to these similarities and differences. **2a, 2c, 2d, 1a, 3a, 3c, 4a**

S3 Earth and Space Sciences Concepts

The student demonstrates conceptual understanding by using a concept accurately to explain observations and make predictions and by representing the concept in multiple ways (through words, diagrams, graphs or charts, as appropriate). Both aspects of understanding—explaining and representing—are required to meet this standard.

The student produces evidence that demonstrates understanding of:

S3a Properties of Earth materials, such as water and gases; and the properties of rocks and soils, such as texture, color, and ability to retain water.

S3b Objects in the sky, such as Sun, Moon, planets, and other objects that can be observed and described; and the importance of the Sun to provide the light and heat necessary for survival.

S3c Changes in Earth and sky, such as changes caused by weathering, volcanism, and earthquakes; and the patterns of movement of objects in the sky.

Examples of activities through which students might demonstrate conceptual understanding of Earth and space sciences include:

- Investigate how the properties of soil can affect the growth of a plant. **3a, 1a, 2a, 2b, 2c, 4a**
- Predict what kinds of materials would be useful for different purposes, such as in buildings or as sources of fuel, because of their physical and chemical properties. **3a, 1a**
- Observe and keep a record of the shape of the Moon for several months; and then make drawings predicting what will happen during the next week. **3b, 3c**
- Make observations of the changes in an object's shadow during the course of a day and investigate the source of the variation. **3b, 3c**
- Write a story that describes what happens to a drop of water and the physical environment through which it flows as it travels from a lake to a river via the Earth's atmosphere. **3a, 3b, 1a, 4a**
- Collect information from a weather station and use the information to explain the patterns of change from fall to winter in terms of weather and the position and movement of objects in the sky. **3b, 3c, 4a, M1a, M1c, M1f, A1a**

S4 Scientific Connections and Applications

The student demonstrates conceptual understanding by using a concept accurately to explain observations and make predictions and by representing the concept in multiple ways (through words, diagrams, graphs or charts, as appropriate). Both aspects of understanding—explaining and representing—are required to meet this standard.

The student produces evidence that demonstrates understanding of:

S4a Big ideas and unifying concepts, such as order and organization; models, form and function; change and constancy; and cause and effect.

S4b The designed world, such as development of agricultural techniques; and the viability of technological designs.

S4c Personal health, such as nutrition, substance abuse, and exercise; germs and toxic substances; personal and environmental safety.

S4d Science as a human endeavor, such as communication, cooperation, and diverse input in scientific research; and the importance of reason, intellectual honesty, and skepticism.

Examples of activities through which students might demonstrate conceptual understanding of scientific connections and applications include:

- Conduct an experiment to determine which brand of paper towel is the best in terms of form and function, cause and effect, cost and personal preference, and write an advertisement for the brand highlighting findings of the experiment. **4a, 4b, 1a, 3a**
- Earn the Webelos Engineer Badge (Boy Scouts of America) or the Brownie Building Art Try-It (Girl Scouts of the U.S.A.) and explain the design of the model. **4b, 4d, 1a, 1b, 1c**
- Explain why people should wash their hands when preparing food. **4c, 3c**
- Make recommendations to improve the selection of food in the school vending machines so that students can make healthier choices. **4c, 2b, M8a, A1b**
- Build a solar cooker and explain what foods can or cannot be cooked safely within the temperature range achieved. **4b, 4c, 2a**
- Interview a person who has a job that interests you and write a report explaining how studying science helped the person prepare for the job. **4d**

Samples of student work that illustrate standard-setting performances for these standards can be found on pages 136-158.

The examples that follow the performance descriptions for each standard are examples of the work students might do to demonstrate their achievement. The examples also indicate the nature and complexity of activities that are appropriate to expect of students at the elementary level.

The cross-references that follow the examples highlight examples for which the same activity, and possibly even the same piece of work, may enable students to demonstrate their achievement in relation to more than one standard. In some cases, the cross-references highlight examples of activities through which students might demonstrate their achievement in relation to standards for more than one subject matter.

Performance Descriptions *Science*

S5 Scientific Thinking

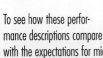

To see how these performance descriptions compare with the expectations for middle school and high school, turn to pages 232-239.

The Science standards are founded upon both the National Research Council's *National Science Education Standards* and the American Association for the Advancement of Science's Project 2061 *Benchmarks for Science Literacy.* These documents, each of which runs to several hundred pages, contain detail that amplifies the meaning of the terms used in the performance descriptions.

The student demonstrates scientific inquiry and problem solving by using thoughtful questioning and reasoning strategies, common sense and conceptual understanding from Science Standards 1 to 4, and appropriate methods to investigate the natural world; that is, the student:

S5 a Asks questions about natural phenomena; objects and organisms; and events and discoveries.

S5 b Uses concepts from Science Standards 1 to 4 to explain a variety of observations and phenomena.

S5 c Uses evidence from reliable sources to construct explanations.

S5 d Evaluates different points of view using relevant experiences, observations, and knowledge; and distinguishes between fact and opinion.

S5 e Identifies problems; proposes and implements solutions; and evaluates the accuracy, design, and outcomes of investigations.

S5 f Works individually and in teams to collect and share information and ideas.

Examples of activities through which students might demonstrate scientific thinking include:

▲ Evaluate the claims of a new product: describe the questions and evidence required to substantiate the claims; conduct an investigation to test ideas; and evaluate the accuracy of the conclusions. **5a, 5b, 5c, 5e**

▲ Work with others to examine the changes in the flora, fauna, and environment in a one square meter plot, caused by recent construction, explain the observations, and make predictions about the future of this microsystem. **5a, 5b, 5c, 5d, 5f, 2a, 2b, 2c**

▲ Use data from one investigation to generate a prediction and conduct a new investigation. **5a, 5b, 5c, 5e**

▲ Summarize a series of newspaper and magazine articles on a current topic, e.g., El Niño; use multiple sources to evaluate accuracy in the articles; and write a revised article putting all the relevant ideas together. **5a, 5b, 5c, 5d, 3a**

S6 Scientific Tools and Technologies

The student demonstrates competence with the tools and technologies of science by using them to collect data, make observations, analyze results, and accomplish tasks effectively; that is, the student:

S6 a Uses technology and tools (such as rulers, computers, balances, thermometers, watches, magnifiers, and microscopes) to gather data and extend the senses.

S6 b Collects and analyzes data using concepts and techniques in Mathematics Standard 4, such as average, data displays, graphing, variability, and sampling.

S6 c Acquires information from multiple sources, such as experimentation and print and non-print sources.

Examples of activities through which students might demonstrate competence with the tools and technologies of science include:

▲ Collect information from the United States Geological Survey and use the information to identify trends in geologic movement in your hometown or state. **6c, 3a, 3c, 5c**

▲ Conduct a survey of students' electricity and gas use at home, compare the data to that of other students, and select an appropriate way to display the comparative data. **6b, 2c, 4b**

▲ Use telecommunications to compare data on similar investigations with students in another school. **6c**

▲ Use electronic data bases to find out about the nutritional value of food available in the cafeteria and compare with alternative selections or snack foods. **6c, 4c**

S7 Scientific Communication

The student demonstrates effective scientific communication by clearly describing aspects of the natural world using accurate data, graphs, or other appropriate media to convey depth of conceptual understanding in science; that is, the student:

S7 a Represents data and results in multiple ways, such as numbers, tables, and graphs; drawings, diagrams, and artwork; and technical and creative writing.

S7 b Uses facts to support conclusions.

S7 c Communicates in a form suited to the purpose and the audience, such as writing instructions that others can follow.

S7 d Critiques written and oral explanations, and uses data to resolve disagreements.

Examples of activities through which students might demonstrate competence in scientific communication include:

▲ Write and illustrate a creative story to explain the food chain to a younger brother or sister. **7a, 7c, 2c**

▲ Make a poster of charts and graphs to communicate effective nutrition and health habits. **7a, 2a, 4b**

▲ Work with other students to create a skit depicting the sequence of events and the characters in an important scientific discovery. **7c, 4d**

▲ Prepare a report, with graphs, charts, and diagrams, on the optimal number and placement of recycling containers, based on trash disposal data from the classroom and the entire school. **7a, 4b, 6b, M7, A1b**

S8 Scientific Investigation

The student demonstrates scientific competence by completing projects drawn from the following kinds of investigations, including at least one full investigation each year and, over the course of elementary school, investigations that integrate several aspects of Science Standards 1 to 7 and represent all four of the kinds of investigation:

S8 a An experiment, such as conducting a fair test.

S8 b A systematic observation, such as a field study.

S8 c A design, such as building a model or scientific apparatus.

S8 d Non-experimental research using print and electronic information, such as journals, video, or computers.

A single project may draw on more than one kind of investigation. A full investigation includes:

• Questions that can be studied using the resources available.

• Procedures that are safe, humane, and ethical; and that respect privacy and property rights.

• Data that have been collected and recorded (see also Science Standard 6) in ways that others can verify and analyze using skills expected at this grade level (see also Mathematics Standard 4).

• Data and results that have been represented (see also Science Standard 7) in ways that fit the context.

• Recommendations, decisions, and conclusions based on evidence.

• Acknowledgment of references and contributions of others.

• Results that are communicated appropriately to audiences.

• Reflection and defense of conclusions and recommendations from other sources and peer review.

Examples of projects through which students might demonstrate competence in scientific investigation include:

▲ Design, make, and fly kites; modifying the kites so they fly higher, maneuver more easily, or achieve some other goal. **8a, 8c**

▲ Investigate why different plants live in the cracks of the sidewalk in different areas around the school. **8b, 2a**

▲ Design and build a Rube Goldberg device and explain how changing aspects of the design made it work better. **8c, 4b**

▲ Research a particular disease; compare local with national risk factors; and produce an information pamphlet that communicates the characteristics and risk associated with the disease. **8d, 4c**

▲ Make a series of drawings and explain the seasonal succession of plants in a field near the school. **8d, 2b**

▲ With a partner, select an endangered plant or animal in your area; collect information from reference books, magazines, video; debate whether the plant or animal should be saved or allowed to disappear, and why. **8d, 2c, 6c**

Samples of student work that illustrate standard-setting performances for these standards can be found on pages 136-158.

The examples that follow the performance descriptions for each standard are examples of the work students might do to demonstrate their achievement. The examples also indicate the nature and complexity of activities that are appropriate to expect of students at the elementary level.

The cross-references that follow the examples highlight examples for which the same activity, and possibly even the same piece of work, may enable students to demonstrate their achievement in relation to more than one standard. In some cases, the cross-references highlight examples of activities through which students might demonstrate their achievement in relation to standards for more than one subject matter.

Work Sample & Commentary: *Flinkers*

The task

Students were instructed to complete a laboratory activity in which they adjusted the mass and/or the volume of an object so that the object would not float on top of water or sink...it would "flink."

The task calls for the student to explore the range of available floating and sinking objects. In order to accomplish the task, it is necessary to combine floating and sinking objects to construct one of the correct density.

The quotations from the Science performance descriptions in this commentary are excerpted. The complete performance descriptions are shown on pages 132-135.

Circumstances of performance

This sample of student work was produced under the following conditions:

alone	√ in a group
in class	√ as homework
with teacher feedback	with peer feedback
timed	opportunity for revision

What the work shows

S1a **Physical Sciences Concepts:** The student produces evidence that demonstrates understanding of properties of objects and materials, such as similarities and differences in the size, weight, and color of objects....

The drawings provide evidence of sorting objects by observable properties and representing the findings.

A The students sorted common objects into those that floated and those that sank and recorded their findings.

B They used trial and error to find combinations that were neutrally buoyant (that "flinked") and drew the results.

The written summary provides evidence of conceptual understanding of density, an observable and measurable property of objects and materials.

Physical Sciences Concepts

Life Sciences Concepts

Earth and Space Sciences Concepts

Scientific Connections and Applications

Scientific Thinking

Scientific Tools and Technologies

Scientific Communication

Scientific Investigation

SCIENCE ENTRY SLIP
Your name_____
Date work was completed Feb. 6
Date work placed in portfolio Feb. 6

What was the assignment? (Attach a copy if possible)

To get the mass and volume of an object to equal 1 so it wouldn't float or sink, it would flink.

Is this part of a long-term investigation or a shorter task?
A short task.

Who selected this piece of work?

What tools or resources did you use? How much feedback or help did you get from your teacher or other adults?

We used things from home that would float and others that sank and put them together just right. My partners mom helped us try out different combinations.

Did you work alone or with a group?

I worked with a partner.

What do you want the reader to notice about this work? Why did you select this piece of work?

That it took determination and patience to get an object to flink, but it was also fun.

What were the important scientific ideas in this task?

To learn about floating, sinking, and density.

> **This work sample illustrates a standard-setting performance for the following part of the standards:**
>
> **S1**a **Physical Sciences Concepts: Properties of objects and materials.**

C The statement, "To make something flink, the mass and volume had to equal one," is acceptable for the elementary school level. At the middle school level, one would expect the student to discuss density in terms of a ratio; for example, "To make something flink, the ratio of the mass and the volume had to equal one," or "To make something flink, the mass divided by the volume had to equal one." Further, and although this is perhaps taken for granted, an adequate middle school response would make explicit the density of water, which equals one.

D Additional evidence of understanding the concept of density is provided in this sentence which

Flinkers

says that the addition of mass changes the buoyancy of the object.

E The final sentence completes the summary with reference to observable properties.

This work is an unrevised piece of homework. There are three spelling errors ("prosess," "absorbe," and "detirmination") and a missing apostrophe.

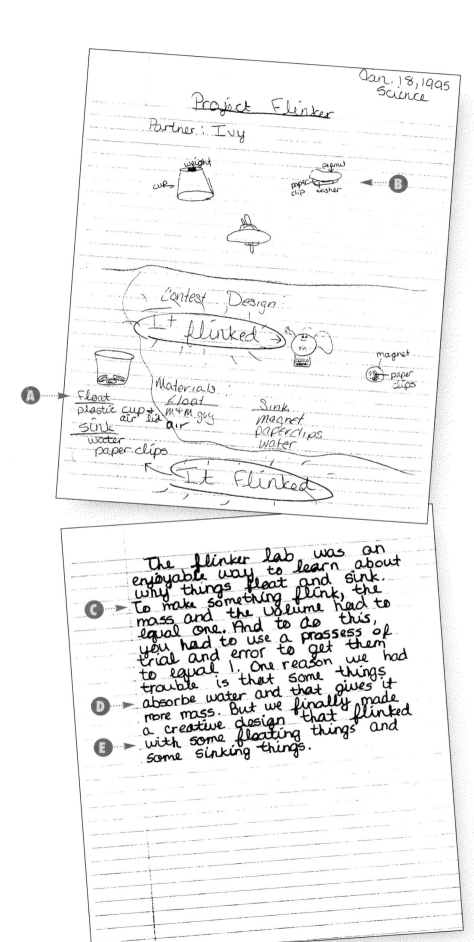

Work Sample & Commentary: *The Growing Tree*

The task

A small tree is planted in a meadow. After 20 years it has grown into a big tree, weighing 250 kg more than when it was planted. Where do the extra 250 kg come from? Explain your answer as fully as you can.

Circumstances of performance

These samples of student work were produced under the following conditions:

√ alone	in a group
√ in class	as homework
with teacher feedback	with peer feedback
√ timed (20 minutes)	opportunity for revision

The task was part of a state assessment program and unrelated to the curriculum that the students were studying.

What the work shows

S2a   Life Sciences Concepts: The student produces evidence that demonstrates understanding of characteristics of organisms, such as survival and environmental support....

These samples effectively explain and represent the key components of photosynthesis at an appropriate level using simple text.

Sample 1

A   Most of the components of photosynthesis are mentioned in the text: energy from the sun, carbon dioxide from the air, and water from the soil; though minerals are omitted.

B   The drawing elaborates the text.

The quotations from the Science performance descriptions in this commentary are excerpted. The complete performance descriptions are shown on pages 132-135.

Physical Sciences Concepts

Life Sciences Concepts   **S2**

Earth and Space Sciences Concepts

Scientific Connections and Applications

Scientific Thinking

Scientific Tools and Technologies

Scientific Communication   **S7**

Scientific Investigation

Sample 1

C Plants grow just like I do Thats how the tree became 250 kg. The plant gets the weight from the food it eats, **D** wich is sugar. The plants food is made from the suns energy, carbon **A** dioxide from the air, and water from the soil.

air gives carbon dioxide

energy comes from the sun

B

Roots get water from the soil

C This statement shows an understanding of the comparable ways that plants and animals grow. A more refined understanding would include the mechanism of adding cells, which is not mentioned in this work, and clarify the differences between plant and animal growth, i.e., that plants can and do make their own food while animals cannot. On the latter point, the idea that plants "eat" sugar is a common statement at the elementary level. The significance of the statement depends on what is meant by "eat." If, for example, the student means "take into their cells and use for growth and other life processes," this would be an accurate understanding.

D By recognizing that the plant makes sugar, this statement shows a high level of conceptualization for an elementary student.

These work samples illustrate standard-setting performances for the following parts of the standards:

S2a   **Life Sciences Concepts: Characteristics of organisms.**

S7a   **Scientific Communication: Represent data and results in multiple ways.**

The Growing Tree

S7 a Scientific Communication: The student represents data and results in multiple ways, such as...drawings, diagrams, and artwork....

Sample 1 was produced by a student in a special education reading program. Despite the punctuation, capitalization, and spelling errors, this sample effectively uses drawing to strengthen the written response.

Sample 2

E This work also includes three of the four major ingredients of photosynthesis—minerals, water, and light. Mentioning the fourth ingredient and the necessity for the presence of chlorophyll would be required in a middle school response. (See also the high school work sample entitled "Photosynthesis" in Volume 3 of these Performance Standards.)

F The elaboration, that the food is used to make cells and that the plant is made up of cells, shows progress from the elementary level, anticipating the middle school level, where structure and function are more extensively explored.

Sample 2

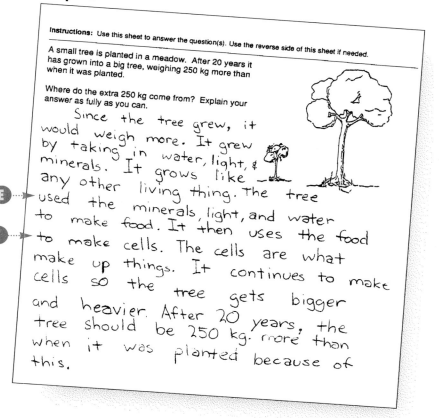

Instructions: Use this sheet to answer the question(s). Use the reverse side of this sheet if needed.

A small tree is planted in a meadow. After 20 years it has grown into a big tree, weighing 250 kg more than when it was planted.

Where do the extra 250 kg come from? Explain your answer as fully as you can.

Since the tree grew, it would weigh more. It grew by taking in water, light, & minerals. It grows like any other living thing. The tree used the minerals, light, and water to make food. It then uses the food to make cells. The cells are what make up things. It continues to make cells so the tree gets bigger and heavier. After 20 years, the tree should be 250 kg. more than when it was planted because of this.

Physical
Sciences
Concepts

S2 ▶ Life
Sciences
Concepts

Earth and
Space Sciences
Concepts

Scientific
Connections and
Applications

Scientific
Thinking

Scientific Tools
and
Technologies

S7 ▶ Scientific
Communication

Scientific
Investigation

Work Sample & Commentary: *Inside the Rain Forest*

The quotations from the Science performance descriptions in this commentary are excerpted. The complete performance descriptions are shown on pages 132-135.

Physical
Sciences
Concepts

Life
Sciences
Concepts **S2**

Earth and
Space Sciences
Concepts

Scientific
Connections and **S4**
Applications

Scientific
Thinking

Scientific Tools
and
Technologies

Scientific
Communication

Scientific
Investigation

The task

Students in a self-contained class participated in two units of study including poetry and nonfiction. During the poetry unit, they read and analyzed a wide variety of poems and learned how to write poetry. The nonfiction unit was focused on producing informational writing.

Two students asked if they could combine the informational writing assignment with their poetry using a topic that interested them. The product of that assignment was a book of poems on the rain forest which is excerpted here.

Circumstances of performance

This sample of student work was produced under the following conditions:

alone	√ in a group
√ in class	√ as homework
√ with teacher feedback	√ with peer feedback
timed	√ opportunity for revision

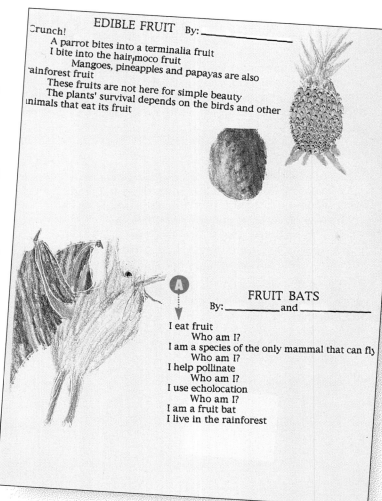

EDIBLE FRUIT By:_____

Crunch!
A parrot bites into a terminalia fruit
I bite into the hair moco fruit
Mangoes, pineapples and papayas are also rainforest fruit
These fruits are not here for simple beauty
The plants' survival depends on the birds and other animals that eat its fruit

A

FRUIT BATS
By:_____and_____

I eat fruit
Who am I?
I am a species of the only mammal that can fly
Who am I?
I help pollinate
Who am I?
I use echolocation
Who am I?
I am a fruit bat
I live in the rainforest

What the work shows

S2a Life Sciences Concepts: The student produces evidence that demonstrates understanding of characteristics of organisms, such as survival and environmental support; the relationship between structure and function....

A **B** Each specific first person ("I" and "My") statement identifies characteristics of a specific organism.

C The importance of bright colors for flower reproduction is evidence of understanding of form and function.

This work sample illustrates a standard-setting performance for the following parts of the standards:

S2a Life Sciences Concepts: Characteristics of organisms.

S2c Life Sciences Concepts: Organisms and environments.

S4a Scientific Connections and Applications: Big ideas and unifying concepts.

Inside the Rain Forest

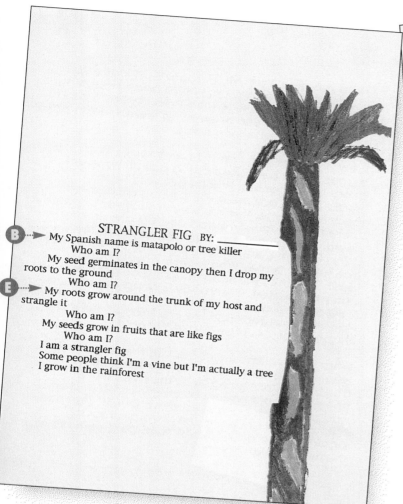

STRANGLER FIG   BY: _____

B ► My Spanish name is matapolo or tree killer
  Who am I?
My seed germinates in the canopy then I drop my
roots to the ground
    Who am I?
E ► My roots grow around the trunk of my host and
strangle it
    Who am I?
My seeds grow in fruits that are like figs
    Who am I?
I am a strangler fig
Some people think I'm a vine but I'm actually a tree
I grow in the rainforest

CAULIFLORY   By: _____
You walk past a rainforest tree with brightly colored ◄ **C**
flowers on its trunk
    You know the flowers are here because
    Here flowers are easily seen by animals who help
pollinate

COCKROACH   By: _____
    Once there was a cockroach
its shell was brown and hard
it crawled around
searching for guano
the food cockroaches eat
    Its home is in the tropical rainforests
    The kind of this cockroach is the Blaberus giganteus
    Its so big it can fit into your hand
    This cockroach is not alive anymore
for trees falling down on it

S2 ◄ Life Sciences Concepts: The student produces evidence of understanding organisms and environments, such as the interdependence of animals and plants in an ecosystem....

D This statement correctly illustrates the dependent relationships between and among the tank, the insects, and the bromeliad.

S4 a Scientific Connections and Applications: The student produces evidence that demonstrates understanding of big ideas and unifying concepts, such as...form and function....

E The reference to the roots strangling a host tree illustrates understanding of the connection between form and function. This is also evident in a number of places in the remainder of the work.

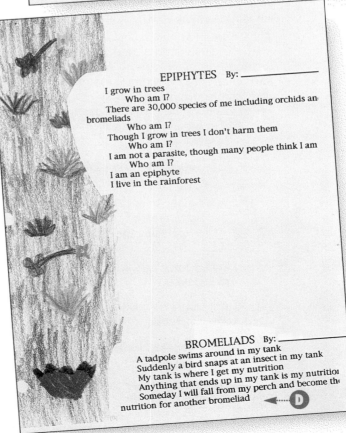

EPIPHYTES   By: _____
    I grow in trees
    Who am I?
    There are 30,000 species of me including orchids an
bromeliads
    Who am I?
    Though I grow in trees I don't harm them
    Who am I?
I am not a parasite, though many people think I am
    Who am I?
I am an epiphyte
I live in the rainforest

BROMELIADS   By: _____
    A tadpole swims around in my tank
    Suddenly a bird snaps at an insect in my tank
    My tank is where I get my nutrition
    Anything that ends up in my tank is my nutritio
    Someday I will fall from my perch and become th
nutrition for another bromeliad ◄ **D**

Work Sample & Commentary: *Drop of Water*

The task

Students who had been studying weather were asked to write a story about a drop of water that goes through the water cycle.

Circumstances of performance

This sample of student work was produced under the following conditions:

√ alone   in a group

√ in class   as homework

√ with teacher feedback   with peer feedback

    timed   √ opportunity for revision

What the work shows

In an engaging story, this work sample shows conceptual understanding for parts of three standards.

S3 b Earth and Space Sciences Concepts: The student produces evidence that demonstrates understanding of objects in the sky, such as…the importance of the Sun to provide the light and heat necessary for survival.

A The story begins with the important role of the sun.

S1 a Physical Sciences Concepts: The student produces evidence that demonstrates understanding of properties of objects and materials, such as…different states of materials.

B Conceptual understanding of different states of matter is demonstrated in the consistent and accurate relationships among phase, temperature, and volume, particularly the recognition that gases rise, and in the descriptions of how it feels to be a gas ("getting bigger"), to be a solid ("smaller"), and to condense from gas to liquid ("getting really crowded").

The quotations from the Science performance descriptions in this commentary are excerpted. The complete performance descriptions are shown on pages 132-135.

Physical Sciences Concepts **S1**

Life Sciences Concepts

Earth and Space Sciences **S3** Concepts

Scientific Connections and **S4** Applications

Scientific Thinking

Scientific Tools and Technologies

Scientific Communication

Scientific Investigation

My Big Trip
by _____

Good morning, I am Mr. H. Tuoh. I just woke up and the sun is coming up. I have been swimming with my friends in a nice lake in Nebraska. Since I am on top of this pile of sleeping friends the sun is going to take me for a ride today. **A**

Wow, that was fast. I am climbing really fast. I feel **B** bigger. That's because I am a gas . It happens every time I get hot. When I get cold I get smaller. They call me a solid. Being solid gives me a headache. This is better than World's of fun! There is a big cloud ahead and we are slowing down. I am getting smaller now because my pants fit better. But, it's getting really crowded!!! I can hardly move. Who let in the ugly dust **C** family? I think I will hang on to this dust guy so I can rest up. Hey, everybody is coppying my idea and we are getting heavy. Oh Noooooooooooooooo we are falling!!! But that's OK because I was getting really cold.

What a trip. I am almost back to the lake. Wait, where is the lake. This looks like a big river . I don't think I am going to hit the river. Oh noooooooooo .I better put on my crash helmet and prepare for a land landing. OUCH! That hurt. But, at least I am down. hey, we are moving again. These dirt and rock hurt. Do they have to come along on MY trip?

This work sample illustrates a standard-setting performance for the following parts of the standards:

S1 a Physical Sciences Concepts: Properties of objects and materials.

S3 a Earth and Space Sciences Concepts: Properties of Earth materials.

S3 b Earth and Space Sciences Concepts: Objects in the sky.

S4 a Scientific Connections and Applications: Big ideas and unifying concepts.

Drop of Water

S3 a Earth and Space Sciences Concepts: The student produces evidence that demonstrates understanding of properties of Earth materials, such as water and gases....

C The role of dust as something upon which water can condense is evidence of understanding the water cycle.

D The arrival in the Mississippi River, not in the original lake in Nebraska, shows further understanding of the water cycle.

S4 a Scientific Connections and Applications: The student produces evidence that demonstrates understanding of big ideas and unifying concepts, such as...change and constancy....

E The final sentences, especially the conclusion, "The End...not really," go beyond an understanding of the water cycle to suggest understanding of a unifying concept, change and constancy.

The response is distinguished by the representation of an abstract concept with clarity (i.e., molecular spacing and movement of water through the water cycle). The discussion of evaporation and condensation provide a more powerful explanation of the water cycle and demonstrates thorough understanding.

D ⤷ Wow, I am in the Mississipi river! There are lots of us and mud and rocks and stuff. I feel kind of dirty. I wish I could go up to sit in the clouds a while. I will just sit back and float a while. Oh, E ⤷ here comes the sun. Here I go again. I wonder where I will end up this time.

The End...not really

S1 Physical Sciences Concepts

Life Sciences Concepts

S3 Earth and Space Sciences Concepts

S4 Scientific Connections and Applications

Scientific Thinking

Scientific Tools and Technologies

Scientific Communication

Scientific Investigation

Work Sample & Commentary: *Erosion*

The task

An elementary class was involved in a year-long, interdisciplinary study of their state. On a field trip to a conservation center, they learned about wind and water erosion. When they returned, they wanted to learn more about erosion and which combinations of soil and grass were most effective in preventing erosion.

The quotations from the Science performance descriptions in this commentary are excerpted. The complete performance descriptions are shown on pages 132-135.

Circumstances of performance

This sample of student work was produced under the following conditions:

alone	√ in a group
√ in class	as homework
with teacher feedback	√ with peer feedback
timed	opportunity for revision

What the work shows

The first page explains that this group of students examined Tall Fescue grass. Other groups in their class studied Perennial Rye, Crested Wheat, and Irrigated Pasture Mix (a mixture of these three and two other types). The second, third, and fourth pages explain the question, hypothesis, and procedures. The fifth page shows the plan for studying soils; the sixth, seventh, and eighth pages show the observa-

---

Native Colorado Soils and Grasses A Water Erosion Experiment

Our class has been studying the effects of erosion. We broke into groups and did erosion experiments. In our group, we had four people, _____, _____, _____, and _____. For our experiment, we decided to plant Tall Fescue grass seeds in three different types of soils. During our experiments we learned how Tall Fescue grows in different soils and how the grass effects soil erosion.

---

tions from the three soil types. The results of the soils' analysis (without grass) are summarized on page 9. The next three pages (10-12) show the results of the same procedure for the same soils planted with Tall Fescue. The final page (13) summarizes the work.

S3 a Earth and Space Sciences Concepts: The student produces evidence that demonstrates understanding of properties of Earth materials, such as...the properties of rocks and soils such as texture, color, and ability to retain water.

A B C There is ample evidence that the students have an understanding of erosion.

S4 a Scientific Connections and Applications: The student produces evidence that demonstrates understanding of big ideas and unifying concepts such as...cause and effect.

A B C D These pieces and the ending also show a good understanding of cause and effect.

S5 a Scientific Thinking: The student asks questions about natural phenomena; objects and organisms; and events and discoveries.

D The entire investigation came from students' questions about natural phenomena. The question and hypothesis are clearly stated.

S5 e Scientific Thinking: The student identifies problems; proposes and implements solutions; and evaluates the accuracy, design, and outcomes of investigations.

E The conclusion shows that students were focused on the best combination of grasses and soils to prevent erosion.

S6 a Scientific Tools and Technologies: The student uses technology and tools....

F G H I J K L The stream table was used effectively to gather data.

Physical Sciences Concepts

Life Sciences Concepts

Earth and Space Sciences Concepts **S3**

Scientific Connections and Applications **S4**

Scientific Thinking **S5**

Scientific Tools and Technologies **S6**

Scientific Communication **S7**

Scientific Investigation

This work sample illustrates a standard-setting performance for the following parts of the standards:

S3 a Earth and Space Sciences Concepts: Properties of Earth materials.

S4 a Scientific Connections and Applications: Big ideas and unifying concepts.

S5 a Scientific Thinking: Ask questions about natural phenomena; objects and organisms; and events and discoveries.

S5 e Scientific Thinking: Identify problems; propose and implement solutions; and evaluate the accuracy, design, and outcomes of investigations.

S6 a Scientific Tools and Technologies: Use technology and tools.

S7 a Scientific Communication: Represent data and results in multiple ways.

S7 b Scientific Communication: Use facts to support conclusions.

S7 c Scientific Communication: Communicate in a form suitable to the purpose and audience.

Erosion

D Question:
What type of soil will erode least with Tall Fescue grass.

Hypothesis:
I think clay soil will erode very little because clay soil absorb water slowly.

O Steps to do experiment

Growing the grass

1. Place soil in growing bin
2. Sprinkle seeds on soil
3. Sprinkle soil on seeds
4. Water with 350 ml every other day

Erosion experiment set-up

1. Collect all of the materials.
2. Spread newspaper over desk or table
3. Place stream table on surface with drain hole over the side.
4. Spread newspaper under drain hole on the ground blow the stream table.
5. Place the collection basin on the newspaper so it can catch the water as it flows out of the drain hole.
6. Remove grass from growing bin and place the grass in the stream.
7. table opposite the drain hole Place ruler on top of the stream table above the grass 6-7 cm from the end of the stream table.
8. Balance flood cup on end of the stream table at the ruler.
9. Fill liter container up to the top (100 ml of water)
10. Place the wooden angle under the stream table opposite the drain hole.

M **N** Attention to accuracy is evident throughout; these are but two examples.

S7 **a** Scientific Communication: The student represents data and results in multiple ways, such as… diagrams…and…writing.

F **G** **H** **I** **J** **K** **L** The diagrams and accompanying explanations clearly describe the results of the investigations.

S7 **b** Scientific Communication: The student uses facts to support conclusions.

C Throughout the work, but particularly in the conclusion, the generalizations follow directly from the data.

S7 **c** Scientific Communication: The student communicates in a form suited to the purpose and the audience, such as writing instructions that others can follow.

O The procedures are well explained.

The attention to detail, and the recording and use of qualitative and quantitative data, support the judgment of this work as standard setting. Evidence of conceptual and applied understanding of Earth science is shown throughout.

Physical Sciences Concepts

Life Sciences Concepts

S3 Earth and Space Sciences Concepts

S4 Scientific Connections and Applications

S5 Scientific Thinking

S6 Scientific Tools and Technologies

S7 Scientific Communication

Scientific Investigation

Names _____ Date _____

STREAM TABLE PLAN

We are trying to find out what happens when We put houses at the end of the sand.

We will need these materials:

stream table   water
cup with hole   duct tape
ruler   3 houses
sand

We will set up our tray like this:

Drain hole

F

GO WITH THE FLOW
This sheet may be reproduced for classroom use.

Landforms Module
PART NO. 542-0106 (no. 7 of 12)

Erosion

G Name _____

Date _____

STREAM TABLE MAP

This is an investigation of _erosion_ .

20 cm

Key	Elapsed time (minutes after start)	mportant events
■ Sand/diatomaceous earth mixture	1	The hole is on the edge sand
□ Sand	2	The sand Land slides
□ Diatomaceous earth	3	It Formed a channel
□	4	Two houses Fell down
□	5	
■	6	

Landforms Module
PART NO. 542-0106 (no. 5 of 12)

GO WITH THE FLOW
This sheet may be reproduced for classroom use.

H Name _____

Date _____

STREAM TABLE MAP

This is an investigation of _erosion_ .

20 cm

Key	Elapsed time (minutes after start)	Important events
■ Sand/diatomaceous earth mixture	1	Holes formed
□ Sand	2	land channeled
□ Diatomaceous earth	3	tunnel closed
□	4	tunnel opened again
□	5	took more sand down
□	6	

Landforms Module
PART NO. 542-0106 (no. 5 of 12)

GO WITH THE FLOW
This sheet may be reproduced for classroom use.

I Name _____

Date _____

STREAM TABLE MAP

This is an investigation of _erosion_ .

20 cm

Key	Elapsed time (minutes after start)	Important events
■ Sand/diatomaceous earth mixture	1	made a little hole
□ Sand	2	hole little bigger
□ Diatomaceous earth	3	water going to side
□	4	water going Forward
□	5	hole's cubic inch
	6	water looks like milk

Landforms Module
PART NO. 542-0106 (no. 5 of 12)

GO WITH THE FLOW
This sheet may be reproduced for classroom use.

M

Experiment Results
(Soils without grass)

The sandy soil eroded through two channels that the water made.

The topsoil eroded through one channel. At the bottom of stream table is where you could find silt and organic materials.

The clay soil eroded just a little bit. A little channel was made and little organic material eroded.

Physical Sciences Concepts

Life Sciences Concepts

Earth and Space Sciences Concepts S3

Scientific Connections and Applications S4

Scientific Thinking S5

Scientific Tools and Technologies S6

Scientific Communication S7

Scientific Investigation

Erosion

Results - Sandy Soil with grass

There was a land slide on the right and in the middle. As the water was coming out of the flood cup, a hole was made in the soil carring a lot of silt and soil materials down the stream table. Most of the water went to the right and a sand bar was formed on the right of the drain hole. The erosion we collected was 2 cm.

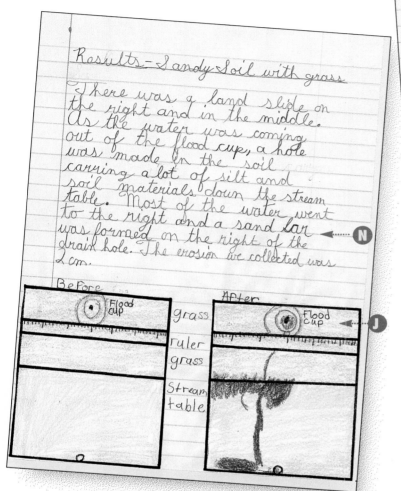

Results - Topsoil with grass

There were channels being made both above ground and below ground. There were pebbles, and rocks deposited into the collection basin. It is carring the silt and lighter materials into the collection basin. The soil did not erode much because the roots are holding the soil and letting the water leak out. The erosin we collected was 1 cm.

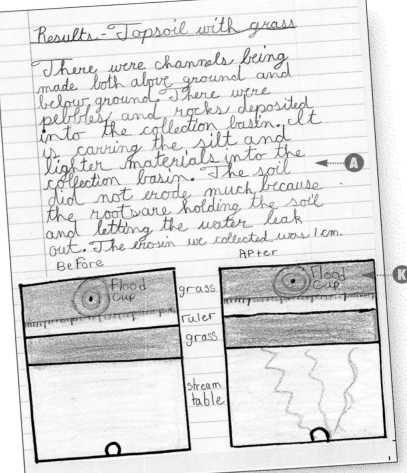

Results - Clay soil with grass

There were under ground tunnels made during the experiment. Little pebbles were carried in the under ground tunnels. It was looking like a land slide would occur. Most of the water went under the soil and it came out clear. There was not enough erosion to measure.

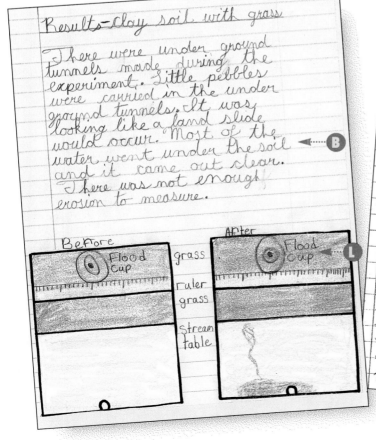

Conclusion

I learned that Tall Fescue grass grows best in clay and topsoil. I also learned that soils erode less with grass growing in them.

I learned that clay soils do not erode a lot and the water that came out of the stream table was pretty clear. Topsoil erodes more than clay soil but less than sandy soil. Sandy soil erodes a lot. I would suggest that people plant Tall Fescue to help pervent erosion. You may plant Tall Fescue in sandy soil at your own risk. You may want to mix sandy soil with clay to help grow grass and pervent erosion.

Work Sample & Commentary: *Yeast Growth*

The task

The National Student Research Center encourages the establishment of student research centers in schools in the United States and around the world. The Center facilitates the exchange of information by publishing a journal of student investigations and by use of the Internet (nsrcmms@aol.com). It provides a standard format that students use to report their results. The format requires that students state a purpose and hypothesis; report their methods, data analysis, and conclusions; and suggest applications for their results.

The quotations from the Science performance descriptions in this commentary are excerpted. The complete performance descriptions are shown on pages 132-135.

Circumstances of performance

This sample of student work was produced under the following conditions:

√ alone   in a group

√ in class   as homework **E**

√ with teacher feedback   with peer feedback **C**

   timed   √ opportunity for revision

What the work shows

By investigating the optimum temperature for the growth of yeast, the investigation explores characteristics of organisms, particularly survival and environmental support, but the report does not explain why temperature or any other variable would be important to investigate, so the work does not illustrate conceptual understanding in Life Sciences Concepts. It does not illustrate misunderstanding either, however. The student does not mention sugar, but has followed the instructions on the package.

TITLE: The Effect of Temperature on Yeast Growth

I. STATEMENT OF PURPOSE AND HYPOTHESIS

I wanted to find out what temperature was best for yeast growth. My hypothesis stated that the yeast would grow best at 110° F because the package said that the water temperature should range from 105° to 115° F. **A** **B**

II. METHODOLOGY

I used 9 different cups of water. The temperature of the water in each cup increased by 10° F starting at 70° F. In each cup, I put the same amount of yeast. I let it rest for 5 minutes to allow the yeast to grow. Then I put a drop of liquid from each cup on a slide and counted the cells. I recorded how many cells I saw from each cup. **D**

III. ANALYSIS OF DATA

I found that I really didn't know how difficult this experiment could be. At 70° F, there were 104 cells; at 80° F, there were 179 cells; at 90° F, there were 156 cells; at 100° F, there were 232 cells; at 110° F, there were 216; at 120° ., there were 96 cells; at 130° F, there were 64 cells; at 140° F, there were 47 cells and at 150° F, there were 35. **F**

IV. SUMMARY AND CONCLUSION

The yeast grew best at 100° F. I cannot believe that the package was incorrect. I should have made a more intelligent hypothesis and shouldn't have relied on the package. Therefore, based on my data I reject my hypothesis. **E** **C**

The Student Researcher. Used by permission of the National Student Research Center, Dr. John I. Swang, Mandeville Middle School, 2525 Soult Street, Mandeville, Louisiana 70448. 504-626-5980 or nsrcmms@aol.com.

Although sugar is necessary for "proofing" yeast, it is not necessary for "activation." The package indicates that the yeast be "dissolved in water (1/4 cup) at a temperature between 105 and 115 degrees Fahrenheit. If it is to be proofed (foamy), a teaspoon of sugar is added. After five minutes in warm water, the yeast will begin to multiply with added food."

S5a Scientific Thinking: The student asks questions about natural phenomena....

A

S5c Scientific Thinking: The student uses evidence from reliable sources to construct explanations.

B The package instructions were used as a reliable source of information.

S5e Scientific Thinking: The student...evaluates the accuracy, design, and outcomes of investigations.

C The testing and questioning of the source provide evidence for evaluation.

Sidebar (left margin)

Physical Sciences Concepts

Life Sciences Concepts

Earth and Space Sciences Concepts

Scientific Connections and Applications

Scientific Thinking **S5**

Scientific Tools and Technologies **S6**

Scientific Communication

Scientific Investigation **S8**

This work sample illustrates a standard-setting performance for the following parts of the standards:

S5a Scientific Thinking: Ask questions about natural phenomena.

S5c Scientific Thinking: Use evidence from reliable sources to construct explanations.

S5e Scientific Thinking: Evaluate the accuracy, design, and outcomes of investigations.

S6a Scientific Tools and Technologies: Use technology and tools.

S6b Scientific Tools and Technologies: Collect and analyze data.

S8a Scientific Investigation: An experiment, such as conducting a fair test.

Yeast Growth

S6a Scientific Tools and Technologies: The student uses technology and tools (such as...microscopes) to gather data and extend the senses.

D "On a slide" implies that a microscope was used. The procedure of using a microscope to count cells and the persistence shown by counting 232 cells while viewing them through a microscope is impressive use of scientific tools and technologies for an elementary student.

S6b Scientific Tools and Technologies: The student collects and analyzes data using concepts and techniques in Mathematics Standard 4, such as... variability....

E The student found the maximum of 100 degrees. At a more advanced level, a more "sophisticated" analysis would be expected: one that shows that the results at 100 degrees and 110 degrees are essentially the same. Further, students might study the way that yeast solutions cool slightly during use, so that it is good to start with a somewhat higher water temperature than recommended on the package; some recipes call for water at 120 to 130 degrees.

S8a Scientific Investigation: The student demonstrates scientific competence by completing an experiment, such as conducting a fair test.

A full investigation includes:

- Questions that can be studied using the resources available.

A

- Procedures that are safe, humane, and ethical; and that respect privacy and property rights.

- Data that have been collected and recorded (see also Science Standard 6) in ways that others can verify and analyze using skills expected at this grade level (see also Mathematics Standard 4).

D **E** **F**

- Data and results that have been represented (see also Science Standard 7) in ways that fit the context.

- Recommendations, decisions, and conclusions based on evidence.

C

- Acknowledgment of references and contributions of others.

The work includes references to the package instructions.

- Results that are communicated appropriately to audiences.

- Reflection and defense of conclusions and recommendations from other sources and peer review.

By sharing the work on the Internet, the student is publishing the work and asking for feedback.

Measurement issues related to repeated sampling from the same container, repeated trials, and checking the temperature of the water would be expected of a middle school student but are not expected at the elementary level. Controlling the time allowed for growth is explicitly mentioned. Controlling the shape of the container and the amount of sugar are not mentioned.

C The conclusion, that the hypothesis should be rejected is correct. The idea that the hypothesis was not intelligent and that the student would have had a basis better than the package instructions is not warranted. The fact that the package could have been correct and the temperature measurements could have been flawed in some way (inaccurate thermometer, for example) is an alternative explanation for the data. As noted above, however, analysis of some of the measurement issues is more sophisticated than would be expected for an elementary student. Finally, the willingness to report a result different from the hypothesis is a major accomplishment for an elementary student.

S6 makes explicit reference to using telecommunications to acquire and share information. A recent National Center on Education Statistics survey recently reported that only 50% of schools and fewer than 9% of instructional rooms currently have access to the Internet. We know this is an equity issue—that far more than 9% of the homes in the United States have access to the Internet and that schools must make sure that students' access to information and ideas does not depend on what they get at home—so we have crafted performance standards that would use the Internet so that people will make sure that all students have access to it. New Standards partners have made a commitment to create the learning environments where students can develop the knowledge and skills delineated here.

Physical Sciences Concepts

Life Sciences Concepts

Earth and Space Sciences Concepts

Scientific Connections and Applications

S5 Scientific Thinking

S6 Scientific Tools and Technologies

Scientific Communication

S8 Scientific Investigation

Work Sample & Commentary: *Smiles*

The quotations from the Science performance descriptions in this commentary are excerpted. The complete performance descriptions are shown on pages 132-135.

The task

The National Student Research Center encourages the establishment of student research centers in schools in the United States and around the world. The Center facilitates the exchange of information by publishing a journal of student investigations and by use of the Internet (nsrcmms@aol.com). It provides a standard format that students use to report their results. The format requires that students state a purpose and hypothesis; report their methods, data analysis, and conclusions; and suggest applications for their results.

Circumstances of performance

This sample of student work was produced under the following conditions:

√ alone   in a group

√ in class   as homework

√ with teacher feedback   with peer feedback

timed   √ opportunity for revision

What the work shows

As part of their work in mathematics, fourth grade students chose to gather data on sizes of different body parts and to compare their data with first grade students. Having done so,

This work sample illustrates a standard-setting performance for the following parts of the standards:

S5a **Scientific Thinking: Ask questions about natural phenomena.**

S5c **Scientific Thinking: Use evidence from reliable sources to construct explanations.**

S5d **Scientific Thinking: Evaluate different points of view using relevant experiences, observations, and knowledge.**

S5f **Scientific Thinking: Work individually and in teams to collect and share information and ideas.**

S6c **Scientific Tools and Technologies: Acquire information from multiple sources.**

S7a **Scientific Communication: Represent data and results in multiple ways.**

S7b **Scientific Communication: Use facts to support conclusions.**

S7c **Scientific Communication: Communicate in a form suited to the purpose and the audience.**

Sidebar navigation:
- Physical Sciences Concepts
- Life Sciences Concepts
- Earth and Space Sciences Concepts
- Scientific Connections and Applications
- Scientific Thinking **S5**
- Scientific Tools and Technologies **S6**
- Scientific Communication **S7**
- Scientific Investigation

TITLE: Body Sizes

I. STATEMENT OF PURPOSE AND HYPOTHESIS:

We want to find out how much bigger a seventh grader is when compared to a fourth grader. Our hypothesis states that the seventh graders will be bigger than the fourth graders by the following amount: head-3 cm, foot-4 cm, ankle-3 cm, and smile-2 cm.

II. METHODOLOGY:

We did a similar project comparing the first graders and the fourth graders. We found a pattern. The fourth grader was bigger in every area by 2 cm except in the measurement of the smile. The fourth grader was only one cm bigger in smile. We used this information to develop our hypothesis. Since we found measurements of students three years younger than us, we now wanted to compare measurements with students three years older than we are. We first found the mean/average head, foot, ankle, and smile size for the fourth graders. Then we did the same thing with seventh graders. Seventh grade students from Nashville, Tenn. helped us out with measurements. We exchanged information through the Internet.

III. ANALYSIS OF DATA:

	Fourth grade	Seventh grade
Head size	54 cm	51.5 cm
Foot size	20 cm	27.0 cm
Ankle size	20 cm	24.1 cm
Smile size	8 cm	7.3 cm

The seventh graders' average head size was 2.5 cm smaller than the fourth graders' average head size. The seventh graders' average foot size was 7.0 cm bigger. The seventh graders' average ankle size was 4.1 cm bigger. The seventh graders' average smile size was .7 cm smaller than the fourth graders' average smile size.

The Student Researcher. Used by permission of the National Student Research Center, Dr. John I. Swang, Mandeville Middle School, 2525 Soult Street, Mandeville, Louisiana 70448. 504-626-5980 or nsrcmms@aol.com.

they then used the Internet to locate a seventh grade class that was willing to provide comparable data to see if the same pattern continued with age. They then "published" their work by reporting it on the Internet in the standard format.

S5a Scientific Thinking: The student asks questions about natural phenomena....

(A) Questions about body sizes are of great interest to children. The value of allowing students to formulate their own questions is demonstrated by their including "smiles" in their list of body parts, something that would not occur to many adults.

S5c Scientific Thinking: The student uses evidence from reliable sources to construct explanations.

(B) The students used data from their previous study with first graders to construct a hypothesis for seventh graders.

Smiles

S5d Scientific Thinking: The student evaluates different points of view using relevant experiences, observations, and knowledge....

C The students checked their data against their prediction, which had been based on a reasonable idea that comparable rates of growth would be observed over three year spans prior to and following their age. They were surprised by their results. Attempting to explain the unexpected results, that the seventh graders had smaller heads and smiles, by critiquing the measurement procedure, would have provided more complete evidence for this standard.

S5f Scientific Thinking: The student works individually and in teams to collect and share information and ideas.

D These students went beyond their immediate experience by seeking out a seventh grade class so that they could extend their study beyond the grade levels contained in their elementary school. Working as a class and with other classes, even classes outside their own school, demonstrates the beginnings of a scientific community that shares data and publishes results.

S6c Scientific Tools and Technologies: The student acquires information from multiple sources such as...non-print sources and from experimentation.

Information was acquired electronically and by direct measurement.

The other aspects of the Scientific Tools and Technologies standard are not fully realized. The tools are not identified, nor are the procedures for measuring (e.g., Were smiles measured at their greatest length? Corner to corner or edge of lips?), but measurements are reported in a reasonable way. The middle school students, who measured themselves, reported with more significant digits, which is probably appropriate. The results of the analysis are reported here but not the procedures. A full report of the data would reveal the adequacy of the sample and the appropriateness of using the average.

S7a Scientific Communication: The student represents data and results in multiple ways, such as numbers, tables, and...writing.

E The data are presented in both a text and a table. A bar graph might have been an effective way to show the contrast from first to fourth to seventh grade, though it would be difficult to convey in many Internet environments.

S7b Scientific Communication: The student uses facts to support conclusions.

IV. SUMMARY AND CONCLUSION:

In our survey, seventh graders tended to have slightly smaller heads and smiles than fourth graders. We are not sure why the seventh graders' heads were smaller than the fourth graders' head. Also, seventh graders tended to have larger feet and ankles than fourth graders. Therefore, we reject our hypothesis in every area.

V. APPLICATION TO LIFE:

Doctors would want to know the average heights for each age group to see if their patients are in the average areas or not. Parents would want to know this information for the same reason. Clothes companies would want to know these measurements for hat sizes, shoe sizes, and sock sizes for each age group. Modeling agencies might be interested in smile sizes.

S7c Scientific Communication: The student communicates in a form suited to the purpose and the audience....

The report is formatted to follow the NSRC guidelines completely and clearly.

The report is not a full investigation consistent with the Scientific Investigation standard. Attempting to explain the unexpected results, that the seventh graders had smaller heads and smiles, by critiquing the measurement procedure, would have provided more complete evidence of an investigation. Attempting to explain the results, by pursuing, for example, developmental reasons for heads attaining their adult size in babies and children more rapidly than limbs do, would have taken the investigation into the Life Sciences Concepts standard. Dealing with the size and representativeness of the sample and the analysis of the data would have addressed parts of Mathematics Standard 4, Statistics and Probability Concepts.

Physical Sciences Concepts

Life Sciences Concepts

Earth and Space Sciences Concepts

Scientific Connections and Applications

S5 Scientific Thinking

S6 Scientific Tools and Technologies

S7 Scientific Communication

Scientific Investigation

Work Sample & Commentary: *Aquarium*

The task

Given a drawing of an aquarium with six labeled items (light, thermometer, castle, rock, snail, and plant), students were told: "In the picture of an aquarium above, six items are labeled. Which of the six items are important to use in or with an aquarium? Explain why each one you name is important."

Circumstances of performance

This sample of student work was produced under the following conditions:

√ alone   in a group

√ in class   as homework

  with teacher feedback   with peer feedback

√ timed (20 minutes)   opportunity for revision

The task was part of a state assessment program and unrelated to the curriculum that the students were studying.

What the work shows

S2a Life Sciences Concepts: The student produces evidence that demonstrates understanding of the characteristics of organisms, such as survival and environmental support....

This response correctly identifies the role each labeled item plays in the environment and connects the item to the needs of the fish. For a fairly straightforward question, the response provides elaborations that show a depth of understanding.

A The explanation of the role of the plant is very complete for the elementary level, since specifying either function would have been adequate.

B The elaboration of the function of the thermometer shows a good degree of accuracy for the elementary level.

C Objects such as the rock and the castle are used in aquaria for decoration as well as protection. From the drawing, one could argue that the fish are large enough not to need protection and that these objects are ornamental. That would also be a correct response.

The quotations from the Science performance descriptions in this commentary are excerpted. The complete performance descriptions are shown on pages 132-135.

Instructions: Use this sheet to answer the question(s). Use the reverse side of this sheet if needed.

In the picture of an aquarium above, six items are labeled. Which of the six items are important to use in or with an aquarium? Explain why each one you name is important.

A The Plant is important because it takes in CO_2 and produces Oxegen it also provides shelter.

B The thermometer is important because it gives an accurate reading of the temp. so it is neteher to hot or to cold.

C The rock and castle are important because they Provide Shelter.

D The snail is important because it eats the decomposing material.

E The light provides warmth

D The language, "decomposing material," is particularly precise for the elementary level.

E This reference to the function of the light is correct. It also helps the plant to grow. Although one might assume that the room's ambient light would suffice for plant growth, this is a refinement appropriate for middle level, not for an elementary student producing a comprehensive response on a timed test.

The systematic treatment of all the items is also a strength at the elementary level. At the middle school level, it would be expected that students could provide a similar analysis for an environment with which they have less first hand experience.

This work sample illustrates a standard-setting performance for the following part of the standards:

S2a **Life Sciences Concepts: Characteristics of organisms.**

Physical Sciences Concepts

Life Sciences Concepts · **S2**

Earth and Space Sciences Concepts

Scientific Connections and Applications

Scientific Thinking

Scientific Tools and Technologies

Scientific Communication

Scientific Investigation

Work Sample & Commentary: *Snow Melt*

The task

This work sample is from a student investigation for a science fair. The instructions asked the students to select a question they wished to investigate and required that some experiment be performed to gather data and come to a conclusion. An explanation of the scientific concepts involved in the experiment was not required. The science fair rules required that data be displayed in a poster presentation format.

Circumstances of performance

This sample of student work was produced under the following conditions:

√ alone   in a group

√ in class   as homework

√ with teacher feedback   with peer feedback

    timed   √ opportunity for revision

PLAN - First, I will collect a tablespoonful of snow from my front yard, and will put it in a half-pint, plastic container. I will place the container of snow in the freezer for 10 minutes. I will do all of my timing using my father's stop watch. Next, I will collect another tablespoonful of snow from the same place, and will put that in a different half-pint, plastic container. Following that, I will place the 2 containers of snow 3 inches away from a fire. I will then wait to see which melts first. I'll also time how long each container of snow will take to melt, and record the difference in melting time of the 2 containers. I will repeat this 9 more times for a total of 10 trials. ◄ D

HYPOTHESIS - I think that fresh snow will melt quicker than frozen snow in front of a fire because the fresh snow wouldn't be as packed together or dense as the frozen snow. The frozen snow may be tight and packed together; when it melts, it might melt in chunks which would cause the snow to take more time in melting. A ---►

This work sample illustrates a standard-setting performance for the following parts of the standards:

S5 a Scientific Thinking: Ask questions about natural phenomena.

S5 c Scientific Thinking: Use evidence from reliable sources to construct explanations.

S5 e Scientific Thinking: Evaluate the accuracy, design, and outcomes of investigations.

S6 a Scientific Tools and Technologies: Use technology and tools.

S6 b Scientific Tools and Technologies: Collect and analyze data.

S7 a Scientific Communication: Represent data and results in multiple ways.

S7 b Scientific Communication: Use facts to support conclusions.

S7 c Scientific Communication: Communicate in a form suited to the purpose and the audience.

S8 a Scientific Investigation: An experiment, such as conducting a fair test.

What the work shows

S5 a Scientific Thinking: The student asks questions about natural phenomena....

S5 c Scientific Thinking: The student uses evidence from reliable sources to construct explanations.

A The statement of the hypothesis includes a rationale based on observation.

S5 e Scientific Thinking: The student...evaluates the accuracy, design, and outcomes of investigations.

B The reasoning about the results, both "I have no reason for it," and "2 possible reason(s)," shows a good degree of self-evaluation for the elementary level.

The quotations from the Science performance descriptions in this commentary are excerpted. The complete performance descriptions are shown on pages 132-135.

Physical Sciences Concepts

Life Sciences Concepts

Earth and Space Sciences Concepts

Scientific Connections and Applications

S5 Scientific Thinking

S6 Scientific Tools and Technologies

S7 Scientific Communication

S8 Scientific Investigation

Snow Melt

S6a Scientific Tools and Technologies: The student uses technology and tools (such as...thermometers, watches)...to gather data and extend the senses.

S6b Scientific Tools and Technologies: The student collects and analyzes data using concepts and techniques in Mathematics Standard 4, such as...data displays, graphing....

B **C** The calculation and display of the differences sets up an interesting analysis in the conclusion.

S7a Scientific Communication: The student represents data and results in multiple ways, such as numbers, tables, and graphs....

S7b Scientific Communication: The student uses facts to support conclusions.

S7c Scientific Communication: The student communicates in a form suited to the purpose and the audience....

The format of the science fair was executed successfully.

Physical
Sciences
Concepts

Life
Sciences
Concepts

Earth and
Space Sciences
Concepts

Scientific
Connections and
Applications

Scientific
Thinking **S5**

Scientific Tools
and
Technologies **S6**

Scientific
Communication **S7**

Scientific
Investigation **S8**

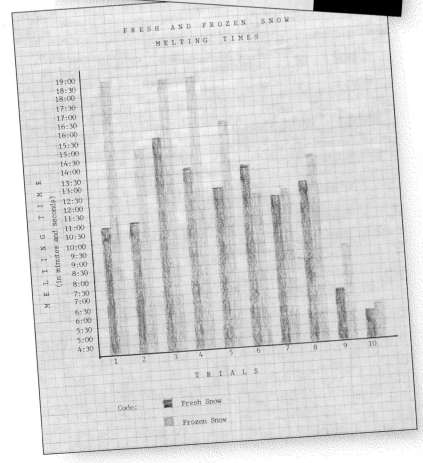

		COLLECTION T			
Trial	Fresh Snow	Time Min:Sec.	Frozen Snow	Time Min:Sec	Difference in Times
1	I	10:55		18:49	7:54
2	I	11:03		15:00	3:57
3	I	15:30		18:39	3:09
4	I	13:48		18:40	4:52
5	I	12:40		16:16	3:36
6		13:46	I	12:13	1:33
7	I	12:00		12:20	0:20
8	I	12:45		14:05	1:20
9	I	6:43		9:13	2:30
10	I	5:31		5:50	0:19

FRESH SNOW WILL MELT QUICKER THAN FROZEN SNOW IN FRONT OF A FIRE.

FRESH AND FROZEN SNOW MELTING TIMES

MELTING TIME (in minutes and seconds)

TRIALS

Code: Fresh Snow

Frozen Snow

Snow Melt

S8 a Scientific Investigation: The student demonstrates scientific competence by completing an experiment, such as conducting a fair test.

A full investigation includes:

• Questions that can be studied using the resources available.

• Procedures that are safe, humane, and ethical; and that respect privacy and property rights.

• Data that have been collected and recorded (see also Science Standard 6) in ways that others can verify and analyze using skills expected at this grade level (see also Mathematics Standard 4).

• Data and results that have been represented (see also Science Standard 7) in ways that fit the context.

• Recommendations, decisions, and conclusions based on evidence.

• Acknowledgment of references and contributions of others.

• Results that are communicated appropriately to audiences.

• Reflection and defense of conclusions and recommendations from other sources and peer review.

D The investigation includes a logical and sequential plan including multiple trials. It uses multiple representations and data displays to communicate scientific findings.

B It explores different interpretations of data and applies the information to potentially relevant environmental conditions in concluding remarks.

E It considers potentially confounding and uncontrolled variables in the experimental design in making appropriate conclusions based on experimental data.

The work touches on the concept of density. More evidence, such as an explanation of the relationship between density and melting times, would be required to meet the standard for Physical Sciences Concepts.

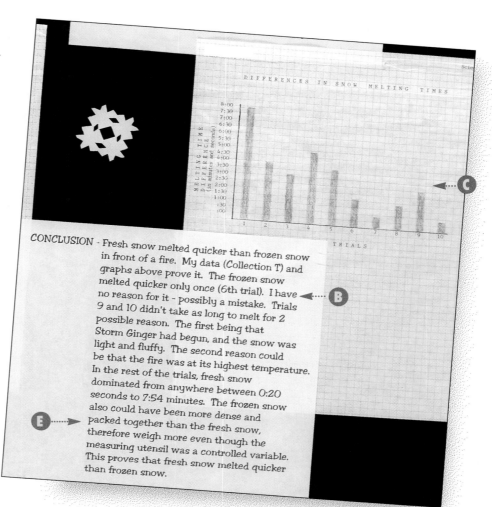

DIFFERENCES IN SNOW MELTING TIMES

CONCLUSION - Fresh snow melted quicker than frozen snow in front of a fire. My data (Collection T) and graphs above prove it. The frozen snow melted quicker only once (6th trial). I have no reason for it - possibly a mistake. Trials 9 and 10 didn't take as long to melt for 2 possible reason. The first being that Storm Ginger had begun, and the snow was light and fluffy. The second reason could be that the fire was at its highest temperature. In the rest of the trials, fresh snow dominated from anywhere between 0:20 seconds to 7:54 minutes. The frozen snow also could have been more dense and packed together than the fresh snow, therefore weigh more even though the measuring utensil was a controlled variable. This proves that fresh snow melted quicker than frozen snow.

Physical
Sciences
Concepts

Life
Sciences
Concepts

Earth and
Space Sciences
Concepts

Scientific
Connections and
Applications

S5 Scientific
Thinking

S6 Scientific Tools
and
Technologies

S7 Scientific
Communication

S8 Scientific
Investigation

Work Sample & Commentary: *Fire-Belly Newts*

The quotations from the Science performance descriptions in this commentary are excerpted. The complete performance descriptions are shown on pages 132-135.

Best practice in science has always included intensive inquiry and investigation, but these are frequently given less emphasis at the elementary level in the face of competing demands from English language arts and mathematics. There are many opportunities to learn science outside of school, including the Girl Scouts of the U.S.A., Boy Scouts of America, Boys and Girls Clubs of America, 4-H, and Future Farmers of America. The work done in these venues can and should be used to provide evidence of meeting these standards.

Physical Sciences Concepts

Life Sciences Concepts **S2**

Earth and Space Sciences Concepts

Scientific Connections and Applications

Scientific Thinking **S5**

Scientific Tools and Technologies

Scientific Communication **S7**

Scientific Investigation **S8**

The task

An elementary student participated in a 4-H program in which she raised an animal, learning about and caring for its needs. The culmination of this project involved a county-wide fair at which the student's project was judged against other similar projects. The task involved observation of the animal, some library research, the production of a display, a report, and an interview with a judge. The student's original report and a follow-up interview are included here.

Circumstances of performance

This sample of student work was produced under the following conditions:

√ alone   in a group

   in class   as homework

   with teacher feedback   √ with peer feedback

   timed   opportunity for revision

The work was done in a 4-H program.

This work sample illustrates a standard-setting performance for the following parts of the standards:

S2a   **Life Sciences Concepts: Characteristics of organisms.**

S2b   **Life Sciences Concepts: Life cycles of organisms.**

S2c   **Life Sciences Concepts: Organisms and environments.**

S5c   **Scientific Thinking: Use evidence from reliable sources to construct explanations.**

S5d   **Scientific Thinking: Evaluate different points of view using relevant experiences, observations, and knowledge.**

S7a   **Scientific Communication: Represent data and results in multiple ways.**

S7b   **Scientific Communication: Use facts to support conclusions.**

S7c   **Scientific Communication: Communicate in a form suited to the purpose and the audience.**

S8b   **Scientific Investigation: A systematic observation, such as a field study.**

What the work shows

S2a   Life Sciences Concepts: The student produces evidence that demonstrates understanding of characteristics of organisms, such as survival and environmental support....

A

S2b   Life Sciences Concepts: The student produces evidence that demonstrates understanding of life cycles of organisms....

B

S2c   Life Sciences Concepts: The student produces evidence that demonstrates understanding of organisms and environments, such as the interdependence of animals and plants in an ecosystem....

C

S5c   Scientific Thinking: The student uses evidence from reliable sources to construct explanations.

C D The student used several sources and was able to identify what information came from which source.

Fire-Belly Newts

S5d Scientific Thinking: The student evaluates different points of view using relevant experiences, observations, and knowledge; and distinguishes between fact and opinion.

E The student differentiated between things she had read and things that she had observed.

S7a Scientific Communication: The student represents data and results in multiple ways, such as…drawings, diagrams, and artwork; and technical and creative writing.

The student communicated with a drawing, a written report, a poster, an oral presentation, and through an interview.

S7b Scientific Communication: The student uses facts to support conclusions.

F

S7c Scientific Communication: The student communicates in a form suited to the purpose and the audience….

Consistent with the context of a 4-H project for presentation at a county fair, the student communicated with a drawing, a written report, a poster, an oral presentation, and an interview with the judge.

S8b Scientific Investigation: The student demonstrates scientific competence by completing a systematic observation, such as a field study.

A full investigation includes:

• Questions that can be studied using the resources available.

A

• Procedures that are safe, humane, and ethical; and that respect privacy and property rights.

C **G**

A

BACKGROUND: Newts are amphibians (can live on land and in water) and are similar to salamanders, not lizards. They have soft toes with four on the front and five on the back. They are very smooth. The tail is flat for swimming purposes. They can regrow missing tails, legs and jaws. They have no eardrums, so they hear through vibrations through their front legs and lower jaw. They are also voiceless. They can locate by means of smell. When picking up a newt, wet your hands so not to tear the skin.

CARE: The newt is fed once a day. I clean its tank twice a month. In doing this I must rinse off the rocks and scrub off the algae from the sides of the tank. I also have to clean off the air pump.

NUTRITION: In the wild newts will eat small insects. If a newt is starving it will eat scraps of meat.

FEEDING : Sarah (my newt) is fed shrimp pellets. We feed her one pellet a day. The pellets smell so bad that we keep them in a ziploc bag. Sarah doesn't usually eat while we are looking. She prefers to be alone. They can be trained to eat right out of your hand. You can also put meat or flies on a stick to make it look like the food is alive.

HOUSING : Sarah (my newt) lives in a tank with a water filter, gravel and 2 large stones. She likes to hide between the two stones. Since Sarah has gone to school and the nursing home we have purchased a small travel tank. The tanks are never completely filled with water. She likes to get on top of the large rocks and out of the water.

HEALTH : I have had Sarah for 4 years, newts seem to live longer then fish. She prefers to be alone. When she walks on land she walks like a crocodile. When they are small they look like a guppy.

B **MATING:** They have a certain ritual that only that species recognizes to mate. They do a dance that other newts will recognize. Some newts have a fluid they put into the water and the females will follow the smell behind the males. Some male newts develop a crest on their heads and a fancy tail during breeding season.

OTHER INFORMATION : Newts skin gets to tight when they grow and they shed it like a snake. Then they eat it. Their enemies in the wild are Hydra, people, and under water animals. When they think they are in danger they turn on their back. Their is black, orange, and gray on their stomach. Then they match their surroundings. They also have a bad taste that their skin gives off.

OTHER TYPES OF NEWTS: Some different kinds of newts are Japanese Newts (black back, bright red belly); Red-Spotted Newts (lives on land as a youth and in the water as an adult; it's brown flecked with red); Smooth or Warty Newt (during mating this newt developes a crest along its back and tail); California Newt (brown with a yellow belly).
Sarah is a fire-belly newt, this is seen by the orange on her stomach.

D Some information on newts I got from these books:
The Little Red Newt by Louise Harris and Norman Harris
Frogs, Toads, Lizards, and Salamanders by Nancy Parker and Joan Wright
Amphibians As Pets by George and Lisbeth Zappler
Lovebirds, Lizards and lammas by Leda and Rhoda Blumberg
Frogs, Toads, Salamanders, and How they Reproduce by Dorthy Hinshaw Patent
Pets by Frances Chrystie

Overall, in taking care of Sarah I have learned that they are easy to care for but are a pretty boring pet. They don't give you love like a dog.

Physical Sciences Concepts

S2 Life Sciences Concepts

Earth and Space Sciences Concepts

Scientific Connections and Applications

S5 Scientific Thinking

Scientific Tools and Technologies

S7 Scientific Communication

S8 Scientific Investigation

Fire-Belly Newts

Student Interview: Fire Belly Newts

Q: Tell me about your 4-H project with the Fire Belly Newt.

A: Her name is Sara and she is an amphibian. I was going to get an iguana, but Mom said I should get a smaller animal.

Q: What did you have to learn to raise the newt?

A: I had to read books. But there weren't a lot of books at the pet store and only one at the library. I got some things out of encyclopedias. I had to learn they are amphibians and need land and water to live. They have soft toes for climbing on land and a tail that helps them swim. Oh, and if they get bitten or caught they can lose a tail or leg and grow it back.

Q: How did you know what to feed her?

C → A: At the pet store, they said to feed her shrimp pellets that smell really bad. In the books I read, they said that in the wild newts will eat insects and, if they are starving, they will eat meat. We put some food on a stick to feed her sometimes. That makes the food look alive. Sara likes to eat when nobody is looking. I feed her only one pellet a day or she will get sick or the tank will get ickey.

I had to keep the tank between 72 and 82 degrees. Sara is cold-blooded and that means she gets sick if it gets too cold or too hot. Like, if it is 72 degrees then she will be that and if it is hot, she will be hot. We got this sticky thermometer so if it gets too hot we would…I mean if it gets too cold we would turn on this heater here. And I have to clean the tank once a week.

Q: How do you do that?

A: I have to take Sara out and I put her in here (*small bowl*). Then I have to clean off the algae with a scraper and clean the filter and it smells sometimes. Then I have to put in new water once in a while. But that's only once or twice so far. And I put this powder in so the stuff in the water doesn't make her sick or die.

Q: Is Sara a female? How could you tell?

E → A: Newts that are male have a crest on their back. I haven't seen a newt with that though. But since my newt doesn't have one I thought she was a female. I want to see if I can find a male newt and breed them. But I can't find any books on how to do that.

Q: How about the pet store people? Could they tell you?

A: They might know. But our pet store has lots of fish and only a few newts and a couple of geckos. I asked them about newts and they didn't know very much except for feeding and they looked that up.

Q: Would you like to tell me how they mate?

B → A: Yes. They have a dance that only other newts will recognize. Then the male newt will spray the water with a liquid and the female will follow the smell and lay her eggs there. It sounds kind of gross. Then the male newt sort of takes off and the female stays

---

there and guards the eggs. I don't know if she guards them until they hatch and I don't know how many baby newts they have.

Q: What about how newts protect themselves?

A: If they think they are in danger they turn on their backs. I think the colors on their stomach maybe are scary to other animals. But the newt can grow back a leg or a tail if it gets eaten and one book says they taste really bad in their skin.

Q: Tell me about raising your newt as a 4-H project.

A: Well, I had to learn all about my newt and I had to tell a 4-H judge about my newt at the fair. I had this paper I wrote about Sara on my table and I had Sara there, too.

Q: Did the judge ask you questions and how did you answer them?

A: Yes. I said, "My name is…" and "Would you like to know about my newt?" Then he said, "Yes." I told him, "My newt is named Sara and she is an amphibian…"

Q: So you pretty much had this whole report memorized?

H → A: Yeah, my Mom helped me with the subjunctive mood and went over and over it a lot.

Q: What else did you do with Sara in this project? Did you have to watch her over time or anything like that?

A: Oh yeah, I had to learn about her from books and from watching her every day. I sometimes kept notes on what she did to see if she was like the newts in the books.

Q: What did you learn from watching Sara?

A: I learned that she likes to spend a lot of time under this rock and she likes to stay away from the bubble thing. But she likes to come out on this rock so she can be out of the water. Oh, and we had to make sure the lid was on this tank because she would get out.

Q: Did she get out?

G → A: Once she almost got out and my Dad saw her and put her back in. Oh, and you have to make sure your hands are wet, because newts have really thin skin and it can tear.

Q: Does she stay underwater for a long time?

A: Yeah, I timed her sometimes and she stayed under about 30 minutes and sometimes more. She breathes air but when she was really little I think she had what fish have.

Q: Gills?

F → A: Yeah, and now she can breathe air which is different and she's an amphibian and can go underwater and on land too.

- Data that have been collected and recorded (see also Science Standard 6) in ways that others can verify and analyze using skills expected at this grade level (see also Mathematics Standard 4).

- Data and results that have been represented (see also Science Standard 7) in ways that fit the context.

- Recommendations, decisions, and conclusions based on evidence.

- Acknowledgment of references and contributions of others.
  C D G H

- Results that are communicated appropriately to audiences.

- Reflection and defense of conclusions and recommendations from other sources and peer review.

wood. Float. Now I will teach some steps.
① Shuffle. Here's how you do it with your right foot up in
② Hit the ball of your foot the ground.
③ Then bring your foot in to your left standing foot. It not be touching the ground
④ Then hit the ball of your toes while bringing it behind left standing foot. It shouldn't be touching the ground....
⑤ Now try it in one motion

which is sugar.
The plants get from the suns energy. Ca DISX ide from the air water from the soil.
air gives carbon dioxide

2,000 hear at event st

By Bob Mahlburg
Fort Worth Star Telegram

About 2,000 grade school kid and teachers gathered in Fort Worth Authors' Conference yesterday to h tips from two authors and tales from storytellers.

"It's fun to listen to them," grader Dana ____, 8, a student at Carlson Applied Learning Center w plan the event.

Featured authors included books writers Caroline Arnold of L

Introduction to the performance standards for

Applied Learning

Applied Learning focuses on the capabilities people need to be productive members of society, as individuals who apply the knowledge gained in school and elsewhere to analyze problems and propose solutions, to communicate effectively and coordinate action with others, and to use the tools of the information age workplace. It connects the work students do in school with the demands of the twenty-first century workplace.

As a newer focus of study, Applied Learning does not have a distinct professional constituency producing content standards on which performance standards can be built. However, the Secretary's Commission on Achieving Necessary Skills (SCANS) laid a foundation for the field in its report, *Learning a Living: A Blueprint for High Performance* (1992) which defined the concept of "Workplace Know-how." We worked from this foundation and from comparable international work to produce our own "Framework for Applied Learning" (New Standards, 1994). That framework delineated nine areas of competence and spelled out their elements. The nine areas of competence were as follows:

• Collecting, analyzing, and organizing information;

• Communicating ideas and information;

• Planning and organizing resources;

• Working with others and in teams;

• Solving problems;

• Using mathematical ideas and techniques;

• Using technology;

• Teaching and learning on demand;

• Understanding and designing systems.

The Applied Learning performance standards have been built upon this framework. The standards have also been built on the experience of the Fort Worth Independent School District's applied learning initiative and the application projects developed by Mountlake Terrace High School in Washington.

We adopted the approach of developing distinct standards for Applied Learning rather than weaving them through the standards for the core subject areas. The advantage of establishing distinct standards for Applied Learning is that it focuses attention on the requirements of these standards and asserts an explicit role for Applied Learning as a domain for assessment and reporting of student achievement. "Cross-curricular" standards run the risk of being absorbed and lost within the expectations of the different subjects. However, the disadvantage of this approach is that it may be interpreted as advocating the development of Applied Learning as a subject in its own right to be studied in isolation from subject content. That is not the intention of these standards. We do not advocate development of Applied Learning as a separate subject. We expect that the work students do to meet the Applied

Learning performance standards will take place generally within the context of a subject or will draw on content from more than one subject area. This expectation is stated in the performance description for **A1**, Problem Solving.

There are five performance standards for Applied Learning:

A1 **Problem Solving;**

A2 **Communication Tools and Techniques;**

A3 **Information Tools and Techniques;**

A4 **Learning and Self-management Tools and Techniques;**

A5 **Tools and Techniques for Working With Others.**

A1, Problem Solving is the centerpiece of the standards. The performance description defines problem solving projects focused on productive activity and organized around three kinds of problem solving:

• Design a product, service or system in which the student identifies needs that could be met by new products, services, or systems and creates solutions for meeting them;

• Improve a System in which the student develops an understanding of the way systems of people, machines, and processes work; troubleshoots problems in their operation and devises strategies for improving their effectiveness;

• Plan and organize an event or an activity in which the student takes responsibility for all aspects of planning and organizing an event or an activity from concept to completion.

The performance description specifies the criteria for each kind of problem solving project. These criteria become progressively more demanding from elementary school to high school.

The four "tools and techniques" standards are designed to work in concert with the Problem Solving standard. Each of these standards describes tools and techniques that are needed for success in completing projects of the kinds outlined above.

The tools and techniques described in **A2**-**A5** (such as gathering information, publishing information, learning from models, and working with others to complete a task) are only meaningful when considered in the context of work that has a genuine purpose and audience. The key to effective use of these tools and techniques is the capacity to put them to use in an integrated way in the course of completing a real task. It is critical, therefore, that they be learned and used in such contexts rather than practiced in a piecemeal way as skills for their own sake. Students are expected to demonstrate their achievement of the tools and techniques standards in the context of problem solving projects. This is reflected in the examples listed under the performance descriptions. At the same time, it is unlikely that any one project will allow students to demonstrate their achievement in relation to all of the standards. This is evident from the work samples and commentaries. In fact, it is likely that a project that attempts to cover all of the parts of the standards will accomplish none of them well.

The Applied Learning performance standards reflect the nine areas of competence defined in the Framework for Applied Learning. But the match is not complete. **M6**, **M8**, **S6**, and **S8** embody many of the competencies that were defined by the "Framework for Applied Learning" in "Using mathematical tools and techniques" and "Using technology." These competencies have not been duplicated in Applied Learning. However, the Applied Learning standards do include an explicit requirement that students use information technology to assist in gathering, organizing, and presenting information. Given the importance of ensuring all students develop the capacity to make effective use of information technology, we resolved that the overlap among the standards in this area was warranted. (See "Introduction to the performance standards for Science," page 130, for disscussion of the resource issues related to this requirement.)

Another area in which we decided that some overlap was warranted relates to **A2**. The first part of this standard, which requires an oral presentation, is similar to one of the requirements of the Speaking, Listening, and Viewing standard in English Language Arts, **E3**. The difference is that the Applied Learning standard focuses explicitly on presenting project plans or results to an audience, whereas the purpose of the presentation is not specified in **E3**. As the cross-referencing of examples under the performance descriptions indicates, oral presentations that meet the requirements of **A2**a may also satisfy the requirements of **E3**c; however, the reverse would not necessarily be the case.

The capacities defined by the tools and techniques standards (**A2** - **A5**) are difficult to pin down. There is a tendency to describe them in terms of general dispositions that render them almost impossible to assess in any credible way. Each part of these standards is defined in terms of a work product or performance that students can use to provide concrete evidence of their achievement. The overall set of products and performances required to meet the standards is similar at each grade level, but the specific requirements differ and grow in demand from elementary to high school. (See "Appendix IV: The Grade Levels Compared: Applied Learning," page 240.)

The first year of developmental testing of Applied Learning portfolios in 1995-96 provided an opportunity to test these performance standards (as they were presented in the *Consultation Draft*) in practice. Students in about 50 classrooms conducted projects designed around the standards. Their experience and the experience of the teachers who supported them was a valuable source of information for refining the performance descriptions. Refinements were also made in response to reviews by representatives of business and industry groups and community youth organizations such as 4-H, Girl Scouts of the U.S.A., Boy Scouts of America, Junior Achievement, and Girls and Boys Clubs of America. The refinements were largely confined to the detail of the performance descriptions, but there were two more significant changes, both related to **A3**. The first was the definition of more explicit requirements for using information technology, especially at the high school level, in response to comments from business and industry representatives. The second was the inclusion of a specific requirement for "research" as set out in **A3**a. Research was implicit in the draft performance standards. The decision to make it explicit arose in the process of review of student projects where it was clear that the successful projects were those in which students had invested energy in research and could demonstrate that research in the work they produced.

Experience in using the standards to shape student work raised several issues. It was notable that most projects focused on "design" and on "planning and organizing." There were fewer examples of "improving a system." This was not surprising, but indicates the need to focus attention on gathering examples of such projects.

The circumstances in which the projects were conducted varied markedly. Some projects were initiated by the teacher and some were initiated by students; some projects were conducted by whole classes, some by small groups of students, and some by individuals; some projects were conducted as part of classwork and some were conducted largely outside class. It was clear, however, that regardless of how a project was initiated, a critical part of its success was the development of a sense of responsibility among the students involved for figuring out the work that needed to be done to complete the project and for making sure that the work got done. What was less clear were the relative merits of different arrangements of whole class, small group, and individual projects. A further question was the appropriate level of scaffolding of projects by teachers and the degree of scaffolding that is appropriate at different grade levels. Our capacity to resolve this last issue was complicated by the fact that, for most of the teachers and students involved, these were the first projects of this sort they had ever undertaken. The work samples and commentaries should be read with this fact in mind. These are issues that can only be resolved through practice and experience.

A1 Problem Solving

To see how these performance descriptions compare with the expectations for middle school and high school, turn to pages 240-245.

The examples that follow the performance descriptions for each standard are examples of the work students might do to demonstrate their achievement. The examples also indicate the nature and complexity of activities that are appropriate to expect of students at the elementary level.

The cross-references that follow the examples highlight examples for which the same activity, and possibly even the same piece of work, may enable students to demonstrate their achievement in relation to more than one standard. In some cases, the cross-references highlight examples of activities through which students might demonstrate their achievement in relation to standards for more than one subject matter.

Apply problem solving strategies in purposeful ways, both in situations where the problem and desirable solutions are clearly evident and in situations requiring a creative approach to achieve an outcome.

The student conducts projects involving at least two of the following kinds of problem solving each year and, over the course of elementary school, conducts projects involving all three kinds of problem solving.

- Design a Product, Service, or System: Identify needs that could be met by new products, services, or systems and create solutions for meeting them.
- Improve a System: Develop an understanding of the way systems of people, machines, and processes work; troubleshoot problems in their operation and devise strategies for improving their effectiveness.
- Plan and Organize an Event or an Activity: Take responsibility for all aspects of planning and organizing an event or an activity from concept to completion, making good use of the resources of people, time, money, and materials and facilities.

Each project should involve subject matter related to the standards for English Language Arts, and/or Mathematics, and/or Science, and/or other appropriate subject content.

Design a Product, Service, or System

A1a   The student designs and creates a product, service, or system to meet an identified need; that is, the student:

- develops ideas for the design of the product, service, or system;
- chooses among the design ideas and justifies the choice;
- establishes criteria for judging the success of the design;
- uses an appropriate format to represent the design;
- plans and carries out the steps needed to turn the design into a reality;
- evaluates the design in terms of the criteria established for success.

Examples of designing a product, service, or system include:

▲ Design a library system to manage classroom resources. **3a, 3b**
▲ Design a tree house, accounting for physical and financial constraints. **2d, M8c**
▲ Design a guide to the school library for younger children. **3b, 4a, 5c, E2d**
▲ Design and produce a weekly school news service for broadcast on the PA system or closed circuit video network. **4a, 5a, E3d**
▲ Design a classroom work area for ongoing project work.
▲ Design a weather station and provide a daily weather reporting service for the school. **2b, 2c, 4a, 5a, 5b, M1a, M1c, M1f, M6h, S3b, S3c**
▲ Design a musical instrument. **3b, S1b**

Improve a System

A1b   The student troubleshoots problems in the operation of a system in need of repair or devises and tests ways of improving the effectiveness of a system in operation; that is, the student:

- identifies the parts of the system and the way the parts connect with each other;
- identifies parts or connections in the system that have broken down or that could be made to work better;
- devises ways of making the system work again or making it work better;
- evaluates the effectiveness of the strategies for improving the system and supports the evaluation with evidence.

Examples of troubleshooting problems in the operation of a system or improving the effectiveness of a system in operation include:

▲ Repair a bicycle, skateboard, or other means of transportation. **5b**
▲ Improve the system for distributing sports equipment during recess and lunch times. **2b**
▲ Clean up an aquarium. **2a, 3b, S2a, S2c**
▲ Improve the system for collecting trash in the school. **2a, 5c, M7b, S4b, S6b, S7a**
▲ Investigate the food choices of students buying food from vending machines near the school and make recommendations for ways of improving the nutritional value of the food available. **3a, 3b, M8a, S4c**

Plan and Organize an Event or an Activity

A1c   The student plans and organizes an event or an activity; that is, the student:

- develops a plan for the event or activity that:
  – includes all the factors and variables that need to be considered;
  – shows the order in which things need to be done;
  – takes into account the resources available to put the plan into action, including people and time;
- implements the plan;
- evaluates the success of the event or activity by identifying the parts of the plan that worked best and the parts that could have been improved by better planning and organization;
- makes recommendations to others who might consider planning and organizing a similar event or activity.

Examples of planning and organizing an event or an activity include:

▲ Organize a storytelling conference. **2b, 2c, 3a, 5a, E2c, E5b**
▲ Plan a class excursion to the zoo or museum.
▲ Organize a drive to raise money for a specific purpose. **2a, 2c, 3b, M1a, M4b**
▲ Plan a camping expedition, including all necessary supplies and a budget. **2a, M6h, M8d, S2a, S2c, S4b, S4c, S4d**

A2 Communication Tools and Techniques

Communicate information and ideas in ways that are appropriate to the purpose and audience through spoken, written, and graphic means of expression.

A2 a The student makes an oral presentation of project plans or findings to an appropriate audience; that is, the student:

- organizes the presentation in a logical way appropriate to its purpose;
- speaks clearly and presents confidently;
- responds to questions from the audience;
- evaluates the effectiveness of the presentation.

Examples of oral presentations include:

▲ A presentation to the custodian of proposals for improving the system of collecting trash in the school. **1b, 5c, E3c**

▲ A presentation to the principal of a proposal for an overnight camping trip. **1c, E3c**

▲ A presentation to a school assembly of results of a fund raising drive. **1c, 3b, E3c**

▲ A presentation to the class of the results of a project to clean up an aquarium. **1b, 3b, E3c, S7c**

A2 b The student composes and sends correspondence, such as thank-you letters and memoranda providing information; that is, the student:

- expresses the information or request clearly;
- writes in a style appropriate to the purpose of the correspondence.

Examples of letters and memoranda include:

▲ A letter inviting students at another school to a storytelling conference. **1c, 2c, 3a, 5a**

▲ A letter of thanks to a visiting speaker. **1c, 2c, 4a, 5a, 5b**

▲ A memorandum asking teachers to explain to their classes new procedures for distributing sports equipment during recess and lunch times. **1b**

▲ The use of E-mail to send the daily weather reports to teachers, parents, and community members. **1a, 2c, 4a, 5a, 5b**

A2 c The student writes and formats information for short publications, such as brochures or posters; that is, the student:

- organizes the information into an appropriate form for use in the publication;
- checks the information for accuracy;
- formats the publication so that it achieves its purpose.

Examples of publishing information include:

▲ Design a format for publishing daily weather reports. **1a, 2b, 4a, 5b, 5c**

▲ Design a poster advertising a fund raising drive. **1c, 3b**

▲ Produce a program for a storytelling conference. **1c, 2b, 3a, 5a**

▲ Create and maintain a Web site for the duration of the fund raising drive. **1c, 3b**

A3 Information Tools and Techniques

Use information gathering techniques, analyze and evaluate information and use information technology to assist in collecting, analyzing, organizing, and presenting information.

A3 a The student gathers information to assist in completing project work; that is, the student:

- identifies potential sources of information to assist in completing the project;
- uses appropriate techniques to collect the information, e.g., considers sampling issues in conducting a survey;
- distinguishes relevant from irrelevant information;
- shows evidence of research in the completed project.

Examples of gathering information to assist in completing project work include:

▲ Investigate the systems used to manage library collections, e.g., through interviews with librarians and field visits to libraries, in order to inform a project to design a library. **1a, 3b**

▲ Research the nutritional value of foods available in the vending machines near the school to inform a project to make recommendations for improving the nutritional value of food available. **1b**

▲ Conduct surveys to identify the reading interests and preferences of intended participants at a storytelling conference in order to inform the design of the conference program. **1c, 2b, 2c, 5a**

A3 b The student uses information technology to assist in gathering, organizing, and presenting information; that is, the student:

- acquires information for specific purposes from on-line sources, such as the Internet, and other electronic data bases, such as an electronic encyclopedia;
- uses word-processing, drawing, and painting programs to produce project reports and related materials.

Examples of using information technology to assist in gathering, organizing, and presenting information include:

▲ Use word-processing and drawing programs to design a guide to the library for younger students. **1a, 4a, 5c**

▲ Use a drawing program to present daily results of a fund raising drive. **1c, 2a, 2c**

▲ Use an electronic card catalogue to research information on sound for the design of a musical instrument or to find out about the requirements of freshwater animals and plants for a project to clean up an aquarium. **1a, 1b, 2a**

▲ Use the Internet to obtain advice from professional librarians during the project to design a library. **1a, 3a**

Samples of student work that illustrate standard-setting performances for these standards can be found on pages 165-209.

The cross-references that follow the examples illustrate some of the ways by which a single Applied Learning project may provide a vehicle for demonstrating achievement of several parts of the standards. The cross-references are based on the examples that are linked to the Problem Solving standard. It is intended that students demonstrate their achievement of the four Tools and Techniques standards in conjunction with Problem Solving projects.

Performance Descriptions *Applied Learning*

To see how these performance descriptions compare with the expectations for middle school and high school, turn to pages 240-245.

The examples that follow the performance descriptions for each standard are examples of the work students might do to demonstrate their achievement. The examples also indicate the nature and complexity of activities that are appropriate to expect of students at the elementary level.

The cross-references that follow the examples highlight examples for which the same activity, and possibly even the same piece of work, may enable students to demonstrate their achievement in relation to more than one standard. In some cases, the cross-references highlight examples of activities through which students might demonstrate their achievement in relation to standards for more than one subject matter.

A4 Learning and Self-management Tools and Techniques

Manage and direct one's own learning.

A4a The student learns from models; that is, the student:

- consults with or observes other students and adults at work, and identifies the main features of what they do and the way they go about their work;
- examines models for the results of project work, such as professionally produced publications, and analyzes their qualities;
- uses what he or she learns from models to assist in planning and conducting project activities.

Examples of learning from models include:

▲ Examine published guides similar in design to the students' proposed guide to the library. **1a, 3b, 5c**

▲ Study the way news reports are presented on radio and television to inform development of the students' own newscasts. **1a, 2c, 5a, 5c**

▲ Visit a meteorological station and observe the work of forecasters to inform the weather station project. **1a, 2b, 2c, 5a, 5b**

A4b The student keeps records of work activities in an orderly manner; that is, the student:

- sets up a system for storing records of work activities;
- maintains records of work activities in a way that makes it possible to find specific materials quickly and easily.

Examples of tools and techniques for keeping records of work activities include:

▲ Maintain a project log book.
▲ Create and use a table of contents.
▲ Use dividers or colored tabs to categorize material.

A4c The student identifies strengths and weaknesses in his or her own work; that is, the student:

- understands and establishes criteria for judging the quality of work processes and products;
- assesses his or her own work processes and products.

Examples of tools and techniques for identifying strengths and weaknesses in one's own work include:

▲ Make a list of the desirable qualities of a piece of work before starting and use the list to review and revise the work at the end.
▲ Use a review of previous project work to guide planning of a new project.
▲ Ask a friend to critique a piece of work in draft form.

A5 Tools and Techniques for Working With Others

Work with others to achieve a shared goal, help other people learn on-the-job, and respond effectively to the needs of a client.

A5a The student works with others to complete a task; that is, the student:

- reaches agreement with group members on what work needs to be done to complete the task and how the work will be tackled;
- takes a share of the responsibility for the work;
- consults with group members regularly during the task to check on progress in completing the task, to decide on any changes that are required, and to check that all parts have been completed at the end of the task.

Examples of working with others to complete a task include:

▲ Work on the production of a weekly school news service. **1a, 4a, 5c**

▲ Share responsibility for collecting information from a weather station and preparing daily reports. **1a, 2b, 2c, 4a, 5b**

▲ Organize a storytelling conference. **1c, 2b, 2c, 3a**

A5b The student shows or explains something clearly enough for someone else to be able to do it.

Examples of showing or explaining something to someone else include:

▲ Show how to fix a specific breakdown in a bicycle. **1b**
▲ Explain how to figure out the average morning temperature recorded at school during the winter. **1a, 2b, 2c, 4a, M4c**
▲ Show how to operate a video camera. **1a, 4a, 5a**

A5c The student responds to a request from a client; that is, the student:

- interprets the client's request;
- asks questions to clarify the demands of a task.

Examples of responding to a request from a client include:

▲ Talk with the custodian to determine problems to be solved in a system for collection of trash in the school. **1b, 2a**

▲ Respond to a written request from a teacher to include some information in a weekly school news broadcast. **1a, 2c, 4a, 5a**

▲ Interview younger children to identify sections they use in the library and things they find confusing about accessing information and use the interview to inform the design of the guide to the library. **1a, 3b, 4a**

Work Sample & Commentary: *Designing and Building a Bike Trailer*

The task

Students were asked to devise a project that would advance their study of a school subject and involve obtaining the assistance of experts from outside the school. The project proposal had to be approved by the teacher and the building principal. Students could work individually or in groups of two or three. This project was undertaken by two students: the work shown here is drawn from the portfolio prepared by one of the students. The students decided to design and build a bike trailer, and to produce a guide to making a bike trailer.

Circumstances of performance

The project was completed both in and out of school time. It occupied about one hour each day for two days per week for most of the year. The students sought assistance from two mentors. They received peer and teacher feedback on drafts of their guide prior to publication.

What the work shows

A1 a Problem Solving: The student designs and creates a product, service, or system to meet an identified need; that is, the student:

- develops ideas for the design of the product, service, or system;
- chooses among the design ideas and justifies the choice;
- establishes criteria for judging the success of the design;
- uses an appropriate format to represent the design;
- plans and carries out the steps needed to turn the design into a reality;
- evaluates the design in terms of the criteria established for success.

This work sample illustrates a standard-setting performance for the following parts of the standards:

A1 a **Problem Solving: Design a product, service, or system.**

A2 b **Communication: Compose correspondence.**

A2 c **Communication: Publish information.**

A3 a **Information: Gather information.**

A4 a **Learning and Self-management: Learn from models.**

A4 b **Learning and Self-management: Keep records of work activities.**

A5 b **Working With Others: Show or explain something so someone else can do it.**

A

September 5, 1995

Mr. _____

Dear Mr. _____,

Have you ever woken up and your parents were gone? You have to ride your bike to school. You just remembered that you have to carry a big heavy project to school. This product will solve those problems.

My audience is Bike owners and school students. This product is a BikeTrailer. It is usable to haul heavy stuff to school or a nearby house or place.

Kids can relax and talk with a friend. You will be able to carry back boards for products to and from school. It can haul luggage to a friends house. It will save gas and energy. It also builds muscle. This product will make life simpler. If you're tired you can rest in the trailer. You can do things better and easier.

In the school library, I found a picture of a motorcycle and its trailer with its parts labeled. This will serve as my adult model.

I will start to build this product with your permission.

I am inventing something to haul almost anything you want useing your bike. I can tell when this project is done because it will be able to haul almost anything or anybody. I will assess this project by if I did my best and if it works. When it is done if it hauls well enough I will sell the plans to a manufacturer. I hope this project will be used in a good way. I wanted to make things easier without using motorized vehicles.

If you are worrying about what you do with this product once you get wherever you are going, all you have to do is lock it to your bike. This product will make life easier in hauling short distances.

Doing this project will be a very wonderful learning experience for me. So far this project is a success. When we finish it will be great.

Sincerely,

A The proposal establishes the need for the new duct. It shows evidence of some initial research into ideas for completing the project, and establishes a criterion for judging the success of the design.

B This working document demonstrates some of the students' planning for the project. It identifies some of the problems they needed to solve in the design and production of the bike trailer.

C **D** **E** These sketches represent early steps in the design process, and suggest some initial ideas (such as an umbrella to shade the trailer) that were rather more ambitious than the final design.

The documentation presented from this project is not a comprehensive record of all work done as part of the project. It would be neither reasonable nor appropriate to ask students to keep detailed written records of every aspect of a project. This would defeat part of the purpose of applied learning which is for students to put their academic learning to work and to learn from projects that connect what they do at school to the demands of the twenty-first century workplace. Some of these standards lend themselves to assessment through observation and other less formal methods than through written work.

A1 Problem Solving

A2 Communication Tools and Techniques

A3 Information Tools and Techniques

A4 Learning and Self-management Tools and Techniques

A5 Tools and Techniques for Working With Others

Designing and Building a Bike Trailer

B

Planning

My partener and I are going to do a project to help people carry stuff on their bike short distances a bike trailer.

Materials-
6 – 4ft – 2in. boards   screws   money
2 – 1ft – 2in. boards
2 – 4by 1 inche wheels. (two pairs)

Steps-
Call _____ .   Interview carpenter.
Investigate cost. Get money. cut wood
mesure wagon hook up hitch.

Problems-
Were to put the hitch? not enough money?
Where to get a turn signal. May not find right materails? not enough materails?

1. How big is it?
2. How heavy is it?
3. How long will it take to build it?
4. Howmuch can it carry il be built.
5. How many trailers should be built.
6. How will wood cost.
7. How does it help.
8. How much to sell it for.
9. what kinds of tools to get
10. Where do we get the money?

C

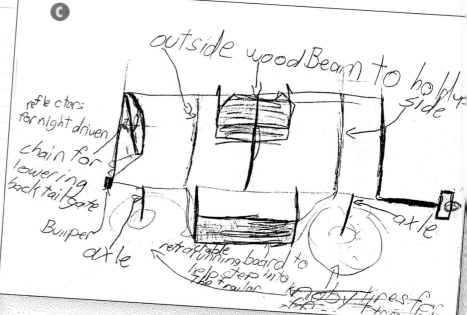

D

Problems

cut boards to short? migh fall apart?
get wrong materails? wagon trailer might notwork.

E

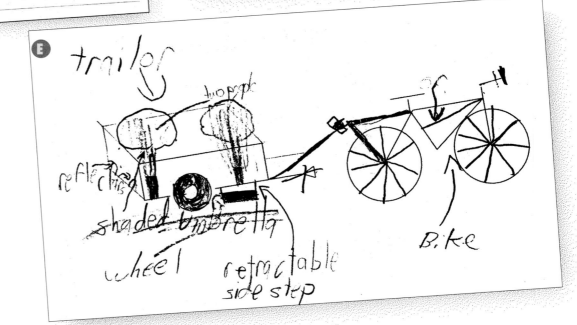

Designing and Building a Bike Trailer

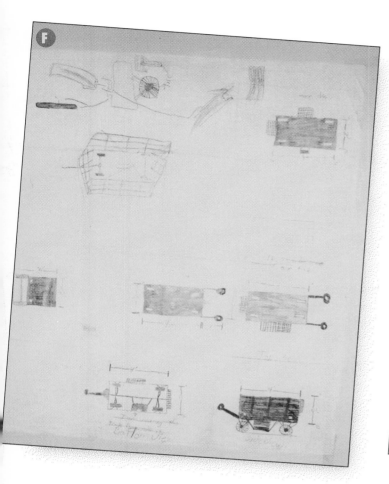

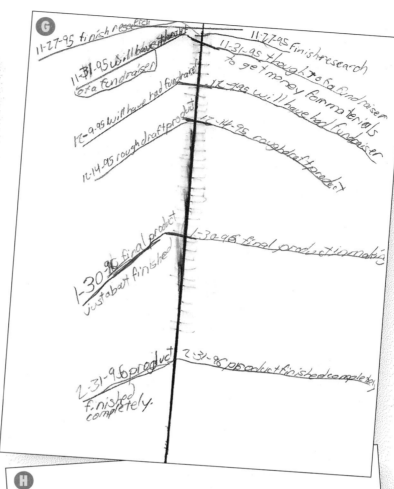

F The students produced scale drawings of the final design, including drawings from several different perspectives. Their carpenter mentor helped them to learn how to produce scale drawings. The results do not have the polish of professional quality but show a clear grasp of the nature and requirements of scale drawings. No paper trail remains to show the decisions the students made during the process of design, though some of the questions they considered are evident in their correspondence with their mentor.

G This extract from the student's log demonstrates development of a schedule for the work.

H The students' guide to making a bike trailer includes a photo of their finished product on the cover and contains detailed instructions for building a bike trailer.

BIKE TRAILER GUIDE
"BIKE'S BEST FRIEND"

BY: _____ & _____

A1 ▶ Problem Solving

A2 ▶ Communication Tools and Techniques

A3 ▶ Information Tools and Techniques

A4 ▶ Learning and Self-management Tools and Techniques

A5 ▶ Tools and Techniques for Working With Others

Designing and Building a Bike Trailer

H

The Student - Pleasing Project

"Bike's Best Friend"

Introduction

This project is one that is created by two students at _____ Elementary. With the help of John, a professional carpenter, to assist them in their project, they have created a bike trailer. Step by step, they worked very hard to complete and construct their product.

This product is helpful to students and bike riders. This product will help students move projects such as backboards and inventions for the invention convention to school. This will also help you carry stuff such as a suit case, and other equipment when you go to a friend's house or a nearby relative's house to spend the night.

Tools And Materials

The following is the Tools and the Materials you will need to build this product.

1	Router
22	Wood-2x4's
8	Wood-4x6's
10	Wood-1x8's
1	Power Plainer
1	Nail Gun
50	Gun Nails
5	Sheets of Coarse Sand Paper
1	Power Saw
1	Power Drill
1	Electric Sander
1	Giant Table Saw
1	Work Mate Work Bench
25	1" Screws
25	1" Nuts
25	1" Bolts
1	Pre-Drilling Bit
1	Pre-Sinker Bit
2	Pints of The Paint of Your Choice
1	Cup of Black Paint to write an inscription (optional)
2	Rubber Wheels with axle and cotter pins
2	Stand Alone Swivel Wheels
1	Bottle of Carpenter's Glue
10	Brackets
1	Carpenter's ruler

Procedure

After you have all your materials you are ready to build the trailer. Once you have finished these steps, you will have a perfectly built trailer for your bike.

Step 1
Smoothing Wood

A. First, use your Power Plainer to smoothen out all the pieces of wood.

B. Then, use 1 sheet of your coarse sand paper to sand the ends of all the pieces of wood.

Step 2
Body

A. Next, on your outside trim, use your Router to make a 1/2" wide and 1/2" thick hole. The hole should be no farther than 1/3" away from one of the sides. No closer than 1/2" away from the same side. You should do this on all four outside trim pieces.

B. Use your Jigsaw to make sure that all of the pieces are the correct length.

C. Next, lay down 8 2x4's on a level surface. Then put one 2x4 across the 8 bottom pieces of wood about 1" away from the side. Do the same with the other side of the bottom pieces.

D. Then take another 2x4 and lay it down about 5" away from one 2x4 that you have already laid down. Nail them with you staple gun, twice on each side.

E. Then, lay a 4x6 from one end of one to the other end of the one that is on the other side of the trailer.

F. Put the outside trim around the sides according to size.

G. Use your driller bit to drill a whole(line) about 3/4" into the wood. Use your pre-sinker bit and pre-sink the wood about 1/4" into the wood.

H. Put three screws in each corner.

Step 3
Fence Work

A. Then you will start working on the fences. You will need your nail gun, gun nails , 4 1x8's , and 5 pieces of 2x4's.

B. Push the 2x4's together real tight. Then place one 1x8 on the pieces of wood with one end at the top and the other side past the last piece of wood

Designing and Building a Bike Trailer

 C. Then, hold down the 1x8 and take your staple gun and put two staples at the top on the first piece of wood.

D. Then, on the third piece of wood (2x4) put two more staples at the middle of the 1x8. Then, remove the second piece of wood (2x4) from the five that are there.

E. Then, on the fifth piece of wood (2x4) put two staples in the bottom about a half inch away from the edge.

F. Then take out the fourth piece of wood (2x4) and then you will have one side completed of the front fence. Then do that with the other side of the fence. You now have the front fence finished. Repeat the steps 10 through 15 and you will have both the front and back fences completed.

G. Then, for the two side fences, it is the same procedure as the front and back fences, but instead of using 2x4's, you will use 4x6's and put another 1x8 in the middle of the fence on the side of the fence that has the 1x8's on it.

Step 4
Assembling The Wheels

A. To be able to put on the front wheels, you need to cut two 4"x4" square pieces of wood. You also need to have two 6x4" pieces of wood. Form a box-like figure, and

nail it to the bottom of the wagon in the front. You now put on your front wheels. Screw the wheels onto the box-like figure. The screws should be bigger than regular screws. You should now put on the rear wheels.

B. You should put on the rear wheels very carefully. Bend and assemble 1" angle aluminum with rivets.

C. Attach rear wheel assembly to trailer with screws.

D. Drill 3/4" holes in assembly for the axle.

E. Run axle through assembly.

F. Attach wheels on axle in secure with cotter pins.

Now, you should start working on your hitch.

Step 5
Hooking On The Hitch

A. First, drill 3/8" hole into the lower, back of the bicycle frame, and both ends of 24" x 1/2" x 18" steel rod.

B. Place hitch plate to trailer with 3/8"x1" machine screws, lock washers, and nuts on tightly.

C. Attach steel rod to bike and trailer with 3/8" x 1" screws, lock washers, and nuts on tightly.

Now, you can use any colors of paint to do any design you want on your now built bike trailer.

A2 b Communication Tools and Techniques: The student composes and sends correspondence, such as thank-you letters and memoranda providing information; that is, the student:

- expresses the information or request clearly;
- writes in a style appropriate to the purpose of the correspondence.

I This is an example of the letters the students wrote seeking help with their project. The letter states the students' request clearly and is written in an appropriate style.

A2 c Communication Tools and Techniques: The student writes and formats information for short publications, such as brochures or posters; that is, the student:

- organizes the information into an appropriate form for use in the publication;
- checks the information for accuracy;
- formats the publication so that it achieves its purpose.

H The guide is organized into an appropriate form to provide a step by step guide and is formatted effectively for its purpose. Close inspection reveals that it omits some of the steps in the sequence of making the bike trailer, refers to components that are not listed at the beginning, and does not provide full information about dimensions of the building materials. Nevertheless, it is an effective piece of communication based on the information the students collected and their direct experience.

Dear John,

Hi, its me again. _____ and my partner _____. We are writing this letter to you with a rough draft procedure in side. Please read it and make any corrections and an good explanation that you feel would make a difference in this project. See if you think it would build and send it back. Also send a name that you think would be a good name. If you think that our name is a good name please say that in the letter that you will hopefully send. Please send it to

_____

Sincerely,

_____

_____

P.S. Send a recommendation for the final name of the trailer. Thank you for the time that you have given up to help us with our project!

John is our mentor. He helped us build the a trailer and put our brochure together.

A1 Problem Solving

A2 Communication Tools and Techniques

A3 Information Tools and Techniques

A4 Learning and Self-management Tools and Techniques

A5 Tools and Techniques for Working With Others

Designing and Building a Bike Trailer

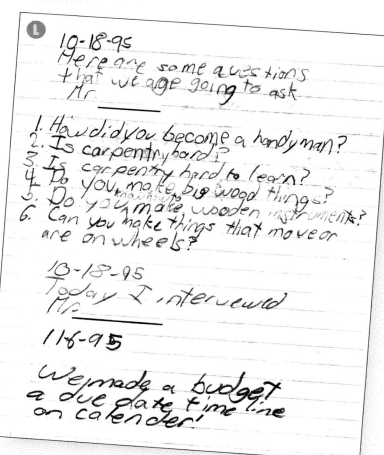

J

10-16-95

1. Carpenters (John)
2. Dad
3. Interview somebody at a hardware store, the builder at 249-live
4. get the builder at 249-live
5. Nicklaus ____ dad

Tomorrow I plan to finish writing our own materials and Blue Print (the booklet)

10-17-95
Today we started typing are letter to Mr. ___ we finished our booklet thing today.

10-18-95
Sent Mr. ___ a second letter to ask when we should come. He said today would be ok.

K

Questions for John

1. Do you mind if we videotape and take snap shots throughout this interview?

2. Can you help us buy our materials?

3. Can you help us draw a model to scale?

4. Can you give us any suggestions on what kind of wood to buy?

5. Do you know a good place to buy rebare? If so, where?

6. Can you help us build a model and or our final product?

7. If we need to have another interview with you, when would be the best time around your schedule? Please tell the time and place.

8. Would you suggest to have a fenced side or solid side?

9. Would you like to have a side step to step into the trailer or not?

L

10-18-95
Here are some questions that we are going to ask Mr. ___

1. How did you become a handyman?
2. Is carpentry hard?
3. Is carpentry hard to learn?
4. Do you make big wood things?
5. Do you make wooden instruments?
6. Can you make things that move or are on wheels?

10-18-95
Today I interviewed Mr. ___

11-6-95

We made a budget a due date time line on calender!

A3 a **Information Tools and Techniques:** The student gathers information to assist in completing project work; that is, the student:

- identifies potential sources of information to assist in completing the project;
- uses appropriate techniques to collect the information, e.g., considers sampling issues in conducting a survey;
- distinguishes relevant from irrelevant information;
- shows evidence of research in the completed project.

B J The planning record and a journal entry provide evidence of identifying potential sources of information for the project.

K L The questions the students prepared for the initial discussions with their carpenter mentor and with the handyman show evidence of their preparatory research.

Problem Solving **A1**

Communication Tools and Techniques **A2**

Information Tools and Techniques **A3**

Learning and Self-management Tools and Techniques **A4**

Tools and Techniques for Working With Others **A5**

Designing and Building a Bike Trailer

A4a Learning and Self-management Tools and Techniques: The student learns from models; that is, the student:

- consults with or observes other students and adults at work, and identifies the main features of what they do and the way they go about their work;
- examines models for the results of project work, such as professionally produced publications, and analyzes their qualities;
- uses what he or she learns from models to assist in planning and conducting project activities.

The project documentation provides evidence of learning from models. There are several references to things the students learned from their carpenter mentor. The preparations the students made for interviewing the carpenter included questions about the nature of his work.

M The students used a commercially produced guide to caring for wounds as a model for their guide. This project log extract demonstrates analysis of the qualities of this model. In other evidence the student also referred to using a picture of a motorcycle and its trailer with the parts labeled as a model for the design of the bike trailer and a blueprint for a playground as a model for the scale drawing for the bike trailer. There is ample evidence that the students used these models of results of project work to assist them to do their work.

A4b Learning and Self-management Tools and Techniques: The student keeps records of work activities in an orderly manner; that is, the student:

- sets up a system for storing records of work activities;
- maintains records of work activities in a way that makes it possible to find specific materials quickly and easily.

J L M The student used a small composition book to keep his records of work on the project. He used dates to identify his records. The book contains a comprehensive record of the project and is easily referenced, especially with regard to the sequence of events involved in completing the project.

A5b Tools and Techniques for Working With Others: The student shows or explains something clearly enough for someone else to be able to do it.

H The guide the students developed on the basis of their experience provides a step by step guide to building a bike trailer. It is explained clearly enough for someone else to be able to do it. The omission of some details (as noted above) does not detract from the accomplishment at the elementary level of a clear and logical explanation of a complicated set of procedures.

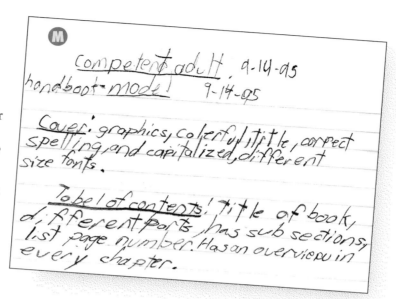

The written work included with this project contains some errors. For the main part the errors are confined to journal entries and other planning documents which were produced for personal use only and were not intended for publication. The three pieces of finished writing are the proposal, the letter to the mentor, and the guide. These contain almost error free writing.

A1 Problem Solving

A2 Communication Tools and Techniques

A3 Information Tools and Techniques

A4 Learning and Self-management Tools and Techniques

A5 Tools and Techniques for Working With Others

Work Sample & Commentary: *Educating People About Tuberculosis*

The task

Students were asked to identify something in their community on which they wanted to work to bring about change. They could work individually or in small groups. This project was undertaken by one student. The student identified the increasing incidence of tuberculosis (TB) in the community as the issue on which he wished to work.

Circumstances of performance

The project was completed over a period of about eight weeks, mainly outside class time. The class worked together initially to develop organizing questions to help structure their project plans. They kept their teacher informed of progress on the projects and sought advice on resolving problems they encountered. Otherwise they worked independently.

The documentation presented from this project is not a comprehensive record of all work done as part of the project. It would be neither reasonable nor appropriate to ask students to keep detailed written records of every aspect of a project. This would defeat part of the purpose of applied learning which is for students to put their academic learning to work and to learn from projects that connect what they do at school to the demands of the twenty-first century workplace. Some of these standards lend themselves to assessment through observation and other less formal methods than through written work.

Physical Sciences Concepts

Life Sciences Concepts

Earth and Space Sciences Concepts

Scientific Connections and Applications **S4**

Scientific Thinking **S5**

Scientific Tools and Technologies **S6**

Scientific Communication **S7**

Scientific Investigation

Problem Solving **A1**

Communication Tools and Techniques **A2**

Information Tools and Techniques **A3**

Learning and Self-management Tools and Techniques

Tools and Techniques for Working With Others

This work sample illustrates a standard-setting performance for the following parts of the standards:

A1a **Problem Solving: Design a product, service, or system.**

A2a **Communication: Make an oral presentation.**

A2c **Communication: Publish information.**

A3a **Information: Gather information.**

A3b **Information: Use information technology.**

S4c **Scientific Connections and Applications: Personal health, personal and environmental safety.**

S5c **Scientific Thinking: Use evidence from reliable sources to construct explanations.**

S6c **Scientific Tools and Technologies: Acquire information from multiple sources.**

S7a **Scientific Communication: Represent data and results in multiple ways.**

S7c **Scientific Communication: Communicate in a form suited to the purpose and the audience.**

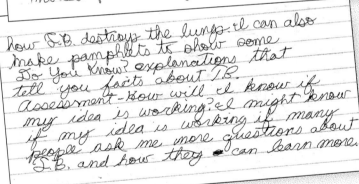

A Community Research

What is needed? People must not spit on the street because T.B. is airborne. To many people are sick in the street, especially homeless people who need medical help to get well. How can we get it? We can get it by giving free checkups at homeless shelters and by encouraging people to cough or spit in a tissue. What do I need to know first? I need to know if homeless shelters give treatments and how many people aren't aware that they could be spreading T.B.

I must do:
Written Research
March 17th < Surveys
Interviews
Observations

What is my design or system? I will try to put up posters and show some examples to people with a clay model of the lungs and a pin showing

how T.B. destroy the lungs. I can also make pamphlets to show some Do you know? explanations that tell you facts about T.B. Assessment- how will I know if my idea is working? I might know if my idea is working if many people ask me more questions about T.B. and how they can learn more.

What the work shows

A1a Problem Solving: The student designs and creates a product, service, or system to meet an identified need; that is, the student:

• develops ideas for the design of the product, service, or system;

• chooses among the design ideas and justifies the choice;

• establishes criteria for judging the success of the design;

• uses an appropriate format to represent the design;

• plans and carries out the steps needed to turn the design into a reality;

• evaluates the design in terms of the criteria established for success.

Educating People About Tuberculosis

C

Dear Ms. _____,
I'd like to tell about what I am doing on my project. So far I have gotten 4 pieces of information, one of those pieces of info has fourteen pieces of info that I can call for place that I still need to contact info. I still need to contact a homeless shelter to ask if they have free T.B. testing. I also have to ask my doctor if I can perform a demonstration on how T.B. destroys the body. I have already made my model to work with of the lungs. My model to work with is what I am going to try to basically replicate, using materials such as clay, foil and pipe cleaners. I will take a pin when I'm done a poke it into the lung to show what T.B. does.
If I can start my final model on Thursday then I will be on a good start.

C

1. My design is a model of the lungs and internal organs located in the ribcage. I want to be able to show people how Tuberculosis affects the lungs by causing a cavity, which is a hole. When my project is complete then I will be able to take a pin and (before a group of children) start poking it into the lungs. That will show how it stops or makes breathing difficult.

P

2. I have only really experienced one difficulty, and that was trying to decide what information that I had collected to keep and what to throw out. Since everything on the internet was almost the same I had a hard time remembering what pages I already had and what I didn't have.

D

For my demonstration I had to prepare it by sending a request to demonstrate to the doctor and the permission from Ms. _____ to verify that I am doing it for a school project. I will use my audio tape to record my conversation at home, then (after I play it at the office) I will show TB destroys lung tissue. After that I will ask for questions. Then I will hand out my pamphlet and tell the audience that I will hand out surveys in two weeks.
Unfortunate Unfortunately, I had to cancel the presentation at my doctor's office because of problems with my mom and the secretary, so this time I am going to go to the other doctor's office and present to them a slip showing that I have the schools permission to do this project.

This student set out to design a service for his community: to educate people about the dangers of tuberculosis. The records of the project do not fit neatly with the features of a "Design" project as set out above; in particular, it suffers for lack of an overall plan and does not include evidence of the way the project was brought to closure. This is, in part, due to the difficulties the student encountered in seeing through his plan to make a presentation to patients at his doctor's office. The particular strength of the project is the research on which the student based his work and its relationship to science content.

A The student's description of the project identifies the problem he identified, his initial plans for the project, and the criteria he intended to use to judge his success.

B Here, the student explained his reasons for choosing to work on this problem.

C **D** These documents explain the student's plan to design a model of the lungs to show people the effects of TB, to rehearse his explanation with his doctor, and then give a presentation to an audience.

Physical Sciences Concepts

Life Sciences Concepts

Earth and Space Sciences Concepts

S4 Scientific Connections and Applications

S5 Scientific Thinking

S6 Scientific Tools and Technologies

S7 Scientific Communication

Scientific Investigation

A1 Problem Solving

A2 Communication Tools and Techniques

A3 Information Tools and Techniques

Learning and Self-management Tools and Techniques

Tools and Techniques for Working With Others

Educating People About Tuberculosis

E   Lung Model

1. First I gathered up materials, such as seven pieces of oak tag, a 37½ box of foil and tape. I also found some scissors.

2. I then looked in one of my medical books and found a diagram ~~showing~~ showing the placement of the lungs and ribs.

3. I took my scissors and cut out a spine and some strips of rectangular shapes. One strip was thicker than the rest.

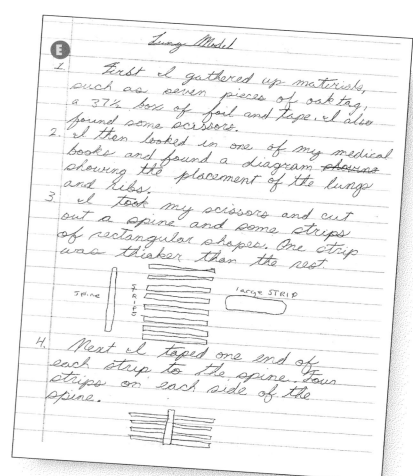

SPine   STRIPS   large STRIP

4. Next I taped one end of each strip to the spine. Four strips on each side of the spine.

5. I then took the large strip and placed it horizontally over the spine. I next began to tape the = eight sides on to the large strip.

6. I used my extra oak tag to make some parts that were curved for better detail of the ribs.

7. I then coated it all with aluminum foil.

8. I started the lungs by drawing them on oak tag.

9. I cut them out and traced them. I cut them out again.

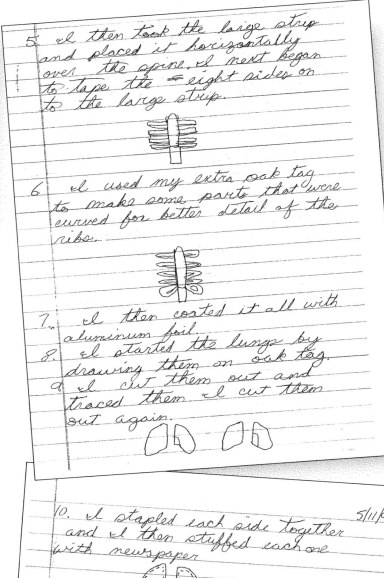

F   Lung Plan

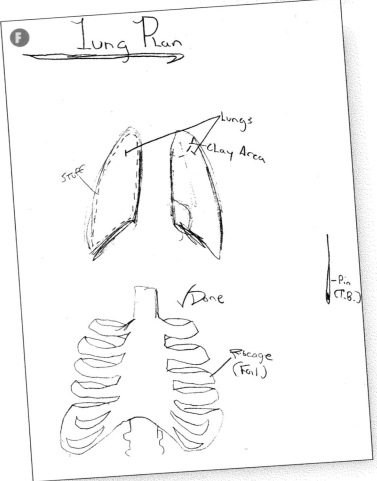

Lungs
Clay Area
Stuff
Done
Ribcage (Foil)
Pin (T.B.)

10. I stapled each side together and I then stuffed each one with newspaper   5/11/96

11. My final step was to paint them an orangy-red.

G

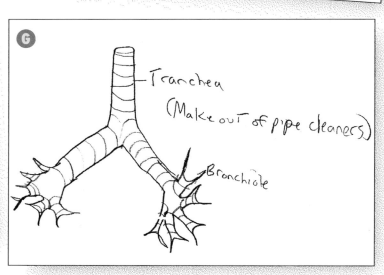

Tranchea (Make out of pipe cleaners)

Bronchiole

Educating People About Tuberculosis

H

Assessment

The best way for me to assess my project is to see if people ask me questions when I talk about TB, therefore I would know that they had some interest in what I said. If people read my pamphlet and do well on my survey then I'll know that they understood what I wrote and what I'm trying to say. Finally if I see people actually stopping to observe my poster then I'll know that it's attractive.

B

I decided to do my project on TB because of my neiborhood. In my neiborhood a lot of people are homeless, and they cough everywhere, so since we were supposed to do a project based on problems in the community I picked TB, because it's spread through the air.

I R

I had given out my surveys to teenagers and adults, forty-two surveys were filled out. I wanted to give my surveys to teens and up because of the material in my survey. I based it on the older grades, such as sixth and up because of their knowledge of diseases, and certain abbreviations. Since they had that knowledge I could see how much of their knowledge was based on TB, and that

E F G "The Lung Model," sets out the design for the model of the lungs and the materials the student used to make it. The accompanying drawings show how the model was made.

H This document sets out a series of criteria for judging success. The criteria are achievable and relate directly to the parts of the service the student designed.

I As noted above, the records of evaluation are incomplete. One problem the student encountered was in his efforts to inform people by putting up posters in the local area warning of the dangers of TB. When he went back, the posters had been torn down. However, the student's comments on the survey demonstrate reflection on the information he gathered through surveys.

J This journal entry suggests the student's commitment to continue to work to reduce the incidence of TB.

would then give me a good idea of how aware they are of it.

I I found from my surveys that many people know what TB is, but they don't know how it's spread or that it's a top killer. They also didn't know the symptoms of TB but most of the surveys filled out showed that close to half of all forty-two people had a friend with TB.

Q Well, I had gone on the Internet about seven times to find topics on tuberculosis, and they all were basically the same, so I had to look through all of the sheets in order to find things that were different, so that I didn't have seven sheets of the same topic. When I found single individual topics I then tossed the others aside, and used them to give out as

Physical Sciences Concepts

Life Sciences Concepts

Earth and Space Sciences Concepts

S4 Scientific Connections and Applications

S5 Scientific Thinking

S6 Scientific Tools and Technologies

S7 Scientific Communication

Scientific Investigation

A1 Problem Solving

A2 Communication Tools and Techniques

A3 Information Tools and Techniques

Learning and Self-management Tools and Techniques

Tools and Techniques for Working With Others

Educating People About Tuberculosis

reference to my classmates.

(S) At my library they have a computer set up, connected to the Internet. It's fairly simple, you use the mouse to click on Internet, then Net search or Net directory. Then you type in phrases or words, like "tuberculosis" and click on Search. I entered tuberculosis, some listings came up, and the one that worked best was "Ask NOAH about Tuberculosis."

(I) I put my posters up at 33rd Street and 2nd Ave and at various bus stops, but when I went to see if they were still up they had been torn down!

(O) My pin is like TB because TB pokes holes in your lungs in order to survive, so the closest thing I could find to poke

a hole into something was a pin.

(P) The arrows connecting the words on my paper are showing the parts of the chest and head in which air travels through.

When someone gets TB not everyone gets it because you would to visit that person on a regular basis, and breath in their air every time.

You should not get worried if you're coughed on because, (as I said in question #10) you would have to visit that person regularly and breath in their air every time to fully get the TB germ. If you get TB your immune system builds a wall around the germ.

TB especially affects the lungs because its cold and damp, and that's exactly what the germ needs in order to survive. It may also affect the brain, genital organs, lymph nodes, etc.

(J) Community Research

Recently I have called the American Lung Association to find out how I can raise money to find new ~~some~~ drugs and research to treat TB. They told me that they have special projects which involve ~~sponsers~~ which I need to find. I must get more surveys done and I must do my TB demonstration. I am falling behind on these activities, that's why I need to properly make time for everything else I got to do

A2a Communication Tools and Techniques: The student makes an oral presentation of project plans or findings to an appropriate audience; that is, the student:

• organizes the presentation in a logical way appropriate to its purpose;
• speaks clearly and presents confidently;
• responds to questions from the audience;
• evaluates the effectiveness of the presentation.

(K) The student evaluated his presentation to the class, and identified both strengths and aspects of the presentation that could have been improved.

(L) This evaluation of the student's performance, prepared by another student, relates some of the content of the presentation.

Educating People About Tuberculosis

K

I think that I did my presentation fairly well. I stuttered a lot and I think I could ha told more information. I should ha already done my presentation to the patients at my doctor's office. I was pretty loud, but I think I didn't speak that clearly. I think I told a good piece of information, and had a good tempo. I also made a lot of eye contact.

I would ~~but~~ put myself under the Admirable category.

Later on I visited my ~~doctors~~ doctor's to give them

L

——————— did a wonderful project on Tuberculosis. He made a great model of the rib cage and the lungs. He said that he would cover the lungs with clay and poke holes in the lungs. He said that it show what tuberculosis does to the lungs

A2c Communication Tools and Techniques: The student writes and formats information for short publications, such as brochures or posters; that is, the student:

• organizes the information into an appropriate form for use in the publication;
• checks the information for accuracy;
• formats the publication so that it achieves its purpose.

M The poster is eye catching and informative.

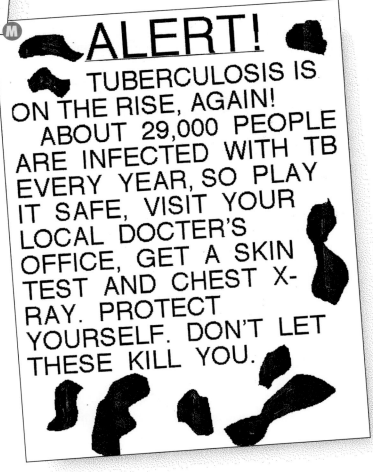

Educating People About Tuberculosis

N Log

March 14, 1996:
This past week I have found a lot more information on tuberculosis, TB disease and TB infection. I learned that a person who has TB disease and H.I.V. is diagnosed as having A.I.D.S. I could have gotten more information on TB but I didn't get a chance to go back to the library this week. Today I am going to call 1-800-LUNG LUNG-USA to find out if they can mail me some pamphlets on how the lungs work. From the information that I found I have fourteen places to call for more pamphlets.

March 15, 1996:
Today I found some information on the internet.

March 18, 1996:
I started making a survey. My lung model to work with

done. All my plans should go right.

March 25, 1996:
Today I found the steps for the breathing process, so that I could find out how TB affects breathing.

March 26, 1996:
I saved my survey work on the class computer and I'm ready to transfer it on to the computer in the computer lab, to print it.

April 14, 1996:
Today I handed surveys out at the corner of 18th street, and got fourteen filled out.

April 22, 1996:
Today I called the American Lung Association to find out how I can raise money to support them in order to find new drugs and research to treat TB.

May 1, 1996:
I am still waiting to hear from the American Lung

Association to see what info they're going to give me.

May 4, 1996:
Today I tallied up my survey results.

May 7, 1996:
I am now unable to do my demonstration at my doctors office. I will now try to start writing my pamphlet.

May 15, 1996:
I have finished my pamphlet and I will start my poster.

A3a Information Tools and Techniques: The student gathers information to assist in completing project work; that is, the student:

- identifies potential sources of information to assist in completing the project;
- uses appropriate techniques to collect the information, e.g., considers sampling issues in conducting a survey;
- distinguishes relevant from irrelevant information;
- shows evidence of research in the completed project.

The student contacted numerous organizations for information to support his project and used the Internet to search for relevant information.

N The project log provides a record of the student's research.

O P These are notes the student made from the materials he collected and notes he made to explain parts of his presentation.

Q In these records, the student explained how he sorted the information he had collected and determined which materials to retain and which to discard.

The research is evident in the design of the model, the survey, and in the poster.

R The student developed and administered a survey to collect information on people's knowledge about TB before giving his presentation. His notes on the survey reflect some attention to sampling issues, his reasons for selecting older students to survey, and ways to structure the survey to achieve its purpose.

The questions in the survey itself are limited in that they do not actually probe the respondents' knowledge.

Educating People About Tuberculosis

A3b Information Tools and Techniques: The student uses information technology to assist in gathering, organizing, and presenting information; that is, the student:

- acquires information for specific purposes from on-line sources, such as the Internet, and other electronic data bases, such as an electronic encyclopedia;
- uses word processing, drawing, and painting programs to produce project reports and related materials.

S The student made extensive use of the Internet and demonstrated his knowledge of how to gain access.

R The survey and poster demonstrate use of word processing and drawing programs.

S4c Scientific Connections and Applications: The student produces evidence that demonstrates understanding of personal health…, personal and environmental safety.

The project is a study of a public health problem in the student's neighborhood that could pose a threat to the student's personal health.

P As the student learned, with a healthy immune system, the likelihood of illness is low.

S5c Scientific Thinking: The student uses evidence from reliable sources to construct explanations.

S6c Scientific Tools and Technologies: The student acquires information from multiple sources such as experimentation and print and non-print sources.

A S The student used a wide range of sources for the research in this project, including print materials, a survey, and searching on the Internet.

O The information is summarized in the student's own words.

Tuberculosis

- caused by Mycobacterium tuberculosis
- attacks any part of body, but usually lungs
- T.B disease once leading cause of death in U.S.
- any person, rich or poor, black or white old or young may get T.B.
- T.B. is spread through air
- T.B may travel ~~through~~ to the lungs, throat, kidney, spine or brain
- travels through ~~b~~ blood
- spread by talking, coughing, or sneezing
- TB disease people may spread to family members, friends or coworkers
- most cases immune system controls T.B., then becomes T.B. infection.
- T.B bacteria multiplies like white blood cells.
- T.B disease - bacteria is active
- **March 24ᵀᴴ National T.B. day.**
  <u>Lungs</u>
- Sections - Bronchus, Tranchea, ~~Bronchus~~ Bronchiole, Alveolus, Left Lung, Right Lung.

- Lung contains thousands branches.
- Air Way: ~~Tranchea → Bronchus →~~ Bronchiole → Alveolus → Left Lung
- ~~Co : Right lung Alveolus → Bronchiole → Bronchus → Tranchea~~
- Lung consists: spongy texture millions of air chambers.
- pharynx (back of nose and mouth) → larynx (voice box) → airways → tranchea → bronchi → bronchus → bronchioles → terminal bronchioles → respiratory ~~units~~ → alveolar sacs → pulmonary capillaries GAS EXCHANGE

Physical Sciences Concepts

Life Sciences Concepts

Earth and Space Sciences Concepts

S4 Scientific Connections and Applications

S5 Scientific Thinking

S6 Scientific Tools and Technologies

S7 Scientific Communication

Scientific Investigation

A1 Problem Solving

A2 Communication Tools and Techniques

A3 Information Tools and Techniques

Learning and Self-management Tools and Techniques

Tools and Techniques for Working With Others

Educating People About Tuberculosis

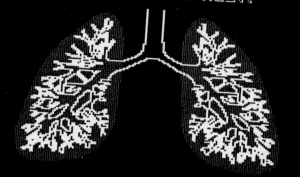

TUBERCULOSIS SURVEY

DO YOU KNOW.............

What is tuberculosis?
YES SOMEWHAT NO

What it does to the lungs, brain or genital organs?
YES SOMEWHAT NO

How it is spread?
YES SOMEWHAT NO

That TB is one of the top killer diseases in the U.S.?
YES SOMEWHAT NO

What is MDR tuberculosis?
YES SOMEWHAT NO

The name of the test most commonly used to treat TB patients?
YES SOMEWHAT NO

The name of the drugs used to treat TB patients?
YES SOMEWHAT NO

The symptoms of TB?
YES SOMEWHAT NO

Anyone with TB?
YES NO

THANK YOU FOR TAKING THIS SURVEY. FOR MORE INFO ON TB READ MY PAMPHLET!

S7 a Scientific Communication: The student represents data and results in multiple ways, such as…diagrams, and artwork; and technical…writing.

The student used a poster, a model of the lungs, a pamphlet, and speaking to get his ideas across.

S7 c Scientific Communication: The student communicates in a form suited to the purpose and the audience….

The student used a variety of communication forms, increasing the likelihood of getting the message to different audiences.

The written work included with this project contains some errors. For the main part the errors are confined to journal entries and other records which were produced for personal use only and were not intended for publication. The only pieces of finished writing are the poster and the survey. These contain almost error free writing.

Community Research
—Survey—

what? So find out what people know about your topic.

Sample—large enough to make conclusion.

who? Community—School
Students—Teachers—Parents.
Stores
Clubs
Building

Survey
Survey
Organize it
Design new system
or improve a system

Purpose is clear to you
To find out what people
think, do, buy, eat, learn, love, hate, etc.

Creating it:
Questions are clear
Questions give you the information you need

User-friendly
Logical
Limit questions (9-12)

Work Sample & Commentary: *Bike Helmet Ordinance*

The task

As part of their social studies program, students undertook a project to research the development of a new ordinance in their city. The ordinance would require children to wear bicycle helmets. The students became interested in this project after a local middle school student was hit by a car while riding his bicycle and sustained serious head injuries. Reports of the accident suggested that the boy's injuries would have been reduced had he been wearing a helmet. The project involved learning about the respective responsibilities of federal, state, and local government, learning how an ordinance is prepared, learning the process by which an ordinance passes through local government, and researching other local government laws regarding bicycle helmets. The project resulted in the City Council passing a new ordinance based closely on the one the students drafted.

Circumstances of performance

The project was completed over a period of about six months. It involved a combination of class time and work outside class. The project involved the whole class in the initial stages of planning and in preparation for presentation of the ordinance to the City Council. Groups of students took responsibility for specific aspects of the project, such as drafting the ordinance. The work shown here was drawn from several students' portfolios.

What the work shows

A1 b Problem Solving: The student troubleshoots problems in the operation of a system in need of repair or devises and tests ways of improving the effectiveness of a system in operation; that is, the student:

• identifies the parts of the system and the way the parts connect with each other;
• identifies parts or connections in the system that have broken down or that could be made to work better;

This work sample illustrates a standard-setting performance for the following parts of the standards:

A1 b Problem Solving: Improve a system.

A2 a Communication: Make an oral presentation.

A2 b Communication: Compose correspondence.

A3 a Information: Gather information.

A4 a Learning and Self-management: Learn from models.

A4 c Learning and Self-management: Identify strengths and weaknesses in own work.

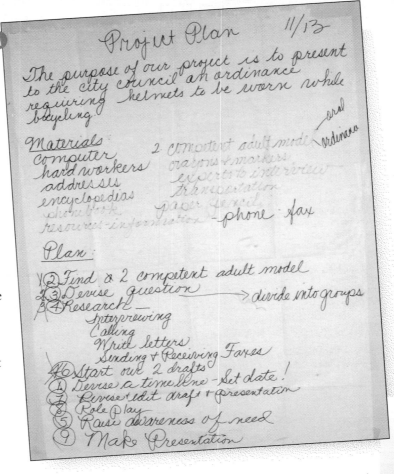

A Project Plan 11/13

The purpose of our project is to present to the city council an ordinance requiring helmets to be worn while bicycling.

Materials:
computer
hard workers
addresses
encyclopedias
resource information
2 competent adult model — oral ordinance
crayons + markers
experts to interview
transportation
paper + pencil
— phone · fax

Plan:
1. (2) Find a 2 competent adult model
2. (3) Devise question → divide into groups
3. (4) Research —
   Interviewing
   Calling
   Write letters
   Sending + Receiving Faxes
4. (6) Start our 2 drafts
(1) Devise a timeline — Set date!
(7) Revise + edit draft + presentation
(8) Role Play
(5) Raise awareness of need
(9) Make Presentation

• devises ways of making the system work again or making it work better;
• evaluates the effectiveness of the strategies for improving the system and supports the evaluation with evidence.

The students investigated the system by which local government passes new laws, including the process of petitioning for a new law, and how laws are drafted. They researched information about the need for a new ordinance covering the use of bicycle helmets to support their petition and drafted their own ordinance for presentation to the City Council. (See **A4 a** below for details of the students' research.)

The students' records of the project do not fit neatly with the features of an "Improving a System" project as set out above; nevertheless, the project provides an example of a successful effort aimed at helping to make a system work more effectively.

A The students worked together to create a plan for the project.

The documentation presented from this project is not a comprehensive record of all work done as part of the project. It would be neither reasonable nor appropriate to ask students to keep detailed written records of every aspect of a project. This would defeat part of the purpose of applied learning which is for students to put their academic learning to work and to learn from projects that connect what they do at school to the demands of the twenty-first century workplace. Some of these standards lend themselves to assessment through observation and other less formal methods than through written work.

A1 Problem Solving

A2 Communication Tools and Techniques

A3 Information Tools and Techniques

A4 Learning and Self-management Tools and Techniques

Tools and Techniques for Working With Others

Bike Helmet Ordinance

B ORDINANCE NO. _____
AN ORDINANCE ESTABLISHING A HELMET
TO BE WARN WHILE RIDING A BICYCLE FOR
MINORS; SETTING FORTH DEFINITIONS,
CREATING OFFENSES FOR MINORS,
PARENTS AND GUARDIANS

WHEREAS, People are being ~~injur~~ *injured* or killed on bicycles each year, in the United States 8,000 children are killed and 50,000 more are permanently disabled 75% of all bike related injuries include trauma to the head, ; and

WHEREAS, our environment is becoming a risk to bicycle riders, streets are widening which will increase traffic flow, the speed limit has increased from 55 to 65 south of _____ and 820, most families in _____ have two or more cars in use, this increase the risk to children being hit by a car coming in and out of their driveways and or neighborhoods, ; and

WHEREAS, a bicycle helmet ordinance would increase the safety of the minors in _____ which will attract homeowners and businesses, this means more taxes, there will be less deaths.

SECTION 1 - DEFINITIONS

1. *Bicycle* means a two wheeled vehicle powered by its rider

2. *Helmet* means a thick covering that fits the head, and is strapped under the head

3. *Wearing a Helmet* means the person's helmet is strapped tightly under the chin

4. *Minor* ~~anyone under~~ *means* the age of 15 (fifteen) *or under the age of*

5. *Private Property* means any property that is owned or operated - residents, apartment buildings, and business

C WHEREAS, People are being injured or killed on bicycles; each year, in the United States; 8,000 children are killed and 50,000 more are permanently disabled; 75% of all bike related injuries include trauma to the head; and

WHEREAS, our environment is becoming a risk to bicycle riders, streets are being widened which will increase traffic flow; the speed limit has increased from 55 to 65 mph south of _____ and 820; most families in _____ have two or more cars in use, which increases the risk to children being hit by a car coming in and out of their driveways and or neighborhoods; and

WHEREAS, a bicycle helmet ordinance would increase the safety of the minors in _____, which will attract homeowners and businesses; this means a wider tax base for _____.

NOW THEREFORE, BE IT ORDAINED BY THE CITY COUNCIL OF THE CITY OF _____, TEXAS:

B C This is an extract from the near-to-final draft of the proposed ordinance and an extract from the final draft of the ordinance that the students presented to the City Council. These demonstrate the process of editing and revision the students followed as they researched and polished their proposed ordinance.

D This cover letter accompanied the agenda for the City Council meeting at which the students presented the ordinance.

D **city** of _____

May 13, 1996

HAND-DELIVERED

Students of Linda _____ Elementary School
_____, TX

Re: **Bicycle Safety Ordinance**

Dear Young Men and Women:

Enclosed for your information are copies of the _____ City Council Agenda for May 16, 1996, City Manager's report to Council, the ordinance you drafted, a revised draft prepared by Police Chief Sam _____, and supporting data (much of which came from you). All this material appears in the discussion packets sent to each Councilmember.

The proposed ordinance is being presented to Council as an action item. That means the ordinance has been published in the newspaper and the Council will be able to vote on it at the meeting.

All this is a direct result of the hard word and dedication shown by you and your teacher. Although children have presented their views to lawmakers on various issues before, I am unaware of any instance locally where a law has been enacted solely due to the impact of a student-driven initiative. I am proud of each of you and honored to represent you as your Councilmember.

I invite each of you to be present Thursday at both the worksession and council meeting. You will be given an opportunity to make any individual presentations you desire before the Council votes. You may also contact any Councilmember individually prior to the meeting to express your views.

Since you have learned that you can make a difference, I hope that you will remain actively involved in the social and political process throughout your lives. Margaret Mead said, "Never doubt that a small group of thoughtful, committed citizens can change the world. Indeed, it's the only thing that ever does." You have proven her correct.

Very truly yours,

Pamela

Pamela _____
Councilmember, Place 7

PHB/ceb

Enclosures

cc: Mr. Bill _____

Bike Helmet Ordinance

students petition City Council

JOURNAL PHOTOS/Karen Barber

Students from Linda

Students from _____ class at _____ Elementary School presented a draft for a bicycle helmet ordinance to the _____ City Council at its April 11 meeting. The presentation was the final chapter of an applied learning social studies project the class had been working on for the entire school year, Mrs. _____ said. The twenty-five students did the research and writing for the proposed ordinance, and all but four attended the presentation, most with their parents. "It was standing room only," Mrs. _____ said of the council meeting. "We packed the room." Students used an overhead projector to illustrate portions of the proposal, and one student, _____, demonstrated the proper use of a bike helmet for council members. The presentation included testimony from a Fort Worth woman whose son was critically injured in a bike-related accident. Council members praised the students for a thorough and thought-provoking presentation.

class at _____ Elementary School delivered a presentation to the _____ City Council on a proposed bike helmet ordinance recently. It was the culmination of a yearlong applied learning project.

Reprinted by permission of *The Journal*.

E *The Journal* reports the students' presentation to the City Council. A subsequent edition reported the Council's decision to pass the ordinance.

A2a Communication Tools and Techniques: The student makes an oral presentation of project plans or findings to an appropriate audience; that is, the student:

- organizes the presentation in a logical way appropriate to its purpose;
- speaks clearly and presents confidently;
- responds to questions from the audience;
- evaluates the effectiveness of the presentation.

F This is a working document prepared early in the process of preparing to present the proposed bicycle helmet ordinance to the City Council. It shows evidence of considering the interests of the audience in planning the presentation.

G This is an extract of the script students prepared for their presentation to the City Council. The students used cue cards when making the actual presentation.

H Each student prepared a rubric for assessment of his or her part of the presentation to the Council. This example reflects the students earlier work on the features of an effective presentation to a City Council.

City Council
Audience

Needs/Want -

"want to be elected/re-elect
please - people
more businesses

Value -

safety of community (homes)

Know - Do they know the fact
Safe community - attract people
Recognize a well researched
presentation

In summary, we honestly believe making this ordinance would be helpful for our community, reducing the number of bicycle accidents by many. We all would benefit from protecting _____ children. Because your decisions have been in consideration of the health and well being of _____ the past, we know you will know make the right decision now.

Members of the City Council Thank you for your attention. As you can see, we children of _____, feel very strongly about this issue.

We respectfully request that you instruct city staff to purpose an ordinance requiring children to wear bicycle helmets in _____, using our work as a model, and to present it to you for action at the earliest possible date.

We would be happy to answer any questions.

Thank you!

A1 Problem Solving

A2 Communication Tools and Techniques

A3 Information Tools and Techniques

A4 Learning and Self-management Tools and Techniques

Tools and Techniques for Working With Others

Bike Helmet Ordinance

H

	4	3	2	1
Introduction:				
Grabs attention				
States purpose				
Addresses Council correctly				
States desired outcome				
Strong topic statement				
Rational				
Plenty information given				
3 reasons stated				
3 examples stated				
Reasons match councils values				
Elaborated reasons				
Reasons ranked by importance				

I

April 26%

first half of legal definition to help understand the ordinance

	E	S	N	4
1. Eye contact				
2. speaking				
3. loud				
4. clear				
5. slowly				

Why
1. I looked down some
2. ok
3. Not terribly
4. Voice high
5. pretty fast

Notes
I could improve on my eye contact. I need to speak up and slow down.

J

I worked pretty hard but not as hard as I was supposed to but it still went on perfectly.

	E	S	N	V
Eye Contact				
Speaking clearly				
Speaking loud				
Speaking slowly				
small slide				

The reason I gave myself then a 1 is because I didn't then give the audience a glimpse. The reason I gave myself a 1 in speaking clearly I spoke good but not to good. I spoke loud and good. This why I gave myself an C. I spoke slowly but a tad to fast thats why I gave myself an needs improvement. I gave myself an S. my usual aide because I wasn't more nervous then in usually am so thats why gave myself a S.

K

Name _____
Project _____

Please rank 4, 3, 2, or 1
4 is outstanding and 1 is unsatisfactory

Introduction:
Grabs attention 4 yes, gave facts
States purpose 4 yes, told exactly what we were doing and what we intended to do
Addresses council properly 4 yes, Shannon (our speaker) addressed everyone
States desired outcome 4, yes, told probably exactly what we were doing.
Strong topic statement 4, yes we told what we intended to

Rationale:
Informative - 4 yes it had alot of information in it
Reasons stated 4 yes, we stated 3 reasons
Reasons elaborated 4 yes, we elaborated them alot
Reasons match councils values 4 yes, we spend a lot of time matching the councils values
Reasons ranked by importance 3, I am not really sure we did that much

Conclusion:
Summary statement 4- yes, I believe we had a very good summary
Restate purpose 2½-3, we didn't really restate the purpose (that statement I know)
Makes formal request of city council for action - 4-yes, we told them we were really were interested in this ordinance
Compliment audience - 2½-3, I am not sure we did much on that

Comments:
We worked really hard on this ordinance and I believe this ordinance should be passed

Bike Helmet Ordinance

I J K The students conducted self evaluations of their individual parts of the presentation during rehearsal and evaluated the final presentation. The examples of the self evaluations reveal a willingness to identify strengths and weaknesses, and to work for improvement: "...I gave myself a U because I didn't even give the audience a glimps (sic)...I spoke slowly but a tad to (sic) fast...I was more nervous than I usually am..." and "I need to speak up and slow down." The evaluation of the overall presentation is supported with reasons and observations.

A2 b Communication Tools and Techniques: The student composes and sends correspondence, such as thank-you letters and memoranda providing information; that is, the student:

- expresses the information or request clearly;
- writes in a style appropriate to the purpose of the correspondence.

L M N These are examples of correspondence the students prepared to request information to assist in their research. The letters state their purpose clearly and are written in an appropriate style.

L

10117 _____
_____ TX , 76 _____
December 11,1995

Chief _____
328 _____
_____ TX 76 _____

Dear Chief _____
Our class is doing a project on bicycle safety. We have questions for you to answer below:

1) How many bike injuries have occurred in the past 6 years?
2) What were their ages?
3) Were there any deaths?
4.) Do you think there needs to be a law requiring children to wear helmets while riding a bike?

Now that you have read the letter could you please take the time to answer these questions and if you have any other information on bicycle safety please send it to _____

Sincerely,

_____
_____
_____

M

10117 _____
_____ TX. 76 _____
Nov. 29, 1995

Senator _____
1701 _____
_____ TX. 76 _____

Dear Senator _____.

Mrs. _____'s _____ class, in _____ Elementary, are trying to to pass a city ordinance to require the children of _____ to wear helmets while biking. We have read about you in the newspaper and would like you to come to our school so we can interview you, and you could address our class and possibly our school and community.

There are many reasons why you should come to our school. Our first reason is you can help make a small part of Texas into a bicycle safety zone. Our second reason is after we have completed this project we can help you make it a state law. Finally, our school mates and community need to hear the information that you gathered on this topic.

We have some questions for you. Here they are: Why do you want there to be a bicycle helmet law? How do you intend to pass a state law? Our final question is can you come to our school and talk to us about passing state laws, specifically the bicycle safety law? Would it be possible for you to come sometime in January? We will make our presentation in March to the _____ City Council.

So please send us the answers and some information back to us.

We are on a tight schedule. Send information to us as soon as possible to _____ _____ If you come to our school we will both be a step closer to our goal.

Sincerely,

_____
_____

N

11-27-95

final copy

Dear _____
We are writing to you from _____ School _____ District. We are in Mrs. _____ Elementary. _____ class at _____
Our project is to pass a law in our city (_____) that requires children to wear helmets while riding their bike.
We are aware of some of the advantages and disadvantages of this ordinance.
Since you have already passed an ordinance we would greatly appreciate if you could send us the steps on how you passed this ordinance, and if possible a copy of your presentation.
This help us a lot if you could send us this information as soon as possible, because we are on a shedule.
Thank-you,

A1 Problem Solving

A2 Communication Tools and Techniques

A3 Information Tools and Techniques

A4 Learning and Self-management Tools and Techniques

Tools and Techniques for Working With Others

Bike Helmet Ordinance

O This document provides evidence of the students' work on establishing the features of correspondence designed to suit their purpose.

A3a Information Tools and Techniques: The student gathers information to assist in completing project work; that is, the student:

- identifies potential sources of information to assist in completing the project;
- uses appropriate techniques to collect the information, e.g., considers sampling issues in conducting a survey;
- distinguishes relevant from irrelevant information;
- shows evidence of research in the completed project.

P This is an example of the lists of questions the students developed to guide their research. The lists were prepared by students working in groups.

Q This list of potential sources of information was produced by the students through class discussion. Individual students took responsibility for working on specific parts of the research.

O

> #9
>
> Persuasive   Descriptive
> I. Introduction
>   A. State your position
>   B. Compliment reader
>   C. State sources of information
>   D. Beg for readers' open mindedness
> II. Body / Reason
>   A. Why / how
>   B. Specific examples   } each reason
> III. Conclusion
>   A. Restate position
>   B. "Beg" reader to
> Consider ———

P

> 1. Can a citizen pass a law?
> 2. If they can't, Why?
> 3. What would be the first step?
> 4. What would we do after that?
> 5. Who will we talk to through letters and phone calls?
> 6. How long will it take to get the law?
> 7. Would we have to make the _____ citizens vote?
> 8. What do you think the punishment should be?
> 9. Do we really need a punishment?
>
> ④

Q

> Where can we look for information:
>
> call city council - date
> newspaper
> Write Houston, Arlington
> Senator _____
> Rep. _____
> Think A Head Foundation
> _____ County Safe Kid
> Coalition +
> _____ / Children's Hospital
> Police Dept -

Problem Solving **A1**

Communication Tools and Techniques **A2**

Information Tools and Techniques **A3**

Learning and Self-management Tools and Techniques **A4**

Tools and Techniques for Working With Others

Bike Helmet Ordinance

R

Mayor _____:

1Q. Hello. We are from westpark. We are doing reaserch proect and we would like to ask you few questions.

1q: How do you right a law?

2q: How long should a law be?

3q: What kind of consaqunces should there be for a bike safty law?

4q: What the positions in ~~the office~~ city hall

Put first < q5 Could you please more info on local goverement,

q5. What kind of laws are there?

q6. What different branches are there in the local level of gove ent

q7. What type of law would you consider this?

q8 How would you pass this type of bar?

q9. and question

Thanks for your help It will be vary helpfull in our project

S

	zip code	Question 1 Yes	Question 1 No	Question 2 Yes	Question 2 No	Question 3 Yes	Question 3 No
	A	B	C	D	E	F	G
1	zip code	Question 1 Yes	Question 1 No	Question 2 Yes	Question 2 No	Question 3 Yes	Question 3 No
2	76103	2		2		2	
3							
4	76104	2	4	5	3	3	
5				2		3	
6	76105	1	1	2			
7				5		3	
8	76107	3	1	1		3	1
9	76083						
10	76108						
11							
12	76109	3	1	2		2	
13							
14	76111		2	2			
15							
16	76112	1	3	3	2	2	
17							
18	76114	1	3	4	1	1	7
19	76115	2		2		4	
20	76116	3		4			
21	76118	3	3				
22	76119	2					
23				3	2	5	
24	76120	3	1				
25							
26	76123						
27			20	16	3	19	7
28	76126	26 15	12			6	
30	76127						
31							
32	76132						
33							
34	76133						
35							
36	76134						
37							
38	76135						
39							
40	76136						
41							
42	76137						
43							
44	76155						
46	76008						
47							
48							
49							
50							

Column header notes:
1 Does your child wear a bicycle helmet?
2 Should children be required to wear helmets?
3 Should there be a law that requires helmets to be worn?

T

Penalties for Breaking Law

Ideas

#1. Ticket ~~$10-$50~~ setting price on how bad it is.

~~2 Take them home~~

★3. Suspended from bicycle - 1 ~~week~~ - 1 month

★4. Warning ticket

Put together

★ warning ticket ⟩ gone
★ ~~ticket~~ ⟩ ticket
★ ticket ⟩
★ suspended from bike for 1 week ⟩
★ suspended from bike for 1 week ⟩ week
★ suspended from bike for 1 week ⟩
★ suspended from bike for 1 week ⟩
★ susi ended from bike for 1 month ⟩ month
★ suspended from bike for 1 month ⟩
★ then big fines $100 - $500 ⟩

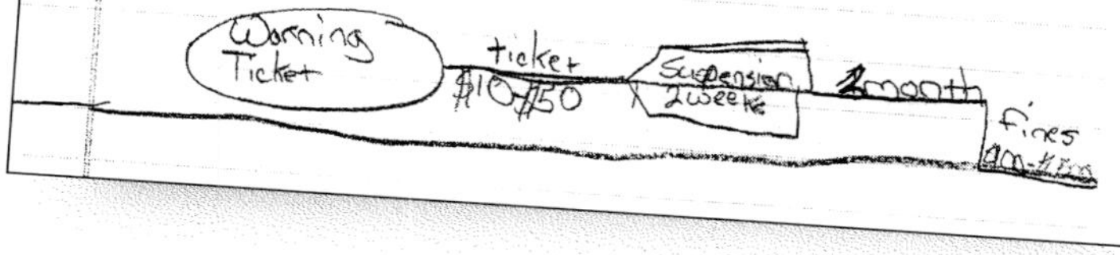

Warning Ticket — ticket $10/$50 — Suspension 2 weeks — 2 month — fines

---

R The students made telephone calls seeking information to assist their research and conducted interviews. This is an example of the texts they prepared for making telephone calls.

S To develop material to support their case for the new ordinance, the students conducted a survey of visitors to the local fair. This is an example of the record sheets they used to record responses.

A1 Problem Solving

A2 Communication Tools and Techniques

A3 Information Tools and Techniques

A4 Learning and Self-management Tools and Techniques

Tools and Techniques for Working With Others

Bike Helmet Ordinance

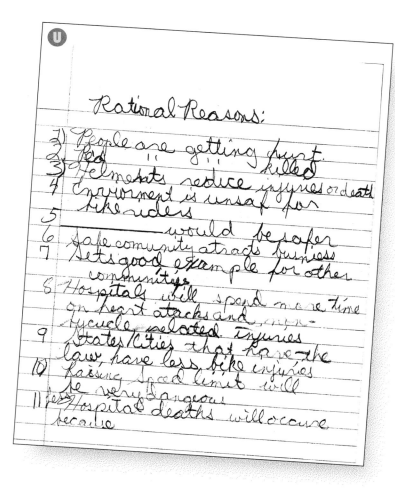

T This working document on penalties for inclusion in the new ordinance illustrates efforts to develop an appropriate sequence of penalties to encourage adherence to the new law. Figuring out how to shape a law so as to encourage adherence was one of the issues the students researched in preparing the ordinance. These notes reflect the student's study of other similar ordinances.

U This list of reasons for passing the proposed ordinance was produced by the class during the process of their research.

A4a Learning and Self-management Tools and Techniques: The student learns from models; that is, the student:

• consults with or observes other students and adults at work, and identifies the main features of what they do and the way they go about their work;

• examines models for the results of project work, such as professionally produced publications, and analyzes their qualities;

• uses what he or she learns from models to assist in planning and conducting project activities.

V The students researched a variety of models, including models of ordinances passed by other city councils and state governments and models of presentations.

Problem Solving **A1**

Communication Tools and Techniques **A2**

Information Tools and Techniques **A3**

Learning and Self-management Tools and Techniques **A4**

Tools and Techniques for Working With Others

Bike Helmet Ordinance

X

(1) I think one of my strengths was the definitions because it just came real easy to me. For me it is easy for me to look up words in the dictionary. I think one of my weaknesses is understanding government. Government is just real boring to me so it goes in one ear and out the other. I can understand things better if I see it instead of reading it and listening to someone talk. But I have admitt I do understand local government a little more because of our speech.

Y

My strengths and weaknesses were a big deal. My strengths were good and my weaknesses were bad. My strengths were getting all the writing done. Another one was standing infront of the city council speaking to them. And the biggest strength I did was completing all the things I had to do to complete this project. And that was about all of my strengths. Now my weaknesses were very bad. One of my weaknesses was didn't finish the letter when we needed it. Another one is when I called Barry he wasn't there so he had to call me back when we needed him to tell me an address so we could send a letter to that place. And that is all my strengths and weaknesses. I did very good on this project. This was a cool project because we got to speak to the city council and write letters and make phone calls. This is my best project ever.

W This document demonstrates an analysis of a model ordinance (an ordinance relating to teen curfew) that a group of students prepared on an overhead transparency for presentation to the class. The acronym "CAP" refers to "Competent Adult Model," the term used by the class to refer to models to guide their work.

A4‹ Learning and Self-management Tools and Techniques: The student identifies strengths and weaknesses in his or her own work; that is, the student:

• understands and establishes criteria for judging the quality of work processes and products;
• assesses his or her own work processes and products.

H I J K These documents demonstrate the criteria the students developed for judging the quality of their work and assessing the strengths and weaknesses of their performances. The students' self-assessments go beyond general comments and demonstrate a willingness and capacity to critique their performances and to identify areas for improvement.

X Y In these final comments on the project, the students described their contributions to the overall work and assessed their strengths and weaknesses. Though some of the comments tend to be wordy and repetitive, the students showed a capacity to analyze their work in some depth and to cite both their perceived strengths and the weaknesses they needed to work on. These reflections contain some spelling errors. The reflections were intended only for personal use and were not edited.

The written work included with this project contains some errors. For the main part the errors are confined to journal entries and other planning documents which were produced for personal use only and were not intended for publication. The pieces of finished writing are the final draft of the ordinance, the script for presentation to the Council, and the letters seeking information. These contain almost error free writing.

A1 ▶ Problem Solving

A2 ▶ Communication Tools and Techniques

A3 ▶ Information Tools and Techniques

A4 ▶ Learning and Self-management Tools and Techniques

Tools and Techniques for Working With Others

Work Sample & Commentary: *Improving the Bathrooms*

The task

Students were asked to identify something in their community on which they wanted to work to bring about change. They could work individually or in small groups. This project was undertaken by three students: the work shown here is drawn from the portfolio prepared by one of the students. The students identified the cleanliness of the boys' bathrooms in the school as the issue on which they wished to work.

Circumstances of performance

The project was completed over a period of about eight weeks, mainly outside class time. The class worked together initially to develop organizing questions to help structure their project plans, and kept their teacher informed of progress on the project and problems as they arose. Otherwise they worked independently.

What the work shows

A1 b Problem Solving: The student troubleshoots problems in the operation of a system in need of repair or devises and tests ways of improving the effectiveness of a system in operation; that is, the student:

- identifies the parts of the system and the way the parts connect with each other;
- identifies parts or connections in the system that have broken down or that could be made to work better;
- devises ways of making the system work again or making it work better;
- evaluates the effectiveness of the strategies for improving the system and supports the evaluation with evidence.

The student's records of the project do not fit neatly with the features of an "Improving a System" project as set out above; nevertheless, the project provides an example of a tenacious effort at working to make a system more effective. A particular strength of the project is the student's effort to make sense of the parts of the system and the way they connect with one another.

The documentation presented from this project is not a comprehensive record of all work done as part of the project. It would be neither reasonable nor appropriate to ask students to keep detailed written records of every aspect of a project. This would defeat part of the purpose of applied learning which is for students to put their academic learning to work and to learn from projects that connect what they do at school to the demands of the twenty-first century workplace. Some of these standards lend themselves to assessment through observation and other less formal methods than through written work.

Problem Solving ◀ **A1**

Communication Tools and Techniques ◀ **A2**

Information Tools and Techniques ◀ **A3**

Learning and Self-management Tools and Techniques

Tools and Techniques for Working With Others

A *Community Research*

I think the bathrooms in this school are terrible. We want a bathroom that is clean and fully equipped for our needs. We would like the bathrooms moped more. We would like new tissue holder, paper towels and soap to dry and wash our hands. If possible we would like air fresheners in the bathroom.

There is a need for cleaner bathrooms because it is very unhealty. In the boys bathroom there is urine all over the floor that you step in when you go to the urinal. You also get allo of the disgusting smelling aroma because it seems like the bathrooms aren't moped.

We have observed the bathrooms at different times. Sometimes it is worse than the day before.

We have also interviewed Lerie to ask about problems that we have in the bathrooms. We also started to give out surveys. We are focusing on the children because they are the ones who are doing this to the bathroom.

A The student's description of the project identifies the problem he planned to tackle and his initial efforts to address the task.

This work sample illustrates a standard-setting performance for the following parts of the standards:

A1 b **Problem Solving: Improve a system.**

A2 a **Communication: Make an oral presentation.**

A2 c **Communication: Publish information.**

A3 a **Information: Gather information.**

Improving the Bathrooms

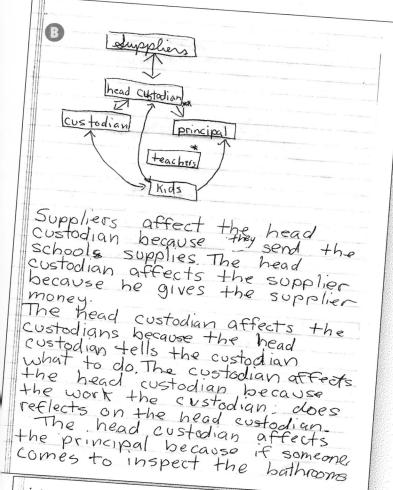

B

Suppliers affect the head custodian because they send the schools supplies. The head custodian affects the supplier because he gives the supplier money.

The head custodian affects the custodians because the head custodian tells the custodian what to do. The custodian affects the head custodian because the work the custodian does reflects on the head custodian.

The head custodian affects the principal because if someone comes to inspect the bathrooms it will reflect on the principal's school.

The Kids can go to the principa head custodian or custodian to complain and put pressure to buy supplies

The custodian affect the Kids because if they don't do their jobs the Kids go to dirty bathrooms.

* - Principal doesn't effect teachers

** The principal doesn't effect the custodian

C

Log

3/18 - Wrote letter to Louie
3/23 - Went to bathrooms to observe them. Decided to interview Louie instead of sending him a letter. Made up the questions for the interview.
3/26 - I went to interview Louie. I got info. from him about the bathrooms. Tommorow I am going to make an appointment with Ms. _____ to interview her.
3/27 - I did my observations of the bathrooms. Were not going to interview Ms. _____
4/22 - Did observations of bathroom. I asked the head custodian if we can make an appointment said he needs to talk to teacher improvment
4/25 - I did a picture of the bathroom
5/5 - Made observations of bathroom. We also took pictures of the bathroom
5/16 - Today we observed the bathrooms. We also made a flier.

C This extract from the student's project log reveals a sequence of project activity and some of the strategies he adopted: making systematic observations of the bathrooms; interviewing key people affecting the condition of the bathrooms; and creating fliers to appeal to students to keep the bathrooms clean.

B This working document shows the student's efforts to identify the people who influence the state of the bathrooms and how the parts of the system connect with one another.

A1 Problem Solving

A2 Communication Tools and Techniques

A3 Information Tools and Techniques

Learning and Self-management Tools and Techniques

Tools and Techniques for Working With Others

Improving the Bathrooms

D

Community Research

~~The~~ Update

We have started to make out observations again. We have seen much improvement. New toilet tissue holders were ordered. They have started to put paper towels in the bathroom. Also the bathrooms do not smell like usual. We tried to make an appointment with the head costodian, but he said that he needs to talk to the teacher.

E

Community Projects

I think if the conditions greatly improve then you get an outstanding. If everything stays the same you should get a try again or failing. If the conditions improve but not much you should get a satisfactory.

Also if people like a principal or custodian paid attention to you, you have succeed. If people like a principal or custodian did something to help you, you would have succeed.

D Several documents provide evidence of evaluation of the effectiveness of the strategies adopted to improve the system. The "Update" includes an evaluation of the effects of the project supported by evidence.

E **F** A further record prepared on the same day indicates recognition of the need to influence key people in the system to bring about change. This issue is picked up again in the piece on problems encountered in the project.

F

Cleaning the Bathrooms

A problem we ran into was interviewing the head custodian. A way to solve this problem is to bring a letter from the teacher to show that you aren't making a joke. You also have to stay on top of a person to get info.

Getting people to cooperate was a problem. You have to keep on them to help you. You have to put lots of posters up. You also have to make several announcement.

Improving the Bathrooms

G

Self-Assessment

I think I did an okay job. I did most of what I wanted to do except for getting paper towels in the bathroom and getting the floors cleaner. We saw new tissue holders in the bathroom but there are still two missing. We have seen soap go into the bathrooms. We still have to do a couple of more things like interviewing the head custodian and putting up posters.

H

To improve something you have to stay on top of everyone who is involved in the system. If your in a job and you need something to be done and somebody keeps forgetting you have to stay on top of him/her to do a better job.

Homeless shelters aren't working because on T.V. they show homeless people in the freezing cold on the street instead of in shelters. I wonder why this happens but I don't know much about the system. To learn more about the system I would interview someone in the shelter.

G The student's "Self-Assessment" provides further evidence of evaluation of the effects of the project and indicates further work needed to improve the system.

H This reflection on the project shows the student's attempt to generalize from his experience and extrapolate to other contexts.

I The interview with the head custodian finally took place the day after the reflection was written. The record of interview reveals new information about the factors affecting the system, especially factors operating beyond the school and beyond the students' capacity to make an impact. Unfortunately, this new information came too late to be incorporated into the student's reflections on the system and his efforts to improve it.

I

The Interview with the Head Custodian

Today we interviewed the head custodian. We asked him how much money is spent per year on the bathrooms but he couldn't answer because they spend more money on workers. We asked were do they get the supplies from he said that there was a scandel in the _____ so supplies are being shiped in. _____ is negotiating right now. We asked what do you spend the money on he said they spend the little money on supplies. We asked why were there no doors on the stalls he said when the school was built that is how it was made. We asked how much the doors cost but he didn't know. He also told us that custodial staff bought rods and metal, which they made toilet paper holders because they were not getting the shipment that they ordered. We asked about the paper towels but he said because of the scandal the paper towels weren't coming in.

Improving the Bathrooms

J

<u>Oral Presentation</u>

I think _____ did a great job presenting his project. He spoke loud and clearly. He made me aware of how dirty the bathroom was. He made it sound intresting so that people stayed intrested. That is why I think _____ did a good job.

K

Bathroom Alert!!

It's your bathroom yet you dirty it. Why do you do this. You're the one who goes to the bathroom. So, it's your duty to keep them clean. Please be considerate, others use the bathrooms.

A2a Communication Tools and Techniques: The student makes an oral presentation of project plans or findings to an appropriate audience; that is, the student:

- organizes the presentation in a logical way appropriate to its purpose;
- speaks clearly and presents confidently;
- responds to questions from the audience;
- evaluates the effectiveness of the presentation.

J The students made oral presentations of their findings of their project's findings to the class. This in an evaluation of this student's presentation provided by another student.

A2c Communication Tools and Techniques: The student writes and formats information for short publications, such as brochures or posters; that is, the student:

- organizes the information into an appropriate form for use in the publication;
- checks the information for accuracy;
- formats the publication so that it achieves its purpose.

K This flier was prepared to inform fellow students of the project. Despite the missing question mark, it is an effective piece of communication that addresses its audience directly and makes an appeal for a change in behavior.

L This is the text for a PA announcement to appeal to students to help with the task of keeping the bathrooms clean. It also demonstrates effective communication: it is informative; addresses its audience directly; and makes a strong appeal for a change in behavior.

Problem Solving **A1**

Communication Tools and Techniques **A2**

Information Tools and Techniques **A3**

Learning and Self-management Tools and Techniques

Tools and Techniques for Working With Others

L

<u>P.A. Announcement</u>

Hello students of _____. My name is _____. I am working with John _____ and Andrew _____. We are working to improve the Bathrooms. We have been making observations for several months. We found out that they are very dirty. You can help be keeping the floors clean. You can also help by not throwing paper towels around. We can't do it alone. So please give us a hand. Remember these are your bathrooms.

Improving the Bathrooms

A3a Information Tools and Techniques: The student gathers information to assist in completing project work; that is, the student:

- identifies potential sources of information to assist in completing the project;
- uses appropriate techniques to collect the information, e.g., considers sampling issues in conducting a survey;
- distinguishes relevant from irrelevant information;
- shows evidence of research in the completed project.

M The students conducted systematic observations of the bathrooms over a period of weeks. This is an extract from the record. The record is detailed and specific.

N They collected information from interviews with key people. This is a record of interview with one of the custodians.

D **E** **G** This research is evident in the student's evaluations of the project.

The written work included with this project contains some errors. For the main part the errors are confined to journal entries and other records which were produced for personal use only and were not intended for publication. The only piece of finished writing is the flier. It contains almost error free writing.

M

Observations

10:44 3rd floor
- no paper towels
- no garbage bag
- no soap

10:53 2nd floor
- paper towels
- no hot water
- no garbage bag
- no soap

10:41 1st floor
- garbage bag
- no paper towels
- no soap
- no hot water

11:02 Basement
- no soap
- paper towels
- no hot water
- garbage bag

N

Interview with Louie

1. Why are there no doors in the boys bathroom? Is it a fire hazard? It's not a fire hazard. Boys bathroom usually dosen't have doors. The girls bathroom has doors.
2. Can we put posters in the bathroom to tell you to wash your hands? No because it is a fire hazard and kids might put the posters down the toilet.
3. How many days a week do you mop the bathroom? Everyday after the kids go home.
4. How many days a week do you change the toilet paper? The paper is checked everyday.
5. Why is there no papy towels in the bathroom? Running short.
6. Why is there no soap in the bathroom? There is plenty of soap but they forget to put it in.
7. Why is there no bathrooms on the 4th and 5th floor? There was offices up there.
8. Has anyone ever changed the toilet paper holder? There is no more. There was a lock order.

A1 ▶ Problem Solving

A2 ▶ Communication Tools and Techniques

A3 ▶ Information Tools and Techniques

Learning and Self-management Tools and Techniques

Tools and Techniques for Working With Others

Work Sample & Commentary: *Sock Hop/Zoo Field Trip*

The task

Students were asked to devise a project that would advance their study of a school subject and involve obtaining the assistance of experts from outside the school. The project proposal had to be approved by the teacher and the building principal. Students could work individually or in groups of two or three. This project was undertaken by three students: the work shown here is drawn from the portfolios prepared by two of the students. The students decided to organize a field trip to the zoo to study animals. To raise funds for the overnight camping trip at the zoo they sold popcorn and held a sock hop dance for the school.

Circumstances of performance

The project was completed both in and out of school time. It occupied about one hour each day for two days each week for most of the year. The students sought assistance from parents and other adult experts as they needed it. They received peer and teacher feedback on most of their finished work prior to publication.

What the work shows

A1c Problem Solving: The student plans and organizes an event or an activity; that is, the student:

• develops a plan for the event or activity that:
– includes all the factors and variables that need to be considered;
– shows the order in which things need to be done;
– takes into account the resources available to put the plan into action, including people and time;
• implements the plan;
• evaluates the success of the event or activity by identifying the parts of the plan that worked best and the parts that could have been improved by better planning and organization;
• makes recommendations to others who might consider planning and organizing a similar event or activity.

The documentation presented from this project is not a comprehensive record of all work done as part of the project. It would be neither reasonable nor appropriate to ask students to keep detailed written records of every aspect of a project. This would defeat part of the purpose of applied learning which is for students to put their academic learning to work and to learn from projects that connect what they do at school to the demands of the twenty-first century work place. Some of these standards lend themselves to assessment through observation and other less formal methods than through written work.

A

Dear Mr._____ and Mrs._____,

We have a problem. The wildlife here in _____ is very limited. There is not a lot of opportunity to learn about conservation and wildlife preservation. If we took a field trip to Fossil Rim our problem would be solved. Shanon _____, Lindsey _____, Karin _____ and I would like to take our class for a great learning experience. In addition, we will provide a study guide to Fossil Rim to identify the animals and provide information about conservation of endangered wildlife.

If we went of a field trip, we will learn about the wildlife from around the world and how Fossil Rim provides a natural habitat for them to live and breed. This information would help us to understand the importance of science in our day to day life. We would use math to make a budget and figure out a way to earn money. These skills will be very useful again and again. We will learn how to make a schedule with target dates. This will provide us with a plan that covers the entire project from start to finish. The preparation of the study guide will require lots of research and organization of information.

The first thing to do is research, research, research! Next, we will choose a fund raiser (with your approval, of course). This will earn money for the field trip. The parents will hopefully chip in their time and money, if we don't get enough. We will prepare a plan schedule. This will provide the dates that team members will need to accomplish the steps toward our goal. My competent adult model is the <u>Unofficial Guide to Walt Disney World.</u> It shows us step by step how to plan a trip and what to see.

Now, you are asking why should I approve a trip to Fossil Rim? How does this help _____ and the students? Besides the fact that the project planning, fund raising, budgeting and reporting will provide an excellent learning opportunity, it will provide education. It will also provide awareness of wildlife and the importance of conservation. This project will be evaluated by its successful planning and its ability to involve our class in wildlife conservation. The trip will

---

be evaluated by the student participation on the trip and a plan of conservation that identifies what we can all do to protect and respect wildlife so they will still be around when we have children.

Sincerely,

_____

A The proposal establishes the need for the field trip and its connection to the students' science studies. It demonstrates consideration of the factors and variables to be taken into account, including the need to raise funds to finance the trip. It also includes reference to the use of a model to assist in planning the trip.

This work sample illustrates a standard-setting performance for the following parts of the standards:

A1c Problem Solving: Plan and organize an event or an activity.

A2b Communication: Compose correspondence.

A2c Communication: Publish information.

A3a Information: Gather information.

A3b Information: Use information technology.

A4a Learning and Self-management: Learn from models.

A4b Learning and Self-management: Keep records of work activities.

Sock Hop/Zoo Field Trip

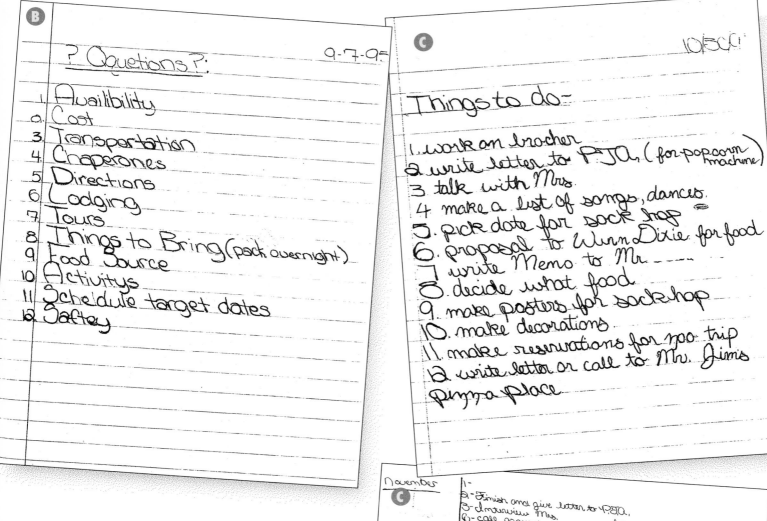

B

? Qquestions?:   9-7-9=

1. Availibility
2. Cost
3. Transportation
4. Chaperones
5. Directions
6. Lodging
7. Tours
8. Things to Bring (pack overnight)
9. Food Source
10. Activitys
11. Schedule target dates
12. Saftey

C   10/5/9?

Things to do-

1. work on brocher
2. write letter to P.T.A. (for popcorn machine)
3. talk with Mrs.
4. make a list of songs, dances.
5. pick date for sock hop
6. proposal to Winn Dixie for food
7. write Memo to Mr. _____
8. decide what food
9. make posters for sock hop
10. make decorations
11. make reservations for zoo trip
12. write letter or call to Mr. Jim's Pizza place

B This list of questions extracted from one of the student's logs shows attention to the factors that needed to be taken into account in planning the zoo field trip.

C D These are extracts from one of the students' project logs showing evidence of planning, including putting together a budget for the sock hop. The students sold pop corn to raise funds for the sock hop.

C

November

1-
2- Finish and give letter to P.T.A.
3- interview Mrs.
6- call around to see who will give us supplies for popcorn   between 11:40 to 1:10
7- pick songs or dances
8- finish memo to Mr.
9- talk about what food to have.
13- talk to food places suchas,

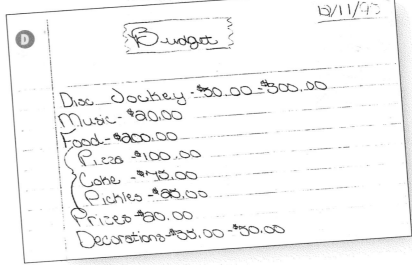

D   12/11/9?

Budget

Disc Jockey - $50.00 - $300.00
Music - $20.00
Food - $200.00
  Pizza - $100.00
  Coke - $75.00
  Pickles - $25.00
Prizes - $20.00
Decorations - $35.00 - $50.00

A1 Problem Solving
A2 Communication Tools and Techniques
A3 Information Tools and Techniques
A4 Learning and Self-management Tools and Techniques
Tools and Techniques for Working With Others

Sock Hop/Zoo Field Trip

E Dear binder,
For my _____ project my group is trying to get an overnight field trip to the zoo. To do this we sold pop-corn to raise money for a school sock hop, the school sock hop will raise money for the field trip. To go to the zoo over-night, for our whole class, will be over $700.00.

My competent adult model is the Unofficial Guide to Disney World and Epcot. It is not exactly what we are doing, but the table of contents is almost exactly alike. We also have a few of the same sections.

To do this project I have learned skills such as:
How to write a script for a phone call
How to write a script for a interview
How to write a good persuasive letter and proposal
How to make and use a schedule
How to make a time line
How to have a conflict resolution discussion
How to make a budget
How to use a phone directory

To do this project we are solving problems and facing these head on such as:
Seeking a reasonably priced DJ (which we did not find so we are having people donate tapes and have a radio DJ to play them);
We have had to get along and cooperate with each other in spite of our differences to make the project successful; and
Finding a good price on pizza that will stick to our budget and not blow all our money on it.

To fully say what I have done, you must realize that a group project means that you work in a group with each member doing certain jobs alone, and certain jobs together. The jobs I can remember doing alone are making phone calls to party places, writing many scripts, talking on the phone, looking up phone numbers, making our sock hop budget, figuring menu prices, and volunteer job descriptions. I did these with none or little help from the group while the other members did other jobs.

If I had to give myself a rating between 1 and 10 I would say a 9. I have done my best to get along with everyone and have done well with my skills. If I had to give my group members a grade, not one would get higher but most about the same. The most valuable thing that I have learned is that you do not have to be best friends to work successfully together for the good of the group and the project.

sincerely,

F By: _____ , _____
_____ , _____

Hasting A Sock Hop

E This interim report on the project contains evidence of the students' evaluation of their planning and organization.

F The students made recommendations to others who might consider planning a similar activity in the form of a guide entitled, "Hosting A Sock Hop."

G They also produced a guide called, "How To Plan your Class Trip." This is the handwritten draft of the table of contents.

These manuals provide evidence that the students understood the process they had developed and the order in which things needed to be done, and that they were aware of possible pitfalls and had developed solutions for them.

Problem Solving **A1**

Communication Tools and Techniques **A2**

Information Tools and Techniques **A3**

Learning and Self-management Tools and Techniques **A4**

Tools and Techniques for Working With Others

 # Food at the Sock - Hop

When we bought food most of it was donated by generous companies in and around _____. We spent $117.56 at _____ to get what wasn't donated. Some generous donors we found were:

_____ $50 gift certificate,

_____ all napkins, straws, 135 plastic tea - spoons, and 100 cups 20 oz.

_____ the gift certificates that we used as prizes for the trivia questions and the contests,

_____ $25 gift certificate with which we purchased their P.C. colas for refreshments,

_____ $20 gift certificate with which we purchased their Sam's Choice cola (2L bottles) for our floats 10 Cola (Coke), 5 Southern Lightning (Dr. Pepper) and 5 Root Beer,

_____ 65 cups and an equal number of plastic iced tea spoons,

_____ 24 pk. of their _____ cola for refreshments,

_____ 25 20 oz cups,

_____ 1 gallon of vanilla ice cream for the floats.

Sock Hop/Zoo Field Trip

As you see many things were donated. We went out during our lunch period as a group. I would definitely put an emphasis on going as a group because we found "power in numbers."

We purchased 10 gallons of ice cream at the start and soon ran out. I would recommend purchasing at least 20 - 25 gallons - if planning for 300 in attendance. We had around 300 people in attendance the night of the sock - hop and had hot dogs, condiments, soda used for floats (2 L bottles), and chips left over.

A way to judge the attendance is by how intensely you advertised; we had daily announcements the last week before the sock - hop, put up flyers around the school 3 weeks before the sock - hop. We wore our costumes to "tempt" the kids to come and see the costumes that everyone would be wearing and join some good honest family fun; Please note in our advertisement we stressed the emphasis of family fun (It's something hard to come by these days.) 300 worked well for us, so just judge the amount of food you will need by advertisement. The sock - hop was well liked by the public and popular with the attenders so a large attendance for a future sock - hop is very probable, especially if you advertise this event thoroughly.

Written by _____

Music/Disc Jockeys

Finding the right Disc Jockey is crucial. Allow plenty of time to research Disc Jockeys. Decide what your budget is for this part of the dance. Come up with a list of questions that include; do they do school dances, how much do they charge, do they have their own music, do they have their own equipment, and are they available on the night you need them. Go through the phone book and call several Disc Jockeys.

Here is a list of Disc Jockeys I called:

\# _____

$ 200.00
They have their own music and equipment

\# _____

$ 350.00 (We got a $ 50.00 discount, which made it $ 300.00)
They have their own equipment and music.

\# _____

$ 395.00 (We got a hundred dollar discount)
They have their own 1000 watt stereo sound system, PA microphones, strobe lights, bubble machines, mirror ball, and fog machine.

_____

$ 60.00
He does not own equipment or music.

If you choose a Disc Jockey that provides their own music and equipment, make all the necessary arrangements with them and you're ready for your dance.

If you choose a Disc Jockey that does not have their own music and equipment (as I did) you will need to make arrangements to get these

Music is a very important part of the Sock-Hop. Without the right music your Sock- Hop will not be a success.

I sent home a note to all the students in my school asking them to send in 50s music. This method proved to be very successful. I collected numerous tapes, cds, and records. I made sure that they all had their names on them.

I listened to all the music and selected a collection of songs that I thought would be appropriate for our Sock-Hop. I made a list of these songs, in the order I wanted them played, to give to the Disc Jockey. I then transferred the the music to cassette tapes. Make sure you have more than enough music to last throughout the dance. Don't forget to return what you borrowed!

You will also have to make arrangements to get the proper equipment. Look through the phone book for companies that rent equipment. You can also check with local schools to see if you can borrow their equipment. I was able to borrow equipment from our local high school.

Our Sock-Hop was a big success. The Disc Jockey I choose did a great job. The 50s music had everyone dancing all night long. Everyone had a good time!

By:

_____

Dear Parents,

We are needing 50's music for our Sock Hop!!!!!!!

Please send in either tapes or records with you child's name on it to Karin Billerbeck. I would greatly appreciate it. I am planning to record these onto tapes and will play them at the Sock-Hop. I will take Excellent care of them and return them when I am through (which will be as soon as possible)

Thank-you,

Sample of note asking for music

_____, Disc Jockey

with _____ and _____

Sock Hop/Zoo Field Trip

I bought music notes in a set, and copied them on a paper, and then cut them out. We used a old motorcycle as a prop. We used the cardboard jukebox as a prop. I bought a roll of pink paper from the werehouse to cover the tables. I glued black construction paper recordsn to make the table cover more attractive. You can make jukeboxes, and 50's car cutouts out of white poster board. I threw steamers around some things. I tied balloons to the decorated table. All 50's membrobilia is fun to hang. I hope you liked the tips and Just think back and you wont believe what you will come up with!!!

Here are some places you can go to find these thing:

_____
_____

a place that sells paper

By: _____

DECORATING

To start on decorating, you should begin three to five weeks ahead. This is a list of things I used.

Plastic records
Real records and there covers
Music notes
Old motorcycle
Life size cardboard jukebox
A roll of pink paper
Black poster board
White poster board
Streamers
Balloons

Most of the items were donated by a parent. I spent $80 total. You can get decoration at most party places. Plastic records cost the most. Real records can be normally found around the house. Hanging them looks great.

CONTEST/GAMES

At our Sock Hop we had a Hoola-Hoop contest, Elvis look alike contest, Dance contest, and a Costume contest.

For the hoola-hoop contest we borrowed the hoola-hoops from the P.E. teacher. When it came time for the contest there was not enough hoola-hoops for everybody. When the kids' hoola-hoop dropped they would either leave the game, or they would pick it up and continue. If I had to do it over, I would have grouped the participates by grades : K-1, 2-3, and 4-5.

The Elvis look-alike contest the kids came up on stage. While Elvis music was playing they tried to do the moves of Elvis. If I had to change something it would be that only students who dressed like Elvis could participate.

During the dance contest it was hard to choose because people had all different ways of dancing. When we would tell somebody they were out, some of them would cry or get mad. If I had to do this over I would do it by age or if you had an adult dancing with you.

The costume contest, kids were running up on the stage with no costumes on. So what we did was take all the kids who did not have costumes on out of the contest. We had separate boy and girl contests. We lined the girls up and went through the line trying to find the people who got the loudest applause. Then we did the same thing through the boys line. Then finally got a winner for both. If I had to do it over, I would have passed out coupons to people who wanted to be in the contest and were dressed in 50's style The coupons would have been little slips of paper that say "I'm part of the costume contest K-2 or 3-5" you would circle which grade level they are in.

When we judged all the contest we did it by applause, but that did ot seem to work because people would pick their friends as the winner. If I had to change that mistake I would of had four volunteer to help contribute for the judge.

Besides all the mistakes we made the Sock Hop went really smooth and it was great family fun.

_____

A2b Communication Tools and Techniques: The student composes and sends correspondence, such as thank-you letters and memoranda providing information; that is, the student:

• expresses the information or request clearly;
• writes in a style appropriate to the purpose of the correspondence.

Problem Solving **A1**

Communication Tools and Techniques **A2**

Information Tools and Techniques **A3**

Learning and Self-management Tools and Techniques **A4**

Tools and Techniques for Working With Others

Sock Hop/Zoo Field Trip

G

Table of Contents

Page 1- Table of Contents

Page 2- Deciding on your destination

Page 3- Getting Information

Page 4- Writing a Proposal

Page 5- How to write a script for phone calls

Page 6- Deciding what to do to raise money for your trip

Page 7- How to get donations for fundraisers

Page 8- How to plan a Schedule for your trip

Page 9- Notification to parents

Page 10 - Supplies to bring with you on your trip.

H

Dear Mrs._____and the PTA Board,

For our_____Applied Learning Project, we are planning an overnight class trip to the_____Zoo. We are planning to raise the money to this ourselves.

We would like to borrow the PTA popcorn machine so that we can sell popcorn after school on the following dates: Nov. 17, Nov. 21, Dec.1, and Dec. 8.

We will have two adult volunteers working the popcorn machine, 2 students bagging the popcorn, 1 taking money, and 1 calling out orders. In this project we will be doing a large combination of skills such as counting money, estimating the amount of popcorn needed, scheduling volunteers, creating advertisements and making deposits.

We plan to use the popcorn money made to get us started on our major fund raisers, a sock hop.

We need to know your decision as soon as possible because we need to make arrangements to buy popcorn and get volunteers. The popcorn machine would be greatly appreciated by our class, not mention all the popcorn lovers of_____Elementary.

Sincerely,

_____
_____
_____
_____
_____

H This is an example of correspondence the students composed. The letter expresses the students' request clearly and is written in an appropriate style. Two words are missing which suggests that the work would have been improved by further attention to accuracy. But the errors do not interfere with the communication.

The guide to planning a sock hop includes a memorandum asking parents to lend music for the sock hop.

A2 Communication Tools and Techniques: The student writes and formats information for short publications, such as brochures or posters; that is, the student:

- organizes the information into an appropriate form for use in the publication;
- checks the information for accuracy;
- formats the publication so that it achieves its purpose.

I This is an extract of a brochure the students produced to provide information to parents and students about the arrangements and schedule for the zoo field trip. The brochure was based on information collected from interviews with zoo staff.

I

Come Spend the Night at the Zoo

" Roar, Snore, and Animal Lore " is a program that allows our class to spend the night at the _____ Zoo. Our Class will enjoy the zoo after hours, guided by zoo counselors.

On our overnight expedition, we will discover who is roaring, who is snoring, and who is just hanging around! The program includes evening and morning zoo tours, a late-evening snack, a continental breakfast, and plenty of excitement! Sleeping quarters are in the _____ Education Center. The emphasis will be on bats.

Staff

During the trip our class will have zoo counselors and zoo keepers from the z☐oo to tour with, and we will have 18 adults.

Health and Safety

Your child will be supervised by an adult at all times. If your child becomes ill you will be contacted. Any medication sent for your child will be given by the classroom teacher. Please bring a note if your child has a health problem, and please fill out the attached medical forms.

Sock Hop/Zoo Field Trip

J

COME JOIN THE FAMILY FUN !!!
SOCK-HOP

Date: Febuary 9, 1996
Time: 6:00-9:00
Place:_____Cafeteria
Dress: 50's outfit's [optional]
Food: Hot Dogs, Coke Floats, Pickles, and
          Sodas
Games: Elvis look alike, Elvis sing
      alike [Ain't Nothin' but a Hound-dog]
      dance, hoola hoop, and
      costume contests
Age: ALL   ** It will be ★ great family fun !**
Admission price :$1.00 per person

SPONSORED BY: MRS._____ CLASS

K

Announcement –

Hey, what are you doing Feb. 9?
I don't know yet, I really
haven't thought about it.
I'm going to go to the sock-
hop!
What is a sock-hop?
A sock-hop is where everybody
dances in their socks to 50's
music!
And their even going to have
food, like hotdogs, pickles, drinks,
and coke floats.
They are also going to have
all kinds of contests.
Wow, that sounds like
alot of fun!
Remember to wear a costume!!
And come join the fun!!!

J This is an example of the posters the students prepared to advertise the fund raising activity.

K This text for a PA announcement to publicize the sock hop demonstrates effective communication skills.

A3ₐ Information Tools and Techniques: The student gathers information to assist in completing project work; that is, the student:

- identifies potential sources of information to assist in completing the project;
- uses appropriate techniques to collect the information, e.g., considers sampling issues in conducting a survey;
- distinguishes relevant from irrelevant information;
- shows evidence of research in the completed project.

The students conducted research, both in organizing the sock hop to raise funds for the zoo field trip and in arranging the field trip itself.

L This is an extract from one of the student's project logs showing her initial thoughts about possible sources of information to assist in planning the field trip. The students abandoned their initial plan to go to Fossil Rim. Instead, they chose the zoo.

L

9/5/95

What I know about
taking a trip to Fossil Rim –
- I've been there before
- It's a large project
- It will take a while to get
everything and all the information
together
- It's a long way over to
Fossil Rim

What can I use to get
information.
- books
- by calling
- brosners
- people
- By the people that work
at Fossil Rim.

Sock Hop/Zoo Field Trip

N

Script for Volunteer help at selling popcorn

Hi, (who ever) this is Karin _____ and 3 of my friends and I are trying to get our class an overnight trip to the _____ Zoo. To raise the money for that we are going to hold a sock hop, and to raise the money for that we are going to sell popcorn Nov. 17th, Nov. 21st, and Dec. 1st. I would like to know if you could volunteer on Nov. 21st or Dec. 1st. If you can do both it would help us out a lunch. We have 2 shifts. One starts at 2:00 and goes to 3:00 and the other starts at 3:00 and goes to 4:00.

Do you know how to work the popcorn machine?

Thank-You!

M

10/18/95

Interview with _____

K.1. How long have you been holding an annual sock hop? 4 years

K.2. What kind of refreshments do you serve? hamburgers, hotdogs, potato chip.

K.3. How much do you charge to get in? 4.00 & 2.00

K4. How many people attend each year? 200

B.5. How much over all money do you get? broke even

B.6. Do you have a D.J.? tip 200 yes, hired from party crew $150.00

B.7. Where do you have your concession stand? all out in gym one corner

O

2-22-96

Paragraph on the Music-

I started with researching DJ's. I looked in the yellow pages and it had a free consumer information number, (_____), this number gave me good information on picking our DJ.

After I called around for awhile I found two that I was satisfied with and asked them to send me a package. When I recieved the letters I compared them. I decided to go with the one that was the less expensive. The next day Mrs. _____ said that her friend Alan _____ (The Dude) would do it for cheaper, I decided that was the way to go.

M This is a partial record of an interview with the principal of another school that had recently held a school-wide dance.

N This is an example of the scripts the students prepared to make telephone calls seeking help to organize the sock hop.

O This extract from one of the students' project logs describes the research she undertook to arrange the music for the sock hop.

A1 Problem Solving

A2 Communication Tools and Techniques

A3 Information Tools and Techniques

A4 Learning and Self-management Tools and Techniques

Tools and Techniques for Working With Others

Sock Hop/Zoo Field Trip

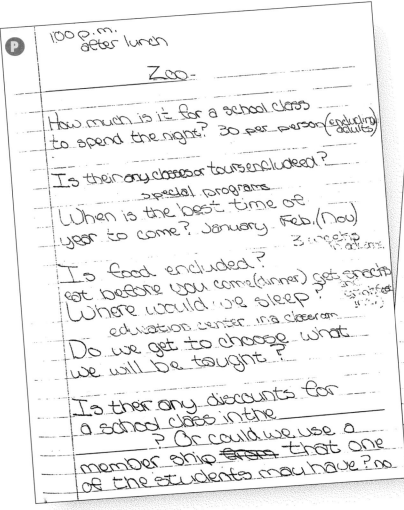

P The brochure setting out the arrangements for the zoo field trip was produced after telephone interviews with zoo staff. This is a partial record of one such interview.

A3 b Information Tools and Techniques: The student uses information technology to assist in gathering, organizing, and presenting information; that is, the student:

- acquires information for specific purposes from on-line sources, such as the Internet, and other electronic data bases, such as an electronic encyclopedia;
- uses word-processing, drawing, and painting programs to produce project reports and related materials.

The students accessed information from a central data base. Not included here, in the interests of space, are records of the requests they made to the district media center (e.g., for information about the 1950's).

Many of the materials produced by the students demonstrate use of a word processing program and several show the capacity to import graphics.

A4 a Learning and Self-management Tools and Techniques: The student learns from models; that is, the student:

- consults with or observes other students and adults at work, and identifies the main features of what they do and the way they go about their work;
- examines models for the results of project work, such as professionally produced publications, and analyzes their qualities;
- uses what he or she learns from models to assist in planning and conducting project activities.

M The students consulted with a person who had experience in organizing an event similar to the sock hop, in this case the principal of another school who had recently organized a school dance.

Q In their proposal the students refer to their intention to use the "Unofficial Guide To Walt Disney World and Epcot" as a model to guide their planning of the zoo field trip. This extract from one of the student's project logs shows her analysis of the qualities of the guide as a model for her own work.

Problem Solving **A1.**

Communication Tools and Techniques **A2**

Information Tools and Techniques **A3**

Learning and Self-management Tools and Techniques **A4**

Tools and Techniques for Working With Others

Sock Hop/Zoo Field Trip

A4b Learning and Self-management Tools and Techniques: The student keeps records of work activities in an orderly manner; that is, the student:

- sets up a system for storing records of work activities;
- maintains records of work activities in a way that makes it possible to find specific materials quickly and easily.

R The students used composition books to store their project records. This student annotated her records by means of tabs to provide easy access to specific information.

The written work included with this project contains some errors. For the main part the errors are confined to journal entries and other planning documents which were produced for personal use only and were not intended for publication. The pieces of finished writing are the proposal, progress evaluation, guide, letter, poster, and brochure. Some of these contain minor errors that could have been corrected with further editing; however, the errors do not interfere with the communication.

A1 ▶ Problem Solving

A2 ▶ Communication Tools and Techniques

A3 ▶ Information Tools and Techniques

A4 ▶ Learning and Self-management Tools and Techniques

Tools and Techniques for Working With Others

Work Sample & Commentary: *Young Authors' Conference*

The task

Students who frequently engage in reading and writing workshops sit "in the author's chair" and present their writing to the class. This experience influenced, in part, the genesis of an annual event in which students sponsor a one-day authors' conference for other elementary students in their school district.

Each year the conference reflects the interests and ideas of the current group. For example, this group set up a pre-conference hot line, arranged for two professional writers to give the conference participants advice on producing effective writing, and for four accomplished storytellers to entertain them. In addition, there were small group "learning sessions" that provided in-depth exploration of successful writing strategies and "sharing sessions" that provided occasion for students to read their original stories and exchange extra copies of their books with other young authors.

Circumstances of performance

This was a class project. The teacher served when necessary as advisor and facilitator, in order to ensure that content objectives were met.

The students had a budget which they supplemented by selling books by the two authors as well as t-shirts the students had designed, which displayed the conference logo. The profits from the conference funded a field trip related to another class project.

The documentation presented from this project is not a comprehensive record of all work done as part of the project. It would be neither reasonable nor appropriate to ask students to keep detailed written records of every aspect of a project. This would defeat part of the purpose of applied learning which is for students to put their academic learning to work and to learn from projects that connect what they do at school to the demands of the twenty-first century workplace. Some of these standards lend themselves to assessment through observation and other less formal methods than through written work.

A   March 24, 1994

Dear Librarian,

Can you please put out a display of books by Deborah Dennard and Caroline Arnold because of the Young Authors' Conference? The Young Authors' Conference is where children come from all over the district to show and trade their books that they made. Since Ms. Dennard and Ms. Arnold are our featured authors for this year's conference, it would be important for the children to know about the authors and their books. We have a list of the books and the publishing companies listed below. Thank you for your time.

Sincerely,

_____
_____
_____

Deborah Dennard

How Wise is an Owl?
Do Cats Have Nine Lives?
Can Elephants Drink Through Their Noses?

Carolrhoda Books 1-800-328-4929

Caroline Arnold

Kangaroo
Flamingo   Cheetah
Penguin   Llama
                                      Giraffe
and many more (including some dinosaur books)

William Morrow   1350 Avenue of the Americas NY,NY 10019

This work sample illustrates a standard-setting performance for the following parts of the standards:

A1 c   **Problem Solving: Plan and organize an event or an activity.**

A2 b   **Communication: Compose correspondence.**

A2 c   **Communication: Publish information.**

A3 a   **Information: Use information technology.**

A4 c   **Learning and Self-management: Identify strengths and weaknesses in own work.**

A5 a   **Working With Others: Work with others to complete a task.**

What the work shows

A1 c   Problem solving: The student plans and organizes an event or an activity; that is, the student:

- develops a plan for the event or activity that:
- includes all the factors and variables that need to be considered;
- shows the order in which things need to be done;
- takes into account the resources available to put the plan into action, including people and time;
- implements the plan;
- evaluates the success of the event or activity by identifying the parts of the plan that worked best and the parts that could have been improved by better planning and organization;
- makes recommendations to others who might consider planning and organizing a similar event or activity.

There is a range of evidence for the planning that took place in preparation for the conference.

A In this letter, the students asked the librarian to mount a display of books by the invited professional authors.

B The students approached a local book store to set up a stall to sell books at the conference.

Young Authors' Conference

B

Alice Carlson
Applied Learning Center
3320 West Cantey
Fort Worth, TX 76109

Book Store
Blvd.
Fort Worth, TX 76110

To whom it may concern,

Alice Carlson's 3rd grade would like to know if you could come to the 4th Annual Young Authors' Conference to sell Caroline Arnold and Deborah Dennard's books. The conference is at Paschal High School on April 16, 1994. If you can come, please write back to Alice Carlson saying that you can. If you can not come, please write back saying that you can not. You can call if it is more convenient. My phone number is _____.

Sincerely,

_____

C

Sunday, April 17, 1994

2,000 hear authors, stories at event students organized

By Bob Mahlburg
Fort Worth Star Telegram

About 2,000 grade school kids, parents and teachers gathered in Fort Worth for a Young Authors' Conference yesterday to hear writing tips from two authors and tales from a series of storytellers.

"It's fun to listen to them," said third-grader _____, a student at the Alice E. Carlson Applied Learning Center who helped plan the event.

Featured authors included children's books writers Caroline Arnold of Los Angeles and Deborah Dennard of Fort Worth.

_____ said she's a big fan of Dennard's books, particularly *Does a Cat Have Nine Lives?* and *Can Elephants Drink Through Their Noses?*

"They are pretty funny," _____ said.

The storytellers, members of the Tejas Storytelling Association, included one who spins African folk tales, one who incorporates music in stories and a bilingual Spanish storyteller, she said.

The all-day conference was "completely planned by students," said Alice E. Carlson teacher _____. "The children have just done an incredible job."

In planning the conference, students learned how to write and edit on computer, and they used math to budget expenses.

The annual event was held at Paschal High School, alma mater of writers including novelist Dan Jenkins, because it was too large for any grade school, _____ said.

Reprint courtesy of the *Fort Worth Star Telegram.*

C D The students arranged publicity for the event. As the article from the *Fort Worth Star Telegram* reports, the conference attracted more than 2,000 students, parents, and teachers.

E F These documents are excerpts from the program the students designed for conference participants. They include evidence of scheduling activities for the conference.

G This account of the preparations for the conference demonstrates awareness of the range of factors that had to be taken into account. The student closes with an offer of advice for any class interested in taking responsibility for planning the event for the following year. See page 28 for commentary on this piece as a narrative procedure within the requirements of the English Language Arts standards.

A2b Communication Tools and Techniques: The student composes and sends correspondence, such as thank-you letters and memoranda providing information; that is, the student:

• expresses the information or request clearly;
• writes in a style appropriate to the purpose of the correspondence.

A B D These are examples of letters the students wrote seeking assistance with the conference. Each is expressed clearly and written in a style appropriate to the purpose of the correspondence. There are some errors, such as, "can not" should be spelled "cannot," but these do not detract from the effectiveness of the communication.

D

Room 5
Alice Carson ALC
3320 W. Cantey
Fort Worth, TX

Channel _____
_____ Street
Fort Worth, TX
_____

Dear Channel __

On April 16, 1994 the third graders at Alice Carlson Applied Learning Center are planning a Young Authors' Conference for all Fort Worth Schools. At the conference two authors are going to tell how they make their books. Also the children that attend the conference bring books that they have written. They share their books with other children and trade them with each other. This conference is being completely planned and organized by Alice Carlson third grade students. It would be an honor if you could come on April 16 from 8:00 a.m. to 12:00 p.m. and cover this event to share with the public. Also you are invited to come to our school any day to watch us while we work on planning the conference.

Sincerely,

_____
_____
_____

A1 Problem Solving

A2 Communication Tools and Techniques

A3 Information Tools and Techniques

A4 Learning and Self-management Tools and Techniques

A5 Tools and Techniques for Working With Others

Young Authors' Conference

E

Welcome to the
Young Authors' Conference

We are glad that you could come to the 1994 YAC. We hope that you have a fun day. Please ask anyone on the staff if you need help. Conference t-shirts and books by the authors will be available during the conference. Here are some questions that we thought you might ask.

What is my schedule?
Look in the program to find the page with your grade level. That is your schedule. In some of the sessions, the people are divided into small groups. Find the first letter of your last name and go to that smaller session.

Do I have to follow <u>my</u> schedule?
We have worked very hard to keep the number of people even in each session. If you change your schedule, you will disturb the plans we have made.

How do I know which Learning or Sharing Session to go to?
The Learning Sessions are in the downstairs classrooms and the Sharing Sessions are in the upstairs classrooms. Each presenter will be giving the same lesson so it does not matter which room you go into. Please choose another room if the room you want to go into is full.

H This handwritten letter of thanks to one of the presenters also contains an error ("the" instead of "that"); nevertheless, it serves its purpose well.

G The account of the preparations for conference refers to a range of other forms of correspondence the students produced.

A2 Communication Tools and Techniques: The student writes and formats information for short publications, such as brochures or posters; that is, the student:
- organizes the information into an appropriate form for use in the publication;
- checks the information for accuracy;
- formats the publication so that it achieves its purpose.

I The students produced posters advertising the conference. This example is eye catching and provides the necessary information.

E F The conference program, from which excerpts are shown here, presents information in a clear and direct manner, while at the same time adopting a welcoming tone.

F

Schedule for Kindergarten and First Grade

8:30 - 9:15	A - J	Author's Session — Deborah Dennard — Small Auditorium
	K - Q	Storyteller's Session — Tom McDermott — Music Room #105
	R - Z	Storyteller's Session — Mary Ann Brewer — Small Cafeteria
9:30 - 10:15	K - Z	Author's Session — Deborah Dennard — Small Auditorium
	A - E	Storyteller's Session — Tom McDermott — Music Room #105
	F - J	Storyteller's Session — Mary Ann Brewer — Small Cafeteria
10:30 - 11:15		Learning Session - Downstairs
11:30 - 12:15		Sharing Session - Upstairs

Schedule for Second Grade

8:30 - 9:15		Sharing Session - Upstairs
9:30 - 10:15		Learning Session - Downstairs
10:30 - 11:15	A - L	Author's Session — Deborah Dennard — Small Auditorium
	M - R	Storyteller's Session — Tom McDermott — Music Room #105
	S - Z	Storyteller's Session — Mary Ann Brewer — Small Cafeteria
11:30 - 12:15	M - Z	Author's Session — Deborah Dennard — Small Auditorium
	A - D	Storyteller's Session — Tom McDermott — Music Room #105
	E - L	Storyteller's Session — Mary Ann Brewer — Small Cafeteria

G

About the Young Authors' Conference

This year is the fourth year that the Fort Worth School District has had a Young Authors' Conference. The first year a grown-up planned it, and the second year a fifth grade class at W. J. Turner planned it. The third year's conference was planned by Deborah _____ s' second graders and Charlotte _____'s first graders. This year, as third graders, Deborah _____ s' class has had complete responsibility for planning and organizing the conference. Everyone at Alice Carlson Applied Learning Center has helped us, such as the kindergarten children sharpened the pencils and made the snack tickets, the fourth graders decorated the stage, and the second and fifth graders made the bookmarks.

To plan the Young Authors' Conference there are a lot of different things involved. Some things that involved math were comparing prices of the supplies and keeping track of the budget of around $8,000. All the way through we have had to do lots of problem solving. For example, we had to decide things like how many reams of paper we needed to buy if there were five bookmarks on a page, 250 pieces of cover stock in a ream, and we needed to make 1,000 bookmarks. We did a lot of estimating, like deciding how many doughnuts to buy and how many t-shirts to order.

Also, it would take a ream of paper to tell all of the writing that is involved in the conference. We did a lot of writing! We had to write memos, business letters, forms, and other things. We wrote news releases and proposals. We have written to the superintendent of the school district, the principals of the schools, the coordinators at each school, and the students who registered. We also had to write to the authors, the storytellers, the presenters, the companies who we got supplies from, book companies, and more.

One of the hardest parts was keeping organized and being responsible. We had to do a whole lot of small things like organize the hot line phone schedule and pack all of the packets. One of the big jobs was to make a database on our computer of all of the participants' names. We had to update the database many, many times. It was difficult for everyone to be responsible for their job and report back to the class.

We learned a lot while planning this conference. If your school or class would like to plan the Young Authors' Conference for 1995, please contact _____ Applied Learning Center. _____ at Alice

Young Authors' Conference

Dear Mary_____,
I would like to thank you for all of your time on being a wonderful presenter. I heard people saying the the presenter sessions were excellent and fun. We all think you did a very good job being a presenter.

Thank You,
Melanie_____

A3b Information Tools and Techniques: The student uses information technology to assist in gathering, organizing, and presenting information; that is, the student:

- acquires information for specific purposes from on-line sources, such as the Internet, and other electronic data bases, such as an electronic encyclopedia;
- uses word-processing, drawing, and painting programs to produce project reports and related materials.

The students used word processing programs to produce their letters and the conference program. The poster includes work produced on a drawing program.

G This account of preparations for the conference includes a reference to "making a database on our computer," though no evidence is provided.

A4c Learning and Self-management Tools and Techniques: The student identifies strengths and weaknesses in his or her own work; that is, the student:

- understands and establishes criteria for judging the quality of work processes and products;
- assesses his or her own work processes and-products.

G This provides one student's account of preparations for the conference. The account focuses on the task as a whole rather than the student's singular role, and it evaluates the activities in terms of their difficulty (for example, "One of the hardest parts was keeping organized and being responsible") rather than in terms of the students' more or less effective management of various elements of the task. Nevertheless, the account does provide evidence for a beginning analysis and review of the work.

A5a Tools and Techniques for Working With Others: The student works with others to complete a task; that is, the student:

- reaches agreement with group members on what work needs to be done to complete the task and how the work will be tackled;
- takes a share of the responsibility for the work;
- consults with group members regularly during the task to check on progress in completing the task, to decide on any changes that are required, and to check that all parts have been completed at the end of the task.

G The account of preparations for the conference describes some of the organizational issues the students needed to resolve in working together to complete the task. It indicates an awareness of the importance in an activity of this kind of everyone taking their share of responsibility for getting the work done.

A1 Problem Solving

A2 Communication Tools and Techniques

A3 Information Tools and Techniques

A4 Learning and Self-management Tools and Techniques

A5 Tools and Techniques for Working With Others

APPENDIX I

The elementary school standards are set at a level of performance approximately equivalent to the end of fourth grade. The middle school standards are set at a level of performance approximately equivalent to the end of eighth grade. The high school standards are set at a level of performance approximately equivalent to the end of tenth grade. It is expected that some students might achieve these levels earlier and others later than these grades.

An array of work is required to achieve any single standard. The work becomes increasing refined and sophisticated as students get older. The complexity of the tasks used to generate the work also increases. This notion of requiring students to hone the sophistication of their performances while simultaneously working with increasingly complex assignments cuts across all the English Language Arts standards.

These standards allow for oral performances of student work whenever appropriate.

Elementary School

E1a The student reads at least twenty-five books or book equivalents each year. The quality and complexity of the materials to be read are illustrated in the sample reading list. The materials should include traditional and contemporary literature (both fiction and non-fiction) as well as magazines, newspapers, textbooks, and on-line materials. Such reading should represent a diverse collection of material from at least three different literary forms and from at least five different writers.

E1b The student reads and comprehends at least four books (or book equivalents) about one issue or subject, or four books by a single writer, or four books in one genre, and produces evidence of reading that:
- makes and supports warranted and responsible assertions about the texts;
- supports assertions with elaborated and convincing evidence;
- draws the texts together to compare and contrast themes, characters, and ideas;
- makes perceptive and well developed connections;
- evaluates writing strategies and elements of the author's craft.

E1c The student reads and comprehends informational materials to develop understanding and expertise and produces written or oral work that:
- restates or summarizes information;
- relates new information to prior knowledge and experience;
- extends ideas;
- makes connections to related topics or information.

E1d The student reads aloud, accurately (in the range of 85-90%), familiar material of the quality and complexity illustrated in the sample reading list, and in a way that makes meaning clear to listeners by:
- self correcting when subsequent reading indicates an earlier miscue;
- using a range of cueing systems, e.g., phonics and context clues, to determine pronunciation and meanings;
- reading with a rhythm, flow, and meter that sounds like everyday speech.

Middle School

E1a The student reads at least twenty-five books or book equivalents each year. The quality and complexity of the materials to be read are illustrated in the sample reading list. The materials should include traditional and contemporary literature (both fiction and non-fiction) as well as magazines, newspapers, textbooks, and on-line materials. Such reading should represent a diverse collection of material from at least three different literary forms and from at least five different writers.

E1b The student reads and comprehends at least four books (or book equivalents) about one issue or subject, or four books by a single writer, or four books in one genre, and produces evidence of reading that:
- makes and supports warranted and responsible assertions about the texts;
- supports assertions with elaborated and convincing evidence;
- draws the texts together to compare and contrast themes, characters, and ideas;
- makes perceptive and well developed connections;
- evaluates writing strategies and elements of the author's craft.

E1c The student reads and comprehends informational materials to develop understanding and expertise and produces written or oral work that:
- restates or summarizes information;
- relates new information to prior knowledge and experience;
- extends ideas;
- makes connections to related topics or information.

E1d The student demonstrates familiarity with a variety of public documents (i.e., documents that focus on civic issues or matters of public policy at the community level and beyond) and produces written or oral work that does one or more of the following:
- identifies the social context of the document;
- identifies the author's purpose and stance;
- analyzes the arguments and positions advanced and the evidence offered in support of them, or formulates an argument and offers evidence to support it;

High School

E1a The student reads at least twenty-five books or book equivalents each year. The quality and complexity of the materials to be read are illustrated in the sample reading list. The materials should include traditional and contemporary literature (both fiction and non-fiction) as well as magazines, newspapers, textbooks, and on-line materials. Such reading should represent a diverse collection of material from at least three different literary forms and from at least five different writers.

E1b The student reads and comprehends at least four books (or book equivalents) about one issue or subject, or four books by a single writer, or four books in one genre, and produces evidence of reading that:
- makes and supports warranted and responsible assertions about the texts;
- supports assertions with elaborated and convincing evidence;
- draws the texts together to compare and contrast themes, characters, and ideas;
- makes perceptive and well developed connections;
- evaluates writing strategies and elements of the author's craft.

E1c The student reads and comprehends informational materials to develop understanding and expertise and produces written or oral work that:
- restates or summarizes information;
- relates new information to prior knowledge and experience;
- extends ideas;
- makes connections to related topics or information.

E6 Public Documents

E6a The student critiques public documents with an eye to strategies common in public discourse, including:
- effective use of argument;
- use of the power of anecdote;
- anticipation of counter-claims;
- appeal to audiences both friendly and hostile to the position presented;
- use of emotionally laden words and imagery;
- citing of appropriate references or authorities.

E6 b The student produces public documents, in which the student:

- examines or makes use of the appeal of a document to audiences both friendly and hostile to the position presented;

- exhibits an awareness of the importance of precise word choice and the power of imagery and/or anecdote;

- identifies or uses commonly used persuasive techniques.

- utilizes and recognizes the power of logical arguments, arguments based on appealing to a reader's emotions, and arguments dependent upon the writer's persona;

E1 e The student demonstrates familiarity with a variety of functional documents (i.e., documents that exist in order to get things done) and produces written or oral work that does one or more of the following:

- uses arguments that are appropriate in terms of the knowledge, values, and degree of understanding of the intended audience;

- identifies the institutional context of the document;

- uses a range of strategies to appeal to readers.

- identifies the sequence of activities needed to carry out a procedure;

E7 Functional Documents

E7 a The student critiques functional documents with an eye to strategies common to effective functional documents, including:

- analyzes or uses the formatting techniques used to make a document user-friendly;

- identifies any information that is either extraneous or missing in terms of audience and purpose or makes effective use of relevant information.

- visual appeal, e.g., format, graphics, white space, headers;

- logic of the sequence in which the directions are given;

- awareness of possible reader misunderstandings.

E7 b The student produces functional documents appropriate to audience and purpose, in which the student:

- reports, organizes, and conveys information and ideas accurately;

- includes relevant narrative details, such as scenarios, definitions, and examples;

- anticipates readers' problems, mistakes, and misunderstandings;

- uses a variety of formatting techniques, such as headings, subordinate terms, foregrounding of main ideas, hierarchical structures, graphics, and color;

- establishes a persona that is consistent with the document's purpose;

- employs word choices that are consistent with the persona and appropriate for the intended audience.

Much writing can be classified as belonging to the public arena. New Standards, however, defines public documents to mean those pieces of text that are concerned with public policy, that address controversial issues confronting the public, or that arise in response to controversial issues or public policy. Public documents are included in the Reading standard at middle school level (**E1 a**) and constitute a separate standard at high school level (**E6**). At the middle school level, the issues students write about come primarily from the school or local community. At high school, students should address issues which are of national importance.

Functional writing is writing that exists in order to get things done. Functional writing is ordinarily considered technical writing and, as such, is often not part of the typical English curriculum. New Standards requires students to demonstrate proficiency with functional writing because such writing is of increasing importance to the complex literacy of our culture. Functional documents are included in the Reading standard at middle school level (**E1 e**) and constitute a separate standard at high school level (**E7**).

APPENDIX I

The number of books required for **E1 a** does not increase as students get older, but the length and complexity of what is read does increase (as indicated by the sample reading lists), so, this standard becomes increasingly formidable.

E1 a assumes an adequate library of appropriate reading material. In some places, library resources are too meager to support the amount of reading required for every student to achieve this standard. Where a shortage of books exists, better use of out-of-school resources must be made, for example, students may have to be assured access to local or county libraries.

Reading twenty-five books a year entails a substantial amount of time. Students may use materials read in conjunction with their regular class work, including courses other than English, to satisfy this requirement.

Elementary School

Fiction

Brink, *Caddie Woodlawn;*
Cleary, *Ramona and Her Father;*
Coerr, *The Josefina Story Quilt;*
Cohen, *Fat Jack;*
De Saint-Exupery, *The Little Prince;*
Hamilton, *Zeely;*
Hansen, *The Gift-Giver;*
Lord, *In the Year of the Boar and Jackie Robinson;*
Mendez and Byard, *The Black Snowman;*
Naidoo, *Journey to Jo'Burg;*
O'Dell, *Zia;*
Ringgold, *Tar Beach;*
Speare, *The Sign of the Beaver;*
Yep, *Child of the Owl.*

Non-Fiction

Aliki, *Corn Is Maize: The Gift of the Indians;*
Baylor, *The Way to Start a Day;*
Cherry, *The Great Kapok Tree;*
Epstein, *History of Women in Science for Young People;*
Fritz, *And Then What Happened, Paul Revere?;*
Godkin, *Wolf Island;*
Greenfield, *Childtimes: A Three-Generation Memoir;*
Hamilton, *Anthony Burns: The Defeat and Triumph of a Fugitive Slave;*
McGovern, *The Secret Soldier: The Story of Deborah Sampson;*
McKissack, *Frederick Douglass: The Black Lion;*
Politi, *Song of the Swallows;*
Sattler, *Dinosaurs of North America.*

Poetry

Ahlberg, *Heard It in the Playground;*
Bishen and Wildsmith, *Oxford Book of Poetry for Children;*
De Regniers, Moore, White, and Carr, eds., *Sing a Song of Popcorn;*
Giovanni, *Ego-Tripping and Other Poems for Young People;*
Greenfield, *Honey, I Love and Other Love Poems;*
Heard, *For the Good of the Earth and Sun;*
Janeczko, *Strings: A Gathering of Family Poems;*
Koch and Farrell, eds., *Talking to the Sun;*
Lobel, ed, *The Random House Book of Mother Goose;*
Manguel, ed., *Seasons;*
Mathis, *Red Dog, Blue Fly: Football Poems;*
Silverstein, *Where the Sidewalk Ends.*

Folklore

French, *Snow White in New York;*
Goble, *Buffalo Woman;*
Griego y Maestas, *Cuentos: Tales From the Hispanic Southwest;*
Huck and Lobel, *Princess Furball;*
Kipling, *The Elephant's Child;*

Middle School

Fiction

Anaya, *Bless Me, Ultima;*
Armstrong, *Sounder;*
Bonham, *Durango Street;*
Cohen, *Tell Us Your Secret;*
Collier, *My Brother Sam Is Dead;*
Cormier, *I Am the Cheese;*
Danziger, *The Cat Ate My Gymsuit;*
Fast, *April Morning;*
Gaines, *A Gathering of Old Men;*
Goldman, *The Princess Bride;*
Greene, *Summer of My German Soldier;*
Hansen, *Which Way Freedom;*
Hinton, *The Outsiders;*
Holman, *Slake's Limbo;*
London, *The Call of the Wild;*
Mathis, *Listen for the Fig Tree;*
Mohr, *Nilda;*
Neufeld, Lisa, *Bright and Dark;*
O'Brien, *Z for Zachariah;*
Schaefer, *Shane;*
Stevenson, *Treasure Island;*
Voigt, *Dicey's Song;*
Walker, *To Hell With Dying;*
Walter, *Because We Are;*
Zindel, *The Pigman.*

Non-Fiction

Amory, *The Cat Who Came for Christmas;*
Berck, *No Place to Be: Voices of Homeless Children;*
Frank, *The Diary of a Young Girl;*
George, *The Talking Earth;*
Gilbreth, *Cheaper by the Dozen;*
Haskins, *Outward Dreams;*
Hautzig, *Endless Steppe: A Girl in Exile;*
Herriott, *All Creatures Great and Small;*
Lester, *To Be a Slave;*
Meyers, *Pearson, a Harbor Seal Pup;*
Reiss, *The Upstairs Room;*
Soto, *Living Up the Street;*
White, Ryan White: *My Own Story;*
Yates, *Amos Fortune, Free Man.*

Poetry

Adams, *Poetry of Earth and Sky;*
Eliot, *Old Possum's Book of Practical Cats;*
Frost, *You Come Too;*
Greenfield, *Night on Neighborhood Street;*
Livingston, *Cat Poems.*

Drama

Blinn, *Brian's Song;*
Davis, *Escape to Freedom;*
Gibson, *The Miracle Worker;*
Lawrence and Lee, *Inherit the Wind;*
Osborn, *On Borrowed Time;*

High School

Fiction

Carroll, *Alice in Wonderland;*
Cisneros, *The House on Mango Street;*
Clark, *The Ox-Bow Incident;*
Golding, *Lord of the Flies;*
Hawthorne, *The Scarlet Letter;*
Hemingway, *For Whom the Bell Tolls;*
Hentoff, *The Day They Came to Arrest the Book;*
Hilton, *Goodbye, Mr. Chips;*
Kinsella, *Shoeless Joe;*
Knowles, *A Separate Peace;*
Lee, *To Kill a Mockingbird;*
McCullers, *The Heart Is a Lonely Hunter;*
Orwell, *1984;*
Paulsen, *Canyons;*
Portis, *True Grit;*
Potok, *Davita's Harp;*
Stoker, *Dracula;*
Wartski, *A Boat to Nowhere;*
Welty, *The Golden Apples.*

Non-Fiction

Angell, *Late Innings;*
Angelou, *I Know Why the Caged Bird Sings;*
Ashe, *Days of Grace;*
Beal, "I Will Fight No More Forever": *Chief Joseph and the Nez Perce War;*
Bishop, *The Day Lincoln Was Shot;*
Bloom, *The Closing of the American Mind;*
Campbell, *The Power of Myth;*
Covey, *Seven Habits of Highly Effective People;*
Galarza, *Barrio Boy;*
Hawking, *A Brief History of Time;*
Houston, *Farewell to Manzanar;*
Kennedy, *Profiles in Courage;*
Kingsley and Levitz, *Count Us In: Growing Up With Down Syndrome;*
Kingston, *Woman Warrior;*
Mazer, ed., *Going Where I'm Coming From;*
Momaday, *The Way to Rainy Mountain;*
Rodriguez, *Hunger of Memory;*
Sternberg, *User's Guide to the Internet;*
Wright, *Black Boy.*

Poetry

Angelou, *I Shall Not be Moved;*
Bly, ed, *News of the Universe;*
Carruth, ed., *The Voice That Is Great Within Us;*
Cummings, *Collected Poems;*
Dickinson, *Complete Poems;*
Hughes, *Selected Poems;*
Knudson and Swenson, eds., *American Sports Poems;*
Longfellow, *Evangeline;*
Randall, ed., *The Black Poets;*
Wilbur, *Things of This World.*

Lee, *Legend of the Milky Way*;
Louie and Young, *Yeh-Shen: A Cinderella Story From China*;
Luenn, *The Dragon Kite*;
Steptoe, *Mufaro's Beautiful Daughters*;
Steptoe, *The Story of Jumping Mouse*.

Modern Fantasy and Science Fiction
Andersen, *The Ugly Duckling*;
Bond, *A Bear Called Paddington*;
Dahl, *James and the Giant Peach*;
Grahame, *The Wind in the Willows*;
Lewis, *The Lion, the Witch and the Wardrobe*;
Norton, *The Borrowers*;
Van Allsburg, *Jumanji*;
White, *Charlotte's Web*.

Children's magazines
Action (Scholastic);
Creative Classroom;
News (Scholastic);
Social Studies for the Young Learner;
Weekly Reader;
World (National Geographic).

Other
Newspapers, manuals appropriate for elementary school children, e.g., video game instructions, computer manuals.

Shakespeare, *A Midsummer Night's Dream*;
Stone, *Metamora, or, the Last of the Wampanoags*.

Folklore/Mythology
Blair, *Tall Tale America*;
Bruchac, *The First Strawberries: A Cherokee Story*;
Bryan, *Beat the Story-Drum, Pum-Pum*;
D'Aulaire, *Norse Gods and Giants*;
Gallico, *The Snow Goose*;
Lee, *Toad Is the Uncle of Heaven: A Vietnamese Folk Tale*;
Pyle, *Merry Adventures of Robin Hood*.

Modern Fantasy and Science Fiction
Babbitt, *Tuck Everlasting*;
Bradbury, *Dandelion Wine*;
Cooper, *The Grey King*;
Hamilton, *The Magical Adventures of Pretty Pearl*;
L'Engle, *A Wrinkle in Time*;
Tolkien, *The Hobbit*;
Yep, *Dragon of the Lost Sea*.

Magazines/Periodicals
Calliope (world history);
Cobblestone (American history);
Faces (anthropology);
Junior Scholastic (Scholastic);
Odyssey (science);
Science World (Scholastic);
Scope (Scholastic);
World (National Geographic);.

Other
Computer manuals; instructions; contracts. See also the reading lists included in award books corresponding to reading provided by the Girl Scouts of the U.S.A. and the Boy Scouts of America.

Drama
Christie, *And Then There Were None*;
Hansberry, *A Raisin in the Sun*;
McCullers, *The Member of the Wedding*;
Pomerance, *The Elephant Man*;
Rose, *Twelve Angry Men*;
Rostand, *Cyrano de Bergerac*;
Shakespeare, *Romeo and Juliet*; *Julius Caesar*;
Van Druten, *I Remember Mama*;
Wilder, *The Skin of Our Teeth*;
Wilson, *The Piano Lesson*.

Folklore/Mythology
Burland, *North American Indian Mythology*;
Evslin, *Adventures of Ulysses*;
Pinsent, *Greek Mythology*;
Stewart, *The Crystal Cave*;
White, *The Once and Future King*.

Modern Fantasy and Science Fiction
Adams, *Watership Down*;
Asimov, *Foundation*;
Bradbury, *The Martian Chronicles*;
Clarke, *2001: A Space Odyssey*;
Clarke, *Childhood's End*;
Frank, *Alas, Babylon*;
Herbert, *Dune*;
Lewis, *Out of the Silent Planet*;
McCaffrey, *Dragonflight*;
Twain, *A Connecticut Yankee in King Arthur's Court*;
Verne, *20,000 Leagues Under the Sea*.

Magazines and Newspapers
Literary Cavalcade (Scholastic);
National Geographic;
Newsweek;
Omni;
Smithsonian;
Sports Illustrated;
Time.

Other
Computer manuals; instructions; contracts; technical materials.

E2 Writing

APPENDIX I

E2b is meant to replace the repertoire of responses that students traditionally write when they respond to literature. This type of response requires an understanding of writing strategies.

The work students produce to meet the English Language Arts standards does not all have to come from an English class. Students should be encouraged to use work from subjects in addition to English to demonstrate their accomplishments. The work samples include some examples of work produced in other classes that meet requirements of these standards.

Elementary School

E2a The student produces a report that:

- engages the reader by establishing a context, creating a persona, and otherwise developing reader interest;
- develops a controlling idea that conveys a perspective on the subject;
- creates an organizing structure appropriate to a specific purpose, audience, and context;
- includes appropriate facts and details;
- excludes extraneous and inappropriate information;
- uses a range of appropriate strategies, such as providing facts and details, describing or analyzing the subject, and narrating a relevant anecdote;
- provides a sense of closure to the writing.

E2b The student produces a response to literature that:

- engages the reader by establishing a context, creating a persona, and otherwise developing reader interest;
- advances a judgment that is interpretive, analytic, evaluative, or reflective;
- supports judgment through references to the text, references to other works, authors, or non-print media, or references to personal knowledge;
- demonstrates an understanding of the literary work;
- provides a sense of closure to the writing.

E2c The student produces a narrative account (fictional or autobiographical) that:

- engages the reader by establishing a context, creating a point of view, and otherwise developing reader interest;
- establishes a situation, plot, point of view, setting, and conflict (and for autobiography, the significance of events);
- creates an organizing structure;
- includes sensory details and concrete language to develop plot and character;
- excludes extraneous details and inconsistencies;
- develops complex characters;
- uses a range of appropriate strategies, such as dialogue and tension or suspense;
- provides a sense of closure to the writing.

Middle School

E2a The student produces a report that:

- engages the reader by establishing a context, creating a persona, and otherwise developing reader interest;
- develops a controlling idea that conveys a perspective on the subject;
- creates an organizing structure appropriate to purpose, audience, and context;
- includes appropriate facts and details;
- excludes extraneous and inappropriate information;
- uses a range of appropriate strategies, such as providing facts and details, describing or analyzing the subject, narrating a relevant anecdote, comparing and contrasting, naming, and explaining benefits or limitations;
- provides a sense of closure to the writing.

E2b The student produces a response to literature that:

- engages the reader through establishing a context, creating a persona, and otherwise developing reader interest;
- advances a judgment that is interpretive, analytic, evaluative, or reflective;
- supports a judgment through references to the text, references to other works, authors, or non-print media, or references to personal knowledge;
- demonstrates an understanding of the literary work;
- anticipates and answers a reader's questions;
- provides a sense of closure to the writing.

E2c The student produces a narrative account (fictional or autobiographical) that:

- engages the reader by establishing a context, creating a point of view, and otherwise developing reader interest;
- establishes a situation, plot, point of view, setting, and conflict (and for autobiography, the significance of events and of conclusions that can be drawn from those events);
- creates an organizing structure;
- includes sensory details and concrete language to develop plot and character;
- excludes extraneous details and inconsistencies;

High School

E2a The student produces a report that:

- engages the reader by establishing a context, creating a persona, and otherwise developing reader interest;
- develops a controlling idea that conveys a perspective on the subject;
- creates an organizing structure appropriate to purpose, audience, and context;
- includes appropriate facts and details;
- excludes extraneous and inappropriate information;
- uses a range of appropriate strategies, such as providing facts and details, describing or analyzing the subject, narrating a relevant anecdote, comparing and contrasting, naming, explaining benefits or limitations, demonstrating claims or assertions, and providing a scenario to illustrate;
- provides a sense of closure to the writing.

E2b The student produces a response to literature that:

- engages the reader through establishing a context, creating a persona, and otherwise developing reader interest;
- advances a judgment that is interpretive, analytic, evaluative, or reflective;
- supports a judgment through references to the text, references to other works, authors, or non-print media, or references to personal knowledge;
- demonstrates understanding of the literary work through suggesting an interpretation;
- anticipates and answers a reader's questions;
- recognizes possible ambiguities, nuances, and complexities;
- provides a sense of closure to the writing.

E2c The student produces a narrative account (fictional or autobiographical) that:

- engages the reader by establishing a context, creating a point of view, and otherwise developing reader interest;
- establishes a situation, plot, point of view, setting, and conflict (and for autobiography, the significance of events and of conclusions that can be drawn from those events);
- creates an organizing structure;
- includes sensory details and concrete language to develop plot and character;
- excludes extraneous details and inconsistencies;
- develops complex characters;
- uses a range of appropriate strategies, such as dialogue, tension or suspense, naming, pacing,

E2 d The student produces a narrative procedure that:

- engages the reader by establishing a context, creating a persona, and otherwise developing reader interest;
- provides a guide to action that anticipates a reader's needs; creates expectations through predictable structures, e.g., headings; and provides transitions between steps;
- makes use of appropriate writing strategies such as creating a visual hierarchy and using white space and graphics as appropriate;
- includes relevant information;
- excludes extraneous information;
- anticipates problems, mistakes, and misunderstandings that might arise for the reader;
- provides a sense of closure to the writing.

- develops complex characters;
- uses a range of appropriate strategies, such as dialogue, tension or suspense, naming, and specific narrative action, e.g., movement, gestures, expressions;
- provides a sense of closure to the writing.

E2 d The student produces a narrative procedure that:

- engages the reader by establishing a context, creating a persona, and otherwise developing reader interest;
- provides a guide to action for a relatively complicated procedure in order to anticipate a reader's needs; creates expectations through predictable structures, e.g., headings; and provides transitions between steps;
- makes use of appropriate writing strategies such as creating a visual hierarchy and using white space and graphics as appropriate;
- includes relevant information;
- excludes extraneous information;
- anticipates problems, mistakes, and misunderstandings that might arise for the reader;
- provides a sense of closure to the writing.

E2 e The student produces a persuasive essay that:

- engages the reader by establishing a context, creating a persona, and otherwise developing reader interest;
- develops a controlling idea that makes a clear and knowledgeable judgment;
- creates and organizes a structure that is appropriate to the needs, values, and interests of a specified audience, and arranges details, reasons, examples, and anecdotes effectively and persuasively;
- includes appropriate information and arguments;
- excludes information and arguments that are irrelevant;
- anticipates and addresses reader concerns and counter-arguments;
- supports arguments with detailed evidence, citing sources of information as appropriate;
- provides a sense of closure to the writing.

and specific narrative action, e.g., movement, gestures, expressions;

- provides a sense of closure to the writing.

E2 d The student produces a narrative procedure that:

- engages the reader by establishing a context, creating a persona, and otherwise developing reader interest;
- provides a guide to action for a complicated procedure in order to anticipate a reader's needs; creates expectations through predictable structures, e.g., headings; and provides smooth transitions between steps;
- makes use of appropriate writing strategies, such as creating a visual hierarchy and using white space and graphics as appropriate;
- includes relevant information;
- excludes extraneous information;
- anticipates problems, mistakes, and misunderstandings that might arise for the reader;
- provides a sense of closure to the writing.

E2 e The student produces a persuasive essay that:

- engages the reader by establishing a context, creating a persona, and otherwise developing reader interest;
- develops a controlling idea that makes a clear and knowledgeable judgment;
- creates an organizing structure that is appropriate to the needs, values, and interests of a specified audience, and arranges details, reasons, examples, and anecdotes effectively and persuasively;
- includes appropriate information and arguments;
- excludes information and arguments that are irrelevant;
- anticipates and addresses reader concerns and counter-arguments;
- supports arguments with detailed evidence, citing sources of information as appropriate;
- uses a range of strategies to elaborate and persuade, such as definitions, descriptions, illustrations, examples from evidence, and anecdotes;
- provides a sense of closure to the writing.

E2 f The student produces a reflective essay that:

- engages the reader by establishing a context, creating a persona, and otherwise developing reader interest;
- analyzes a condition or situation of significance;
- develops a commonplace, concrete occasion as the basis for the reflection, e.g., personal observation or experience;
- creates an organizing structure appropriate to purpose and audience;
- uses a variety of writing strategies, such as concrete details, comparing and contrasting, naming, describing, creating a scenario;
- provides a sense of closure to the writing.

E3 Speaking, Listening, and Viewing

Elementary School

E3a The student participates in one-to-one conferences with a teacher, paraprofessional, or adult volunteer, in which the student:

- initiates new topics in addition to responding to adult-initiated topics;
- asks relevant questions;
- responds to questions with appropriate elaboration;
- uses language cues to indicate different levels of certainty or hypothesizing, e.g., "what if...," "very likely...," "I'm unsure whether...";
- confirms understanding by paraphrasing the adult's directions or suggestions.

E3b The student participates in group meetings, in which the student:

- displays appropriate turn-taking behaviors;
- actively solicits another person's comment or opinion;
- offers own opinion forcefully without dominating;
- responds appropriately to comments and questions;
- volunteers contributions and responds when directly solicited by teacher or discussion leader;
- gives reasons in support of opinions expressed;
- clarifies, illustrates, or expands on a response when asked to do so; asks classmates for similar expansions.

E3c The student prepares and delivers an individual presentation, in which the student:

- shapes information to achieve a particular purpose and to appeal to the interests and background knowledge of audience members;
- shapes content and organization according to criteria for importance and impact rather than according to availability of information in resource materials;
- uses notes or other memory aids to structure the presentation;
- engages the audience with appropriate verbal cues and eye contact;
- projects a sense of individuality and personality in selecting and organizing content, and in delivery.

Middle School

E3a The student participates in one-to-one conferences with a teacher, paraprofessional, or adult volunteer, in which the student:

- initiates new topics in addition to responding to adult-initiated topics;
- asks relevant questions;
- responds to questions with appropriate elaboration;
- uses language cues to indicate different levels of certainty or hypothesizing, e.g., "what if...," "very likely...," "I'm unsure whether...";
- confirms understanding by paraphrasing the adult's directions or suggestions.

E3b The student participates in group meetings, in which the student:

- displays appropriate turn-taking behaviors;
- actively solicits another person's comment or opinion;
- offers own opinion forcefully without dominating;
- responds appropriately to comments and questions;
- volunteers contributions and responds when directly solicited by teacher or discussion leader;
- gives reasons in support of opinions expressed;
- clarifies, illustrates, or expands on a response when asked to do so; asks classmates for similar expansions;
- employs a group decision-making technique such as brainstorming or a problem-solving sequence (e.g., recognize problem, define problem, identify possible solutions, select optimal solution, implement solution, evaluate solution).

E3c The student prepares and delivers an individual presentation, in which the student:

- shapes information to achieve a particular purpose and to appeal to the interests and background knowledge of audience members;
- shapes content and organization according to criteria for importance and impact rather than according to availability of information in resource materials;
- uses notes or other memory aids to structure the presentation;

High School

E3a The student participates in one-to-one conferences with a teacher, paraprofessional, or adult volunteer, in which the student:

- initiates new topics in addition to responding to adult-initiated topics;
- asks relevant questions;
- responds to questions with appropriate elaboration;
- uses language cues to indicate different levels of certainty or hypothesizing, e.g., "what if...," "very likely...," "I'm unsure whether...";
- confirms understanding by paraphrasing the adult's directions or suggestions.

E3b The student participates in group meetings, in which the student:

- displays appropriate turn-taking behaviors;
- actively solicits another person's comment or opinion;
- offers own opinion forcefully without dominating;
- responds appropriately to comments and questions;
- volunteers contributions and responds when directly solicited by teacher or discussion leader;
- gives reasons in support of opinions expressed;
- clarifies, illustrates, or expands on a response when asked to do so; asks classmates for similar expansions;
- employs a group decision-making technique such as brainstorming or a problem-solving sequence (e.g., recognize problem, define problem, identify possible solutions, select optimal solution, implement solution, evaluate solution);
- divides labor so as to achieve the overall group goal efficiently.

E3c The student prepares and delivers an individual presentation, in which the student:

- shapes information to achieve a particular purpose and to appeal to the interests and background knowledge of audience members;
- shapes content and organization according to criteria for importance and impact rather than according to availability of information in resource materials;

3d The student makes informed judgments about television, radio, and film productions; that is, the student:

- demonstrates an awareness of the presence of the media in the daily lives of most people;
- evaluates the role of the media in focusing attention and in forming an opinion;
- judges the extent to which the media provide a source of entertainment as well as a source of information;
- defines the role of advertising as part of media presentation.

- develops several main points relating to a single thesis;
- engages the audience with appropriate verbal cues and eye contact;
- projects a sense of individuality and personality in selecting and organizing content, and in delivery.

3d The student makes informed judgments about television, radio, and film productions; that is, the student:

- demonstrates an awareness of the presence of the media in the daily lives of most people;
- evaluates the role of the media in focusing attention and in forming opinion;
- judges the extent to which the media are a source of entertainment as well as a source of information;
- defines the role of advertising as part of media presentation.

- uses notes or other memory aids to structure the presentation;
- develops several main points relating to a single thesis;
- engages the audience with appropriate verbal cues and eye contact;
- projects a sense of individuality and personality in selecting and organizing content, and in delivery.

3d The student makes informed judgments about television, radio, and film productions; that is, the student:

- demonstrates an awareness of the presence of the media in the daily lives of most people;
- evaluates the role of the media in focusing attention and in forming opinion;
- judges the extent to which the media are a source of entertainment as well as a source of information;
- defines the role of advertising as part of media presentation.

3e The student listens to and analyzes a public speaking performance; that is, the student:

- takes notes on salient information;
- identifies types of arguments (e.g., causation, authority, analogy) and identifies types of logical fallacies (e.g., ad hominem, inferring causation from correlation, over-generalization);
- accurately summarizes the essence of each speaker's remarks;
- formulates a judgment about the issues under discussion.

E4 Conventions, Grammar, and Usage of the English Language

Elementary School

E4a The student demonstrates a basic understanding of the rules of the English language in written and oral work, and selects the structures and features of language appropriate to the purpose, audience, and context of the work. The student demonstrates control of:

- grammar;
- paragraph structure;
- punctuation;
- sentence construction;
- spelling;
- usage.

E4b The student analyzes and subsequently revises work to clarify it or make it more effective in communicating the intended message or thought. The student's revisions should be made in light of the purposes, audiences, and contexts that apply to the work. Strategies for revising include:

- adding or deleting details;
- adding or deleting explanations;
- clarifying difficult passages;
- rearranging words, sentences, and paragraphs to improve or clarify meaning;
- sharpening the focus;
- reconsidering the organizational structure.

Middle School

E4a The student demonstrates an understanding of the rules of the English language in written and oral work, and selects the structures and features of language appropriate to the purpose, audience, and context of the work. The student demonstrates control of:

- grammar;
- paragraph structure;
- punctuation;
- sentence construction;
- spelling;
- usage.

E4b The student analyzes and subsequently revises work to clarify it or make it more effective in communicating the intended message or thought. The student's revisions should be made in light of the purposes, audiences, and contexts that apply to the work. Strategies for revising include:

- adding or deleting details;
- adding or deleting explanations;
- clarifying difficult passages;
- rearranging words, sentences, and paragraphs to improve or clarify meaning;
- sharpening the focus;
- reconsidering the organizational structure.

High School

E4a The student independently and habitually demonstrates an understanding of the rules of the English language in written and oral work, and selects the structures and features of language appropriate to the purpose, audience, and context of the work. The student demonstrates control of:

- grammar;
- paragraph structure;
- punctuation;
- sentence construction;
- spelling;
- usage.

E4b The student analyzes and subsequently revises work to clarify it or make it more effective in communicating the intended message or thought. The student's revisions should be made in light of the purposes, audiences, and contexts that apply to the work. Strategies for revising include:

- adding or deleting details;
- adding or deleting explanations;
- clarifying difficult passages;
- rearranging words, sentences, and paragraphs to improve or clarify meaning;
- sharpening the focus;
- reconsidering the organizational structure;
- rethinking and/or rewriting the piece in light of different audiences and purposes.

APPENDIX I

Elementary School

E5a The student responds to non-fiction, fiction, poetry, and drama using interpretive, critical, and evaluative processes; that is, the student:

- identifies recurring themes across works;
- analyzes the impact of authors' decisions regarding word choice and content;
- considers the differences among genres;
- evaluates literary merit;
- considers the function of point of view or persona;
- examines the reasons for a character's actions, taking into account the situation and basic motivation of the character;
- identifies stereotypical characters as opposed to fully developed characters;
- critiques the degree to which a plot is contrived or realistic;
- makes inferences and draws conclusions about contexts, events, characters, and settings.

E5b The student produces work in at least one literary genre that follows the conventions of the genre.

Middle School

E5a The student responds to non-fiction, fiction, poetry, and drama using interpretive, critical, and evaluative processes; that is, the student:

- identifies recurring themes across works;
- interprets the impact of authors' decisions regarding word choice, content, and literary elements;
- identifies the characteristics of literary forms and genres;
- evaluates literary merit;
- identifies the effect of point of view;
- analyzes the reasons for a character's actions, taking into account the situation and basic motivation of the character;
- makes inferences and draws conclusions about fictional and non-fictional contexts, events, characters, settings, and themes;
- identifies stereotypical characters as opposed to fully developed characters;
- identifies the effect of literary devices such as figurative language, allusion, diction, dialogue, and description.

E5b The student produces work in at least one literary genre that follows the conventions of the genre.

High School

E5a The student responds to non-fiction, fiction, poetry, and drama using interpretive, critical, and evaluative processes; that is, the student:

- makes thematic connections among literary texts, public discourse, and media;
- evaluates the impact of authors' decisions regarding word choice, style, content, and literary elements;
- analyzes the characteristics of literary forms and genres;
- evaluates literary merit;
- explains the effect of point of view;
- makes inferences and draws conclusions about fictional and non-fictional contexts, events, characters, settings, themes, and styles;
- interprets the effect of literary devices, such as figurative language, allusion, diction, dialogue, description, symbolism;
- evaluates the stance of a writer in shaping the presentation of a subject;
- interprets ambiguities, subtleties, contradictions, ironies, and nuances;
- understands the role of tone in presenting literature (both fictional and non-fictional);
- demonstrates how literary works (both fictional and non-fictional) reflect the culture that shaped them.

E5b The student produces work in at least one literary genre that follows the conventions of the genre.

M1 Arithmetic and Number Concepts/Number and Operation Concepts

APPENDIX II

The elementary school standards are set at a level of performance approximately equivalent to the end of fourth grade. The middle school standards are set at a level of performance approximately equivalent to the end of eighth grade. The high school standards are set at a level of performance approximately equivalent to the end of tenth grade or the end of the common core. It is expected that some students might achieve these levels earlier and others later than these grades.

Elementary School

The student produces evidence that demonstrates understanding of arithmetic and number concepts; that is, the student:

M1 a Adds, subtracts, multiplies, and divides whole numbers, with and without calculators; that is:

- adds, i.e., joins things together, increases;
- subtracts, i.e., takes away, compares, finds the difference;
- multiplies, i.e., uses repeated addition, counts by multiples, combines things that come in groups, makes arrays, uses area models, computes simple scales, uses simple rates;
- divides, i.e., puts things into groups, shares equally; calculates simple rates;
- analyzes problem situations and contexts in order to figure out when to add, subtract, multiply, or divide;
- solves arithmetic problems by relating addition, subtraction, multiplication, and division to one another;
- computes answers mentally, e.g., 27 + 45, 30 x 4;
- uses simple concepts of negative numbers, e.g., on a number line, in counting, in temperature, "owing."

M1 b Demonstrates understanding of the base ten place value system and uses this knowledge to solve arithmetic tasks; that is:

- counts 1, 10, 100, or 1,000 more than or less than, e.g., 1 less than 10,000, 10 more than 380, 1,000 more than 23,000, 100 less than 9,000;
- uses knowledge about ones, tens, hundreds, and thousands to figure out answers to multiplication and division tasks, e.g., 36 x 10, 18 x 100, 7 x 1,000, 4,000 ÷ 4.

M1 c Estimates, approximates, rounds off, uses landmark numbers, or uses exact numbers, as appropriate, in calculations.

M1 d Describes and compares quantities by using concrete and real world models of simple fractions; that is:

- finds simple parts of wholes;
- recognizes simple fractions as instructions to divide, e.g., $\frac{1}{4}$ of something is the same as dividing something by 4;
- recognizes the place of fractions on number lines, e.g., in measurement;

Middle School

The student produces evidence that demonstrates understanding of number and operation concepts; that is, the student:

M1 a Consistently and accurately adds, subtracts, multiplies, and divides rational numbers using appropriate methods (e.g., the student can add $\frac{1}{2} + \frac{5}{6}$ mentally or on paper but may opt to add $\frac{13}{24} + \frac{57}{68}$ on a calculator) and raises rational numbers to whole number powers. (Students should have facility with the different kinds and forms of rational numbers, i.e., integers, both whole numbers and negative integers; and other positive and negative rationals, written as decimals, as percents, or as proper, improper, or mixed fractions. Irrational numbers, i.e., those that cannot be written as a ratio of two integers, are not required content but are suitable for introduction, especially since the student should be familiar with the irrational number π.)

M1 b Uses and understands the inverse relationships between addition and subtraction, multiplication and division, and exponentiation and root-extraction (e.g., squares and square roots, cubes and cube roots); uses the inverse operation to determine unknown quantities in equations.

M1 c Consistently and accurately applies and converts the different kinds and forms of rational numbers.

M1 d Is familiar with characteristics of numbers (e.g., divisibility, prime factorization) and with properties of operations (e.g., commutativity and associativity), short of formal statements.

M1 e Interprets percent as part of 100 and as a means of comparing quantities of different sizes or changing sizes.

M1 f Uses ratios and rates to express "part-to-part" and "whole-to-whole" relationships, and reasons proportionally to solve problems involving equivalent fractions, equal ratios, or constant rates, recognizing the multiplicative nature of these problems in the constant factor of change.

M1 g Orders numbers with the > and < relationships and by location on a number line; estimates and compares rational numbers using sense of the magnitudes and relative magnitudes of numbers and of base-ten place values (e.g., recognizes relationships to "benchmark" numbers $\frac{1}{2}$ and 1 to conclude that the sum $\frac{1}{2} + \frac{5}{6}$ must be between 1 and $1\frac{1}{2}$ (likewise, $\frac{13}{24} + \frac{57}{68}$)).

High School

The student produces evidence that demonstrates understanding of number and operation concepts; that is, the student:

M1 a Uses addition, subtraction, multiplication, division, exponentiation, and root-extraction in forming and working with numerical and algebraic expressions.

M1 b Understands and uses operations such as opposite, reciprocal, raising to a power, taking a root, and taking a logarithm.

M1 c Has facility with the mechanics of operations as well as understanding of their typical meaning and uses in applications.

M1 d Understands and uses number systems: natural, integer, rational, and real.

M1 e Represents numbers in decimal or fraction form and in scientific notation, and graphs numbers on the number line and number pairs in the coordinate plane.

M1 f Compares numbers using order relations, differences, ratios, proportions, percents, and proportional change.

M1 g Carries out proportional reasoning in cases involving part-whole relationships and in cases involving expansions and contractions.

M1 h Understands dimensionless numbers, such as proportions, percents, and multiplicative factors, as well as numbers with specific units of measure, such as numbers with length, time, and rate units.

M1 i Carries out counting procedures such as those involving sets (unions and intersections) and arrangements (permutations and combinations).

M1 j Uses concepts such as prime, relatively prime, factor, divisor, multiple, and divisibility in solving problems involving integers.

M1 k Uses a scientific calculator effectively and efficiently in carrying out complex calculations.

M1 l Recognizes and represents basic number patterns, such as patterns involving multiples, squares, or cubes.

- uses drawings, diagrams, or models to show what the numerator and denominator mean, including when adding like fractions, e.g., ⅛ + ⅛, or when showing that ¾ is more than ⅜;

- uses beginning proportional reasoning and simple ratios, e.g., "about half of the people."

M1 e Describes and compares quantities by using simple decimals; that is:

- adds, subtracts, multiplies, and divides money amounts;

- recognizes relationships among simple fractions, decimals, and percents, i.e., that ½ is the same as 0.5, and ½ is the same as 50%, with concrete materials, diagrams, and in real world situations, e.g., when discovering the chance of a coin landing on heads or tails.

M1 f Describes and compares quantities by using whole numbers up to 10,000; that is:

- connects ideas of quantities to the real world, e.g., how many people fit in the school's cafeteria; how far away is a kilometer;

- finds, identifies, and sorts numbers by their properties, e.g., odd, even, multiple, square.

M2 Geometry and Measurement Concepts

APPENDIX II

Elementary School

The student produces evidence that demonstrates understanding of geometry and measurement concepts; that is, the student:

M2a Gives and responds to directions about location, e.g., by using words such as "in front of," "right," and "above."

M2b Visualizes and represents two dimensional views of simple rectangular three dimensional shapes, e.g., by showing the front view and side view of a building made of cubes.

M2c Uses simple two dimensional coordinate systems to find locations on a map and to represent points and simple figures.

M2d Uses many types of figures (angles, triangles, squares, rectangles, rhombi, parallelograms, quadrilaterals, polygons, prisms, pyramids, cubes, circles, and spheres) and identifies the figures by their properties, e.g., symmetry, number of faces, two- or three-dimensionality, no right angles.

M2e Solves problems by showing relationships between and among figures, e.g., using congruence and similarity, and using transformations including flips, slides, and rotations.

M2f Extends and creates geometric patterns using concrete and pictorial models.

M2g Uses basic ways of estimating and measuring the size of figures and objects in the real world, including length, width, perimeter, and area.

M2h Uses models to reason about the relationship between the perimeter and area of rectangles in simple situations.

M2i Selects and uses units, both formal and informal as appropriate, for estimating and measuring quantities such as weight, length, area, volume, and time.

M2j Carries out simple unit conversions, such as between cm and m, and between hours and minutes.

M2k Uses scales in maps, and uses, measures, and creates scales for rectangular scale drawings based on work with concrete models and graph paper.

Middle School

The student produces evidence that demonstrates understanding of geometry and measurement concepts in the following areas; that is, the student:

M2a Is familiar with assorted two- and three-dimensional objects, including squares, triangles, other polygons, circles, cubes, rectangular prisms, pyramids, spheres, and cylinders.

M2b Identifies similar and congruent shapes and uses transformations in the coordinate plane, i.e., translations, rotations, and reflections.

M2c Identifies three dimensional shapes from two dimensional perspectives; draws two dimensional sketches of three dimensional objects that preserve significant features.

M2d Determines and understands length, area, and volume (as well as the differences among these measurements), including perimeter and surface area; uses units, square units, and cubic units of measure correctly; computes areas of rectangles, triangles, and circles; computes volumes of prisms.

M2e Recognizes similarity and rotational and bilateral symmetry in two- and three-dimensional figures.

M2f Analyzes and generalizes geometric patterns, such as tessellations and sequences of shapes.

M2g Measures angles, weights, capacities, times, and temperatures using appropriate units.

M2h Chooses appropriate units of measure and converts with ease between like units, e.g., inches and miles, within a customary or metric system. (Conversions between customary and metric are not required.)

M2i Reasons proportionally in situations with similar figures.

M2j Reasons proportionally with measurements to interpret maps and to make smaller and larger scale drawings.

M2k Models situations geometrically to formulate and solve problems.

High School

The student produces evidence that demonstrates understanding of geometry and measurement concepts; that is, the student:

M2a Models situations geometrically to formulate and solve problems.

M2b Works with two- and three-dimensional figures and their properties, including polygons and circles, cubes and pyramids, and cylinders, cones, and spheres.

M2c Uses congruence and similarity in describing relationships between figures.

M2d Visualizes objects, paths, and regions in space, including intersections and cross sections of three dimensional figures, and describes these using geometric language.

M2e Knows, uses, and derives formulas for perimeter, circumference, area, surface area, and volume of many types of figures.

M2f Uses the Pythagorean Theorem in many types of situations, and works through more than one proof of this theorem.

M2g Works with similar triangles, and extends the ideas to include simple uses of the three basic trigonometric functions.

M2h Analyzes figures in terms of their symmetries using, for example, concepts of reflection, rotation, and translation.

M2i Compares slope (rise over run) and angle of elevation as measures of steepness.

M2j Investigates geometric patterns, including sequences of growing shapes.

M2k Works with geometric measures of length, area, volume, and angle; and non-geometric measures such as weight and time.

M2l Uses quotient measures, such as speed and density, that give "per unit" amounts; and uses product measures, such as person-hours.

M2m Understands the structure of standard measurement systems, both SI and customary, including unit conversions and dimensional analysis.

M2n Solves problems involving scale, such as in maps and diagrams.

M2o Represents geometric curves and graphs of functions in standard coordinate systems.

M2p Analyzes geometric figures and proves simple things about them using deductive methods.

M2q Explores geometry using computer programs such as CAD software, Sketchpad programs, or LOGO.

M3 Function and Algebra Concepts

Elementary School

The student produces evidence that demonstrates understanding of function and algebra concepts; that is, the student:

M3a Uses linear patterns to solve problems; that is:

- shows how one quantity determines another in a linear ("repeating") pattern, i.e., describes, extends, and recognizes the linear pattern by its rule, such as, the total number of legs on a given number of horses can be calculated by counting by fours;

- shows how one quantity determines another quantity in a functional relationship based on a linear pattern, e.g., for the "number of people and total number of eyes," figure out how many eyes 100 people have all together.

M3b Builds iterations of simple non-linear patterns, including multiplicative and squaring patterns (e.g., "growing" patterns) with concrete materials, and recognizes that these patterns are not linear.

M3c Uses the understanding that an equality relationship between two quantities remains the same as long as the same change is made to both quantities.

M3d Uses letters, boxes, or other symbols to stand for any number, measured quantity, or object in simple situations with concrete materials, i.e., demonstrates understanding and use of a beginning concept of a variable.

Middle School

The student produces evidence that demonstrates understanding of function and algebra concepts; that is, the student:

M3a Discovers, describes, and generalizes patterns, including linear, exponential, and simple quadratic relationships, i.e., those of the form $f(n)=n^2$ or $f(n)=cn^2$, for constant c, including $A=\pi r^2$, and represents them with variables and expressions.

M3b Represents relationships with tables, graphs in the coordinate plane, and verbal or symbolic rules.

M3c Analyzes tables, graphs, and rules to determine functional relationships.

M3d Finds solutions for unknown quantities in linear equations and in simple equations and inequalities.

High School

The student produces evidence that demonstrates understanding of function and algebra concepts; that is, the student:

M3a Models given situations with formulas and functions, and interprets given formulas and functions in terms of situations.

M3b Describes, generalizes, and uses basic types of functions: linear, exponential, power, rational, square and square root, and cube and cube root.

M3c Utilizes the concepts of slope, evaluation, and inverse in working with functions.

M3d Works with rates of many kinds, expressed numerically, symbolically, and graphically.

M3e Represents constant rates as the slope of a straight line graph, and interprets slope as the amount of one quantity (y) per unit amount of another (x).

M3f Understands and uses linear functions as a mathematical representation of proportional relationships.

M3g Uses arithmetic sequences and geometric sequences and their sums, and sees these as the discrete forms of linear and exponential functions, respectively.

M3h Defines, uses, and manipulates expressions involving variables, parameters, constants, and unknowns in work with formulas, functions, equations, and inequalities.

M3i Represents functional relationships in formulas, tables, and graphs, and translates between pairs of these.

M3j Solves equations symbolically, graphically, and numerically, especially linear, quadratic, and exponential equations; and knows how to use the quadratic formula for solving quadratic equations.

M3k Makes predictions by interpolating or extrapolating from given data or a given graph.

M3l Understands the basic algebraic structure of number systems.

M3m Uses equations to represent curves such as lines, circles, and parabolas.

M3n Uses technology such as graphics calculators to represent and analyze functions and their graphs.

M3o Uses functions to analyze patterns and represent their structure.

Elementary School

The student produces evidence that demonstrates understanding of statistics and probability concepts in the following areas; that is, the student:

M4a Collects and organizes data to answer a question or test a hypothesis by comparing sets of data.

M4b Displays data in line plots, graphs, tables, and charts.

M4c Makes statements and draws simple conclusions based on data; that is:

• reads data in line plots, graphs, tables, and charts;

• compares data in order to make true statements, e.g., "seven plants grew at least 5 cm";

• identifies and uses the mode necessary for making true statements, e.g., "more people chose red";

• makes true statements based on a simple concept of average (median and mean), for a small sample size and where the situation is made evident with concrete materials or clear representations;

• interprets data to determine the reasonableness of statements about the data, e.g., "twice as often," "three times faster";

• uses data, including statements about the data, to make a simple concluding statement about a situation, e.g., "This kind of plant grows better near sunlight because the seven plants that were near the window grew at least 5 cm."

M4d Gathers data about an entire group or by sampling group members to understand the concept of sample, i.e., that a large sample leads to more reliable information, e.g., when flipping coins.

M4e Predicts results, analyzes data, and finds out why some results are more likely, less likely, or equally likely.

M4f Finds all possible combinations and arrangements within certain constraints involving a limited number of variables.

Middle School

The student produces evidence that demonstrates understanding of statistics and probability concepts; that is, the student:

M4a Collects data, organizes data, and displays data with tables, charts, and graphs that are appropriate, i.e., consistent with the nature of the data.

M4b Analyzes data with respect to characteristics of frequency and distribution, including mode and range.

M4c Analyzes appropriately central tendencies of data by considering mean and median.

M4d Makes conclusions and recommendations based on data analysis.

M4e Critiques the conclusions and recommendations of others' statistics.

M4f Considers the effects of missing or incorrect information.

M4g Formulates hypotheses to answer a question and uses data to test hypotheses.

M4h Represents and determines probability as a fraction of a set of equally likely outcomes; recognizes equally likely outcomes, and constructs sample spaces (including those described by numerical combinations and permutations).

M4i Makes predictions based on experimental or theoretical probabilities.

M4j Predicts the result of a series of trials once the probability for one trial is known.

High School

The student demonstrates understanding of statistics and probability concepts; that is, the student:

M4a Organizes, analyzes, and displays single-variable data, choosing appropriate frequency distributions, circle graphs, line graphs, histograms, and summary statistics.

M4b Organizes, analyzes, and displays two-variable data using scatter plots, estimated regression lines, and computer generated regression lines and correlation coefficients.

M4c Uses sampling techniques to draw inferences about large populations.

M4d Understands that making an inference about a population from a sample always involves uncertainty and that the role of statistics is to estimate the size of that uncertainty.

M4e Formulates hypotheses to answer a question and uses data to test hypotheses.

M4f Interprets representations of data, compares distributions of data, and critiques conclusions of data, and the use of statistics, both in school materials and in public documents.

M4g Explores questions of experimental design, use of control groups, and reliability.

M4h Creates and uses models of probabilistic situations and understands the role of assumptions in this process.

M4i Uses concepts such as equally likely, sample space, outcome, and event in analyzing situations involving chance.

M4j Constructs appropriate sample spaces, and applies the addition and multiplication principles for probabilities.

M4k Uses the concept of a probability distribution to discuss whether an event is rare or reasonably likely.

M4l Chooses an appropriate probability model and uses it to arrive at a theoretical probability for a chance event.

M4m Uses relative frequencies based on empirical data to arrive at an experimental probability for a chance event.

M4n Designs simulations including Monte Carlo simulations to estimate probabilities.

M4o Works with the normal distribution in some of its basic applications.

APPENDIX II

Elementary School

The student demonstrates logical reasoning throughout work in mathematics, i.e., concepts and skills, problem solving, and projects; demonstrates problem solving by using mathematical concepts and skills to solve non-routine problems that do not lay out specific and detailed steps to follow; and solves problems that make demands on all three aspects of the solution process—formulation, implementation, and conclusion.

Formulation

M5 a Given the basic statement of a problem situation, the student:

- makes the important decisions about the approach, materials, and strategies to use, i.e., does not merely fill in a given chart, use a pre-specified manipulative, or go through a predetermined set of steps;

- uses previously learned strategies, skills, knowledge, and concepts to make decisions;

- uses strategies, such as using manipulatives or drawing sketches, to model problems.

Implementation

M5 b The student makes the basic choices involved in planning and carrying out a solution; that is, the student:

- makes up and uses a variety of strategies and approaches to solving problems and uses or learns approaches that other people use, as appropriate;

- makes connections among concepts in order to solve problems;

- solves problems in ways that make sense and explains why these ways make sense, e.g., defends the reasoning, explains the solution.

Conclusion

M5 c The student moves beyond a particular problem by making connections, extensions, and/or generalizations; for example, the student:

- explains a pattern that can be used in similar situations;

- explains how the problem is similar to other problems he or she has solved;

- explains how the mathematics used in the problem is like other concepts in mathematics;

- explains how the problem solution can be applied to other school subjects and in real world situations;

- makes the solution into a general rule that applies to other circumstances.

Middle School

The student demonstrates problem solving by using mathematical concepts and skills to solve non-routine problems that do not lay out specific and detailed steps to follow, and solves problems that make demands on all three aspects of the solution process—formulation, implementation, and conclusion.

Formulation

M5 a The student participates in the formulation of problems; that is, given the basic statement of a problem situation, the student:

- formulates and solves a variety of meaningful problems;

- extracts pertinent information from situations and figures out what additional information is needed.

Implementation

M5 b The student makes the basic choices involved in planning and carrying out a solution; that is, the student:

- uses and invents a variety of approaches and understands and evaluates those of others;

- invokes problem solving strategies, such as illustrating with sense-making sketches to clarify situations or organizing information in a table;

- determines, where helpful, how to break a problem into simpler parts;

- solves for unknown or undecided quantities using algebra, graphing, sound reasoning, and other strategies;

- integrates concepts and techniques from different areas of mathematics;

- works effectively in teams when the nature of the task or the allotted time makes this an appropriate strategy.

Conclusion

M5 c The student provides closure to the solution process through summary statements and general conclusions; that is, the student:

- verifies and interprets results with respect to the original problem situation;

- generalizes solutions and strategies to new problem situations.

High School

The student demonstrates problem solving by using mathematical concepts and skills to solve non-routine problems that do not lay out specific and detailed steps to follow, and solves problems that make demands on all three aspects of the solution process—formulation, implementation, and conclusion.

Formulation

M5 a The student participates in the formulation of problems; that is, given the statement of a problem situation, the student:

- fills out the formulation of a definite problem that is to be solved;

- extracts pertinent information from the situation as a basis for working on the problem;

- asks and answers a series of appropriate questions in pursuit of a solution and does so with minimal "scaffolding" in the form of detailed guiding questions.

Implementation

M5 b The student makes the basic choices involved in planning and carrying out a solution; that is, the student:

- chooses and employs effective problem solving strategies in dealing with non-routine and multi-step problems;

- selects appropriate mathematical concepts and techniques from different areas of mathematics and applies them to the solution of the problem;

- applies mathematical concepts to new situations within mathematics and uses mathematics to model real world situations involving basic applications of mathematics in the physical and biological sciences, the social sciences, and business.

Conclusion

M5 c The student provides closure to the solution process through summary statements and general conclusions; that is, the student:

- concludes a solution process with a useful summary of results;

- evaluates the degree to which the results obtained represent a good response to the initial problem;

- formulates generalizations of the results obtained;

- carries out extensions of the given problem to related problems.

Mathematical reasoning

M5 d The student demonstrates mathematical reasoning by generalizing patterns, making conjectures and explaining why they seem true, and by making sensible, justifiable statements; that is, the student:

- formulates conjectures and argues why they must be or seem true;
- makes sensible, reasonable estimates;
- makes justified, logical statements.

Mathematical reasoning

M5 d The student demonstrates mathematical reasoning by using logic to prove specific conjectures, by explaining the logic inherent in a solution process, by making generalizations and showing that they are valid, and by revealing mathematical patterns inherent in a situation. The student not only makes observations and states results but also justifies or proves why the results hold in general; that is, the student:

- employs forms of mathematical reasoning and proof appropriate to the solution of the problem at hand, including deductive and inductive reasoning, making and testing conjectures, and using counterexamples and indirect proof;
- differentiates clearly between giving examples that support a conjecture and giving a proof of the conjecture.

M6 Mathematical Skills and Tools

Elementary School

The student demonstrates fluency with basic and important skills by using these skills accurately and automatically, and demonstrates practical competence and persistence with other skills by using them effectively to accomplish a task, perhaps referring to notes, books, or other students, perhaps working to reconstruct a method; that is, the student:

M6a Adds, subtracts, multiplies, and divides whole numbers correctly; that is:

- knows single digit addition, subtraction, multiplication, and division facts;

- adds and subtracts numbers with several digits;

- multiplies and divides numbers with one or two digits;

- multiplies and divides three digit numbers by one digit numbers.

M6b Estimates numerically and spatially.

M6c Measures length, area, perimeter, circumference, diameter, height, weight, and volume accurately in both the customary and metric systems.

M6d Computes time (in hours and minutes) and money (in dollars and cents).

M6e Refers to geometric shapes and terms correctly with concrete objects or drawings, including triangle, square, rectangle, side, edge, face, cube, point, line, perimeter, area, and circle; and refers with assistance to rhombus, parallelogram, quadrilateral, polygon, polyhedron, angle, vertex, volume, diameter, circumference, sphere, prism, and pyramid.

M6f Uses $+, -, \times, \div, /, \overline{}$, \$, ¢, %, and . (decimal point) correctly in number sentences and expressions.

M6g Reads, creates, and represents data on line plots, charts, tables, diagrams, bar graphs, simple circle graphs, and coordinate graphs.

M6h Uses recall, mental computations, pencil and paper, measuring devices, mathematics texts, manipulatives, calculators, computers, and advice from peers, as appropriate, to achieve solutions; that is, uses measuring devices, graded appropriately for given situations, such as rulers (customary to the ⅛ inch; metric to the millimeter; graph paper (customary to the inch or half-inch; metric to the centimeter); measuring cups (customary to the ounce; metric to the milliliter), and scales (customary to the pound or ounce; metric to the kilogram or gram).

Middle School

The student demonstrates fluency with basic and important skills by using these skills accurately and automatically, and demonstrates practical competence and persistence with other skills by using them effectively to accomplish a task (perhaps referring to notes, or books, perhaps working to reconstruct a method); that is, the student:

M6a Computes accurately with arithmetic operations on rational numbers.

M6b Knows and uses the correct order of operations for arithmetic computations.

M6c Estimates numerically and spatially.

M6d Measures length, area, volume, weight, time, and temperature accurately.

M6e Refers to geometric shapes and terms correctly.

M6f Uses equations, formulas, and simple algebraic notation appropriately.

M6g Reads and organizes data on charts and graphs, including scatter plots, bar, line, and circle graphs, and Venn diagrams; calculates mean and median.

M6h Uses recall, mental computations, pencil and paper, measuring devices, mathematics texts, manipulatives, calculators, computers, and advice from peers, as appropriate, to achieve solutions.

High School

The student demonstrates fluency with basic and important skills by using these skills accurately and automatically, and demonstrates practical competence and persistence with other skills by using them effectively to accomplish a task, perhaps referring to notes, or books, perhaps working to reconstruct a method; that is, the student:

M6a Carries out numerical calculations and symbol manipulations effectively, using mental computations, pencil and paper, or other technological aids, as appropriate.

M6b Uses a variety of methods to estimate the values, in appropriate units, of quantities met in applications, and rounds numbers used in applications to an appropriate degree of accuracy.

M6c Evaluates and analyzes formulas and functions of many kinds, using both pencil and paper and more advanced technology.

M6d Uses basic geometric terminology accurately, and deduces information about basic geometric figures in solving problems.

M6e Makes and uses rough sketches, schematic diagrams, or precise scale diagrams to enhance a solution.

M6f Uses the number line and Cartesian coordinates in the plane and in space.

M6g Creates and interprets graphs of many kinds, such as function graphs, circle graphs, scatter plots, regression lines, and histograms.

M6h Sets up and solves equations symbolically (when possible) and graphically.

M6i Knows how to use algorithms in mathematics, such as the Euclidean Algorithm.

M6j Uses technology to create graphs or spreadsheets that contribute to the understanding of a problem.

M6k Writes a simple computer program to carry out a computation or simulation to be repeated many times.

M6l Uses tools such as rulers, tapes, compasses, and protractors in solving problems.

M6m Knows standard methods to solve basic problems and uses these methods in approaching more complex problems.

M7 Mathematical Communication

Elementary School

The student uses the language of mathematics, its symbols, notation, graphs, and expressions, to communicate through reading, writing, speaking, and listening, and communicates about mathematics by describing mathematical ideas and concepts and explaining reasoning and results; that is, the student:

M7 a Uses appropriate mathematical terms, vocabulary, and language, based on prior conceptual work.

M7 b Shows mathematical ideas in a variety of ways, including words, numbers, symbols, pictures, charts, graphs, tables, diagrams, and models.

M7 c Explains solutions to problems clearly and logically, and supports solutions with evidence, in both oral and written work.

M7 d Considers purpose and audience when communicating about mathematics.

M7 e Comprehends mathematics from reading assignments and from other sources.

Middle School

The student uses the language of mathematics, its symbols, notation, graphs, and expressions, to communicate through reading, writing, speaking, and listening, and communicates about mathematics by describing mathematical ideas and concepts and explaining reasoning and results; that is, the student:

M7 a Uses mathematical language and representations with appropriate accuracy, including numerical tables and equations, simple algebraic equations and formulas, charts, graphs, and diagrams.

M7 b Organizes work, explains facets of a solution orally and in writing, labels drawings, and uses other techniques to make meaning clear to the audience.

M7 c Uses mathematical language to make complex situations easier to understand.

M7 d Exhibits developing reasoning abilities by justifying statements and defending work.

M7 e Shows understanding of concepts by explaining ideas not only to teachers and assessors but to fellow students or younger children.

M7 f Comprehends mathematics from reading assignments and from other sources.

High School

The student uses the language of mathematics, its symbols, notation, graphs, and expressions, to communicate through reading, writing, speaking, and listening, and communicates about mathematics by describing mathematical ideas and concepts and explaining reasoning and results; that is, the student:

M7 a Is familiar with basic mathematical terminology, standard notation and use of symbols, common conventions for graphing, and general features of effective mathematical communication styles.

M7 b Uses mathematical representations with appropriate accuracy, including numerical tables, formulas, functions, equations, charts, graphs, and diagrams.

M7 c Organizes work and presents mathematical procedures and results clearly, systematically, succinctly, and correctly.

M7 d Communicates logical arguments clearly, showing why a result makes sense and why the reasoning is valid.

M7 e Presents mathematical ideas effectively both orally and in writing.

M7 f Explains mathematical concepts clearly enough to be of assistance to those who may be having difficulty with them.

M7 g Writes narrative accounts of the history and process of work on a mathematical problem or extended project.

M7 h Writes succinct accounts of the mathematical results obtained in a mathematical problem or extended project, with diagrams, graphs, tables, and formulas integrated into the text.

M7 i Keeps narrative accounts of process separate from succinct accounts of results, and realizes that doing so can enhance the effectiveness of each.

M7 j Reads mathematics texts and other writing about mathematics with understanding.

M8 Putting Mathematics to Work

Elementary School

The student conducts at least one large scale project each year, beginning in fourth grade, drawn from the following kinds and, over the course of elementary school, conducts projects drawn from at least two of the kinds.

A single project may draw on more than one kind.

M8 a Data study, in which the student:

• develops a question and a hypothesis in a situation where data could help make a decision or recommendation;

• decides on a group or groups to be sampled and makes predictions of the results, with specific percents, fractions, or numbers;

• collects, represents, and displays data in order to help make the decision or recommendation; compares the results with the predictions;

• writes a report that includes recommendations supported by diagrams, charts, and graphs, and acknowledges assistance received from parents, peers, and teachers.

M8 b Science study, in which the student:

• decides on a specific science question to study and identifies the mathematics that will be used, e.g., measurement;

• develops a prediction (a hypothesis) and develops procedures to test the hypothesis;

• collects and records data, represents and displays data, and compares results with predictions;

• writes a report that compares the results with the hypothesis; supports the results with diagrams, charts, and graphs; acknowledges assistance received from parents, peers, and teachers.

M8 c Design of a physical structure, in which the student:

• decides on a structure to design, the size and budget constraints, and the scale of design;

• makes a first draft of the design, and revises and improves the design in response to input from peers and teachers;

• makes a final draft and report of the design, drawn and written so that another person could make the structure; acknowledges assistance received from parents, peers, and teachers.

Middle School

The student conducts at least one large scale investigation or project each year drawn from the following kinds and, over the course of middle school, conducts investigations or projects drawn from three of the kinds.

A single investigation or project may draw on more than one kind.

M8 a Data study based on civic, economic, or social issues, in which the student:

• selects an issue to investigate;

• makes a hypothesis on an expected finding, if appropriate;

• gathers data;

• analyzes the data using concepts from Standard 4, e.g., considering mean and median, and the frequency and distribution of the data;

• shows how the study's results compare with the hypothesis;

• uses pertinent statistics to summarize;

• prepares a presentation or report that includes the question investigated, a detailed description of how the project was carried out, and an explanation of the findings.

M8 b Mathematical model of physical phenomena, often used in science studies, in which the student:

• carries out a study of a physical system using a mathematical representation of the structure;

• uses understanding from Standard 3, particularly with respect to the determination of the function governing behavior in the model;

• generalizes about the structure with a rule, i.e., a function, that clearly applies to the phenomenon and goes beyond statistical analysis of a pattern of numbers generated by the situation;

• prepares a presentation or report that includes the question investigated, a detailed description of how the project was carried out, and an explanation of the findings.

M8 c Design of a physical structure, in which the student:

• generates a plan to build something of value, not necessarily monetary value;

• uses mathematics from Standard 2 to make the design realistic or appropriate, e.g., areas and volumes in general and of specific geometric shapes;

High School

The student conducts at least one large scale investigation or project each year, over the course of high school, conducts investigations or projects drawn from at least three of the kinds.

A single investigation or project may draw on more than one kind.

M8 a Data study, in which the student:

• carries out a study of data relevant to current civic, economic, scientific, health, or social issues;

• uses methods of statistical inference to generalize from the data;

• prepares a report that explains the purpose of the project, the organizational plan, and conclusions, and uses an appropriate balance of different ways of presenting information.

M8 b Mathematical model of a physical system or phenomenon, in which the student:

• carries out a study of a physical system or phenomenon by constructing a mathematical model based on functions to make generalizations about the structure of the system;

• uses structural analysis (a direct analysis of the structure of the system) rather than numerical or statistical analysis (an analysis of data about the system);

• prepares a report that explains the purpose of the project, the organizational plan, and conclusions, and uses an appropriate balance of different ways of presenting information.

M8 c Design of a physical structure, in which the student:

• creates a design for a physical structure;

• uses general mathematical ideas and techniques to discuss specifications for building the structure;

• prepares a report that explains the purpose of the project, the organizational plan, and conclusions, and uses an appropriate balance of different ways of presenting information.

M8 d Management and planning analysis, in which the student:

• carries out a study of a business or public policy situation involving issues such as optimization, cost-benefit projections, and risks;

• uses decision rules and strategies both to analyze options and balance trade-offs; and brings

M3d Management and planning, in which the student:

- decides on what to manage or plan, and the criteria to be used to see if the plan worked;

- identifies unexpected events that could disrupt the plan and further plans for such contingencies;

- identifies resources needed, e.g., materials, money, time, space, and other people;

- writes a detailed plan and revises and improves the plan in response to feedback from peers and teachers;

- carries out the plan (optional);

- writes a report on the plan that includes resources, budget, and schedule, and acknowledges assistance received from parents, peers, and teachers.

M3e Pure mathematics investigation, in which the student:

- decides on the area of mathematics to investigate, e.g., numbers, shapes, patterns;

- describes a question or concept to investigate;

- decides on representations that will be used, e.g., numbers, symbols, diagrams, shapes, or physical models;

- carries out the investigation;

- writes a report that includes any generalizations drawn from the investigation, and acknowledges assistance received from parents, peers, and teachers.

- summarizes the important features of the structure;

- prepares a presentation or report that includes the question investigated, a detailed description of how the project was carried out, and an explanation of the findings.

M8d Management and planning, in which the student:

- determines the needs of the event to be managed or planned, e.g., cost, supply, scheduling;

- notes any constraints that will affect the plan;

- determines a plan;

- uses concepts from any of Standards 1 to 4, depending on the nature of the project;

- considers the possibility of a more efficient solution;

- prepares a presentation or report that includes the question investigated, a detailed description of how the project was carried out, and an explanation of the plan.

M8e Pure mathematics investigation, in which the student:

- extends or "plays with," as with mathematical puzzles, some mathematical feature, e.g., properties and patterns in numbers;

- uses concepts from any of Standards 1 to 4, e.g., an investigation of Pascal's triangle would have roots in Standard 1 but could tie in concepts from geometry, algebra, and probability; investigations of derivations of geometric formulas would be rooted in Standard 2 but could require algebra;

- determines and expresses generalizations from patterns;

- makes conjectures on apparent properties and argues, short of formal proof, why they seem true;

- prepares a presentation or report that includes the question investigated, a detailed description of how the project was carried out, and an explanation of the findings.

---

in mathematical ideas that serve to generalize the analysis across different conditions;

- prepares a report that explains the purpose of the project, the organizational plan, and conclusions, and uses an appropriate balance of different ways of presenting information.

M8e Pure mathematics investigation, in which the student:

- carries out a mathematical investigation of a phenomenon or concept in pure mathematics;

- uses methods of mathematical reasoning and justification to make generalizations about the phenomenon;

- prepares a report that explains the purpose of the project, the organizational plan, and conclusions, and uses an appropriate balance of different ways of presenting information.

M8f History of a mathematical idea, in which the student:

- carries out a historical study tracing the development of a mathematical concept and the people who contributed to it;

- includes a discussion of the actual mathematical content and its place in the curriculum of the present day;

- prepares a report that explains the purpose of the project, the organizational plan, and conclusions, and uses an appropriate balance of different ways of presenting information.

S1 Physical Sciences Concepts

APPENDIX III

The elementary school standards are set at a level of performance approximately equivalent to the end of fourth grade. The middle school standards are set at a level of performance approximately equivalent to the end of eighth grade. The high school standards are set at a level of performance approximately equivalent to the end of tenth grade. It is expected that some students might achieve these levels earlier and others later than these grades.

The Science standards are founded upon both the National Research Council's *National Science Education Standards* and the American Association for the Advancement of Science's Project 2061 *Benchmarks for Science Literacy*. These documents, each of which runs to several hundred pages, contain detailed explication of the concepts identified here.

Elementary School

The student produces evidence that demonstrates understanding of:

S1 a Properties of objects and materials, such as similarities and differences in the size, weight, and color of objects; the ability of materials to react with other substances; and different states of materials.

S1 b Position and motion of objects, such as how the motion of an object can be described by tracing and measuring its position over time; and how sound is produced by vibrating objects.

S1 c Light, heat, electricity, and magnetism, such as the variation of heat and temperature; how light travels in a straight line until it strikes an object or how electrical circuits work.

Middle School

The student produces evidence that demonstrates understanding of:

S1 a Properties and changes of properties in matter, such as density and boiling point; chemical reactivity; and conservation of matter.

S1 b Motions and forces, such as inertia and the net effects of balanced and unbalanced forces.

S1 c Transfer of energy, such as transformation of energy as heat; light, mechanical motion, and sound; and the nature of a chemical reaction.

High School

The student produces evidence that demonstrates understanding of:

S1 a Structure of atoms, such as atomic composition, nuclear forces, and radioactivity.

S1 b Structure and properties of matter, such as elements and compounds; bonding and molecular interaction; and characteristics of phase changes.

S1 c Chemical reactions, such as everyday examples of chemical reactions; electrons, protons, and energy transfer; and factors that affect reaction rates such as catalysts.

S1 d Motions and forces, such as gravitational and electrical; net forces and magnetism.

S1 e Conservation of energy and increase in disorder, such as kinetic and potential energy; energy conduction, convection, and radiation; random motion; and effects of heat and pressure.

S1 f Interactions of energy and matter, such as waves, absorption and emission of light, and conductivity.

S2 Life Sciences Concepts

Elementary School

The student produces evidence that demonstrates understanding of:

S2 a Characteristics of organisms, such as survival and environmental support; the relationship between structure and function; and variations in behavior.

S2 b Life cycles of organisms, such as how inheritance and environment determine the characteristics of an organism; and that all plants and animals have life cycles.

S2 c Organisms and environments, such as the interdependence of animals and plants in an ecosystem; and populations and their effects on the environment.

S2 d Change over time, such as evolution and fossil evidence depicting the great diversity of organisms developed over geologic history.

Middle School

The student produces evidence that demonstrates understanding of:

S2 a Structure and function in living systems, such as the complementary nature of structure and function in cells, organs, tissues, organ systems, whole organisms, and ecosystems.

S2 b Reproduction and heredity, such as sexual and asexual reproduction; and the role of genes and environment on trait expression.

S2 c Regulation and behavior, such as senses and behavior; and response to environmental stimuli.

S2 d Populations and ecosystems, such as the roles of producers, consumers, and decomposers in a food web; and the effects of resources and energy transfer on populations.

S2 e Evolution, diversity, and adaptation of organisms, such as common ancestry, speciation, adaptation, variation, and extinction.

High School

The student produces evidence that demonstrates understanding of:

S2 a The cell, such as cell structure and function relationships; regulation and biochemistry; and energy and photosynthesis.

S2 b Molecular basis of heredity, such as DNA, genes, chromosomes, and mutations.

S2 c Biological evolution, such as speciation, biodiversity, natural selection, and biological classification.

S2 d Interdependence of organisms, such as conservation of matter; cooperation and competition among organisms in ecosystems; and human effects on the environment.

S2 e Matter, energy, and organization in living systems, such as matter and energy flow through different levels of organization; and environmental constraints.

S2 f Behavior of organisms, such as nervous system regulation; behavioral responses; and connections with anthropology, sociology, and psychology.

S3 Earth and Space Sciences Concepts

Elementary School

The student produces evidence that demonstrates understanding of:

S3 a Properties of Earth materials, such as water and gases; and the properties of rocks and soils, such as texture, color, and ability to retain water.

S3 b Objects in the sky, such as Sun, Moon, planets, and other objects that can be observed and described; and the importance of the Sun to provide the light and heat necessary for survival.

S3 c Changes in Earth and sky, such as changes caused by weathering, volcanism, and earthquakes; and the patterns of movement of objects in the sky.

Middle School

The student produces evidence that demonstrates understanding of:

S3 a Structure of the Earth system, such as crustal plates and land forms; water and rock cycles; oceans, weather, and climate.

S3 b Earth's history, such as Earth processes including erosion and movement of plates; change over time and fossil evidence.

S3 c Earth in the Solar System, such as the predictable motion of planets, moons, and other objects in the Solar System including days, years, moon phases, and eclipses; and the role of the Sun as the major source of energy for phenomena on the Earth's surface.

S3 d Natural resource management.

High School

The student produces evidence that demonstrates understanding of:

S3 a Energy in the Earth system, such as radioactive decay, gravity, the Sun's energy, convection, and changes in global climate.

S3 b Geochemical cycles, such as conservation of matter; chemical resources and movement of matter between chemical reservoirs.

S3 c Origin and evolution of the Earth system, such as geologic time and the age of life forms; origin of life; and evolution of the Solar System.

S3 d Origin and evolution of the universe, such as the "big bang" theory; formation of stars and elements; and nuclear reactions.

S3 e Natural resource management.

S4 Scientific Connections and Applications

Elementary School

The student produces evidence that demonstrates understanding of:

S4a Big ideas and unifying concepts, such as order and organization; models, form and function; change and constancy; and cause and effect.

S4b The designed world, such as development of agricultural techniques; and the viability of technological designs.

S4c Personal health, such as nutrition, substance abuse, and exercise; germs and toxic substances; personal and environmental safety.

S4d Science as a human endeavor, such as communication, cooperation, and diverse input in scientific research; and the importance of reason, intellectual honesty, and skepticism.

Middle School

The student produces evidence that demonstrates understanding of:

S4a Big ideas and unifying concepts, such as order and organization; models, form, and function; change and constancy; and cause and effect.

S4b The designed world, such as the reciprocal nature of science and technology; the development of agricultural techniques; and the viability of technological designs.

S4c Health, such as nutrition, exercise, and disease; effects of drugs and toxic substances; personal and environmental safety; and resources and environmental stress.

S4d Impact of technology, such as constraints and trade-offs; feedback; benefits and risks; and problems and solutions.

S4e Impact of science, such as historical and contemporary contributions; and interactions between science and society.

High School

The student produces evidence that demonstrates understanding of:

S4a Big ideas and unifying concepts, such as order and organization; models, form and function; change and constancy; and cause and effect.

S4b The designed world, such as the reciprocal relationship between science and technology; the development of agricultural techniques; and the reasonableness of technological designs.

S4c Health, such as nutrition and exercise; disease and epidemiology; personal and environmental safety; and resources, environmental stress, and population growth.

S4d Impact of technology, such as constraints and trade-offs; feedback; benefits and risks; and problems and solutions.

S4e Impact of science, such as historical and contemporary contributions; and interactions between science and society.

S5 Scientific Thinking

Elementary School

The student demonstrates scientific inquiry and problem solving by using thoughtful questioning and reasoning strategies, common sense and conceptual understanding from Science Standards 1 to 4, and appropriate methods to investigate the natural world; that is, the student:

S5 a Asks questions about natural phenomena; objects and organisms; and events and discoveries.

S5 b Uses concepts from Science Standards 1 to 4 to explain a variety of observations and phenomena.

S5 c Uses evidence from reliable sources to construct explanations.

S5 d Evaluates different points of view using relevant experiences, observations, and knowledge; and distinguishes between fact and opinion.

S5 e Identifies problems; proposes and implements solutions; and evaluates the accuracy, design, and outcomes of investigations.

S5 f Works individually and in teams to collect and share information and ideas.

Middle School

The student demonstrates scientific inquiry and problem solving by using thoughtful questioning and reasoning strategies, common sense and conceptual understanding from Science Standards 1 to 4, and appropriate methods to investigate the natural world; that is, the student:

S5 a Frames questions to distinguish cause and effect; and identifies or controls variables in experimental and non-experimental research settings.

S5 b Uses concepts from Science Standards 1 to 4 to explain a variety of observations and phenomena.

S5 c Uses evidence from reliable sources to develop descriptions, explanations, and models.

S5 d Proposes, recognizes, analyzes, considers, and critiques alternative explanations; and distinguishes between fact and opinion.

S5 e Identifies problems; proposes and implements solutions; and evaluates the accuracy, design, and outcomes of investigations.

S5 f Works individually and in teams to collect and share information and ideas.

High School

The student demonstrates skill in scientific inquiry and problem solving by using thoughtful questioning and reasoning strategies, common sense and diverse conceptual understanding, and appropriate ideas and methods to investigate science; that is, the student:

S5 a Frames questions to distinguish cause and effect; and identifies or controls variables in experimental and non-experimental research settings.

S5 b Uses concepts from Science Standards 1 to 4 to explain a variety of observations and phenomena.

S5 c Uses evidence from reliable sources to develop descriptions, explanations, and models; and makes appropriate adjustments and improvements based on additional data or logical arguments.

S5 d Proposes, recognizes, analyzes, considers, and critiques alternative explanations; and distinguishes between fact and opinion.

S5 e Identifies problems; proposes and implements solutions; and evaluates the accuracy, design, and outcomes of investigations.

S5 f Works individually and in teams to collect and share information and ideas.

S6 Scientific Tools and Technologies

APPENDIX III

S6 makes explicit reference to using telecommunications to acquire and share information. A recent National Center on Education Statistics survey recently reported that only 50% of schools and fewer than 9% of instructional rooms currently have access to the Internet. We know this is an equity issue—that far more than 9% of the homes in the United States have access to the Internet and that schools must make sure that students' access to information and ideas does not depend on what they get at home—so we have crafted performance standards that would use the Internet so that people will make sure that all students have access to it. New Standards partners have made a commitment to create the learning environments where students can develop the knowledge and skills delineated here.

Elementary School

The student demonstrates competence with the tools and technologies of science by using them to collect data, make observations, analyze results, and accomplish tasks effectively; that is, the student:

S6 a Uses technology and tools (such as rulers, computers, balances, thermometers, watches, magnifiers, and microscopes) to gather data and extend the senses.

S6 b Collects and analyzes data using concepts and techniques in Mathematics Standard 4, such as average, data displays, graphing, variability, and sampling.

S6 c Acquires information from multiple sources, such as experimentation and print and non-print sources.

Middle School

The student demonstrates competence with the tools and technologies of science by using them to collect data, make observations, analyze results, and accomplish tasks effectively; that is, the student:

S6 a Uses technology and tools (such as traditional laboratory equipment, video, and computer aids) to observe and measure objects, organisms, and phenomena, directly, indirectly, and remotely.

S6 b Records and stores data using a variety of formats, such as data bases, audiotapes, and videotapes.

S6 c Collects and analyzes data using concepts and techniques in Mathematics Standard 4, such as mean, median, and mode; outcome probability and reliability; and appropriate data displays.

S6 d Acquires information from multiple sources, such as print, the Internet, computer data bases, and experimentation.

S6 e Recognizes sources of bias in data, such as observer and sampling biases.

High School

The student demonstrates competence with the tools and technologies of science by using them to collect data, make observations, analyze results, and accomplish tasks effectively; that is, the student:

S6 a Uses technology and tools (such as traditional laboratory equipment, video, and computer aids) to observe and measure objects, organisms, and phenomena, directly, indirectly, and remotely, with appropriate consideration of accuracy and precision.

S6 b Records and stores data using a variety of formats, such as data bases, audiotapes, and videotapes.

S6 c Collects and analyzes data using concepts and techniques in Mathematics Standard 4, such as mean, median, and mode; outcome probability and reliability; and appropriate data displays.

S6 d Acquires information from multiple sources, such as print, the Internet, computer data bases, and experimentation.

S6 e Recognizes and limits sources of bias in data, such as observer and sample biases.

S7 Scientific Communication

APPENDIX III

Elementary School

The student demonstrates effective scientific communication by clearly describing aspects of the natural world using accurate data, graphs, or other appropriate media to convey depth of conceptual understanding in science; that is, the student:

S7 a Represents data and results in multiple ways, such as numbers, tables, and graphs; drawings, diagrams, and artwork; and technical and creative writing.

S7 b Uses facts to support conclusions.

S7 c Communicates in a form suited to the purpose and the audience, such as writing instructions that others can follow.

S7 d Critiques written and oral explanations, and uses data to resolve disagreements.

Middle School

The student demonstrates effective scientific communication by clearly describing aspects of the natural world using accurate data, graphs, or other appropriate media to convey depth of conceptual understanding in science; that is, the student:

S7 a Represents data and results in multiple ways, such as numbers, tables, and graphs; drawings, diagrams, and artwork; and technical and creative writing.

S7 b Argues from evidence, such as data produced through his or her own experimentation or by others.

S7 c Critiques published materials.

S7 d Explains a scientific concept or procedure to other students.

S7 e Communicates in a form suited to the purpose and the audience, such as by writing instructions that others can follow; critiquing written and oral explanations; and using data to resolve disagreements.

High School

The student demonstrates effective scientific communication by clearly describing aspects of the natural world using accurate data, graphs, or other appropriate media to convey depth of conceptual understanding in science; that is, the student:

S7 a Represents data and results in multiple ways, such as numbers, tables, and graphs; drawings, diagrams, and artwork; technical and creative writing; and selects the most effective way to convey the scientific information.

S7 b Argues from evidence, such as data produced through his or her own experimentation or data produced by others.

S7 c Critiques published materials, such as popular magazines and academic journals.

S7 d Explains a scientific concept or procedure to other students.

S7 e Communicates in a form suited to the purpose and the audience, such as by writing instructions that others can follow; critiquing written and oral explanations; and using data to resolve disagreements.

S8 Scientific Investigation

Best practice in science has always included extensive inquiry and investigation, but these are frequently given less emphasis at the elementary level in the face of competing demands form English language arts and mathematics. There are many opportunities to learn science outside of school, including Scouts, Boys and Girls Clubs, 4-H, and Future Farmers of America. The work done in these venues can and should be used to provide evidence of meeting the standards.

Elementary School

The student demonstrates scientific competence by completing projects drawn from the following kinds of investigations, including at least one full investigation each year and, over the course of elementary school, investigations that integrate several aspects of Science Standards 1 to 7 and represent all four of the kinds of investigation:

S8 a An experiment, such as conducting a fair test.

S8 b A systematic observation, such as a field study.

S8 c A design, such as building a model or scientific apparatus.

S8 d Non-experimental research using print and electronic information, such as journals, video, or computers.

A single project may draw on more than one kind of investigation.

A full investigation includes:

• Questions that can be studied using the resources available.

• Procedures that are safe, humane, and ethical; and that respect privacy and property rights.

• Data that have been collected and recorded (see also Science Standard 6) in ways that others can verify and analyze using skills expected at this grade level (see also Mathematics Standard 4).

• Data and results that have been represented (see also Science Standard 7) in ways that fit the context.

• Recommendations, decisions, and conclusions based on evidence.

• Acknowledgment of references and contributions of others.

• Results that are communicated appropriately to audiences.

• Reflection and defense of conclusions and recommendations from other sources and peer review.

Middle School

The student demonstrates scientific competence by completing projects drawn from the following kinds of investigations, including at least one full investigation each year and, over the course of middle school, investigations that integrate several aspects of Science Standards 1 to 7 and represent all four of the kinds of investigation:

S8 a Controlled experiment.

S8 b Fieldwork.

S8 c Design.

S8 d Secondary research, such as use of others' data.

A single project may draw on more than one type of investigation.

A full investigation includes:

• Questions that can be studied using the resources available.

• Procedures that are safe, humane, and ethical; and that respect privacy and property rights.

• Data that have been collected and recorded (see also Science Standard 6) in ways that others can verify, and analyzed using skills expected at this grade level (see also Mathematics Standard 4).

• Data and results that have been represented (see also Science Standard 7) in ways that fit the context.

• Recommendations, decisions, and conclusions based on evidence.

• Acknowledgment of references and contributions of others.

• Results that are communicated appropriately to audiences.

• Reflection and defense of conclusions and recommendations from other sources and peer review.

High School

The student demonstrates scientific competence by completing projects drawn from the following kinds of investigation, including at least one full investigation each year and, over the course of high school, investigations that integrate several aspects of Science Standards 1 to 7 and represent all four of the kinds of investigation:

S8 a Controlled experiment.

S8 b Fieldwork.

S8 c Design.

S8 d Secondary research.

A single project may draw on more than one type of investigation.

A full investigation includes:

• Questions that can be studied using the resources available.

• Procedures that are safe, humane, and ethical; and that respect privacy and property rights.

• Data that have been collected and recorded (see also Science Standard 6) in ways that others can verify, and analyzed using skills expected at this grade level (see also Mathematics Standard 4).

• Data and results that have been represented (see also Science Standard 7) in ways that fit the context.

• Recommendations, decisions, and conclusions based on evidence.

• Acknowledgment of references and contributions of others.

• Results that are communicated appropriately to audiences.

• Reflection and defense of conclusions and recommendations from other sources and peer review.

A1 Problem Solving

The elementary school standards are set at a level of performance approximately equivalent to the end of fourth grade. The middle school standards are set at a level of performance approximately equivalent to the end of eighth grade. The high school standards are set at a level of performance approximately equivalent to the end of tenth grade. It is expected that some students might achieve these levels earlier and others later than these grades.

Elementary School

The student conducts projects involving at least two of the following kinds of problem solving each year and, over the course of elementary school, conducts projects involving all three kinds of problem solving.

- Design a Product, Service, or System: Identify needs that could be met by new products, services, or systems and create solutions for meeting them.

- Improve a System: Develop an understanding of the way systems of people, machines, and processes work; troubleshoot problems in their operation and devise strategies for improving their effectiveness.

- Plan and Organize an Event or an Activity: Take responsibility for all aspects of planning and organizing an event or an activity from concept to completion, making good use of the resources of people, time, money, and materials and facilities.

Each project should involve subject matter related to the standards for English Language Arts, and/or Mathematics, and/or Science, and/or other appropriate subject content.

Design a Product, Service, or System

A1 a The student designs and creates a product, service, or system to meet an identified need; that is, the student:

- develops ideas for the design of the product, service, or system;

- chooses among the design ideas and justifies the choice;

- establishes criteria for judging the success of the design;

- uses an appropriate format to represent the design;

- plans and carries out the steps needed to turn the design into a reality;

- evaluates the design in terms of the criteria established for success.

Improve a System

A1 b The student troubleshoots problems in the operation of a system in need of repair or devises and tests ways of improving the effectiveness of a system in operation; that is, the student:

- identifies the parts of the system and the way the parts connect with each other;

Middle School

The student conducts projects involving at least two of the following kinds of problem solving each year and, over the course of middle school, conducts projects involving all three kinds of problem solving.

- Design a Product, Service, or System: Identify needs that could be met by new products, services, or systems and create solutions for meeting them.

- Improve a System: Develop an understanding of the way systems of people, machines, and processes work; troubleshoot problems in their operation and devise strategies for improving their effectiveness.

- Plan and Organize an Event or an Activity: Take responsibility for all aspects of planning and organizing an event or an activity from concept to completion, making good use of the resources of people, time, money, and materials and facilities.

Each project should involve subject matter related to the standards for English Language Arts, and/or Mathematics, and/or Science, and/or other appropriate subject content.

Design a Product, Service, or System

A1 a The student designs and creates a product, service, or system to meet an identified need; that is, the student:

- develops a range of ideas for design of the product, service, or system;

- selects one design option to pursue and justifies the choice with reference, for example, to functional, aesthetic, social, economic, or environmental considerations;

- establishes criteria for judging the success of the design;

- uses appropriate conventions to represent the design;

- plans and carries out the steps needed to create the product, service, or system;

- makes adjustments as needed to conform with specified standards or regulations regarding quality and safety;

- evaluates the quality of the design in terms of the criteria for success and by comparison with similar products, services, or systems.

High School

The student conducts projects involving at least two of the following kinds of problem solving each year and, over the course of high school, conducts projects involving all three kinds of problem solving.

- Design a Product, Service, or System: Identify needs that could be met by new products, services, or systems and create solutions for meeting them.

- Improve a System: Develop an understanding of the way systems of people, machines, and processes work; troubleshoot problems in their operation and devise strategies for improving their effectiveness.

- Plan and Organize an Event or an Activity: Take responsibility for all aspects of planning and organizing an event or activity from concept to completion, making good use of the resources of people, time, money, and materials and facilities.

Each project should involve subject matter related to the standards for English Language Arts, and/or Mathematics, and/or Science, and/or other appropriate subject content.

Design a Product, Service, or System

A1 a The student designs and creates a product, service, or system to meet an identified need; that is, the student:

- develops a design proposal that:

- shows how the ideas for the design were developed;

- reflects awareness of similar work done by others and of relevant design standards and regulations;

- justifies the choices made in finalizing the design with reference, for example, to functional, aesthetic, social, economic, and environmental considerations;

- establishes criteria for evaluating the product, service, or system;

- uses appropriate conventions to represent the design;

- plans and implements the steps needed to create the product, service, or system;

- makes adjustments as needed to conform with specified standards or regulations regarding quality or safety;

- evaluates the product, service, or system in terms of the criteria established in the design proposal, and with reference to:

- information gathered from sources such as impact studies, product testing, or market research;

- comparisons with similar work done by others.

Improve a System

A1 b The student troubleshoots problems in the operation of a system in need of repair or devises and tests ways of improving the effectiveness of a system in operation; that is, the student:

• explains the structure of the system in terms of its:

- logic, sequences, and control;

- operating principles, that is, the mathematical, scientific, and/or organizational principles underlying the system;

• analyzes the way the system works, taking account of its functional, aesthetic, social, environmental, and commercial requirements, as appropriate, and using a relevant kind of modeling or systems analysis;

• evaluates the operation of the system, using qualitative methods and/or quantitative measurements of performance;

• develops and tests strategies to put the system back in operation and/or optimize its performance;

• evaluates the effectiveness of the strategies for improving the system and supports the evaluation with evidence.

Plan and Organize an Event or an Activity

A1 c The student plans and organizes an event or an activity; that is, the student:

• develops a planning schedule that:

- is sensible in terms of the goals of the event or activity;

- is logical and achievable;

- reflects research into relevant precedents and regulations;

- takes account of all relevant factors;

- communicates clearly so that a peer or colleague could use it;

• implements and adjusts the planning schedule in ways that:

- make efficient use of time, money, people, resources, facilities;

- reflect established priorities;

- respond effectively to unforeseen circumstances;

• evaluates the success of the event or activity using qualitative and/or quantitative methods;

• makes recommendations for planning and organizing subsequent similar events or activities.

Improve a System

A1 b The student troubleshoots problems in the operation of a system in need of repair or devises and tests ways of improving the effectiveness of a system in operation; that is, the student:

• describes the structure and management of the system in terms of its logic, sequences, and control;

• identifies the operating principles underlying the system, i.e., mathematical, scientific, organizational;

• evaluates the way the system operates;

• devises strategies for putting the system back in operation or improving its performance;

• evaluates the effectiveness of the strategies for improving the system and supports the evaluation with evidence.

Plan and Organize an Event or an Activity

A1 c The student plans and organizes an event or activity; that is, the student:

• develops a plan that:

- reflects research into relevant precedents and regulations;

- includes all the factors and variables that need to be considered;

- shows the order in which things need to be done;

- takes into account the resources available to put the plan into action, including people and time;

• implements the plan in ways that:

- reflect the priorities established in the plan;

- respond effectively to unforeseen circumstances;

• evaluates the success of the event or activity;

• makes recommendations to others who might consider planning and organizing a similar event or activity.

• identifies parts or connections in the system that have broken down or that could be made to work better;

• devises ways of making the system work again or making it work better;

• evaluates the effectiveness of the strategies for improving the system and supports the evaluation with evidence.

Plan and Organize an Event or an Activity

A1 c The student plans and organizes an event or an activity; that is, the student:

• develops a plan for the event or activity that:

- includes all the factors and variables that need to be considered;

- shows the order in which things need to be done;

- takes into account the resources available to put the plan into action, including people and time;

• implements the plan;

• evaluates the success of the event or activity by identifying the parts of the plan that worked best and the parts that could have been improved by better planning and organization;

• makes recommendations to others who might consider planning and organizing a similar event or activity.

A2 Communication Tools and Techniques

Elementary School

A2 a The student makes an oral presentation of project plans or findings to an appropriate audience; that is, the student:

- organizes the presentation in a logical way appropriate to its purpose;
- speaks clearly and presents confidently;
- responds to questions from the audience;
- evaluates the effectiveness of the presentation.

A2 b The student composes and sends correspondence, such as thank-you letters and memoranda providing information; that is, the student:

- expresses the information or request clearly;
- writes in a style appropriate to the purpose of the correspondence.

A2 c The student writes and formats information for short publications, such as brochures or posters; that is, the student:

- organizes the information into an appropriate form for use in the publication;
- checks the information for accuracy;
- formats the publication so that it achieves its purpose.

Middle School

A2 a The student makes an oral presentation of project plans or findings to an audience beyond the school; that is, the student:

- organizes the presentation in a logical way appropriate to its purpose;
- adjusts the style of presentation to suit its purpose and audience;
- speaks clearly and presents confidently;
- responds appropriately to questions from the audience;
- evaluates the effectiveness of the presentation.

A2 b The student conducts formal written correspondence with an organization beyond the school; that is, the student:

- expresses the information or request clearly for the purpose and audience;
- writes in a style appropriate to the purpose and audience of the correspondence.

A2 c The student publishes information using several methods and formats, such as overhead transparencies, handouts, and computer generated graphs and charts; that is, the student:

- organizes the information into an appropriate form for use in the publication;
- checks the information for accuracy;
- formats the published material so that it achieves its purpose.

High School

A2 a The student makes an oral presentation of project plans or findings to an audience with expertise in the relevant subject matter; that is, the student:

- organizes the presentation in a logical way appropriate to its purpose;
- adjusts the style of presentation to suit its purpose and audience;
- speaks clearly and presents confidently;
- responds appropriately to questions from the audience;
- evaluates the effectiveness of the presentation and identifies appropriate revisions for a future presentation.

A2 b The student prepares a formal written proposal or report to an organization beyond the school; that is, the student:

- organizes the information in the proposal or report in a logical way appropriate to its purpose;
- produces the proposal or report in a format similar to that used in professionally produced documents for a similar purpose and audience.

A2 c The student develops a multi-media presentation, combining text, images, and/or sound; that is, the student:

- selects an appropriate medium for each element of the presentation;
- uses the selected media skillfully, including editing and monitoring for quality;
- achieves coherence in the presentation as a whole;
- communicates the information effectively, testing audience response and revising the presentation accordingly.

A3 Information Tools and Techniques

Elementary School

A3 a The student gathers information to assist in completing project work; that is, the student:

- identifies potential sources of information to assist in completing the project;
- uses appropriate techniques to collect the information, e.g., considers sampling issues in conducting a survey;
- distinguishes relevant from irrelevant information;
- shows evidence of research in the completed project.

A3 b The student uses information technology to assist in gathering, organizing, and presenting information; that is, the student:

- acquires information for specific purposes from on-line sources, such as the Internet, and other electronic data bases, such as an electronic encyclopedia;
- uses word-processing, drawing, and painting programs to produce project reports and related materials.

Middle School

A3 a The student gathers information to assist in completing project work; that is, the student:

- identifies potential sources of information to assist in completing the project;
- uses appropriate techniques to collect the information, e.g., considers sampling issues in conducting a survey;
- interprets and analyzes the information;
- evaluates the information for completeness and relevance;
- shows evidence of research in the completed project.

A3 b The student uses information technology to assist in gathering, analyzing, organizing, and presenting information; that is, the student:

- acquires information for specific purposes from on-line sources, such as the Internet, and other electronic data bases, such as a scientific data base on CD ROM;
- uses word-processing, graphics, data base, and spreadsheet programs to produce project reports and related materials.

High School

A3 a The student gathers information to assist in completing project work; that is, the student:

- identifies potential sources of information to assist in completing the project;
- uses appropriate techniques to collect the information, e.g., considers sampling issues in conducting a survey;
- interprets and analyzes the information;
- evaluates the information in terms of completeness, relevance, and validity;
- shows evidence of research in the completed project.

A3 b The student uses on-line sources to exchange information for specific purposes; that is, the student:

- uses E-mail to correspond with peers and specialists in the subject matter of their projects;
- incorporates into E-mail correspondence data of different file types and applications.

A3 c The student uses word-processing software to produce a multi-page document; that is, the student:

- uses features of the software to create and edit the document;
- uses features of the software to format the document, including a table of contents, index, tabular columns, charts, and graphics;
- uses features of the software to create templates and style sheets for the document.

A3 d The student writes, adds content to, and analyzes a data base program that uses a relational data base; that is, the student:

- writes a program capable of handling data with at least two files;
- creates macros to facilitate data entry, analysis, and manipulation;
- creates multiple report formats that include summary information;
- merges data from the data base with other files.

A3 e The student creates, edits, and analyzes a spreadsheet of information that displays data in tabular, numeric format and includes multiple graphs; that is, the student:

- creates a spreadsheet that displays the use of formulas and functions;
- uses features of the software to sort, arrange, display, and extract data for specific purposes;
- uses features of the software to create multiple spreadsheets and to synthesize the spreadsheets into a single presentation.

A4 Learning and Self-management Tools and Techniques

Elementary School

A4 a The student learns from models; that is, the student:

- consults with or observes other students and adults at work, and identifies the main features of what they do and the way they go about their work;

- examines models for the results of project work, such as professionally produced publications, and analyzes their qualities;

- uses what he or she learns from models to assist in planning and conducting project activities.

A4 b The student keeps records of work activities in an orderly manner; that is, the student:

- sets up a system for storing records of work activities;

- maintains records of work activities in a way that makes it possible to find specific materials quickly and easily.

A4 c The student identifies strengths and weaknesses in his or her own work; that is, the student:

- understands and establishes criteria for judging the quality of work processes and products;

- assesses his or her own work processes and products.

Middle School

A4 a The student learns from models; that is, the student:

- consults with or observes other students and adults at work, and identifies the main features of what they do and the way they go about their work;

- identifies models for the results of project work, such as professionally produced publications, and analyzes their qualities;

- uses what he or she learns from models to assist in planning and conducting project activities.

A4 b The student develops and maintains a schedule of work activities; that is, the student:

- establishes a schedule of work activities that reflects priorities and deadlines;

- seeks advice on the management of conflicting priorities and deadlines;

- updates the schedule regularly.

A4 c The student sets goals for learning and reviews his or her progress; that is, the student:

- sets goals for learning;

- reviews his or her progress towards meeting the goals;

- seeks and responds to advice from others in setting goals and reviewing progress.

High School

A4 a The student learns from models; that is, the student:

- consults with and observes other students and adults at work and analyzes their roles to determine the critical demands, such as demands for knowledge and skills, judgment and decision making;

- identifies models for the results of project work, such as professionally produced publications, and analyzes their qualities;

- uses what he or she learns from models in planning and conducting project activities.

A4 b The student reviews his or her own progress in completing work activities and adjusts priorities as needed to meet deadlines; that is, the student:

- develops and maintains work schedules that reflect consideration of priorities;

- manages time;

- monitors progress towards meeting deadlines and adjusts priorities as necessary.

A4 c The student evaluates his or her performance; that is, the student:

- establishes expectations for his or her own achievement;

- critiques his or her work in light of the established expectations;

- seeks and responds to advice and criticism from others.

A5 Tools and Techniques for Working With Others

APPENDIX IV

Elementary School

A5 a The student works with others to complete a task; that is, the student:

- reaches agreement with group members on what work needs to be done to complete the task and how the work will be tackled;
- takes a share of the responsibility for the work;
- consults with group members regularly during the task to check on progress in completing the task, to decide on any changes that are required, and to check that all parts have been completed at the end of the task.

A5 b The student shows or explains something clearly enough for someone else to be able to do it.

A5 c The student responds to a request from a client; that is, the student:

- interprets the client's request;
- asks questions to clarify the demands of a task.

Middle School

A5 a The student takes responsibility for a component of a team project; that is, the student:

- reaches agreement with team members on what work needs to be done to complete the task and how the work will be tackled;
- takes specific responsibility for a component of the project;
- takes all steps necessary to ensure appropriate completion of the specific component of the project within the agreed upon time frame.

A5 b The student coaches or tutors; that is, the student:

- assists one or more others to learn on the job;
- analyzes coaching or tutoring experience to identify more and less effective ways of providing assistance to support on-the-job learning;
- uses the analysis to inform subsequent coaching or tutoring activities.

A5 c The student responds to a request from a client; that is, the student:

- consults with a client to clarify the demands of a task;
- interprets the client's request and translates it into an initial plan for completing the task, taking account of available resources;
- negotiates with the client to arrive at an agreed upon plan.

High School

A5 a The student participates in the establishment and operation of self-directed work teams; that is, the student:

- defines roles and shares responsibilities among team members;
- sets objectives and time frames for the work to be completed;
- establishes processes for group decision making;
- reviews progress and makes adjustments as required.

A5 b The student plans and carries out a strategy for including at least one new member in a work program; that is, the student:

- plans and conducts an initial activity to introduce the new member to the work program;
- devises ways of providing continuing on-the-job support and advice;
- monitors the new member's progress in joining the program, and revises the kinds and ways of providing support and advice accordingly;
- reviews the success of the overall strategy.

A5 c The student completes a task in response to a commission from a client; that is, the student:

- negotiates with the client to arrive at a plan for meeting the client's needs that is acceptable to the client, achievable within available resources, and includes agreed-upon criteria for successful completion;
- monitors client satisfaction with the work in progress and makes adjustments accordingly;
- evaluates the result in terms of the negotiated plan and the client's evaluation of the result.

STANDARDS DEVELOPMENT STAFF

Harold Asturias, Academic Advancement, University of California Office of the President

Pam Beck, Academic Advancement, University of California Office of the President

Ann Borthwick, Learning Research and Development Center, University of Pittsburgh

Bill Calder, Fort Worth Independent School District, TX

Shannon C'de Baca, Thomas Jefferson High School, Council Bluffs, IA

Janet Coffey, Edmund Burke School, Washington, DC

Duane A. Cooper, Center for Mathematics Education and Department of Mathematics, University of Maryland

Phil Daro, Academic Advancement, University of California Office of the President

Mishaa DeGraw, Academic Advancement, University of California Office of the President

Diana Edwards, Learning Research and Development Center, University of Pittsburgh

Gary Eggan, Learning Research and Development Center, University of Pittsburgh

JoAnne Eresh, Learning Research and Development Center, University of Pittsburgh

Sally Hampton, Fort Worth Independent School District, TX

Drew Kravin, Cornell Elementary School, Albany, CA

Georgia Makris, Academic Advancement, University of California Office of the President

Mary Marsh, Fort Worth Independent School District, TX

Megan Martin, Academic Advancement, University of California Office of the President

Evy McPherson, Academic Advancement, University of California Office of the President

Kate Nolan, Learning Research and Development Center, University of Pittsburgh

Andy Plattner, National Center on Education and the Economy

Lonny Platzer, Learning Research and Development Center, University of Pittsburgh

Mark Rasmussen, Cornell Elementary School, Albany, CA

Jennifer Regen, Fort Worth Independent School District, TX

Christine Ross, Learning Research and Development Center, University of Pittsburgh

Annette Seitz, Learning Research and Development Center, University of Pittsburgh

Ann Shannon, Academic Advancement, University of California Office of the President

Liz Spalding, National Council of Teachers of English

Elizabeth Stage, Academic Advancement, University of California Office of the President

Dick Stanley, Dana Center, University of California at Berkeley

Cathy Sterling, Academic Advancement, University of California Office of the President

John Tanner, Fort Worth Independent School District, TX

Ginny Van Horne, Education and Human Resources, American Association for the Advancement of Science

ACKNOWLEDGMENTS

Peter Afflerbach, University of Maryland

Bob Anderson, California Department of Education

Laura Arndt, Eaglecrest High School, Aurora, CO

Rob Atterbury, San Diego City Schools, CA

Linda Ballenger, West Park Elementary, Fort Worth, TX

Jerry Bell, Education and Human Resources, American Association for the Advancement of Science

Neal Berkin, White Plains Schools, White Plains, NY

Victoria Bill, Institute for Learning, Learning Research and Development Center, University of Pittsburgh

Linda Block-Gandy, Mountainview Elementary, CO

Greg Bouljon, Bettendorf Middle School, IL

Rupi Boyd, Taft Junior High School, CA

Diane Briars, Pittsburgh Public Schools, PA

Melanie Broujos, Frick International Studies Academy, Pittsburgh, PA

Shirley Patton Brown, West Memphis High School, West Memphis, AR

Hugh Burkhardt, Shell Centre for Mathematics Education, Nottingham, England

Charlotte Burrell, Trimble Tech High School, Fort Worth, TX

Jill Calder, Wedgwood Sixth Grade School, Fort Worth, TX

Ruben Carriedo, San Diego City Schools, CA

Linda Carstens, San Diego City Schools, CA

Cynthia Carter, New York City Lab School, NY

Sharon Chambers, Forbes Elementary School, Penn Hills, PA

Miriam Chaplin, National Council of Teachers of English

Phyllis Chapman, Linden Elementary School, Pittsburgh, PA

Lynda Chittenden, Park Elementary, Mill Valley, CA

Fran Claggett, Forestville, CA

Doug Clarke, Australian Catholic University, Australia

Gill Close, King's College, University of London, England

Laurel Collins, Linton Middle School, Pittsburgh, PA

Kathy Comfort, California Department of Education

John Davis, Langley High School, Pittsburgh, PA

Marshé DeLain, Delaware Department of Public Instruction

Dot Down, Dublin High School, CA

Mark Driscoll, Education Development Center, Newton, MA

Xandra Williams Earlie, Aldine Independent School District, Houston, TX

Phyllis Eisen, National Association of Manufacturers

Marcia Elliott, Somers Public Schools, CT

Ed Esty, Independent Consultant, Chevy Chase, MD

Alan Farstrup, International Reading Association

Harry Featherstone, Featherstone & Associates, Wooster, OH

Susan Fineman, East Hill ISA, PA

Donna Foley, Parker School, Chelmsford, MA

Amanda Frohberg, PS 41, New York, NY

Karen Fujii, Bucher Middle School, Santa Clara, CA

Matt Gandal, American Federation of Teachers

Don Geary, Linton Middle School, Pittsburgh, PA

Roger Gehman, Linton Middle School, Pittsburgh, PA

Karrie Gengo, Meadowdale High School, Lynnwood, WA

Judy Goldfeder, PS 116, New York, NY

Amy Granatire, Penn Hebron Elementary School, Pittsburgh, PA

Eunice Greer, University of Illinois

Susan Halbert, National 4-H Council

Mike Hale, Council Bluffs Community Schools, Council Bluffs, IA

Jerry Halpern, Langley High School, Pittsburgh, PA

Shirley Brice Heath, Stanford University

Rae Ann Hirsh, Penn Hebron Elementary School, Pittsburgh, PA

Bonnie Hole, Princeton Institute for Research, New Haven, CT

Bill Honig, San Francisco State University

Kathy Howard, Reizenstein Middle School, Pittsburgh, PA

David Hughes, Linton Middle School, Pittsburgh, PA

Beth Hulbert, Barre City Elementary School, VT

Sharon Woods Hussey, Girl Scouts of the U.S.A.

Robin Ittigson, Minadeo Elementary School, Pittsburgh, PA

Tom Jones, National Alliance for Restructuring Education

Nancy Kellogg, CONNECT, Colorado Department of Education

Don King, Department of Mathematics, Northeastern University, Boston, MA

Denis Krysinski, Vann Elementary School, Pittsburgh, PA

Brian Lawler, Eaglecrest High School, Aurora, CO

Lyn Le Countryman, Price Lab School, IA

Steve Leinwand, Connecticut State Department of Education

Jane Lester, New York City Lab School, NY

Denise Levine, New York City Community District 2, NY

Linda Lewis, Fort Worth Independent School District, TX

Debra Liberman, Fells High School, Philadelphia, PA

Bob Livingston, Pennsylvania Department of Education

Anthony Lucas, Duquesne University, Pittsburgh, PA

Denise Lutz, Peabody High School, Pittsburgh, PA

Susan MacArthur, South Portland High School, South Portland, ME

Gary MacDonald, Junior High School, Greely, CO

Shirley Malcom, American Association for the Advancement of Science

Kelly Maloney-Fermoile, Carrie E. Tompkins School, Croton-on-Hudson, NY

Rich Matthews, Pittsburgh Public Schools, PA

Ken McCaffrey, Brattleboro Union High School, VT

Jim Meadows, Mountlake Terrace High School, Mountlake Terrace, WA

David Mintz, National Alliance for Restructuring Education

Harriet Mosatche, Girl Scouts of the U.S.A.

Jo Ann Mosier, Kentucky Department of Education

Tim Moynihan, Mountlake Terrace High School, Mountlake Terrace, WA

Monty Multanen, Edmonds School District, WA

Sandy Murphy, University of California at Davis

Martha Murray-Zinn, Wedgwood Middle School, Fort Worth, TX

Miles Myers, National Council of Teachers of English

Tienne Myers, Hancock Elementary School, Philadelphia, PA

Christina Myren, Acacia Elementary School, Thousand Oaks, CA

Joseph Newkirk, School for the Physical City, New York, NY

Lee Odell, Rensselaer Polytechnic Institute, Troy, NY

Gary Oden, Institute for Learning, Learning Research and Development Center, University of Pittsburgh

Alan Olds, Standley Lake High School, Westminster, CO

Marian Opest, Penn Hills Senior School, Pittsburgh, PA

Ann Osborne, Linton Middle School, Pittsburgh, PA

Jean O'Shell, Linton Middle School, Pittsburgh, PA

Kevin Padian, Department of Integrative Biology, University of California at Berkeley

Dennie Palmer Wolf, Harvard PACE

Tim Patterson, Mountlake Terrace High School, Mountlake Terrace, WA

Risa Payne, Wedgwood Middle School, Fort Worth, TX

David Pearson, University of Illinois

Charles Peters, Oakland Michigan Schools, MI

Marge Petit, Vermont Institute for Mathematics, Science, and Technology

Cindy Phillips, Tri City Elementary, Myrtle Creek, OR

Marcia Pink, Newport High School, WA

John Porter, National Alliance for Restructuring Education

Robert Probst, University of Georgia

Fred Quinonez, Overland Trail Middle School, Brighton, CO

Susan Radley, Teachers College Writing Project at Columbia University, NY

Donald Raintree, Universal Dynamics Inc., Woodbridge, VA

Lynn Raith, Pittsburgh Public Schools, PA

Ginny Redish, Redish & Associates, Inc.

Eeva Reeder, Mountlake Terrace High School, Mountlake Terrace, WA

Susan Rowe, Bonnieville School, CT

Don Rubin, University of Georgia

Carmen Rubino, Eaglecrest High School, Aurora, CO

Robert Rueda, University of Southern California

Marge Sable, National Alliance for Restructuring Education

Sandy Short, Hillview Crest Elementary School, New Haven Unified School District, CA

Cheryl Sims, School for the Physical City, New York, NY

Sandy Smith, Harrison High School, Aurora, CO

Dave Steward, John Evans Jr. High School, Greely, CO

John Swang, National Student Research Center, Mandeville, LA

Carol Tateishi, Bay Area Writing Project

Johnny Tolliver, Delaware State University

Cathy Topping-Wiese, U-32 Junior/Senior High School, Montpelier, VT

Lora Turner, A. Leo Weil School, Pittsburgh, PA

Ann Tweed, Eaglecrest High School, Aurora, CO

Zalman Usiskin, The University of Chicago School Mathematics Project

John Vibber, Mt. Abraham Union High School, Briston, VT

Dale Vigil, San Diego City Schools, CA

Rhonda Wagner, Cherry Creek Schools, Englewood, CO

Brenda Wallace, New York, NY

Anne Weinstock, PS 116, New York, NY

Eric Weiss, U-32 Junior/Senior High School, Montpelier, VT

Sandra Wilcox, Michigan State University

Arnold Willens, PS 41, New York, NY

Ann Marie Williams, PS 41, New York, NY

Darby Williams, Sacramento County Office of Education, CA

Scott J. Wolff, Davenport West High School, IA

Victoria Young, Texas Education Agency

Judi Zawojewski, National-Louis University, Evanston, IL

MATERIALS USED WITH PERMISSION

"Sharing 25" task. From *Writing in Math Class*, pp. 76-78. Copyright 1995 by Math Solutions Publications. Marilyn Burns Education Associates, 150 Gate 5 Road, Suite 101, Sausalito, CA 94965; student work reprinted with permission from the Balanced Assessment Project, University of California, Berkeley, CA 94720.

"More Cube Buildings" task. From *Seeing Solids and Silhouettes* by Michael T. Battista and Douglas H. Clements. Student activity sheets #15 and #16. Copyright 1995 by Dale Seymour Publications.

"Creatures" task. From "Crazy Mixed-Up Animals" excerpted from *Posing Open-Ended Questions in the Primary Classroom* by Christina Wyren. Published in 1995 by Teaching Resource Center, P.O. Box 1509, 14023 Catalina Street, San Leandro, CA 94577. Tel. 800-833-3389.

"The Great Fish Dilemma" task. From *Learning How to Show Your Best*, Marge Petit and Beth Hulbert. Published in 1993 by Exemplars: A Teachers Solution, RR 1 Box 7390, Underhill, VT 05489.

"Aquarium" task and student response, and "The Growing Tree" task and student response. Copyright 1989 by California Department of Education, 721 Capital Mall, 4th Floor, Sacramento, CA 95814.

"Erosion" task. From *FOSS Landforms Module*, Activity 3, "Go with the Flow," 1992: The Regents of the University of California. Developed by the Lawrence Hall of Science, University of California at Berkeley, CA 94720-5200. Published and distributed by Encyclopaedia Britannica Educational Corporation, 310 South Michigan Avenue, Chicago, IL 60604.

"Yeast Growth" and "Smiles" research format and student work. From *The Student Researcher*. Reprinted with permission from the National Student Research Center, Dr. John I. Swang, Mandeville Middle School, 2525 Soult Street, Mandeville, LA 70448. Tel. 504-626-5980 or nsrcmms@aol.com.

"Bike Helmet Ordinance" newspaper article titled "Westpark students petition City Council." Reprinted with permission from *The Journal*, 3412 Marquita Drive, Fort Worth, TX 76116.

"Young Authors' Conference" newspaper article titled "2000 hear authors, stories of event students organized" by Bob Mahlburg. Reprinted courtesy of the *Fort Worth Star-Telegram*.

REFERENCES

American Association for the Advancement of Science. (1993). *Benchmarks for Science Literacy: Project 2061.* New York: Oxford University Press.

American Federation of Teachers. (1994). *Defining World Class Standards: A Publication Series.* Vol. 1-3. Washington, DC: Author.

American Federation of Teachers. (1995). *Making Standards Matter: A Fifty-State Progress Report on Efforts to Raise Academic Standards.* Washington, DC: Author.

Balanced Assessment Project. (In preparation). Schoenfeld, A.H., et al. *Twenty Plus Assessment Packages at Grades Four, Eight, Ten and Twelve.* Berkeley, CA: Graduate School of Education, University of CA at Berkeley.

Black, Paul, and Atkin, Myron, eds. (1996). *Changing the Subject: Innovations in Science, Mathematics, and Technology Education.* London and New York: Organisation for Economic Co-operation and Development.

Boy Scouts of America. (1990). *The Boy Scout Handbook.* Irving, TX: Author.

Burns, Marilyn. (1987). *A Collection of Math Lessons: From Grades 3 through 6.* New Rochelle, NY: Math Solutions Publications.

The Business Task Force on Student Standards. (1995). *The Challenge of Change: Standards To Make Education Work For All Our Children.* Washington, DC: Business Coalition for Education Reform.

Commission on Standards for School Mathematics. (1989). *Curriculum and Evaluation: Standards for School Mathematics.* Reston, VA: National Council of Teachers of Mathematics.

Dale Seymour Publications. (1995). *Seeing Solids and Silhouettes.* Palo Alto, CA: Author.

Girl Scouts of the U.S.A. (1994). *Junior Girl Scout Handbook.* New York: Author.

National Council of Teachers of English & International Reading Association. (1996). *Standards for the English Language Arts.* Urbana, IL and Newark, DE: NCTE and IRA.

National Education Goals Panel, Technical Planning Group. (1993). *Promises to Keep: Creating High Standards for American Students.* Washington, DC: Author.

National Research Council. (1996). *National Science Education Standards.* Washington, DC: National Academy Press.

New Standards Project. (1994). *The New Standards Framework for Applied Learning.* Discussion draft. Washington, DC: Author.

Petit, M. and Hulbert, B. (1993). *Learning How to Show Your Best.* Underhill, VT: Exemplars.

Secretary's Commission on Achieving Necessary Skills. (1992). *Learning A Living: A Blueprint for High Performance—A SCANS Report For America 2000.* Washington, DC: U.S. Department of Labor.

SELECT BIBLIOGRAPHY

Australian Education Council and Curriculum Corporation. (1991). *A National Statement on Mathematics for Australian Schools.* Carlton, Victoria: Curriculum Corporation.

California State Board of Education. (1987). *English-Language Arts Framework for California Public Schools.* Sacramento: Author.

California State Board of Education. (1985). *Mathematics Framework for California Public Schools.* Sacramento: Author.

California State Board of Education. (1990). *Science Framework for California Public Schools.* Sacramento: Author.

Colorado State Department of Education. (Draft). *Model Content Standards for Mathematics.* Denver: Author.

Colorado State Department of Education. (Draft). *Model Content Standards for Reading and Writing.* Denver: Author.

Colorado State Department of Education. (Draft). *Model Content Standards for Science.* Denver: Author.

Commission on Maine's Common Core of Learning. (1990). *Maine's Common Core of Learning: An investment in Maine's future.* Augusta, ME: Maine Department of Education.

Curriculum Corporation. (1994). *English—a curriculum profile for Australian schools.* Carlton, Victoria: Author.

Curriculum Corporation. (1994). *Mathematics—a curriculum profile for Australian schools.* Carlton, Victoria: Author.

Curriculum Corporation. (1994). *Science—a curriculum profile for Australian schools.* Carlton, Victoria: Author.

Der Kultusminister des Landes Nordrhein-Westfalen. (1989). *Grundschule in Nordrhein-Westfalen.* Köln, Bundesrepublik Deutschland: Greven Verlag Köln.

Dutch Ministry of Education and Science. (1993). *The Dutch National Curriculum for Primary School.* Typescript provided in translation by the Dutch Ministry of Education and Science.

Dutch Ministry of Education and Science. (1993). *Mathematics: General and Core Objectives.* Typescript provided in translation by the Dutch Ministry of Education and Science.

Educational and Cultural Exchange Division, UNESCO and International Affairs Department, Science and International Affairs Bureau, Ministry of Education, Science and Culture. (1983). *Course of Study for Elementary Schools in Japan.* (Notification No. 155 of Ministry of Education, Science and Culture.) Tokyo: Printing Bureau, Ministry of Finance.

Educational and Cultural Exchange Division, UNESCO and International Affairs Department, Science and International Affairs Bureau, Ministry of Education, Science and Culture. (1983). *Course of Study for Lower Secondary Schools in Japan.* (Notification No. 156 of Ministry of Education, Science and Culture.) Tokyo: Printing Bureau, Ministry of Finance.

Educational and Cultural Exchange Division, UNESCO and International Affairs Department, Science and International Affairs Bureau, Ministry of Education, Science and Culture. (1983). *Course of Study for Upper Secondary Schools in Japan.* (Notification No. 163 of Ministry of Education, Science and Culture.) Tokyo: Printing Bureau, Ministry of Finance.

Girl Scouts of the U.S.A. (1993). *Brownie Girl Scout Handbook.* New York: Author.

Girl Scouts of the U.S.A. (1995). *Cadette Girl Scout Handbook.* New York: Author.

Girl Scouts of the U.S.A. (1995). *A Resource Book for Senior Girl Scouts.* New York: Author.

Illinois Academic Standards Project of the Illinois State Board of Education. (Draft). *Illinois Academic Standards, State Goals 1-10: English Language Arts and Mathematics.* Springfield, IL: Author.

Illinois Academic Standards Project of the Illinois State Board of Education. (Draft). *Illinois Academic Standards, State Goals 11-18: Science and Social Studies.* Springfield, IL: Author.

Iowa Department of Education. (1994). *Education is Iowa's Future: The State Plan for Educational Excellence in the 21st Century.* Des Moines, IA: Author.

Kentucky Department of Education. (1993). *Transformations: Kentucky's Curriculum Framework.* Frankfort, KY: Author.

Maine Department of Education. (Draft). *Learning Results.* Augusta, ME: Author.

Ministère de l'Éducation Nationale. (1985). *Colléges: Programmes et Instructions.* Paris: Centre National de Documentation Pédagogique.

Ministère de l'Éducation Nationale. (1994). *Évaluation à l'entrée en seconde générale et technologique:* Français. Paris: Direction de l'Évaluation et de la Prospective.

Ministère de l'Éducation Nationale de la Jeunesse et des Sports, Direction des Écoles. (1991). *Les cycles à l'école primaire.* Paris: Centre National de Documentation Pédagogique & Hachette Écoles.

Ministère de l'Éducation Nationale. (1991). *Baccalauréat Professionel: Enseignements généraux.* Paris: Centre National de Documentation Pédagogique.

Ministry of Education, New Zealand. (1994). *English in the New Zealand Curriculum.* Wellington, New Zealand: Learning Media Ltd.

Ministry of Education, New Zealand. (1994). *Mathematics in the New Zealand Curriculum.* Wellington, New Zealand: Learning Media Ltd.

Ministry of Education, New Zealand. (1994). *Science in the New Zealand Curriculum.* Wellington, New Zealand: Learning Media Ltd.

Ministry of Education and Research. (1987). *Curriculum Guidelines for Compulsory Education in Norway.* W. Nygaard, Norge: H. Aschehoug & Co.

Ministry of Education of the Russian Federation and the General School Education Institute of the Russian Academy of Education. (1993). *The Provisional State Education Standards, General Secondary Education: Mathematics.* Moscow: Author.

Ministry of Education and Training, Canada. (1993). *Provincial Standards: Mathematics.* Toronto, Ontario: Queen's Printer for Ontario.

Ministry of Education and Training, Canada. (1993). *The Common Curriculum, Grades 1-9.* Toronto, Ontario: Queen's Printer for Ontario.

Missouri Department of Education. (Draft). *Academic Performance Standards and Curriculum Frameworks.* Jefferson City, MO: Author.

National Science Teachers Association. (1992). *Scope, Sequence, and Coordination Content Core.* Washington, DC: Author.

Nolan, Kate. (1994). *Mathematics in Five Countries.* Pittsburgh, PA: New Standards.

Oregon Department of Education. (1993). *21st Century Schools: Information Packet.* Salem, OR: Author.

Oregon Department of Education. (1986). *English Language Arts: Common Curriculum Goals.* Salem, OR: Author.

Oregon Department of Education. (1986). *Essential Learning Skills.* Salem, OR: Author.

Oregon Department of Education. (1987). *Mathematics: Common Curriculum Goals.* Salem, OR: Author.

Rhode Island Department of Education. (1994). *First Draft: Mathematics Framework for Grades K-12.* Providence, RI: Author.

School Curriculum and Assessment Authority. (1994). *Design & Technology in the National Curriculum.* Draft Proposals. London: Author and the Central Office of Information.

School Curriculum and Assessment Authority. (1994). *English in the National Curriculum.* Draft Proposals. London: Author and the Central Office of Information.

School Curriculum and Assessment Authority. (1994). *Science in the National Curriculum.* Draft Proposals. London: Author and the Central Office of Information.

Scottish Office Education Department. (1991). *Curriculum and Assessment in Scotland, National Guidelines: English Language 5-14.* Edinburgh: Author.

Southern Examining Group. (1992). *English: General Certificate of Secondary Education, National Curriculum Syllabus, 1994 Examinations.* Surrey, England: Author.

State of Delaware. (1995). *English Language Arts Curriculum Framework: Volumes One and Two.* Dover, DE: Author.

State of Delaware. (1995). *Mathematics Curriculum Framework: Volumes One and Two.* Dover, DE: Author.

State of Delaware. (1995). *Science Curriculum Framework: Volumes One and Two.* Dover, DE: Author.

The State of Vermont Department of Education. (1995). *Content Standards: Working Draft.* Montpelier, VT: Author.

The State of Vermont Department of Education. (1995). *Performance Standards: Working Draft.* Montpelier, VT: Author.

The State of Vermont Department of Education. (1995). *Vermont's Common Core Framework for Curriculum and Assessment: Draft.* Montpelier, VT: Author.

School-to-Work Transition Team. (1994). *Education for Employment in Rhode Island: The Report of the School-to-Work Opportunities Transition Team.* Providence, RI: Author.

Speech Communication Association. (1996). *Speaking, Listening, and Media Literacy Standards For K through 12 Education.* Annendale, VA: Author.

Texas Education Agency. (1995). *English Language Arts Essential Elements: Chapter 75, Texas Administrative Code.* Austin, TX: Author.

Texas Education Agency. (1995). *Mathematics Essential Elements: Chapter 75, Texas Administrative Code.* Austin, TX: Author.

Texas Education Agency. (1995). *Science Essential Elements: Chapter 75, Texas Administrative Code.* Austin, TX: Author.

Stigler, J. and Stevenson, H. W. (1991). "How Asian Teachers Polish Each Lesson to Perfection." *American Educator.* Spring, 1991, 12-20, 43-47.

The University of the State of New York and The State Education Department. (1995). *Preliminary Draft Framework for Career Development and Occupational Studies.* Albany, NY: Authors.

The University of the State of New York and The State Education Department. (1994). *Preliminary Draft Framework for English Language Arts.* Albany, NY: Authors.

The University of the State of New York and The State Education Department. (1995). *Preliminary Draft Framework for Mathematics, Science and Technology.* Albany, NY: Authors.

Utbildningsdepartmentet. (1993). *Kursplaner för Grundskolan.* Stockholm: Nordstedts Tryckeri AB.

NEW STANDARDS PRODUCTS AND SERVICES: WHERE TO FIND WHAT YOU NEED

These performance standards serve as the basis of design specifications for the New Standards reference examinations and portfolios, which in turn provide information about performance to students, teachers, and parents.

But the performance standards cannot by themselves provide all of the information students and teachers will need in order to improve student performance in the core subjects.

Therefore, we include here some of the common requests we encounter from people who have begun to use the performance standards, along with information about the New Standards resources available to answer those requests.

- **Where can I find samples of student work that do not yet meet the standards? What about rubrics and scoring guides?**

New Standards Released Tasks contain sample tasks, scoring rubrics, and samples of student work at all of the score points given in the rubrics. Released Tasks can be ordered from Harcourt Brace Educational Measurement (Tel. 800-228-0752).

- **Clearly, many parts of the performance standards can only be assessed through some kind of portfolio system. Does New Standards offer portfolios?**

Yes—the New Standards portfolios in Mathematics, Science, English Language Arts, and Applied Learning are constructed to link directly to the performance standards. Portfolios are available individually, in classroom sets, and in sampler packets. Portfolios can be ordered directly from New Standards (Tel. 888-361-6233).

- **Our school district is using the performance standards to improve teaching and learning. We want standardized tests that can tell us how our students are doing based on the standards. What does New Standards offer?**

The New Standards reference examinations are available in English Language Arts and Mathematics for grades 4, 8, and 10. The examinations are designed using the performance standards as their foundation. Score reports for the reference examinations tell teachers and students about the quality of student work by referring to the performance standards. To order reference examinations, call Harcourt Brace Educational Measurement (Tel. 800-228-0752).

- **In order to move to a standards-based district, we need professional development and consulting for teachers and central office staff. Can New Standards help us with this?**

New Standards consultants can provide on-site services in several areas, including professional development, public engagement, strategic planning, standards linking, and technical issues involved with performance assessment. To discuss services needed by your school or district, call the Office of State and Local Relations, located at the National Center on Education and the Economy (Tel. 202-783-3668).